I0605225

Wyche Fowler

A Political Life in Georgia, Congress, and Abroad

In this richly detailed book, R. William Johnstone—one of the most talented staff members of Congress in modern times—presents an authoritative and enthralling biography of Senator Wyche Fowler. Fowler served the State of Georgia with great skill, compassion, and success in both the US House and Senate. He has always been one of the most intelligent and witty of Georgia's distinguished public servants in Congress over the years, and among the most thoughtful and ethical. This impressive study not only brings Fowler's phenomenal political career alive, but also manages to capture the essence of key policy issues that have been—and remain—front and center in the American polity. Johnstone's handling is judicious, thorough, and lively. The result is an extraordinary book, befitting a special individual who guided Georgia well during his many outstanding years in Washington, DC. Here is a book for every Georgian, and anyone else who wants to know more about Fowler's thoughtful, timeless views on domestic and foreign policy.

—Loch K. Johnson, Regents Professor of International Affairs emeritus, University of Georgia

Early in life, Wyche Fowler caught the bug—the desire to serve—and, like a stubborn cold, it never let him go. From "night mayor" to alderman to city council president to congressman to senator to ambassador, he was driven by his belief that government can be a force for good in the lives of its constituents. Moreover, at a time when the "dog whistle" politics of division were commonplace for Southern politicians, Fowler insisted on pursuing his work within the context of multi-racial coalitions, building together what Martin Luther King, Jr. called "the beloved community." This compelling political biography is not only his story, but in many ways the story of the New South coming of age and making its impact amidst the winds of change following the Civil Rights Movement on to the turn of a new century.

—Reverend Raphael Warnock, U.S. Senator from Georgia

This wonderful volume is really two books in one. William Johnstone, who served as Wyche Fowler's right-hand man in his campaigns and throughout his consequential career in Congress, has written a lively textbook on the doings in Washington back when Washington did things (important things!) with our budget, taxes, social programs, and international affairs. But this is also an autobiography written by Fowler himself, a truly magnetic figure who managed to combine a wicked sense of humor with a razor-sharp intelligence and a passion for improving the lot of others. I've had the privilege of knowing Wyche Fowler for more than a half-century and I've marveled at the twinkle in his eye and the love in his heart.

—Frederick Allen, author of *Secret Formula: The Inside Story of How Coca-Cola Became the Best-Known Brand in the World*

Wyche Fowler is a pleasure to read. Sprinkled amid a full account of one of the most fun, dedicated, and hard-working politicians in Georgia's history are many of the senator's personal and often hilarious stories. Johnstone provides many details about Senator Fowler's career, including morsels about Atlanta's local government, the Clarence Thomas-Anita Hill hearings, the Persian Gulf War, and the 1986 and 1992 senate campaigns. But no matter which chapter you're reading, Fowler's sparkling personality shines through.

—Mark Weston, author of *The Runner-Up Presidency: The Elections That Defied America's Popular Will*

MUP/ H1054

Published by Mercer University Press
1501 Mercer University Drive
Macon, Georgia 31207

29 28 27 26 25 5 4 3 2 1

Books published by Mercer University Press are printed on acid-free paper that meets the requirements of the American National Standard for Information Sciences—Permanence of Paper for Printed Library Materials.

Printed and bound in Canada.

This book is set in Adobe Caslon Pro.

Cover/jacket design by Burt&Burt.

ISBN 978-0-88146-969-1 (Print)
978-0-88146-970-7 (eBook)

Cataloging-in-Publication Data is available from the Library of Congress

Wyche Fowler

A Political Life in Georgia,
Congress, and Abroad

R. William Johnstone

With an Introduction by

Ambassador Wyche Fowler Jr.

MERCER UNIVERSITY PRESS
Macon, Georgia

Contents

Preface

In 2012, Wyche Fowler approached me about working with him to compile a collection of his achievements, observations, and other highlights of his life and career. This would result in a modest-sized volume intended only for his family and closest friends. He would supply the main narrative, complete with the storytelling that has been a hallmark of his interactions with people over the years, whereas I would add—from my own notes and recollections—documentation of his achievements, primarily from the period that I worked for him in the US House of Representatives (1977–1986) and Senate (1987–1992). From the outset, my chief goal in this project was to preserve such records for future researchers, especially on key events in which Fowler played a major role, including the Nicaragua-contra war and the associated issue of congressional oversight of intelligence operations (mid-1980s) and the 1990 budget summit.

Work on the book proceeded intermittently over the years due to competing priorities and changing views as to the structure and objectives of the project. As the effort progressed, however, it became clear that I had much more relevant material than anticipated, and I continuously expanded the scope and details of my portion of the work. The result is the present work, which is primarily concerned with one time period—1977 to 1992—and one aspect—Wyche's campaigns for and service in the US Congress. Furthermore, I am no disinterested, objective reporter, as I was a direct participant in many of the events described herein as Fowler's legislative director in the House, chief of staff in the Senate, and campaign manager in almost all of those campaigns.

The major controversial elements of the Fowler record, however, such as his conflicts with Maynard Jackson, the Clarence Thomas nomination, and the House bank scandal used in the 1992 campaign against him, are addressed, and I have tried to further compensate, to a degree, for my pro-Fowler bias by including many contemporary third-party reports (primarily from newspapers) describing and assessing Fowler's activities.

With regard to sources, the period before my association with Wyche—discussed in chapters 1 and 2 and providing most of the work's "personal" details—is heavily dependent on the extraordinarily comprehensive set of scrapbooks of photos, articles, or mentions of Wyche Fowler in the Atlanta and local community newspapers maintained by family friend Judy Merkle. My records and notes, as well as selections from the *Congressional Record*, newspaper articles (primarily but not exclusively the *Atlanta Journal-Constitution*), newsletters, and other written material (such as Richard Fenno's *Senators on the Campaign Trail*) constitute the major sources for those portions covering Fowler's congressional career (chapters 3 through 13). The final chapter, covering his post-congressional career, is largely based on media accounts as well as recent reflections by Ambassador Fowler himself. We supplemented our own records and memories by reviewing the collection of Fowler's papers located at Emory University.

Hundreds of individuals helped staff Wyche Fowler during his years in local and congressional service, while thousands more worked on his various campaigns for those offices. Consequently, it is not possible to recognize many of them by name in the work that follows. However, the accomplishments detailed herein would not have been possible without their contributions, and it was my privilege to work with them.

—RWJ

Introduction

by Ambassador Wyche Fowler Jr.

> "Life is short. Do not forget about the most important things in our life, living for other people and doing good for them."
>
> —Marcus Aurelius

Bill Johnstone's biography of my public life, chronicling my campaigns for office and my public policy involvements in the US Congress, could easily have been *his* autobiography. As my legislative director in the House and chief of staff in the Senate, our work together was so close, so exhaustive, and so complete that the finished product—whether speeches, amendments, or policy initiatives—was the result of two minds working as one.

As my campaign manager in all my races after 1977, his guidance (and polling) kept me focused and resilient when times were tough and my spirits sagged. Bill also followed my directive that we have no debt after my elections, win or lose, a standard learned from my mentor, Charles Longstreet Weltner, while working as his assistant in the Congress. Money was always hard to come by, as whatever my political talents, soliciting funds for campaigning was not one of them. As you will read, in my successful 1986 campaign we were dramatically outspent by the incumbent and behind by double digits until the final weekend when my campaign surged and we squeaked out a victory. We had won and had no debt. For his leadership, Bill was named national campaign manager of the year.

This book should fascinate future historians who seek detailed records of major national public policy initiatives, and "how our laws are made." Readers will be astonished at how relevant—even prescient—much of the work of the Ninety-Fifth through 102nd

Congresses have become. Today's budget and tax policies, and certainly our country's alternative energy policies, were debated and evolved during those years. And lessons learned from the Iraq War still inform today's US policy about using ground forces abroad.

I have led an adventurous and fortunate life, enhanced by a curiosity about other people, other cultures, other lands. As a political candidate, I tried to treat all I met as equals, explaining my reasons for seeking public office and listening to their responses. I was not one to look over the citizen's shoulder for the next hand to shake. In short, I became a politician because I like people and wanted to be a part of a government that gave them faith and confidence. I was also fortunate to have completed my army service and law education (1969) at a time when political candidates did not seek office for power or money but wanted to work together—Republicans and Democrats—passing legislation by consensus on policies that benefited our people and our country. Sadly, that is not the case today.

As a proper biographer, Bill has included many of my accounts of experiences unique to my personality and public efforts. Campaigning to me was never drudgery, but fun and exciting, as every day presented new scenarios for new friends and new stories to tell. I also learned that humor can glide you over rough spots on public issues, convincing the citizen that you would make a worthy neighbor—one step away from being a worthy neighborhood representative.

In Peter Shaffer's 1990 play *Lettice and Lovage*, I accidently discovered the secret of successful public speakers. Lettice, an ambitious tour guide for England's National Trust, had been assigned a 400-year-old castle where nothing of historical note ever happened—no treaties, no plots, no assassinations—nothing. So, Lettice, sensing tourists should at least be entertained, showered them with made-up tales of madness, intrigue, and mayhem in the castle. Word traveled back to her superior, Lovage, in London. Lettice was called on the carpet to explain her perfidy. "My mother told me that the secret of life was the three E's: enlarge, enliven, enthuse." It got her fired. It got me thinking...

"Enlarge, Enliven, Enthuse." Albeit subconsciously, these words informed my public performances—before a Sunday school class, a jury, a town meeting, or a public rally. I was an entertainer, an adventurer, a performer. People are especially attracted to enthusiasm, I believe, which often leads to acceptance and trust. In my twenty-five-plus years in public office described herein, I was always conscious of the precariousness of public trust and did my utmost to never betray it.

> "Be like the bird who, pausing in her flight awhile
> on boughs too slight,
> Feels them give way beneath her, and yet sings,
> Knowing she hath wings."
> —Victor Hugo

Figure 1. Fowler's "proudest accomplishment" in public service was in securing placement of a MARTA transit station, which opened June 18, 1988, within the Hartsfield Atlanta International Airport terminal.

Source: Wikimedia Commons

Figure 2. Re-enactment of Fowler's swearing-in to the U.S. House of Representatives by Speaker of the House Thomas P. "Tip" O'Neill on April 6, 1977.

Source: U.S. House of Representatives; Courtesy of Wyche Fowler, Jr. papers, Stuart A. Rose Manuscript, Archives, and Rare Book Library, Emory University

Figure 3. Fowler with UN Ambassador Andrew Young.

Source: U.S. House of Representatives, undated; Courtesy of Wyche Fowler, Jr. papers, Stuart A. Rose Manuscript, Archives, and Rare Book Library, Emory University

Figure 4. Fowler shaking hands with President Jimmy Carter.

Source: White House photographer, July 20, 1978; Courtesy of Wyche Fowler, Jr. papers, Stuart A. Rose Manuscript, Archives, and Rare Book Library, Emory University

Figure 5. Fowler shaking hands with Egyptian President Anwar Sadat after conclusion of Camp David Accords peace treaty between Egypt and Israel.

Source: White House photographer, September 1978; Courtesy of Wyche Fowler, Jr. papers, Stuart A. Rose Manuscript, Archives, and Rare Book Library, Emory University

Figure 6. Fowler shaking hands with People's Republic of China leader Deng Xiaoping during Deng's 1979 visit to the United States.

Source: White House photographer, February 1, 1979; Courtesy of Wyche Fowler, Jr. papers, Stuart A. Rose Manuscript, Archives, and Rare Book Library, Emory University

Figure 7. Fowler (3rd from right) greeting Vice President Walter Mondale (at left), accompanied by Andrew Young (3rd from left) and Coretta Scott King (at right).

Source: White House photographer, October 19, 1979; Courtesy of Wyche Fowler, Jr. papers, Stuart A. Rose Manuscript, Archives, and Rare Book Library, Emory University

Figure 8. From left, Atlanta Mayor Andrew Young, Wyche Fowler, and Vice President George Bush at dedication of Morehouse School of Medicine Building, July 21, 1982.

Source: White House photographer; Courtesy of Wyche Fowler, Jr. papers, Stuart A. Rose Manuscript, Archives, and Rare Book Library, Emory University

Figure 9. Fowler (3rd from left) and members of the House Intelligence Committee in White House meeting with President Ronald Reagan (2nd from right).

Source: White House photographer, April 26, 1983; Courtesy of Wyche Fowler, Jr. papers, Stuart A. Rose Manuscript, Archives, and Rare Book Library, Emory University

Figure 10. Fowler was "the leading catalyst in securing funding" for reconstruction of the Talmadge Bridge in Savannah, Georgia.

Source: U.S. Army Corps of Engineers, 2013 photo

Figure 11. Fowler with parents and daughter Katherine in front of U.S. Capitol after being sworn in as a U.S. Senator.

Source: Wyche Fowler, Jr., January 6, 1987; Courtesy of Wyche Fowler, Jr. papers, Stuart A. Rose Manuscript, Archives, and Rare Book Library, Emory University

Figure 12. Gov. Zell Miller, Fowler, and Sen. Sam Nunn at press conference at Fort Stewart, Georgia, February 1, 1991.

Source: U.S. Army; Courtesy of Wyche Fowler, Jr. papers, Stuart A. Rose Manuscript, Archives, and Rare Book Library, Emory University

Figure 13. King Fahd bin Abd al-Aziz Al Saud (right) receives a visit from Ambassador Fowler and Secretary of Defense William Cohen at the palace in Jeddah, Kingdom of Saudi Arabia.

Source: Department of Defense, February 8, 1998

Figure 14. From left, Vice President Gore, Ambassador Fowler, unidentified individual, and President Clinton in an Oval Office meeting at the White House.

Source: White House photographer, September 24, 1998; Courtesy of Wyche Fowler, Jr. papers, Stuart A. Rose Manuscript, Archives, and Rare Book Library, Emory University

MERCER UNIVERSITY PRESS

Endowed by

Tom Watson Brown

and

The Watson-Brown Foundation, Inc.

Wyche Fowler

Chapter 1

Early Years (1940–1962): "Ch" like in "Church"

In 1940, much of the world was at war, and though still ostensibly neutral, the United States was being drawn inexorably into that conflict. Back at home, Americans were still struggling to overcome the effects of the Great Depression. The population of Atlanta, Georgia, was 302,288, making it the twenty-eighth largest city in the United States. Approximately one-third of its people were African Americans, but the city spent less than one-sixth of its school funds on Black students. The Ku Klux Klan was still active in the area, with ten members indicted that year for floggings in Fulton County. And on September 4, Atlanta's first-term Mayor William Hartsfield was defeated in his first try for reelection.

Hartsfield's victorious opponent, Roy LeCraw, resigned from office to enlist in the army after the Pearl Harbor attack, and Hartsfield won the May 1942 special election to replace him. He was reelected for four more terms, serving as Atlanta's mayor until 1961, and leaving behind a legacy that included being one of the first white politicians to build biracial coalitions after the outlawing of Georgia's "whites only" primary system by the United States Supreme Court in 1946. Historian Clarence Bacote called Hartsfield's 1949 election "a turning point, as Blacks and Northside whites became part of a biracial political coalition that controlled city politics over the next twenty years."

Family Life

On October 6, 1940, seventh-generation Georgian William Wyche Fowler Jr. was born at Emory University Hospital in DeKalb County just outside Atlanta. His father hailed from Warrenton, Georgia, near Augusta, and received his college degree from Mercer University in Macon before serving as a Navy lieutenant during the Second World War. His mother, Emelyn Barbre, began life in Albany but grew up in Washington,

Georgia, located between Augusta and Macon. She attended Brenau College in Gainesville, Georgia. Both parents began their careers as educators (he was principal at Tennille and Carrollton High Schools), but they moved to the metro Atlanta area when Mr. Fowler found higher-paying work, first as a textbook salesman and then as an insurance agent with the Travelers Insurance Company from which he retired after sixteen years.

A 1985 story in the *Atlanta Constitution* recounted Wyche Fowler's recollections of his parents: "From his father, a stern disciplinarian, Fowler learned discipline and dedication. From his mother, whom many say he favors, he gained wit. 'They taught me to do right, to try to do right, no matter what the consequences.'"[1] More recently, he elaborated.

> This is a good juncture to try and capture my father, his strengths and weaknesses, and my unwavering love and admiration for him. My spankings and whippings through my formative years were never considered by me to be cruel—or unusual—punishment but proportionate to my failure to maintain the high standards he had for me, and his understanding that I would not willingly do anything amiss that would embarrass me or the family. In other words, I never, never felt that I was the victim of rage or pre-meditated violence. Although he drank regularly and excessively at times (a trait I inherited from him, I suppose), he never punished me or lectured me when he had been drinking. My mother did form a barrier, assuring that conflict between us did not get out of control, understanding that my misconduct was not caused by malice, but more often by spontaneous irrepressibility.
>
> My father was born in 1910 in Warren County, Georgia, still noted as the poorest county in the state. He excelled in track, and on the debate team, winning a partial grant to go to Mercer College, the Baptist school in Macon, Georgia. He was not the first in our family to go to college as his father had been a proud Mercer graduate. Daddy, as I called him throughout his life, excelled in his studies and won the school's award as champion debater. I never asked him if he would have liked to have gone to law school, as that was not a possibility at the time. He graduated at the height (or depth) of the Great Depression, and he scrambled to find a job teaching school in the adjoining county. He taught English, Latin,

and math, while coaching the school's sports teams. He was known as a popular teacher, but a severe disciplinarian, as several of his former students told me as I campaigned the state for the U.S. Senate. I can attest that his insistence on disciplined behavior continued throughout his life.

In 1935, at a school dance in the adjacent county, Wilkes, he met my mother-to-be, Emelyn Barbre, and was apparently smitten. By now the principal of Warren County High, he was looking for teachers, he told her, and offered her a job. It did not take her long to accept and a two-year courtship secretly began, as my father thought it unseemly to be seen wooing one of his teachers. My mother, irrepressibly vivacious and winsome from youth, finally compromised their efforts at concealment. They were married in Washington, Georgia, in 1938 and I was born two years later.

To supplement their sparse teachers' salaries, my father sold World Book Encyclopedias door-to-door for a few years but found that could not support the family after I arrived. Rural Georgia—and most of the South—had not recovered from the Depression. On what Daddy maintained was a stroke of luck, he landed a job with Travelers Insurance in Atlanta and we moved to Marietta, twenty miles away, where a small apartment was affordable. He enjoyed his work, and after a few years was appointed regional manager for the company.

I have tried many times to capture the essence of my mother, but always failed. After I was born, she never worked outside of the home, yet to me she was a larger-than-life constant presence in my life, a lodestar in my consciousness wherever I was. She could be witty, irreverent, or ironic. She was vivacious and mischievous, charmed by anyone who came into her orbit. And she loved me unconditionally, often to the detriment of her relationship with my father. When I was home, it was my preferences that were satisfied, and I could detect when Daddy thought that he had been ignored. My friends say that my personality is most like my mother's, and I do not dispute it. She taught me to make friends, respect all, and to live life with joy and laughter. Six months after her death, drinking with friends at a neighborhood bar, when asked about her death I broke into tears.

The Fowlers were living in Decatur when Wyche Jr. came into the world. (Like his father, he has always been called by his distinctive middle name, which is pronounced "Y-ch," with the "ch" sounding like the "ch" in "church"—as was proclaimed somewhat famously in a 1986 campaign ad—derived from the Old English word *wic*, meaning someone living in an outlying community, and which first appeared as a family name in England in the period after the Norman Conquest of 1066.) Five years later, his sister Gerald was born, and the family moved to Marietta. When Fowler Jr. was in the fourth grade, the family moved again, this time to the Northside Atlanta home where the elder Fowlers lived for the rest of their lives.

Today, Fowler fondly recalls his early years, and in so doing, reveals his characteristic penchant for finding humor in many of his life's experiences.

> Many memoirists have written about the delights of growing up in the "innocent" years after WWII and before the sexual revolution of the 1960s and the Vietnam War created anxiety and protests throughout the nation. My experience was equally as positive, filled with friendship, laughter, sports, experimenting with girls, Christian proselytizing—and mischievousness. Words that parents and their children customarily use today to describe school and extracurricular activities—such as anxiety, stress, despondency, and fatigue—never entered my vocabulary, much less my mind. I do remember occasionally neglecting my homework or an assigned science project, but I was always confident that with a spurt of late effort, the work would be done, and on time. I did not worry or fret. My mother commented to her weekly bridge club that "she had never seen me bring a book home from school." Although not entirely accurate, I managed to make the honor society with minimal effort outside of the school day.
>
> During the war, my father, a Navy man, spent most of his three years' service in the Philippines and was home on leave only twice, which I do not remember. From about age three to six, I was in the care of my mother and her two older sisters, Pauline Cooke and Lucile Lindsey, readers all. I was constantly read to, encouraged to read aloud, and to memorize nursery rhymes. They taught me to

spell, a talent which has remained. There was no television, as yet, to distract and dismay. All parents and surrogates think their children are prodigies, and mine were no exception—a judgement I seriously doubt.

I could talk in complete sentences at an early age—an ability my namesake grandson also possessed—and I memorized some 300-plus birds in a bird encyclopedia, which I promptly displayed (performed) upon demand. But other than early indications of mental competence, I was a happy, healthy, and unremarkable child. I brimmed with excitement as I was taken by my mother to my first-grade classes in Marietta, only to have my enthusiasm dashed in the first few minutes. When the books were distributed, I shoved them away: "I read all these books before I was born." (Is this an argument for homeschooling?) Eager for school every day, much like Sunday school, I was unremarked upon by my teacher until one day she called to request a conference with my parents. "Wyche is doing extremely well, and is bright, but for the last few days, when it rains, he leaves his seat, goes to the window and stares at the rain. He refuses to stay in his seat and pay attention." My parents said they would take care of it, as he will obey when they tell him to mind the teacher.

A week or so later, rain fell, and I went to the window, watching. Promptly sent to the principal, at the subsequent conference it was recommended that I have some sort of psychological evaluation. My parents were disturbed, but knowing of no alternative, agreed. Emory was chosen, and I can still remember the youthful psychologist—probably an intern—who spent several "sessions" with me. I liked him and had no hesitancy in answering his many questions. His analysis completed, he sent his report to the school and my parents. The conclusion: "This child's psyche understands the cleansing power of the rain. He is refreshing his soul." Often thereafter, on rainy days I did not have to go to school. One such day I was allowed to remain home and stare at the rain. It was my mother's bridge-club day. "Why is little Wyche at home today," one asked. "Is he sick?" "Sick," my mother injected, "I'll have you know he's refreshing his soul."

> Years later, in a public debate for presidency of the Atlanta City Council, one of my opponents characterized my position as nutty. "He's insane," he declared of me. "Insane?" I responded, "I have a doctor's certificate of sanity," daring him to produce one of his own. The certifiably sane candidate won. For the rest of my life, I have remained captivated by rain and have my sunniest disposition on rainy days.

Early Influences: Religion and Music

Religion played a significant role in Wyche Jr.'s early years when, as he later recalled, "the Baptist side of my family [from his father's side] and the Methodist side [from his maternal grandmother] fought over my soul," with the Baptist side winning out. As a member of the Second-Ponce de Leon Baptist Church in Atlanta, Fowler says, "They couldn't have anything at the church that I wasn't there. I believed with all my heart that I was going to be a minister. I had this absolute determination that that's what the Lord wanted me to do." He helped start an interfaith fellowship group in high school, and his father reported that his young son was a faithful practitioner of tithing, the practice of providing one-tenth of one's earnings to the church, when he donated ten percent of his wages from bagging groceries. Years later, Fowler recalled a Christmas pageant at Second-Ponce de Leon when he was a member of the youth choir. The stage upon which the choir members were standing collapsed a short distance to the floor, but the choir continued singing. This phase of the future senator's development also provided him with an all-important political skill.

> Sometime mid-ninth grade, I decided that I wanted to be a preacher. Or rather, I was convinced that *God* had called me to be a preacher. This revelation had matured over time, as from the first grade onward, I had loved going to church and Sunday school at every opportunity, while memorizing the books of the Bible and hundreds of quotable verses. By studying maps of the Holy Land, I absorbed the wars and tribulations of ancient Israel, my first unwitting exposure to foreign policy in the Middle East. Entering high school, I began carrying a pocket New Testament and "witnessing"

to any classmate who would listen—mostly girls. With the permission of Northside's principal, Weddington Kelley, I organized a monthly Christian Youth fellowship, held at Trinity Presbyterian Church with the encouragement of its longtime pastor, Allison Williams. Attendance grew to an average of more than a hundred a month and attracted many from all grades. Even a few Jewish students attended; we had no Black students during those days.

Looking back, I suspect my motivation was one of public performance more than theological impulse, but I possessed a Christian faith without doubts, and God's call to "spread the gospel" was one I enthusiastically embraced. Shortly after my sixteenth birthday, my own pastor, Dr. Monroe Swilley, invited me to preach the morning service on Youth Day at Second Ponce de Leon Baptist Church. Church attendance was at an all-time high in the late fifties, and more than a thousand people were in attendance. Having closely modeled my preaching style after Dr. Swilley (with occasional rhetorical flourishes from Billy Graham), I used no notes and spoke no longer than twenty minutes. The choir sang the hymn of invitation, and I uttered the call.

Twenty-three people came forward to join the church. God had spoken through me! I privately exulted. Years later, I learned from a deacon that Dr. Swilley had secretly asked those who were intending to join to wait until my Sunday sermon to "make me look good." It certainly did. Although unaware at the time, my homilies at the monthly fellowship, spoken prayers at morning devotions, and several sermons in churches had made me a confident public speaker by the time of my high school graduation.

Music was an important factor in Fowler's formative years as well and provided him with his first brush with public acclaim.

At approximately age eight, I persuaded my parents to let me take guitar lessons. I had already memorized many of the traditional Baptist hymns, and I wanted to accompany myself on the guitar. In other words, I didn't want to become a serious guitar musician, with flourishes of individual notes, but to sing and strum with nothing more difficult than chord groups and alternating strumming techniques. My large hands and long fingers enabled me to encircle the guitar neck quite easily, and after learning the chord groups I was on my way past self-entertaining to—performing!

A neighborhood lady who catered children's birthday parties soon had me on the "circuit," armed with guitar and cowboy hat, for a whopping three dollars a gig. My father, already pleased with my love of the Bible, suggested that I give a quarter dollar of my earnings to the church, resulting in a lifelong habit of philanthropy—albeit at a modest level. "Red River Valley," "Clementine," "Detour, There's a Muddy Road Ahead," "There's a Church in the Valley by the Wildwood," and ofttimes "What a Friend We Have in Jesus" followed the cake and ice cream to the subdued applause of the birthday congregants.

When I was eleven, I was asked to appear on a local version of Ted Mack's *Amateur Hour* titled *Stars of Tomorrow* and hosted by a gregarious former weatherman named Freddie Miller. The show was live on Sunday afternoons, and each week's winner won the prize of twenty-four Brock candy bars from the Brock Candy Company in Chattanooga. I sang "Red River Valley" and won. The following week, a seven-year-old with a husky alto from Augusta, Brenda Lee, accompanied by her mother on the piano, won the candy.

The show had a rule against repeats, but cards and letters poured in urging that Brenda and I be brought back to possibly sing a duet. The producers evidently liked the idea, so a "gospel interlude" was introduced, with Brenda and me invited to inaugurate the new programming. Brenda's mother suggested "The Old Rugged Cross," with me as the tenor and Brenda as bass. It was one of my favorites, so I readily agreed. I sat and smiled and strummed while tiny Brenda (she only grew to five feet two) stood on the piano bench to sing as her mother accompanied us both. A few months later, my voice changed. Brenda's matured and deepened, and she rocketed to stardom as a country music favorite. I realized that if I were to continue to perform, it would not be as a soloist.

Thirty-five years later, Brenda and I reunited on stage, right after my election to the United States Senate. My election was not expected, nor anticipated in many quarters, so, many corporate clients—and their lobbyists—were eager to help me "pay off my campaign debt," the euphemism for putting money in the pocket of an election winner in hopes of ensuring future access and possibly favoritism. (Irony: I had no campaign debt. Although outspent by more than three to one by my opponent, I had never spent more than I raised in any of my multitude of city and congressional races. My rule was ironclad, and my staff ensured that I emerged from each contest—winner or loser—with no debt.)

Two days after my victory, a prominent Atlanta law firm hosted a victory/pay-off-the-debt party at the Commerce Club attended by one hundred or more of my "new" supporters. I enjoyed it, greeting comfortably those who were uncomfortably trying to appear comfortable in my presence. As the party was breaking up, a Cobb County official reminded me that the Cobb County Chamber of Commerce was holding its annual event at Cobb's convention center that evening and there would be a big crowd. He mischievously suggested that, since the county had overwhelmingly supported my opponent, I might make a surprise appearance, demonstrating that I held no grudges.

When I arrived, dinner was over and the lights had been dimmed for the program. The crowd was huge, well over a thousand. I seated myself just inside the door at the back of the hall, and in the dimness, nobody saw me except the African American waiters—probably my only voters present. The speaker suddenly announced that in celebration of the county's extraordinary growth and tax base this year, there would be no speeches, but instead announced a surprise entertainment: "Direct from Nashville, Georgia's own Little Brenda Lee and her band!"

Wow! The lights were still not on, and three spotlights filled the stage. Nobody knew I was there, so I signaled a waiter for a double scotch and sat back to enjoy the show. All her hits came roaring out, and I was enjoying my second (or was it my third?) drink, when suddenly the music stopped and Brenda stepped forward with her hand cupped over her eyes, searching the audience. "I understand my old singing buddy Wyche Fowler—excuse me, Senator Wyche—is in the audience. Come on up here, Wyche, and let's sing together after so long." Spotlights crisscrossed the darkened room as I cringed in fear. Suddenly, they found me, the accused now exposed. What was I to do? Rising, I began approaching the stage among the applauding audience, all standing in tribute or politeness or derision.

In the glare of the stage, the petite Brenda extended the microphone upward as if interviewing an NBA all-star. "What'll it be, Wyche?" I swallowed hard, turned toward the band, and blurted, "Rockin' Robin in C!" Varoom! As we shouted out "he rocks in the treetops all the day long, hoppin' and a-boppin' and a-singing his song. Rockin' robin, oh, rockin' robin," I found myself skip—hopping around the stage on one leg, imitating Chuck Berry in his Johnny B Good glory. Suddenly, I came to my—addled—senses. As Brenda was demanding another song, I bolted off the stage, staggered down the central aisle, rammed the exit doors, stumbled into the parking lot, and vomited all party foods, alcohol, and pride before fleeing. The next morning's headline in the Cobb County newspaper trumpeted NEW SENATOR FOWLER STEALS SHOW AT ANNUAL CHAMBER OF COMMERCE EVENT.

Elementary School and High School

Fowler attended Atlanta's Morris Brandon Elementary School and Northside High School, where his grades were "decent," but his major interests, besides the church, were sports and music. He played guard on the basketball team and ran track, excelling at the latter as a two-time winner of All-State honors in cross-country. In his high school yearbook, he was described as possessing "a world of wit and heart of purest gold." His favorite singers were Buddy Holly and Chuck Berry, and it was his appreciation for African American music that led him, as a teenager during the highly segregated 1950s, to regularly attend performances at Black clubs such as the Royal Peacock and the Waluhaje. Fowler still possesses vivid memories of these occasions.

Throughout my high school years, I was a rock and roll fanatic, enthralled with the Black pioneers of this new music rage: Chuck Berry, Fats Domino, Chubby Checker, as well as Howlin' Wolf, Muddy Waters, B. B. King, and Clyde McPhatter and the Drifters.

I listened constantly to WAOK, the Black music and news station in Atlanta.

The highlight of our entertainment universe was the frequent weekend rock and roll concerts at the Municipal Auditorium, featuring many of the stars mentioned above. Ironically, these concerts became an unforeseen revelation to me into biracial politics. The auditorium had been constructed with two stories, the top story reached by a circular walkway, not unlike today's modern stadiums. Unusual was the concession area, built as a platform between the upper and lower floors, reached by the walkway, and servicing Black and white patrons together at the concert's intermission. In a reversal of the Old South plantation church seating arrangements, the whites were seated UPSTAIRS, and all Blacks were seated downstairs, stage center, where they were allowed to dance during the concert. Not us whites. We were to remain in our seats, cheering wildly, but no dancing. We mingled, over hot dogs and Cokes, at intermission.

If I saw a young man downstairs with a particular distinctive dance move, I would seek him out at intermission, introduce myself, and ask him to show me his technique. In that way I made my first African American friends, Ben Brown and Julian Bond, both of whom went on to be elected to the Georgia legislature, and the latter of whom became a nationally prominent figure in the civil rights and anti-war movements.

On one special summer's night in 1957, my friends and I had tickets to see Fats Domino, the unique vocal and musical stylist, at the top of his popularity. "Blueberry Hill" was my current favorite, but he had just reached the top of the charts with "Yes It's Me and I'm in Love Again," a catchy blues-doused rhythm impossible to absorb sitting still. And no one could. We whites bounced in our seats, while the Blacks were dancing in the aisles. Fats played the song THIRTY-TWO straight times before the crowd would let him go. It was a performance I can still see with clarity, all these many years later.

The following year, I went to a concert at the old Paramount Theater, in downtown Peachtree near Five Points, to hear a young phenom named Elvis Presley. Elvis wiggled and jerked with manic energy, and the teenage girls screamed with abandonment, but I was not impressed. Somehow, he seemed a poor substitute for Chuck Berry, Little Richard, or Fats Domino. Of course, I hadn't concentrated on his incredible voice: to me, he wasn't Black, therefore not authentic. How little I knew.

Many years later, in early August 1977, I led a delegation of young elected officials to five countries in East Africa on behalf of the American Council of Young Political Leaders. After bidding them adieu, I stayed in Tanzania to climb Mount Kilimanjaro. Upon completing that adventure, I arrived at the airport in Dar es Salaam for the flight to New York and home. The airport was jammed with Tanzanians in every possible combination of dress and color and headgear, pushing and shoving and singing. If I saw another white person, I don't remember it. Over the airport speaker system flights were being announced, gate changes were called, all in a cacophony of tribal-tinged English, virtually unintelligible to my ears.

Suddenly, as if a bomb had burst, everyone in the crowd dropped to their knees as one and began wailing and "gnashing of teeth" (as the Bible reports). I was the only human standing, a white man like the last colonialist, standing in a sea of a thousand crying Black Africans, unaware of the announcement that had caused the simultaneous collapse. "Elvis Presley has died," it was announced. The King had died on August 16. The mourning and shouted grief was still ringing in my ears as I boarded the plane for New York.

Fowler's formative years were not just about church, school and sports, however, and he displayed a penchant for occasional outbursts of anarchy. Even today, he can recall them (or at least his own version thereof) in some detail. For example, there was an incident in high school, involving a betting scheme on lunchroom attendance.

I was popular in school, despite my religious proclivities, which I'm sure some thought prudish or self-righteous. I was rewarded for my wit and mischievousness. In the 10th-grade homeroom one morning a sheet began appearing listing the absentees from the previous day as well as an item recording how many hot lunches were sold in the school cafeteria that day. Why, I wondered, as I mulled over the averages for the first week. Suddenly, I bet a friend a quarter that I could come closer to tomorrow's lunch count than he could. I lost and paid him his due. The idea came to me in a flash. I would enlist four to five of my colleagues to go to other homerooms and quietly get others to bet: the reward being still a quarter. By the end of the day, I had over fifteen dollars in quarters, and had paid out less than five dollars. Over the next school day, I enlisted over twenty collectors, then paid the quarter reward to the winners at the end of the day. After two weeks, I had over $300 in quarters in my basement at home, when over the loudspeaker Dr. Kelley intoned: "Wyche Fowler come immediately to the office." When I arrived, he accused: "I have evidence that you have been running a lottery over lunch sales." I had never heard that word in my life. Dumbfounded, I confessed the error of my ways, pleading innocent to any immoral or illegal purpose. Kelley was sympathetic, I think, and I only received a one-day suspension. The pain came from my father, who gave me quite a whipping. Thankfully, no one knew of my stash in the basement, and I emerged from the incident quite a rich man.

Or his pigeon release in the Fox Theatre...

The Fox Theatre in Atlanta is now on the National Register of Historic Places, but in high school it was the premier dating facility, enormous with its 1,500 seats, many dark alcoves, and opportunities to steal a kiss from a reluctant first date. (It also hosted the Metropolitan Opera's first stop on their national tour for over forty years.) It had the city's largest silver cinemascope screen, which became my undoing.

On a lazy Saturday in summer, Harold Wells, Harry Lange, and I were eating hot dogs in Harold's convertible at the Varsity, another Atlanta legend, which was founded in 1928. We had no dates for the evening. Pigeons proliferate at the Varsity, and today was no exception as they circled our car, picking the scraps thrown at them. I had an idea. I bet the two of them that I could catch a pigeon before them on a two-hour time limit. They accepted and began making traps of Varsity boxes using a stick prop and a string for capture. What they didn't know is that I had seen a butterfly net in a pawn shop window across the street on North Avenue. That became my weapon. My pigeon was easily entrapped first. Their traps were ingenious and succeeded. Suddenly, we had three birds!

What to do? A Jimmy Stewart movie was playing at the Fox and someone—could it have been me?—suggested that we release our birds in the theater. In those days, one could take food into the theater, and after purchasing our tickets, we approached the young ticket-taker with our Varsity boxes in hand. I was first. Peeep! came a sound from my box. "What did you say?" said the kid. I said "Peeep" and marched forward into the theater, as did the other two.

To reach the balcony, or loge, as it was named, we had to walk up fifteen or twenty stairs, then descend approximately the same number to reach the front row of the loge. It was around 5 P.M. and the crowd was sparse. No one else was on our row and we nervously sat with our boxes in our laps. Going first, I slipped my hands under the pigeon's breast and launched it upward with a whispered, "Shoooo." The bird landed on the rail in front of me with a flutter. Panicking, I grabbed it and flung it downward into space. It was followed instantly by Harold and Harry's birds. Suddenly, all three birds—in full flight—headed towards the $20,000 cinemascope screen. Bam! One of them hit Jimmy Stewart on his nose. Crash! The next one hit his horse. We were off and running, with moviegoers cheering wildly as the birds cartwheeled toward the screen's light. We almost made it, but having to run up the stairs to reach the downward stair exit gave the redcoats, as the formally attired ushers wearing red jackets were known, time to surround us. When Harold was tackled, Harry and I surrendered.

The authorities took us to the Fulton County Juvenile Court. Which parent to be called confirming our arrest? Not mine; no way. I would rather be jailed than face my father and his belt. Harry's father, a medical doctor with a sense of humor, as it turned out, came to get us. After much discussion outside of our presence—and with Dr. Lange agreeing to pay any damage to the screen—we were released with no record of the incident, preserving our chances of going to college. My parents never found out until years later and were not amused. No bill for damages to the theater ever arrived.

I realized that I had dodged a bullet and understood that my impulsive mischievousness was thoughtless, as serious property damage could have occurred. It was time to curb my instincts and reflect the mature individual I—and my parents—thought myself to be. For the rest of the school year, I sought redemption in serious study, hoping to make the National Honor Society.

Alongside these isolated incidents of mischief, Fowler's natural curiosity also led him to more constructive pursuits, though even in recalling these, he cannot resist the urge to add drama and humorous twists.

The summer between my junior and senior year at Northside High School was spent with my aunt Lucile (one of two of my mother's older sisters) in Washington, Georgia. She was jovial and playful, not unlike my mother, and I always enjoyed her company. Lucile's stately and grand Georgian home was always on the national tour of homes, and Lucile often regaled us with the story of opening the door one morning in her pajamas and curlers to confront a startled Adlai Stevenson, who had mistaken the dates of the tour and arrived a week early. She, of course, welcomed him in.

Also in residence that summer were Patti and Peggy Lindsey, my first cousins, twin daughters of Lucile's son Willis. The twins were studying medicine at Duke Medical School, anticipating graduation in December upon completion of mandatory gynecological training to be held at a rural public clinic in the town. The clinic was supervised by Dr. Charles Willis, revered by all and the only general practitioner in a four-county area. Throughout that part of the state, it was known that the clinic would deliver for free all babies whose mothers agreed to the teaching atmospherics of medical students in training. This being the rural South in 1957, it was known as a "Black clinic," since no self-regarding white supremacist would tarnish their family reputation by having their child born into amateur hands in a facility that also birthed African American babies.

Each night over dinner, Patti and Peggy would delight us with the day's births, the obstacles to be overcome in natural birth, and finally the overwhelming emotional experience of assisting in the miracle of life. I was overcome with curiosity and asked Lucile if I might come watch. She did not hesitate, picking up the phone, reaching Dr. Willis, and simply declaring, "Little Wyche wants to come watch the babies being born." (My father was always "Big Wyche.") "That'll be fine; send him with the girls tomorrow."

There were seven of us, six medical students and me. The students, under Dr. Willis' careful supervision were arranged around the birthing table, complete with available oxygen and stirrups. Each took turns in a delivery, with six to eight births a day. Problems, we were told, were minimal, as many babies were born at home "or in the fields," Dr. Willis exclaimed, with no assistance "except the Divine." Our major intervention, we learned, must come when the baby's neck is crooked to the side in the cervix and must be straightened inside the womb, or when the umbilical cord has somehow wrapped the child's neck and must be untangled. We had several such incidents over the four days of my participation, but all were resolved by the students, and healthy babies were born.

After two or three rounds of birth (eighteen to twenty babies), Dr. Willis looked at me with a mirthful grin, "Would you like to deliver the next one?" Surprisingly, I was not nervous. And after pulling out a slippery boy, cleaning his mouth, slapping him upside down on his bottom, clipping the chord, and with assistance tying it, I was in the rotation, part of the team, and delivered five more babies the next two days.

When I returned to high school my senior year, I was convinced my adventure would titillate the girls and enhance my sexiness with them. Instead, everyone I told was horrified, and immediately branded me a weirdo to be shunned, one even breaking a date to an upcoming Saturday night dance. Needless to say, I did not make that mistake with college girls, relegating the thrill of my experience to the secret category of my "little bag of tricks."

In addition to elucidating details about his life before it came under the scrutiny and documentation of public service, which will largely predominate in later chapters, these tales provide ample proof of one of Mr. Fowler's lifelong traits: his affinity for, and skills in, storytelling, which here is not meant to convey any notion of untruth, but rather stories in the sense of the National Storyteller's Network definition: "Storytelling is the interactive art of using words and actions to reveal the elements and images of a story while encouraging the listener's imagination." And for all of those who have *heard* and *seen* Fowler deliver these accounts, it must be said that reducing them to the printed word loses much of the impact of his oral delivery, which comes complete with changing facial expressions, sound effects, gesticulations, and other performance accompaniments.

College, Citibank, and Army Intelligence

In 1958, Fowler enrolled at Davidson College just outside of Charlotte, North Carolina, majoring in English, with a minor in biblical studies. Among his extracurricular activities were serving on the student council, joining the Phi Delta Theta fraternity, volunteering at an orphanage, teaching a Sunday school class, coaching a basketball team of African American teenagers, and participating in the campus Reserve Officers Training Corps (ROTC), a college-based program that provided preparatory training for commissioned officers of the US Armed Forces in exchange for government-funded tuition assistance. His time at Davidson caused him to "really examine my [religious] faith, make it stronger, and be able to back it up," and he became, and remains, a Presbyterian. Davidson was founded by Presbyterians in 1837, and its church ties were still strong when Fowler was there. His theological history, which began as a Baptist, led Fowler to quip, "That makes me something rare in the religious world: a totally immersed Presbyterian."

His religious faith remained strong, but by the time Fowler graduated from college in 1962, he was no longer inclined toward a career in the ministry. Instead, he was beginning to look toward serving the public in another capacity, though his first experience here resulted in failure.

> I absorbed my first lesson in politics my junior year at Davidson when I ran for student body president. Voters vote against a candidate more frequently than they vote for him. I was defeated by a ghost, my friend George Trask, who was away in France for his entire junior year. Whereas I campaigned constantly, going from one fraternity house to another seeking to persuade, George merely sent in written responses on campaign issues prepared by the school newspaper. He was invisible, could not be questioned, and had an aura around his candidacy that I could not challenge from the trenches. I lost by a handful of votes, defeated by a friendly "ghost." George remained a wonderful friend and was forever proud of the fact that he was the first to contribute to my initial campaign for Congress.

Upon graduation, Fowler moved to New York City and worked at Citibank for eighteen months in 1962 and 1963. While there, he got another opportunity to use the lessons he had learned at Dr. Willis's clinic years before.

> I landed my first real job at First National City Bank (now branded Citibank) in New York, headquartered at 399 Park Avenue. I was enrolled in the bank's executive training program and shared my first apartment with two other trainees over the Lexington Avenue subway at 96th and Lexington. On pretty days, we often skipped down the forty-four blocks to our office and in the evening sampled the local bars, ate at Tad's Steaks (steak and baked potato for $1.29), and saw our first foreign films, which were far sexier and complicated than the Hollywood offerings. Upon occasion, a senior executive would invite one of us to lunch in the executive dining room on the 39th floor. This was the heyday of the three-martini lunch.
>
> I had never had anything more potent than a beer during my college days, so when I had my first sip of a straight-up gin martini, I could feel the dizziness coming on. I must say my superiors usually stopped at two, and I, at two sips, but it slowed me for the rest of the day. Until I arrived in London for a brief stint at the London School of Economics (LSE) after my army service, I had never seen

more serious drinking over lunch. But British journalists, many of whom became my closest friends, made my banker executives look like teetotalers and initiated me into a lifestyle of tippling that I have found hard to shake.

On a hot summer afternoon at the bank in 1963, I was watching the clock in anticipation of a second date with a girl I had met at a party. I had worn my white seersucker suit, purchased at great expense from Brooks Brothers, to impress her. Shortly before 5 P.M., a huge thunderstorm erupted, with cascades of rain drenching Park Avenue, ensnaring the traffic, and making cabs impossible to obtain. I waited outside under shelter for more than thirty minutes, but the rain did not slow and traffic was at a standstill. Suddenly, a man emerged from a cab in the far lane, and I raced to it and dived in, already soaked.

Nothing moved, but suddenly, a distraught Hispanic woman pounded on the taxi door, screaming and pleading for admittance. "Don't let her in," the driver yelled. But I did. She dived over me, moaning, "Hospital, hospital," as I realized that she was hugely pregnant. Subconsciously, I began to time her contractions and realized the time was upon us. I yelled at the driver to get us to a hospital "even if you have to drive on the sidewalk." She would not calm down, so finally I put my arm around her and breathed, "Doctore, doctore." Her crying ceased and she swooned into my chest.

We still searched for a lane to advance, when I felt her legs jumping and sensed her water break. Reflexively I got to my knees and caught the baby boy as he emerged, as drenched in blood as we were drenched in water. Instantly, I cleared his mouth, and holding him by the ankles, gave him a good slap which bashed his head against the closed window. Holding my breath in terror, I released it when the wail of the newborn's salutation filled the cab.

The next fifteen to thirty minutes—who knows how long—passed with me holding the crying child complete with afterbirth, the mother passed out on my shoulder, and the cabbie screaming at me over the cost of cleaning his cab. There was blood everywhere, and I bemoaned the demise of my beautiful white suit. There were no cell phones in those days, so I had no way of calling my date. When I reached her hours later, she accused me of lying. I never saw her again. Finally, we reached Presbyterian Hospital on the Upper East Side. As the stretchers arrived in the emergency entrance, mother and child were taken. I had persuaded the driver to take me home to get money for his cleanup, when an administrative functionary dragged me inside to sign forms. She assumed I was the father of the child. Finally, I was released. Days later, while doing the hospital paperwork, I regretted that I had not named the child. Maybe name him Jose Wyche Gonzalez. Today he might be the multi-million-dollar shortstop of the New York Yankees. What a windfall my descendants might have had.

After his time at the bank and fulfilling his ROTC commitment, Fowler was called into the US Army in February of 1964 as a second lieutenant intelligence officer. After basic training at Fort Benning near Columbus, Georgia, he went on to Fort Holabird in Baltimore, Maryland, where he received intelligence training during the summer of 1964. In the fall of that year, he was assigned to the Pentagon, where his focus was on assessing domestic terrorism, which at that time included surveillance of civil rights leaders. Thus began Fowler's long-term interest in intelligence policy, including the need for appropriate accountability and oversight.

Chapter 2

A Life in Public Service (1963–1977): A Change in Plans

Charles Weltner

While he was still in the army, in 1963 Fowler volunteered to work in the Washington, DC, office of US Representative Charles Longstreet Weltner, a first-term congressman representing Atlanta's Fifth Congressional District. It would prove to be a pivotal moment that strongly influenced the future course of his life and career.

Weltner was thirty-four years old when elected to Congress in 1962, defeating eight-term incumbent and avowed segregationist James C. Davis in the Democratic primary and going on to win in the general election as well. His two terms in the House of Representatives (1963–1966) were dominated by the issue of civil rights, and Weltner emerged as one of the most conspicuous figures in the legislative struggles of those years.

Having already earned a reputation as a supporter of civil rights while he was practicing law in the late 1950s and early 1960s, in his first year in office Weltner spoke out in favor of stepping up implementation of the Supreme Court's *Brown v. Board of Education of Topeka* decision that outlawed segregation in public schools. In September 1963, he denounced the bombing of a Birmingham church that killed four Black children, stating, "It happened because those chosen to lead have failed to lead. Those whose task it is to speak have stood mute. And in so doing, we have permitted the voice of the South to preach defiance and disorder. We have stood by, leaving the field to reckless and violent men."[2]

It was the front-page *Washington Post* account of Weltner's speech that caused Lt. Fowler, serving as an army intelligence officer in the Pentagon, to call the congressman, who invited him to his office for coffee. Weltner's first impression was that Fowler "was extremely bright...[and] he was brought up with a sense that you ought to be here to help other people."[3] Fowler began volunteering in Weltner's office shortly thereafter, and when discharged from his military service, he accepted the congressman's offer to become his chief of staff in January 1965, at age twenty-four. Thus began his lifelong friendship with a brilliant mentor, ending only with Weltner's death in 1992 while serving as chief justice of the Georgia Supreme Court.

Perhaps the high point in Weltner's congressional career came in July 1964, when, after having opposed an earlier version, he announced on the House floor that he had changed his mind and would vote for the final version of what became the landmark Civil Rights Act of 1964. Weltner told the House, "We in the South face some difficult decisions. We can offer resistance and defiance, with their harvest of strife and tumult. We can suffer continued demonstrations, with their wake of violence and disorder. Or we can acknowledge this measure as the law of the land." He was one of only seven Southerners—and the only member of the Georgia delegation or from the Deep South—to support the legislation. Weltner also voted in favor of the Voting Rights Act of 1965, a measure that literally helped to change the face of Southern politics and which had an ongoing impact on the Fifth District and Wyche Fowler's political career in the years ahead.

All of this made a deep impression on Fowler during his time in the Weltner office. Years later, Weltner recalled Fowler's work in his office, remembering that it was Fowler who initiated the publication of a newsletter to constituents, and adding, "What Wyche did was outwork everybody else. What he is especially good at is handling a myriad of little details.... He remembers people. Wyche has an engaging personality.... And he has a pleasantly realistic view. He does not take himself overly seriously." This was also the period when Fowler started accumulating a mailing list of key political contacts in Atlanta, the list that would serve as the starting point for his own future campaigns.

After winning the Democratic primary nomination for reelection in 1966, on October 3, Weltner withdrew from the general election contest rather than fulfill the newly developed oath that he and all other Democratic candidates had earlier signed pledging to support the entire Democratic ticket. The problem was that arch-segregationist Lester Maddox had unexpectedly won the Democratic gubernatorial primary, prompting Weltner to announce, "While I cannot violate my oath, I cannot violate my principles. I cannot compromise with hate. I cannot vote for Lester

Maddox. Therefore, I am withdrawing as the Democratic nominee for the House of Representatives."[4] Fowler and the rest of Weltner's staff were all out of a job on January 2, 1967.

It was also during this period that Fowler met and befriended Don Anderson, who served as a staffer for the flamboyant and controversial congressman from Harlem Adam Clayton Powell. Anderson later founded and served for many years as executive director of the National Association of the Southern Poor, which sought to organize and enable low-income, predominantly African American Southerners to overcome discrimination and poverty.

Fowler and Anderson remained close friends over many years, as Wyche recently remembered.

> One of my closest friends during my Washington years was a green-eyed Black man from central Florida, Donald Louis Anderson. Don was almost indescribable—and irresistible. He was a Shakespearean scholar, staging complete plays at his horse farm in the mountains of Virginia. He loved and studied grand opera, memorizing famous arias in French, German, and Italian. He trained Tennessee walkers, leading his friends on long rides in the Virginia wilderness. (I was thrown twice while furiously cantering, miraculously surviving with my bones intact.) He cooked elaborate dinners for his friends and strode the mountains surrounding him at dusk dressed in Scottish cap and kilt, playing the bagpipes "for the entertainment of his goats," he said.
>
> Late one summer evening, I arrived at Daniel's Mountain, named after the grave of an enslaved individual Don and I had uncovered on the property some years earlier. Don greeted me looking weak and worn. His prized nanny goat, Matilda, lay pregnant and dying, unable to discharge the baby lodged in her uterus. Having heard my birthing stories many times, Don pleaded, "Can you do something?"
>
> Arriving at the barn, I saw that death was close. Matilda lay on her side, quivering, gnats infesting her eyes. Sending Don to the cabin for Vaseline, I greased my hands and arms, unsure what to do but determined to try something. Don held the goat's hind legs to ensure that my teeth were not kicked out. I knelt and began

slowly to work my hands up and into the birth canal. Matilda whimpered but did not resist. Suddenly, my hands found the head, crooked and lodged sideways. Sweating profusely, and remembering Dr. Willis's instructions, I cradled the baby's head in my hands and tugged down and at an angle, freeing it. Within seconds, the baby goat began to emerge, and suddenly there it was, standing before us, bleating, on all four legs. I was crying; Don was crying; the baby goat was crying. (I'm even crying as I write this.) Matilda had fallen into an exhaustive sleep. We warmed goat's milk we had in the house and fed the baby by bottle for two days before I had to return to Washington. When I left, the baby, its mother, and the grandfather seemed to be doing well. All survived.

It was almost a year before I returned to Daniel's Mountain to attend a performance of *Othello* starring Donald (of course) in the title role. Donald awaited me in front of the cabin. "Come, come quickly, I've got to see if you can pick out Little Wyche," as he had named it. "Don't be ridiculous," I countered, knowing that most goats look alike and wanting a strong whiskey after the four-hour drive from Washington. But Don would not be deterred. He blew a whistle signaling feeding time, and the herd of goats, seventeen of them, came leaping and struggling over the landscape anticipating their evening meal.

I looked and looked and looked from goat to goat, searching frantically for an identity. Suddenly, I recognized *my goat*! Its head was elongated and lop-sided, one eye several inches higher than the other. Its lips were sealed in a crooked smile, made even more sinister as the goat's nose was straightforward and unaffected. I had created a Frankenstein goat, horror of horrors! After laughing and crying and laughing again, I told Don that my medical career was over, and we both praised God that there would be no goat malpractice lawsuit.

In the years that followed, we stayed in close touch, and Don even worked briefly on my congressional staff. Donald died in 2002 and was buried at Daniel's Mountain next to his enslaved forebearers. He was a generous and thoughtful friend. I miss him every day.

After Charles Weltner's decision to resign, Fowler went to England to study at the London School of Economics during the winter of 1966 to 1967. While there, he satisfied his love of theater by taking advantage of cheap student tickets and concentrating on productions of Shakespeare. He also hitchhiked around Ireland, touring sites associated with his favorite poet, William Butler Yeats.

Years later, Fowler amplified his recollections of this transitional period in his life, which reveal an interest in travel as a way of broadening one's perspectives.

> When Charles Weltner resigned from his office the day after winning the Democratic primary, all staff were also "out of office." I was twenty-five in August 1966, and I determined to do something adventurous. Having been an Anglophile since college days, I took off for London, hoping to enroll in the London School of Economics. It turned out to be easy, as English colleges are a vast library for self-study and writing papers. Lectures are sparsely attended.
>
> I made several friends but mostly took advantage of the extraordinary theater, music halls, and museums of London. Come spring break in March, I took a boat to Ireland, intent on following the known paths of W. B. Yeats, my poetic hero. Hitchhiking in Ireland proved easy, as Irish drivers were anxious to lend a hand and hear a new story. A few days into my travels, I spent the day in Sligo, Yeats's birthplace, then caught a ride with a lorry driver who suggested I stay overnight in an inn some distance on the road north. It was dark when I left him at what seemed a crossroads in a tiny village with an unpronounceable name. (I have tried mightily to find it on maps to no avail.) But here was the inn, an ancient pub with four rooms upstairs for rent. I feasted on my usual fare, Irish stew and Guinness, and retired rather early over the pub. At around four in the morning, a cascade of church bells rang out. I leapt from my bed, fearing a fire (my father had been trapped in a hotel fire with one leg badly burned). Thankfully, that was not the case.
>
> Overnight there had been a freak snowstorm, rather late in the season, that deposited four to six inches and threatened the sheep in the county. A region of slowly rolling hills, the sheep wandered

the hillsides, fenced in by dry rock walls along the roads. The snow would have been no threat, but sheep, being God's most stupid creatures, panicked at the first flakes and ran downhill to hunker next to the wall, eventually to be covered by the drifting snow. With the sheep facing suffocation, the clanging bells called the men of the village to the pub to save them.

I joined the volunteer force. Issued the bottoms of Guinness bottles to use as sunglasses against the blinding reflection of the dawning sun off the snow, seven of us walked the stone walls, searching for two nostril holes in the snowbank. If the sheep, in its panic and panting, can melt a passageway for air, there is hope of a rescue. I found my first holes in the snow, and held by my ankles upside down by a strapping Irish shepherd, I dug down to find a sheep, already dead. The same thing happened a second time.

The next time, as I dug feverishly, the lamb emerged almost leaping into my arms. It was alive and was saved, and I suddenly realized that the dumb creature knew that it had been saved. This was a moment of spiritual insight that I had not experienced since my baptism and conversion as a child. Jesus's parable of lostness and salvation was the focus of this insight: "There is more joy in heaven over the one (sheep) that was lost and is found, than over the ninety and nine that were safely in the pen" (Luke 15:3–6). I rescued two more that morning, crying all the time as the real shepherds looked on in bewilderment.

Meantime, Weltner had accepted a position as deputy chairman of the Democratic National Committee. One of his specific roles was to oversee the committee's newly created Young Americans Division, which sought to improve the party's appeal to younger voters. Always restless, Weltner convinced himself he was too old to be recruiting young voters and telephoned Fowler in England, pleading with him to come home and assume that role. Fowler readily obliged, saying it was too cold in London anyway, and he took over as executive director of the division on April 15, 1967. In this capacity, among other duties, he supervised college interns doing policy and political research and represented the DNC at various forums across the country. One of the latter was an October 1967 appearance at Texas A&M University in which the young Georgian appeared with Illinois Republican congressman (and future secretary of defense) Donald Rumsfeld. Both men urged the college students to get involved in public affairs, with Fowler saying, "The major crisis our country faces today is not the Vietnam War or race riots but the changing attitudes of our young people. Your generation is sick of hearing how well off you are, because you can see clearly how far we still have to go. And you can determine how far we go by becoming involved in government."

Rumsfeld and Fowler then outlined their views on the differences between the two parties.

> **Rumsfeld:** "The Democratic Party is an anachronism. It is a marriage of convenience, formed of groups with diverse and conflicting interests. It is an alliance formed, not to govern, but to hold power, and the result has been ineffective government. [The Republican Party] is the party of opportunity."
>
> **Fowler:** "Democrats try to figure out how to do things, while Republicans try to figure out how not to do things. The more the Republicans look to the past, the more we must look to the future. The more they polarize politics around the negative side, the more we must look to the positive side. The more the Republican Party becomes exclusive, the more the Democratic Party must become inclusive."[5]

At the end of the presentations the audience voted and chose Fowler as the winner of the debate.

Law School (1967–1969)

Fowler returned to Georgia in September 1967 to attend Emory University's law school, where he earned his law degree in December 1969 after going straight through for nine consecutive quarters. His father had urged him to go to law school to increase his career options and ensure his independence, believing this path would enable his son to pursue whatever he wanted to do.

> After my two years in the army and my six months at the LSE in London, I decided to please my father by going to law school after

years of procrastination. I had received an acceptance several years previously from Emory law school in Atlanta, but that had expired. I drove to the campus to see Dean Ben Johnson, an acquaintance, but a close friend of Charles Weltner, to tell him of my plans. He expressed excitement and was sure my application would be accepted for the following year. "Sir," I began, "I was hoping to begin this term." "But school began two weeks ago," the dean replied. "Yes, I know, but don't you have several dropouts in the first few weeks?" I smiled. After several back-and-forths, he threw up his hands and said, "You win." I began classes the next morning.

Many faculty were not amused by my breaking and entering. When I entered my first class on civil procedure, Professor William Ferguson threw up his hands in mock delight, proclaiming, "Class, we now have a major constitutional scholar in our midst, straight from the halls of Congress. When challenged I will defer to his judgment." Several other faculty members reacted with undisguised disdain.

While still in law school, Fowler took a first step in his own political career in the summer of 1968 by approaching Atlanta's then-mayor, Ivan Allen Jr., with an unusual offer. Allen was Hartsfield's progressive, handpicked successor, and he had defeated Lester Maddox in the 1961 mayor's race. Observing that there was an unmet need for the city to assist people with problems during the hours when the mayor's office was closed at night and on weekends, Fowler volunteered to serve as an unpaid "ombudsman" who would try to help respond to such problems. Allen went along with the idea, which in practice amounted primarily to Fowler answering the mayor's phone. Displaying the kind of political savvy he would later be noted for, however, Fowler described his position to any who would listen (especially in the news media) as Atlanta's "Night Mayor." After spending ten weeks in that role during that summer, Fowler was employed as an associate with Gerald Horton's Research Group, which specialized in governmental consulting work.

At the beginning of 1970, Fowler began working at the Atlanta law firm of Smith, Cohen, Ringel, Kohler, Martin and Lowe. He specialized in insurance cases, was noted for his trial summations, never lost a case, and generally enjoyed the experience. He remained at Smith Cohen until his election to Congress in 1977, although his interest and involvement in politics remained strong throughout that time.

1969 Atlanta City Elections

The "Night Mayor" resume-builder came in handy when Fowler sought his first elected office in 1969. He ran for a seat on Atlanta's Board of Aldermen, the legislative body that preceded the current city council, at age twenty-nine while still in law school.

> I soldiered on [in law school], with mediocre grades due to the major distraction I created: I announced my candidacy for the Atlanta Board of Aldermen. I do not know how or when my decision was made. As became the pattern in all my subsequent races, I did not consult with anyone or seek any professional advice. I realized my age and lack of a career would be drawbacks, but I had two major advantages: Weltner's congressional mailing lists, including all donors, and a free campaign worker force sitting aside me in class. All I had to do was ask them, and many signed up for the lark. The election was citywide, and the district was almost contiguous with Weltner's congressional district, which I knew well.
>
> One professor, politically astute, was my contracts teacher Tarver Rountree, who was as big around as his name. We became friends after classes, as he was genuinely interested in my politics. The day before my candidacy announcement, I took the handwritten draft to Dr. Rountree to seek his opinion. He read it silently, uttering not a word. "Please, sir, don't spare me. I've never written such a thing before." "Well," he finally said, "Your content is fine and you strike the right notes, but if you're going to have a future in Georgia politics, I think this is the last time that you should match subject and verb." I remembered that advice, especially when campaigning statewide for the U.S. Senate.

Atlanta's political structure at the time, established in 1954, consisted of the unicameral Board of Aldermen, which was comprised of sixteen members: two aldermen representing each of Atlanta's eight wards (or districts); the vice mayor, who served as the presiding officer of the Board of Aldermen; and the mayor. A new Ninth Ward was created prior to the

1969 elections, bringing the total number of aldermanic positions to be elected at that time to eighteen. However, though the aldermen represented specific districts, they, along with the mayor and vice mayor, were elected citywide. Thus, Fowler had to seek support from all across Atlanta.

On April 1, 1969, Wyche Fowler formally launched his first bid for elective office, stating, "Atlanta's reputation for progressive government must continue to be earned, lest like quicksilver it slip from our grasp. The need for vigorous, tough-minded aldermen has never been greater; men of intellectual energy and physical stamina; men not wedded to last year's solution; men who view change as a challenge to be harnessed for the public good."

In a May 1969 article in the *Atlanta Journal and Constitution*, which focused on Fowler, Maynard Jackson, and other "next generation" candidates and potential candidates in the upcoming municipal elections, the twenty-eight-year-old Fowler commented on his objectives in seeking office and the significance of that generational change.

> The major impetus in my decision to run for alderman is my experience in government, which really was given to me at an early age. I feel very strongly about a responsibility for public service, and last summer in the mayor's office I saw the need is as great on the local level, if not greater.... Young people feel very strongly about wanting to participate in the decision-making process. They have the time. They're not caught in possible conflicts of interest, the way some established businessmen may be. They have the flexibility of mind to solve old problems.[6]

Years later, Fowler reflected on the filing of his paperwork to officially qualify as a candidate, which brought to mind another of his adventures.

> In late summer of 1969, I arrived at the Fulton County Court House to file papers and pay a small fee to qualify for a position on the ballot for election to the Atlanta Board of Aldermen, as it was then known. I also deliberately swore to a falsehood. Amidst the litany of questions that had to be answered in the negative—"Have you ever committed a felony," "Have you ever been arrested for

drunk driving," "Have you ever had your driver's license revoked," "Are you, or have you ever been a member of the Communist party"—I discovered the following: "Have you ever been to a nudist colony?" This qualifier was added by the state legislature after a nudist colony was discovered operating in the north Georgia mountains the preceding year. I hesitated, swallowed hard, and lied.

Three years earlier, in the fall of 1966, shortly after Charles Weltner's resignation from Congress, I received a call from Jimmy Goldsmith, who was to achieve wealth and prominence as a corporate raider, inviting me to a party in Nice, France, celebrating his acquisition of a French bank on very favorable terms. Jimmy, who had been expelled from Cambridge for gambling, had gambled big and won big in the bank sweepstakes. This was to be the first of many such successes in Europe and in America.

Jimmy had rented a prominent bistro near the waterfront and had, for the occasion, imported a New Orleans Preservation Hall band along with approximately fifty international guests. Fine wines and champagne were inexhaustible; I danced and drank and flirted with many European socialites, chattering hesitantly in my inadequate high school French. (*Descendants*! This was my earliest realization that to live a full life with all its opportunities one *must* learn a second language.) As 2 A.M. arrived, the exhausted band announced the last number, but Jimmy—and the crowd—wanted more. Suddenly, Jimmy seized the microphone and announced that he had *bought the band*! and that the night would continue.

Finally, shortly before sunrise, those of us who remained standing (about sixteen, as I remember) were led, staggering, on board a yacht that immediately set sail. I collapsed with the others on deck and awoke hours later with a German tuba player's stomach as my pillow. Hungover and hungry, we passengers discovered there was no food on board, only cases of champagne. Suddenly, passing a distant island, somebody yelled that there were nudes playing volleyball on the beach. Jimmy, who just finished berating the captain for his food folly, ordered him to set sail for the island. "Non, non, monsieur, it is forbidden." "*Pour quoi*?" "It is the Ile du Levant (the Isle of the Rising Sun), the oldest private nudist colony in Europe.

No one but members are allowed. We are not allowed." I knew that would not deter Jimmy.

Positioning *his* band on the bow, he ordered the captain to change course, and we drew a bead on the colony as the band played "When the Saints Go Marching In." As we closed in on the harbor, the hills disgorged its nudists, nudists of all shapes, sizes, and physical distortions, which I shall not describe. Meeting us on the dock, the completely naked head nudist recited the rules of the colony, forbidding us to disembark. Jimmy began his negotiation: "We would propose to have lunch with you, and then we will offer a concert." "Non, monsieur, *c'est impossible*." "We will bring you your lunch on board, and then you can serenade us from your ship in the harbor." "Non, monsieur, *c'est impossible*. We will dine with you like gentlemen, and then give you a fine concert."

Jimmy's tenacity won the day, as we knew it would. We agreed to follow the legendary customs of the island and disrobe before proceeding to our lunch. Afterwards we would perform the concert from our yacht, for an audience of approximately three hundred nudists seated on land. Positioning the band to lead us again playing "When the Saints Go Marching In," we wiggled and hopped and danced up a winding path to luncheon on a hilltop. Along the way, the celebrants waved palm fronds and shouted hosannas, a contrast often remarked upon for those who know the conditions under which Jesus entered Jerusalem.

The "restaurant" was in a Quonset hut, windowless and barren of all but long tables and primitive chairs. At the entrance were two boxes, one filled with muumuus for the women, the other with jock straps for us men. It was explained that this protocol was to protect one from "spilled soup." I found myself seated to the left of the head nudist; Jimmy, being the guest of honor, was on his right. Once seated, I noticed a man entering with what looked like an X on his strap. "Why does that man have an X on his strap?" I innocently inquired. "An X?," the leader exclaimed. "That's not an X, that's a cross. He's our parish priest!"

After our concert, twenty to thirty women of all ages and sizes beseeched us to take them cruising, with no requested time of re-

> turn. I can still see Jimmy, in a marvelous imitation of Alec Guinness in *The Bridge on the River Kwai*, trooping the line with an improvised swagger stick, anointing the chosen with a tap on the shoulder, while the rejected slunk away, abandoned. We set sail with our new gleeful passengers. Sadly, the story must end here. Use your imagination.

In the 1969 city elections, Fowler ran for Position 2 in Ward 5, which was located on Atlanta's northeast side. The seat opened up when longtime incumbent G. Everett Millican declared his intention to run for mayor. Fowler faced three opponents in the nonpartisan October 7 election: Terry Ecker, a law school graduate and iron worker; Vito Pulverenti, a taxi driver; and Ed Walters, a graduate of Troy State University and a white staffer at Martin Luther King Jr.'s Southern Christian Leadership Conference (SCLC).

Touting himself as the "Night Mayor," Fowler ran a low-budget campaign, with most of his campaign effort involving personal appearances and many of his campaign volunteers recruited from his law school class. He supported consolidation of the Atlanta and Fulton County governments as a way of improving governmental efficiency and providing an adequate revenue base for the city and prioritizing the preservation of residential neighborhoods in zoning decisions. As the campaign progressed, much of Fowler's support came from African American constituents owing to his affinity for campaigning in the Black community and the belief of many in the white establishment that he was "too young and too liberal." In coming years, more than one observer would comment on Fowler's effectiveness in speaking at African American churches, a setting where perhaps his own earlier religious training and inclinations were most at home. Both of the major Atlanta papers endorsed Fowler, with the *Constitution* calling him the one "who probably has the best leadership potential of any candidate running for the aldermanic board," and the *Journal* citing him as "a bright young man."[7]

Fowler won easily, garnering 37,082 votes, which represented 62.9 percent of all votes cast in the race. He later recalled, "I won the aldermanic race handily, thanks largely to my reputation as the Night Mayor, and the indefatigable campaigning of my Emory classmates. I became the youngest member of the eighteen-member board."

The 1969 city elections also witnessed milestones in the evolution of Atlanta politics. The biracial coalition of the African American and moderate white population and the Atlanta business community that had dominated elections since the time of William Hartsfield began to fall apart. Mayor Allen, the inheritor of the Hartsfield tradition, did not run for reelection, but endorsed Republican alderman Rodney Cook for mayor. Allen's choice was resisted by many liberal and moderate white and African American voters. In the ensuing multi-candidate race for mayor, white citizens split their votes between Cook and Vice Mayor Sam Massell, who was considered the more progressive of the two, whereas Black voters divided their votes between Massell and Horace Tate, an African American educator. The result was that no candidate received the requisite majority, and a runoff election was held two weeks later between the top two finishers, Cook and Massell. In the runoff, the white vote remained divided, but Massell won more than 90 percent of the African American vote, which provided him with the victory.

Of greater long-term significance, Atlanta lawyer Maynard Jackson was able to avoid a runoff in the four-candidate field for vice mayor by winning 58 percent of the vote, including 98 percent of the Black vote and more than a quarter of the white vote. In the process, Jackson became the first African American to hold that post. Thus, in the end, the Black-moderate-white coalition more or less held together, but this time without the business establishment.

Before Fowler took office, Weltner discussed his protégé in an *Atlanta Constitution* article.

> One of [the newly elected members of the Board of Aldermen] is Wyche Fowler, who won his first race for public office by an impressive margin in a field of four.... His legal training, together with extensive experience in governmental and political matters in Washington, combine to make up an unusual combination of talents. He takes office with the psychological advantage of a fine victory, a youthful enthusiasm, and a determination to serve well. There are no encumbrances—either in the form of entangling campaign promises or debilitating campaign debts. Fowler can be counted on to make things happen. He and his new colleagues can

make a substantial and long lasting contribution to the people they serve. Let us hope that they will.[8]

1969 was also the year in which Wyche Fowler married, wedding Sue Skaggs in July. Daughter Katherine was born a little more than a year later, on September 27, 1970, but the marriage ended in divorce in June 1973.

Board of Aldermen (1970–1973)

Fowler and the other newly elected city officials were sworn in on January 5, 1970, in a ceremony at Atlanta's City Hall. He was to continue in public office continuously for the next twenty-two years.

As a member of the Board of Aldermen, Wyche Fowler authored the Atlanta Government-in-the-Sunshine Ordinance that prohibited all closed-door sessions of the city's agencies, and the Safe Streets and Sidewalks Ordinance. He sponsored the first measures to provide significant municipal funding for the arts, and gained approval of an ordinance to protect the environment and enhance the quality of life for city residents by banning the unnecessary removal of trees. He also won unanimous election by his colleagues as vice president of the board, set to preside in the absence of the vice mayor. This was to be the first in a career-long trend in which Fowler won plaudits and votes of confidence from those with whom he served.

It was during his service on the Board of Aldermen that Fowler began to develop an intense interest in international affairs. As part of its longstanding, extensive efforts to retain the American political support that was vital in its struggle with the mainland People's Republic of China (PRC), the government of Taiwan identified Fowler as a rising political figure and invited him on a ten-day tour of the island in August 1970. Part of the tour took him to a spot on Taiwan that looked out on the contested islands of Quemoy and Matsu, which had figured prominently in the US presidential race of 1960. But the most memorable part of the trip came during the farewell dinner, as Fowler has often recounted in the years since then.

The young alderman wanted to show appreciation to his hosts by taking them to a special restaurant in Taipei. Finding such a place wasn't easy because the Taiwanese capital offered—and still offers—a full range of exceptional Chinese cuisines, all concentrated in one place. But during the visit, Fowler had learned of a particular local delicacy: a snake that emerged from its underground dwellings every August, upon which it was quickly harvested for local consumption. Since this coincided with his trip, he thought it would be the perfect choice to honor his hosts.

> And when I told my hosts that I wished to treat them to a farewell dinner at the premier restaurant serving this delicacy, they were indeed delighted. That evening, we went to this little, curvy street—whose name really was Snake Street—where the restaurant was supposed to be located. We were let out at a building with a large aquarium up front—so large in fact that I thought we had been brought to a pet store by mistake. But it turned out to be the right place, and there was an open glass case writhing with living snakes. I was introduced to the head chef, who presented me with silver tongs and told me I was to pick out the snake for him to prepare for us. I went for the smallest of the lot, but the chef demurred and proceeded to pull out one that was six feet long. He was holding this huge, writhing thing and took it over to a cutting counter, where he hooked the snake's head to hold it in place. While it was still writhing all about, he produced a switchblade and made a cut about six inches below the head. One of my hosts then stepped forward to offer a toast. "To Wyche Fowler, a man who has come across the ocean to express love and peace for the people of Taiwan. To symbolize the heart of a great man, we give him the heart of this snake." He then scooped out the still-beating two ventricles of the snake's heart and presented them to me. I was astounded, but trying not to show it, I took the two sticks with the snake heart, pretending in my mind that it was only an oyster, and quickly swallowed it whole. I remember counting backward in my head like you do when you are anesthetized before an operation—100, 99, 98—waiting to die. But I was brought back by my hosts, who made it clear it was now time for me to give *my* toast. So, I regained my composure as best I could and offered, "I can feel in my breast the love of the Chinese people." One of them then said, "You liked it, then. Excellent. We'll get you another." I ran straight out the exit into the street, fleeing my laughing friends.

Fowler's interest in foreign policy intensified when he joined the board of directors of the American Council of Young Political Leaders (ACYPL), a bipartisan organization founded by Fowler friend Spencer Oliver. The ACYPL sponsored foreign trips for young American political officials and, in turn, hosted similar delegations from other countries. In this capacity, Fowler joined US delegations to the Soviet Union in October and November 1971, traveling alongside Nixon aide Pat Buchanan, and to Japan in July 1973, when he took time off from the campaign trail and conducted interviews by phone from Tokyo. It was this last that led one of Fowler's fellow board members, Cecil Turner, to dub him, in a long-remembered phrase, as "the only alderman with a foreign policy." The quote was to have a humorous turn in Fowler's later foray into state politics when a Bainbridge media outlet misinterpreted a garbled version and credited Fowler as the only Atlanta official with a "farm policy."

During the trip to the Soviet Union, Alderman Fowler worked to persuade Soviet authorities to allow Yakov Gluzman, a Ukrainian Jew, to emigrate to Israel so he could be reunited with his wife, Rita, and the two-year-old son he had never seen. Mrs. Gluzman had approached Fowler prior to his departure and informed him that while she had been permitted to leave the USSR in September 1969, a month after their marriage, Yakov, who was a university-trained biologist then being forced to work as a carpenter because of his desire to leave the country, was not allowed to join her.

When the ACYPL delegation reached Kiev, the capital of Ukraine, Fowler asked the local authorities to intervene on behalf of Gluzman. The request came at a time when the Soviet government was beginning to relax its emigration restrictions on Soviet Jews in response to growing global condemnation of its human rights abuses. A reported 7,500 Soviet Jews had been allowed to leave the USSR during the previous year. Before the end of his trip, Fowler was informed that Gluzman's visa had been approved and he would be allowed to leave the country within a few weeks. The Gluzmans were reunited in late November 1971. In March of 1972, Fowler was presented with a special recognition award from the Israeli government for his "humanitarian service" in the Gluzman case, and in

1973, he received the Myrtle Wreath Award from the international Jewish service organization B'nai B'rith for his efforts on behalf of Soviet Jewry.

Sadly, there was to be no happy ending for the Gluzmans, as Fowler discovered many years later.

> I was in my ambassadorial office in Saudi Arabia when an aide announced that a reporter was calling from New Jersey. "Are you the Wyche Fowler that secured freedom for Yakov Gluzman many years ago?" How did you find me, I asked? "Computers are wonderful tools," she responded. Did I know where Rita Gluzman was? No, I had no idea...why? The reporter replied that a couple picnicking on the banks of the Passaic River on Easter Sunday had noticed several tied plastic bags floating down the scenic river. Being sensitive environmentalists, they enlisted a park ranger to retrieve the "trash." Inside the bags was discovered two hundred twenty-seven pieces of Yakov Gluzman! The subsequent trial of Rita confirmed that she and a lover had murdered Yakov with baseball bats, chopped him into 227 parts and dumped him into the river. They were both given life sentences. Suddenly, a chill came over my body. In my attempt to reunite a family, had I been an unwitting accessory to Yakov's murder? Did he know his wife was having an affair in America? Was he glad to be rid of her? Did he not want to leave the U.S.SR? These questions still haunt me.

1972 Congressional Election

While still on the Board of Aldermen, in 1972 Fowler decided to run for Charles Weltner's old seat as Fifth District congressman. Weltner's withdrawal from the 1966 race had led to the election of conservative Republican Fletcher Thompson, who won reelection by defeating Weltner in 1968. In 1970, Thompson won by 57 percent to 43 percent over former Martin Luther King Jr. aide Andrew Young in a contest that polarized sharply along racial lines. However, in 1972, a federal court-ordered redistricting plan removed heavily Republican areas south of Atlanta from the district and increased the African American share of the population to 44 percent. Under these circumstances, and with a competitive US Senate race looming after the death of longtime senator Richard Russell in 1971, Thompson decided to run for the Senate. Those same circumstances, the absence of an incumbent, and the opportunity to follow in the footsteps of his mentor, Charles Weltner, drew Fowler into the '72 Fifth District race.

Fowler announced his candidacy at a February 7, 1972, press conference at City Hall: "I want to be your representative in Washington. I want the opportunity to prove that personal effort combined with understanding of the federal and municipal systems can make things work for the individual citizen."

Four candidates were on the ballot in the August 8 Democratic primary, including H. D. Dodson, an African American who had been elected to the Atlanta Board of Aldermen along with Fowler in 1969, and Howell Smith, a white Atlanta attorney. But Fowler's major opponent in the Democratic primary was Andrew Young.

Fowler's platform was laid out in a response to a questionnaire.

> The key questions facing the voters of urban Atlanta are how we can have food at reasonable prices, how we can once again have streets and parks free of crime and drug-pushing, how we can preserve for ourselves and our posterity a livable and enjoyable environment, and how we can once again have schools where children can simply learn. I support an immediate end to the Vietnam War, concurrent with the return of all American prisoners of war.... The incongruities in the welfare and economic system must be resolved to assure every American the opportunity to earn a paycheck. I will work diligently to close those tax loopholes through which big corporations and wealthier Americans manage to pay little or no taxes.

Fowler also advocated "a strong reassertion of the role of Congress, which is the direct voice of the people, in all war-making decisions." And because of his belief that "the question of defense in this country is as much a question of economics as a question of military strength," he called for "an immediate reassessment of American defense posture with an eye toward weeding out those weapons systems which are useless or obsolete, while, at the same time, maintaining a strong and up-to-date defense posture."

Young and his campaign had learned some valuable lessons from his 1970 defeat, especially in improving his appeal to white voters. For example, he pledged to activists in northeast Atlanta neighborhoods (including Morningside and Virginia-Highlands) that, if elected, he would do all he could to support their efforts to block construction of a major north-south expressway that state highway authorities were planning to build through their area. Those neighborhoods were home to many of the "Northside whites" who had long been part of the progressive, biracial coalitions that had elected officials such as Hartsfield, Allen, Weltner, and Maynard Jackson. Though they also represented a natural constituency for Fowler, his support for the highway in 1972, plus Young's own attractiveness to these voters, produced a sizeable vote for the latter in the primary. This, coupled with Young's near universal appeal to Black voters, resulted in a substantial victory for Young.

Andrew Young	35,926	60.34 percent
Wyche Fowler	19,549	32.84 percent
H. D. Dodson	3,053	5.13 percent
Howell Smith	1,008	1.69 percent

After expending very little in the successful 1969 aldermanic bid, the Fowler campaign budget was also modest in the 1972 race. And learning from Charles Weltner, Fowler did not spend any more than he raised and so emerged from the loss debt-free.

Even in defeat, Fowler won accolades for the way he conducted his campaign, free of attempts to play the "race card" in a district that was still majority white. Though he was ultimately unsuccessful in winning many votes from within the African American community, a Chicago filmmaker chronicling the Young campaign later wrote of "a quite stirring speech that had been made by Fowler at [a Black Baptist church]: an exquisite statement of solidarity with racial justice."[9] Fowler's prompt and unequivocal endorsement of Young was credited with helping Young win the general election 53 percent to 47 percent over Rodney Cook, in part by carrying almost a fourth of the white vote. Indeed, Fowler conceded the race in a joint election-night television appearance with Young, indicating that even though early results showed Fowler ahead, he believed

Young would win the primary and general election and go on to be an excellent congressman.

1973 Atlanta City Council President Election

Returning to city government after his congressional defeat, Fowler set his sights on the upcoming 1973 municipal elections. Those elected would serve under a new governmental structure established by a revised city charter adopted earlier in the year. Under the new charter, the legislative body was changed to a city council, twelve of whom were to be elected by local district, with six at-large members elected by all city voters. The vice mayor position was converted to city council president, and though still elected citywide, was to be an exclusively legislative position. Finally, the citywide election system for mayor was maintained, but the office was given greatly enhanced authority over the city administration.

Mayor Sam Massell ran for reelection, but he was challenged by Vice Mayor Maynard Jackson. Former Congressman Weltner also ran, along with eight other candidates. Fowler sought the city council presidency, where he was pitted against civil rights activist Hosea Williams, fellow aldermen Wade Mitchell and Cecil Turner, African Methodist Episcopal minister Robert Hunter, and Socialist Workers Party candidate Joel Aber.

At his announcement speech on May 15, 1973, Fowler invoked the public concerns arising from the unfolding Watergate scandal and recent ethical misconduct within Atlanta's city government.

> I ask the people of Atlanta to join me as participants, not spectators, in a combined effort to bring hope and confidence and good government to our American city this year.... I make this announcement seeking further public service at a time in which there is an unprecedented exodus from government at all levels. Each day brings new accounts of wrongdoing in the highest branches of the American government. In recent times, Atlanta's city government has known recurrent crises of confidence. Most disturbing is the all-too-frequent reaction of the man in the street: that the misuse of power and even outright corruption is simply "politics as usual." I do not believe that the business of this nation or this city can be conducted in the closets of conspiracy or the drawing rooms of pub-

> lic officials. I do not believe that uncounted dollars from undisclosed sources should ever be able to buy a liquor license or an office in the state house or White House.

Fowler had accumulated significant exposure across Atlanta as Weltner's top aide, in running and winning citywide in his 1969 race for alderman, and in his recent unsuccessful effort in the Fifth District race. His campaign approach closely mirrored that of the 1969 contest, emphasizing personal contact with voters and maintaining a rigorous schedule of speaking appearances at civic and community organizations as well as white and Black churches. On a number of occasions, Fowler drove himself and Hosea Williams to an event because Williams's license had been temporarily suspended.

One campaign issue was Fowler's proposal to ban cheap handguns, known as "Saturday Night specials," by prohibiting the delivery or assembly of any handgun cast from metal that melted at less than 800 degrees Fahrenheit. The ordinance was adopted by the board by a 14–2 vote (with Mitchell voting in favor and Turner voting against) on September 17, 1973, but it was ultimately declared unconstitutional by the Georgia Supreme Court as an overreach of municipal authority. Nonetheless, it represented an attempt to deal with the rapid rise in homicides that Atlanta, along with many other major American cities, was experiencing. The number of murders in Atlanta had risen from sixty-seven in 1960 to 243 in 1970, making it one of the most dangerous places in the country, a status the city maintained for many years thereafter.

A significant change from Fowler's 1972 platform was his full embrace of the neighborhood preservation cause. Perhaps most importantly, this included the fight to prevent construction of a proposed in-town expressway through northeast Atlanta, a position he formally endorsed in June 1973. One campaign letter stated,

> I am writing to you on a matter that I feel is not only important to you and me, but critical to Preservation in Atlanta. That matter is neighborhoods and homes vs. unnecessary highways. We are facing a crisis. *The crisis being what we want Atlanta to be.* I feel, as I'm sure you do, that Atlanta's unique quality must be preserved from those who would have us tear down every home to build another

> highway.... If we cultivate only the cement and asphalt and neglect the human resources of our city, it will be truly tragic, not only for people, but for the city itself.

This approach made sense from a political standpoint, as it aligned with the wishes of many voters in northeast Atlanta on an issue important to them, helping to distinguish him from both Hosea Williams and the business-oriented Mitchell. At the same time, a look at Fowler's record—stretching all the way back to his support for neighborhood preservation in his 1969 campaign for alderman to his later activism in Congress on behalf of such causes as historic preservation and environmental protection—clearly demonstrates that this was a position very much in line with his core beliefs.

In response to questions submitted by *The Northside Neighbor* newspaper in September 1973, Fowler outlined his approach to land use and transportation issues.

> It is imperative that land use plans begin in the neighborhoods affected. A plan must express the hopes and desires of the citizen who has chosen to live in Atlanta, and the professional planning help should be provided by the city to help transfer a neighborhood's thoughts for [the city] council's actions. I will do everything I can to get planners out of city hall and into the neighborhood organizations to help formulate true land use policy.... We have got to orient this city to think public transportation before they think automobile.... Only through hard decisions emphasizing public transportation and public corridors will we make the decisions that will provide a way for everyone—teenagers, old people, housewives and businessmen—to get where they have to go without having to depend on the automobile.[10]

Such stands, especially Fowler's opposition to the in-town expressway (now officially designated as I-485), helped him win the endorsement of the newly created Citywide League of Neighborhoods, a coalition of fifty local civic groups formed by northeastern Atlanta neighborhood leaders and anti-highway activists. (The league backed Maynard Jackson in the mayor's race.)

Both of the major Atlanta dailies again endorsed Wyche Fowler.

> This year the voters once again have a nice choice of candidates for [city council president]. In the Journal's opinion, one candidate, WYCHE FOWLER, is superior. He has been on the board of aldermen...and distinguished himself by his ability to get to the heart of a question. He has a mind like a knife. It cuts through and he has saved the city many hours of aldermanic time by returning debate to the proper path. Mr. Fowler is a debater and a parliamentarian, a born presiding officer. He knows legislators and legislation. This job might have been tailored to suit his talents. The Journal recommends WYCHE FOWLER as President of City Council.
>
> —*Atlanta Journal*
> September 26, 1973

> Wyche Fowler and Wade Mitchell present this city with as difficult—and happy—a choice as it is likely to have in this decade.... Fowler pursues a more open political style. He has worked actively for gun control and for security guards in shopping centers, and for a lot of other programs. As a young law student, he sought out then Mayor Ivan Allen, Jr., and asked for the job of "night mayor." He did it well.... Fowler seems to us to have the edge in this race, more because of the city's needs than for his own personal reasons. The city needs to develop intelligent young men who are interested in political careers. Black and white men alike need to be brought along as the thinkers and planners and doers in the city. Mitchell says candidly that he is not interested in being a full-time politician. There is merit in his attitude, and he is to be admired for feeling that way. Fowler is interested in a political career, and we think he has the potential to develop into a splendid office-holder. At age 32 Fowler's potential for growth is large. His determination that

"we've got to return to public office those politicians who trust people" strikes us as the right attitude. We commend him to Atlanta voters.

—*Atlanta Constitution*
September 28, 1973

With a relatively good turnout of 52 percent of the city's registered voters on October 2, including an estimated turnout of 56 percent among Black voters and 45 percent among white voters, Jackson ran far ahead of the other mayoral candidates, winning 46 percent of the vote, with Massell (20 percent) edging out Weltner (19 percent) for second. In the city council president race, the establishment-backed Mitchell ran third, trailing narrowly behind Fowler and Williams. However, since no candidate won a majority in either race, a runoff was required two weeks later.

Wyche Fowler	30,006	31.02 percent
Hosea Williams	29,009	29.99 percent
Wade Mitchell	25,469	26.33 percent
Cecil Turner	9,957	10.29 percent
Robert Hunter	1,834	1.90 percent
Joel Aber	453	0.47 percent

Williams's strong showing shocked many political observers and was built on his winning approximately 55 percent of Black voters while garnering less than 3 percent of the white vote. Mitchell placed a relatively strong second behind Williams in the African American community with approximately 22 percent, and behind Fowler in the predominantly white and prosperous northwest portion of the city with 40 percent. Fowler ran third among African American voters, with approximately 12 percent. He had a narrow margin over Mitchell in the northwest, winning approximately 49 percent, but secured the overall lead, and in the process knocked Mitchell out of the runoff thanks to solid support in the Buckhead-Northside (56 percent Fowler to 32 percent Mitchell) and especially Atlanta's northeast sections (59 percent Fowler to 21 percent Mitchell), where the highway issue was most salient.

While the first election had been mostly free of racially polarizing campaigning, in the runoff, Mayor Massell made a clear pitch for white votes under the slogan "Atlanta's Too Young to Die," which led the *Atlanta Constitution* to editorialize, "Mayor Sam Massell acts as if he were running for mayor of a South African city which practices apartheid rather than mayor of a fully integrated city."[11] (Even though the city was 52 percent Black in terms of total population, white citizens represented a slight majority of registered voters and [though not in the 1973 contests] also tended to turn out in higher proportions, usually making the electorate majority white.) Fowler went to great pains to separate himself from Massell's approach. In an October 9 speech to the biracial civic group Resurgens Atlanta, he said, "Through a quarter of a century of painful progress...we in Atlanta have steadfastly practiced the politics of faith, not fear. It will be a hollow victory, indeed, if a divided city, torn by racial strife, is the bitter heritage of this election." Fowler and Williams were both praised in the news media and elsewhere for the nonracial tones of their campaigns, and shortly after the runoff vote, Fowler said that Williams's campaign proved that "he thought more of his city than he did of his own election.... He chose the high road knowing it would lose him some votes."

On October 16, 62 percent of Atlanta's registered voters turned out to vote, up 10 points from two weeks earlier, with African Americans once again showing up in higher proportions (an estimated 68 percent) than the white community (57 percent). When the results were in, Maynard Jackson had defeated Sam Massell 59 percent to 41 percent, becoming the first African American elected mayor of a major Southern city. Wyche Fowler won by an even larger margin of 64 percent to 36 percent. Both victors put together significant biracial coalitions, with Jackson winning an estimated 22 percent of the white vote (to go along with 95 percent of the African American vote) and Fowler gaining the support of a third of Black voters (as well as 97 percent of the white vote).

Wyche Fowler	78,209	63.99 percent
Hosea Williams	44,017	36.01 percent

This was to be one of many runoffs and special elections involving Wyche Fowler, who would face as many or more of these contests as any other figure involved in national politics in the twentieth century. Such elections pose particular problems, especially with respect to turnout, given their unusual timing. Over the years, Fowler found himself running in elections scheduled just days near Easter, Passover, and Thanksgiving. Additionally, the lack of other races on the ballot often hindered efforts to generate awareness and interest. In any event, he would prove to be adept at prevailing under these circumstances, winning in all runoffs and special elections until the very last one, the 1992 US Senate runoff, which he lost by just one percentage point.

All told, Fowler spent about $35,000 on his 1973 campaign and ended up with a surplus of $9,800, which was returned to his 1,400 contributors. He said at the time, "I have always given instructions to my people to operate on a cash basis. It's always dangerous to operate on credit in a political campaign." He would retain this philosophy in all subsequent campaigns.

The 1973 elections also significantly boosted African American representation in what was now the city council, which would be evenly divided with nine Black and nine white representatives.

Just after the election, Atlanta Constitution editor Reg Murphy provided his assessment of the newly elected council president.

> Wyche Fowler [is] at 33 emerging to a major southern political career. For the next four years he will be President of the Atlanta City Council. Much of the responsibility for working out the details of the new city charter falls to him. Fowler ran a beautiful race for the council presidency. He started with all the important factors in Atlanta politics committed to other candidates.... You had to scrape around diligently to find much recognizable support. Eventually it became known that former Mayor Ivan Allen Jr. and a handful of others were assisting him.... He had run a campaign for Congress against Andrew Young. People remembered him as a gracious loser, but a loser nonetheless. And then, two weeks ago, he found himself running first. His personal campaign style had fetched up impressive support from the non-aligned. Hosea Williams was his runoff opponent, and suddenly Williams came out of the street to begin running a dignified campaign. Fowler had two choices. He could adopt a campaign of wide-eyed screaming nightmares about the city's future. Or he could push his horn-rimmed glasses back up the bridge of his nose and pursue a responsible campaign.... Cool under

pressure, Fowler pushed up his glasses and became more dignified. He won. Fowler thus is the balance in the racial equation in City Hall. He goes in with impressive support from both whites and Blacks. He'll make it. He's smart.[12]

City Council President (1974–1977)

In remarks delivered at the Atlanta Civic Center ceremony on January 7, 1974, marking the inauguration of the new city government, Fowler pledged to work to create "a city hall which will once and for all rekindle the spirit of the town hall and give us again a government which trusts the people, a government which the people will trust."

That new government that took office on January 7 was bound to face numerous challenges. Both the old governmental system, in which the Board of Aldermen held substantial authority over the city bureaucracy, and the political system, under which the white business leadership had a leading role, had been overturned. Combined with the fact that the two newly elected leaders were both very young (Jackson was thirty-five and Fowler thirty-three) and ambitious, the stage was set for a difficult transition period.

Fowler was asked about possible personality clashes in an interview that appeared in the October 22, 1973, edition of the *Atlanta Constitution*.

> Q—There was a lot of friction between Mayor Sam Massell and Vice Mayor Maynard Jackson, although the vice mayor had an essentially powerless position. The new city charter gives the City Council President almost equal powers with the Mayor. Do you foresee a potential for conflicts between you and Mayor-elect Jackson?
>
> Fowler—I don't. I think that both of us realize if we are to implement the charter, reorganize the government and make our new city government truly representative, it is imperative that we work together. I see no friction between the two of us. I will do everything I can to help the Mayor-elect in the reorganization and the implementation procedures.

> Q—Do you think conflicts would arise from the personalities of the men involved rather than the structure of government the charter sets up?
>
> Fowler—Any charter is only as good as the visions of the men and women who seek to implement it. Personality conflicts are inevitable in any elective system. But I believe that the mandate the Mayor-elect and I received will make it far easier to work harmoniously with the new council, devoid of any conflict.[13]

But conflicts did indeed arise.

Mayor Jackson asserted the enhanced mayoral authority in several areas. Among these were city contracting, where he established a 25 percent set-aside for minority-owned firms; the city's hiring practices, where an affirmative action requirement was established; and the police department, where he attempted to fire the incumbent police chief because of Atlanta's growing crime problem and charges of racial insensitivity within the police force. For his part, city council president Fowler was eager to establish the council as an independent body capable of appropriately discharging its new role of legislating and oversight.

Disagreement between the mayor and city council president became particularly pronounced over Mayor Jackson's attempted firing of Police Chief John Inman in May 1974, and his appointment later that year of A. Reginald Eaves, who had no previous law enforcement experience, as public safety commissioner, a position that oversaw both the police and fire departments.

On May 3, the mayor sent a letter to Chief Inman informing him that he was being dismissed effective three weeks later, and informing him of his right to appeal the decision within that time frame. On May 10, Inman indicated he would fight his removal in the superior courts in Fulton and DeKalb Counties.

At this point, Fowler urged council members to refrain from commenting publicly on the case or taking other action that could compromise the council's potential role in either acting impartially on a potential Inman appeal, or actually administering the police department as under the old charter should a legal impasse develop between the mayor and Inman. On June 1, 1974, the council voted 12 to 4 to impeach Inman and to begin trial proceedings for his alleged defiance of council subpoenas and for planting a spy in the offices of *The Atlanta Voice* newspaper.

In a June 17, 1974, speech to the Atlanta Rotary Club, Fowler urged Atlantans to give the courts time to act on the efforts to fire Inman initiated by the mayor and city council.

> We must choose between the passions and prejudices of the moment and the measured processes of our court system, which often tries our patience but ultimately protects our freedoms. We must choose between our rush to get things settled and our higher duty to get things solved. We must ultimately hold our officials accountable—calmly and deliberately—within the framework of the public good, judging them not by their friends and enemies, but their accomplishments and failures.

Eventually, the Inman matter was indeed resolved by the courts. In an attempt to prevent the reorganization sought by Mayor Jackson and to save his own job, Inman filed several lawsuits seeking to declare the new city charter unconstitutional and to preserve his position as chief of police. These issues were ultimately resolved by the Georgia Supreme Court, which ruled on July 3, 1974, that the new charter was constitutional; as a result, the mayor could proceed with his plan to create a new Department of Public Safety with authority over the police and fire departments, but Inman could not be removed as chief of the police department. Ultimately, Inman continued to serve as Atlanta's police chief until his retirement in 1979, though as a subordinate to the public safety commissioner.

While the proceedings in the Inman case were still playing out, Fowler voiced his concerns about the impending announcement of the mayor's nomination for public safety commissioner, as reported in a July 1974 news story.

> The Atlanta City Council is cranking up full-scale hearings for Maynard Jackson's still unknown choice to be the City's first superchief, Council President Wyche Fowler said Tuesday.... The council president said Jackson's appointee—whose identity is still a tightly guarded secret—will receive "the most careful scrutiny"

> during two public hearings the week of Aug. 12.... "Police-community relations demand the finest, fairest, toughest, experienced administrator to be found," Fowler said. He said the council will quiz Jackson's choice on questions of "his philosophy of law enforcement," methods for fighting crime, ideas for curbing domestic assaults and proposals for "fair, impartial promotion and transfer systems" for his officers. "These are questions that were never asked of Chief Inman," Fowler said. Only 15 minutes elapsed between Inman's nomination as chief by Mayor Sam Massell and his confirmation by the former Board of Aldermen in March 1972.... "I know personally that the Mayor and his staff have made a nationwide search" for a qualified superchief, Fowler said, but he doesn't have a clue as to who Jackson's present candidate is.[14]

On August 5, 1974, Mayor Jackson nominated his executive assistant Reginald Eaves as commissioner of public safety. Eaves, a former college classmate of the mayor, had also worked on Jackson's 1973 mayoral race.

At a press conference later that same day, Fowler stated, "I'm shocked. I'm amazed. I'm very disappointed. I don't believe Mr. Eaves has the background or qualifications this position demands.... [I will fight the appointment] with all the persuasion I can muster." He also compared the choice to then-Mayor Massell's reported consultations with his brother before appointing Inman in 1972. It was this break with the mayor over the Eaves appointment that, more than anything else, led to friction between the two city officials.[15]

Fowler's position was applauded by the *Atlanta Journal* in an August 7 editorial.

> Wyche Fowler, the president of the Atlanta City Council, is a man who has shunned the limelight during his current tenure in office. In contrast to his two immediate predecessors in the City's No. 2 spot, Mr. Fowler has preferred to keep a low profile. He has worked hard and meticulously in his role, and has done so quietly. It is reasonable to assume that he has had his disagreements with Mayor Jackson's administration. But he has not sought to capitalize on those differences. To his credit, he has instead sought to use his influence on behalf of the city without sounding off whenever he

> might disagree with decisions and policies. With that background, Mr. Fowler's decision to take a public stand against Mayor Jackson's choice of Reginald Eaves as Atlanta's first public safety commissioner can only be regarded as significant. It is an unusual step by the council president. And because it is unusual it deserves serious and careful consideration. Mr. Fowler objects to the "political overtones" in the appointment to a job that should be outside the political arena. He questions the absence of "background or qualifications this position demands." Wyche Fowler has a reputation for calmness and coolness, for weighing a matter on its merits rather than emotionally or on the basis of prejudice or snap judgment. It is in this context that Mr. Fowler's decision to take a public stand should be considered.

Since his first election in 1969, Fowler was a proponent of a professional and non-politicized police department and had battled with the Massell administration over what he regarded as its attempts to insert politics into the department's operations. He believed the Jackson administration was trying to do the same thing, and he vigorously resisted it. Fowler told a *Harper's Weekly* reporter,

> This is a bad situation. Some Black elected official has got to rise above color and think in terms of competence. As it is now, all white officials are going to have a difficult time disagreeing with Black officials without being labeled a racist. And the Blacks are afraid they will be called a sell-out. This is potentially dangerous, but it really doesn't threaten the health of the city yet. Atlanta has problems like every city, but I think things are taking off for the better. There is a tremendous new involvement of people in politics here. Neighborhoods are being restored. People are moving back into the city. A big business expansion is on the way. Most of the things happening now are birth pangs, not death pangs.[16]

Despite Fowler's concerns, the Eaves nomination was approved by the council by a 12–6 margin on August 19, 1974.

Fowler joined the mayor and others on October 6, 1974, (Fowler's thirty-fourth birthday) for "Affirmation Atlanta," an event organized by civic and religious leaders to promote cooperation across racial and neighborhood lines. The public gathering was held in downtown Atlanta's Central City Park and drew an estimated crowd of 7,500. The city council president's remarks focused on the future.

> [This event must be] not a celebration of past glories but a blueprint for a hard road ahead. It challenges all of us in Atlanta's leadership to lead, not bully. It challenges Atlanta's citizens to respond, not balk.... Affirmation Atlanta requires that we in this biracial city, once and for all, reject racism in all its myriad forms—and most assuredly in both of its colors. We in this biracial city must remind ourselves that that which unites us is greater than that which divides us, but it asks us also to remember that diversity does not have to mean discord and that honest people of different colors must sometimes disagree. If civility tempers our disagreement then we become not rivals for power but partners for progress.

In January 1975, Fowler called for a shift in Atlanta's crime-fighting strategy, with greater emphasis on violent crime and drug trafficking and less attention devoted to gambling and prostitution raids.

> City Council President Wyche Fowler Tuesday blasted the policy of police raids on gambling and prostitution while assaults rose 22 percent during 1974. "Gamblers and gambling and prostitution do not leave an innocent citizen bleeding in the street," Fowler said. Fowler did not criticize Public Safety Commissioner Reginald Eaves directly, but Eaves has been a frequent and vocal supporter of crackdowns on gambling and prostitution as sources of money for illegal drug trafficking. The City Council President said there is "no evidence that gambling money finances drugs in any greater amount than any other illegal activity." He added, "Cutting off gambling and prostitution in Atlanta would not make a major dent in the drug traffic." Fowler said he will urge Atlanta City Council's Public Safety Committee to set new priorities for detection and prevention of violent crime "even if it means a lessening of our attention to gambling raids and busts at rock concerts...." In addition to new priorities, Fowler called for teams of policemen to work out of

> the 38 fire stations currently being operated by the city. And he said the council "must deal with the establishment of a comprehensive merit system for policemen.... Mr. Eaves has done a good job in establishing a fair test for sergeants. But you cannot develop a professional system piecemeal. We have got to develop an overall structure which insures job security...." Fowler said the "greatest problem we have in the Atlanta Police Department today is a sense of lessening professionalism." He said Eaves "needs the help of the Public Safety Committee and council in swift enactment of a comprehensive merit system." On the subject of gambling and prostitution raids, Fowler said, "It's a matter of what you declare war on. When you have a high crime rate, your first priority should be prevention and detection of assaults and robberies, and if you catch a few gamblers and prostitutes, it should be an extra feather in your cap. We have a headdress full [of feathers] from busting street prostitutes. The heavy stuff—assaults and illegal drugs—have got to be corralled immediately." Fowler's remarks appeared to be an attack on Eaves, who has several times conspicuously ridden at the head of raiding parties on gambling houses. But Fowler said Eaves is not to blame. "The job of setting priorities is the council's," he said. "Mr. Eaves has had virtually no direction from the policy-makers. He cannot be faulted for acting contrary to the city policy, since there isn't a city policy to date."[17]

Commissioner Eaves took public exception to Fowler's comments, but the two "held a bury-the-hatchet meeting" two weeks later that "apparently ended their public fracas over law enforcement strategies."[18]

Throughout most of 1975 and 1976, all Fowler-Jackson disagreements were played out in the news media as a prelude to their anticipated matchup in the 1977 mayoral race, with Fowler widely expected to follow his two immediate predecessors, Sam Massell and Maynard Jackson, in using the city's number two post as a springboard to run for mayor. In January 1975, Fowler spoke to the Buckhead Kiwanis Club, implicitly trying to put his disagreements with the mayor into perspective: "Harmony is not the highest goal to be achieved. Responsible dissent must be the lifeblood of our city...[even though] it does not make for good, calm, tranquil [news reports].... If you want a place where everyone looks alike and thinks alike, they can be found. But they're not cities."

According to press accounts, the mayor and city council president held a private, three-hour meeting at Fowler's house on Haven Ridge Drive in mid-November 1975. The meeting was designed to settle their differences and resulted in "an uneasy truce," according to the reports.[19]

It was during his service as city council president that Fowler obtained what he would later cite as his proudest accomplishment in all his years of public service. The subject was Atlanta's newly authorized rapid rail transit system, called the Metropolitan Atlanta Rapid Transit Authority, or MARTA, and, in particular, the future location of its route and station in the vicinity of the city's international airport.

Several of the region's key real estate developers had purchased land around the airport in anticipation of MARTA being routed there, with shuttle service to be provided to the airport itself. Fowler spoke out publicly against this approach, saying it would be a mistake to compromise passenger convenience and limit the full potential of both the airport and the MARTA system. Instead, he advocated placing a MARTA station inside the airport terminal and lobbied the city council on behalf of that position. Ultimately, the council divided evenly on the question, with no site obtaining the requisite majority, and Fowler used his tie-breaking vote as council president to secure victory for the airport terminal location. This decision has proven to be a very good one for passengers as well as the airport and the MARTA system.

Not all of Fowler's exploits as council president involved weighty matters of public policy.

> Several weeks after taking office, I received a call from a woman identifying herself as Maxine Taylor. She said she had an offer that I could not refuse. Intrigued, I listened as she described herself as president of an organization of astrologers who, considering themselves professionals, were volunteering to pay Atlanta's professional tax of one hundred dollars. It was surprising, but I did not discern the hidden motive. I promised her a hearing on her recommendation, as I was the new City Council President and could set the agenda. A veteran alderman, Q. V. Williamson, when informed of the request, said, "Oh, Wyche, you're being hoodwinked. These

astrologists are willing to pay $100 to be listed with doctors, lawyers, architects and other real professionals." My naiveté was exposed.

The hearing was held two weeks later in the afternoon. I had not thought much about it, and had certainly not notified the press. The hearing room was jammed to overflowing, three deep standing around the walls. As I entered, the TV cameras encircled me and I was suddenly face-to-face with a striking beauty, green-eyed with cascading jet-black hair. Her silhouette approached as she exclaimed, "I am Maxine Taylor and I can tell that you are a Libra rising." Knowing nothing of astrology, I found myself glancing downward to discover that I was, in fact, rising. That night on the news my mortification was complete, as the cameras captured me seemingly bowing to Maxine as we discovered each other with my unwitting greeting.

Maxine got her tax. I liked her immensely, and when she got a weekly astrological radio show, she became famous in her own right. She married a prominent Atlanta lawyer.

Years after the tumultuous 1973 to 1976 era, at a December 8, 1981, tribute dinner held to honor Maynard Jackson, and marking the end of Jackson's first eight-year stint as mayor, Fowler reflected on the mayor's accomplishments as well as the nature of that period in the city's history.

> Mayor Jackson has served Atlanta in what perhaps has been her most difficult hour—a period of transition. And, it has often been the undeserved fate of those who govern in such a period to receive more praise from future historians than from contemporary critics. In the eight years of the Jackson Administration change, swift, sure and sometimes unwelcome, engulfed the city. The structure of city government changed dramatically with the implementation in 1973 of its first new charter in a century. The structure of political power changed dramatically with the stunning political achievements of Atlanta's richly talented and world-renowned Black community.... Maynard Jackson dealt with those challenges and more—with courage, imagination and integrity. He has been a

path-breaker, a role model, an inspiration to others who could choose paths of public service.

In November 1976, *Atlanta* magazine ran a full-length cover story by Roger M. Williams titled "Which Way Wyche: Atlanta Will Elect a Mayor and Tongues Are Wagging Already: Will City Council President Fowler Be a Main Contender—Or Does He Have Other Choices?"

> Fowler has his eye on the mayor's office. Should he gain it in 1977, his election would alter the racial balance of power, and he would become a major figure. Beyond that, Fowler has his eye on statewide offices: lieutenant governor to start, governor or U.S. senator after that. Where's the dilemma? Well, Fowler may not reach any of these goals: because of current cold political realities, he may not even try for those posts. He might not even be able to hold onto the presidency of the Council, which is a long way from becoming successor to Sen. Herman Talmadge. If Fowler fails, Atlanta will have lost one of its most attractive and articulate young leaders—and its white population will, to put it bluntly, have lost its current leading prospect for a "white man's candidate" to unseat Mayor Jackson. Fowler's friends and advisors glumly admit that his fast-moving career is in danger of stalling. "Wyche is stuck," declares one of his longtime counselors who offered a shorthand review of what pols call "the options": "Maynard will run for a second term and will be too strong for any opponent, white or Black. Congress is out: Rep. Andy Young is in solid, and Wyche isn't about to carpetbag into the Fourth District. Gov. Busbee will be able to succeed himself, so Zell Miller, who wants to run for governor, will run for re-election to lieutenant governor instead—and Wyche can't beat Miller. Wyche [would] have a chance at attorney general or secretary of state, but he doesn't want either one." All right, he can always be Council president again. "Can he? He's aggravated Blacks to the point where they might well run a strong candidate against him and win." Then he can be a plain councilman so he can at least hold a political base. "Not Wyche. He wouldn't want a nitty-gritty job like that, not at this point." Well, he can practice law full time

> and make some real money for a change. "Hah. That's the last thing he wants. Wyche doesn't like being a lawyer." [block quote]

Fowler responded to the reporter's questions about his future plans.

> There's no question that what I like best is dealing with important matters of public policy. But elective office aside, there are a lot of things I'd like to do in this life—teach, work in international relations, maybe practice law regularly.... My ideas are still jelling in the public policy area, and when I have a clear picture of where I can do the things I want to see done, I'll commit, I'll start running. At 35, I've still got one big race left in me. I do wonder how you can be a local official and worry about foreign affairs. Your job is to unstop sewers and sweep up dead animals and settle zoning problems. It's damn difficult to talk about all that in relation to the rest of the world without seeming grand or grandiose. But I'm going to keep trying.

Chapter 3

Fifth Congressional District and 1977 Special Election: Crucible of Change

Fifth District History

Georgia's Fifth Congressional District has been the scene of a number of major historical developments, particularly after World War II when it emerged at the forefront of efforts to both expand and restrict the rights of all citizens to participate in the political process.

Republicans twice won the Fifth District seat during Reconstruction. Unlike in other districts in the South, however, neither representative was an African American. From 1874 until Fletcher Thompson's victory in 1966 after Weltner's withdrawal, the Fifth District seat was held by a Democrat, very often with little or no opposition in the general election. This was due in considerable part to an electoral system that disenfranchised not only African Americans, but many other urban Atlanta voters as well. Fifth District residents were to play crucial roles in dismantling that system.

After the Civil War, a small proportion of African Americans were able to vote in Georgia elections until 1929, when participation in the Democratic primary was restricted to whites only. Since the general elections at that time amounted to little more than formalities in which the Democratic nominee always won easily, this effectively deprived Black voters of any meaningful say in Georgia politics. But in 1944, the US Supreme Court declared the white primary unconstitutional. The State of Georgia resisted implementing the ruling.

When longtime Fifth District Congressman Robert Ramspeck resigned in early 1946, a special election was called in February to replace him. Though Georgia was still claiming immunity from the Supreme Court decision outlawing the whites-only primary, that system was not employed in the special election, meaning that Black citizens could participate. The progressive Helen Douglas Mankin was the only one of the seventeen candidates to actively campaign for Black support, and she won by fewer than 800 votes, thanks largely to overwhelming backing from African American voters. Mankin became the second woman elected to Congress from Georgia, but her time in office proved to be short.

In April 1946, the US Supreme Court reaffirmed its 1944 judgment and explicitly struck down Georgia's whites-only Democratic primary system. Running once again in an open primary in July, Mankin easily defeated James C. Davis by more than 11,000 votes. At this point, Georgia's Democratic leadership resorted to another of its methods for circumscribing the voice of certain voters by applying the "county unit system." This was a state-based version of the presidential electoral college under which the decisive votes were tallied at the county level, with each candidate winning a plurality in a given jurisdiction obtaining all of its assigned electoral votes.

Though regularly used at the statewide level, where its bias in favor of less populous parts of the state at the expense of Georgia's cities had long worked to the advantage of segregationist politicians such as Eugene Talmadge, the county unit system had not been used in the Fifth District since 1932. When applied to the July 1946 Democratic primary, it meant that Mankin's large popular vote advantage in Fulton County, where most of the votes were cast, won her the six unit votes assigned to it, while Davis's edge in the less populated other jurisdictions in the district netted him a total of eight unit votes, making him the Democratic nominee. Mankin mounted a write-in campaign in the November general election but lost 62 percent to 38 percent.

Davis, who signed the 1956 Southern Manifesto opposing integration, was reelected until 1962, when he lost in a Democratic primary runoff to Charles Weltner. Prior to that election, Weltner had joined with Atlanta attorney Morris Abram in initiating a lawsuit on behalf of Fulton County voters maintaining that Georgia's county unit system gave disproportionate weight to less populous counties. For example, Fulton County made up 14 percent of Georgia's total population, but its six unit votes represented only 1.5 percent of total unit votes, whereas Echols County, with a population of less than one-tenth of 1 percent of the state's total was awarded 0.5 percent of the total unit votes. Thus, the vote of each resident of Echols County was equivalent to 99 Fulton votes. By an eight to one margin in the 1963 decision of *Gray v. Sanders*, the US Supreme Court agreed with the plaintiffs and struck down the county unit system as a violation of the equal protection clause of the Fourteenth Amendment. Indeed, the Georgia case represented the first time that the crucial principle of "one person, one vote" that has guided the US electoral process ever since was enunciated by the Supreme Court.

But that was not the only landmark court case involving Fifth District voters during this period. According to the 1960 Census, the Fifth District—then consisting of the counties of Fulton, DeKalb, and Rockdale—was home to more than 800,000 residents, whereas the average population of the state's ten congressional districts was less than 400,000. A group of Fulton County voters filed suit on the grounds that their votes for Congress were thus devalued compared to those in other districts. They called on the courts to halt further congressional elections in Georgia until the state redrew boundaries to bring districts more in line with the population distribution. In its *Wesberry v. Sanders* decision of 1964, the Supreme Court again decided for the Fulton County plaintiffs, ruling that the Constitution required

> that as nearly as is practicable one man's vote in a congressional election is to be worth as much as another's.... To say that a vote is worth more in one district than another would not only run counter to our fundamental ideas of democratic government, it would cast aside the principle of a House of Representatives elected 'by the People,' a principle tenaciously fought for and established at the Constitutional Convention.

The *Wesberry* decision had immediate and long-lasting results, causing districts around the country to be redrawn based on the "one person, one vote" requirement. In Georgia, the old Fifth District was subdivided in 1966 into a new Fifth, comprised of most of Fulton County, and a new Fourth District, which was centered on DeKalb and Rockdale Counties.

After his initial triumph in 1972, Andrew Young was easily reelected to the Fifth District post, winning 72 percent of the general election vote in 1974 and 67 percent in 1976. During the 1976 campaign, Representative Young played a key role as one of the early supporters of former Georgia Governor Jimmy Carter in his run for the White House. After the Carter victory, on December 16, 1976, Young was nominated by Carter to be the American ambassador to the United Nations, creating a vacancy in the Fifth District seat that would require a special election to fill.

1977 Congressional Election

Between the 1970 and 1980 censuses, the African American population of the Fifth District rose from 44 percent to 51 percent. Thus, the March 15, 1977, special congressional election took place at a time when the district was changing from majority white to majority Black. In terms of voter registration, however, the district's electorate was 60 percent white, 40 percent Black.

Under Georgia law, the special election took the form of a nonpartisan election in which all candidates who paid the $1,338 filing fee, or qualified as "paupers" by indicating they were unable to afford the fee, were pitted against each other on the same ballot. If no candidate received a majority of the votes cast, a runoff would be held three weeks later.

Twelve candidates qualified for the special election: Democrats Wyche Fowler, John Lewis (executive director of the Voter Education Project), Ralph David Abernathy (president of the Southern Christian Leadership Conference), Marge Thurman (chair of the Georgia Democratic Party), Billy McKinney (state representative), Henrietta Canty (state representative), Wyman Lowe (attorney), Alma Johnson (moderator for the Greater Atlanta Interfaith Movement) and Clennon King (Baptist minister); Republicans Paul Coverdell (state Senate minority leader) and Harry Belfor (retired attorney); and Socialist Workers Party candidate James Harris (carpenter). Five candidates were white—Fowler, Thurman, Lowe, Coverdell, and Belfor—and the remaining seven were African Americans.

Fowler announced his candidacy on December 30, 1976, two weeks after Carter's nomination of Young. "The Fifth District congressional seat from the state of Georgia is not a white seat, and it's not a Black seat. It's not a Democratic seat and it's not a Republican seat. It's a seat that represents a district of vast differences and enormous possibilities.... We don't need a symbol in that seat anymore because now the symbols of the New South are in the White House and are the ambassador to the United Nations. I will work for both white and Black."

Just as the campaign was getting underway, a major cultural phenomenon appeared on American (and Fifth District) television screens.

Each night between January 23 and January 30, 1977, the ABC network aired "Roots," the miniseries based on Alex Haley's book of the same name that dealt frankly with the issue of slavery and its impact on Haley's ancestors. It was watched by an estimated 140 million viewers nationwide, capturing two-thirds of the total TV audience, and its final episode drew 100 million viewers, a figure that still ranks as the third-highest audience for any US television program. Thus, as the candidates for the Fifth District seat previously held by Andrew Young began to seek support, the question of race was prominent in voters' minds.

Most observers believed that the election would be won by one of four top contenders: Ralph David Abernathy, civil rights leader and close associate of Dr. Martin Luther King; Paul Coverdell, Republican state senator and Senate minority leader representing northern Atlanta and north Fulton County; city council president Wyche Fowler; and community organizer and civil rights hero John Lewis. Lewis and Hosea Williams had led six hundred civil rights demonstrators in the 1965 Selma to Montgomery march for voting rights. The severe beating inflicted upon Lewis and others after crossing the Edmund Pettus Bridge in Selma, which received national media coverage, was one of the key events that culminated in the passage of the Voting Rights Act later that year. Some viewed the March 15 election as a two-part contest, with Abernathy and Lewis battling mainly for Black votes, Coverdell and Fowler vying for white votes, and the winners of these two "primaries" making it into the runoff.

The four candidates were interviewed about their approaches in a February 15 *Washington Post* article.

> Abernathy and Lewis both have close ties to Ambassador Young, who has chosen not to interfere in the race. But Lewis has received endorsements from Young's wife, Jean, and the influential Rev. Martin Luther King, Sr., father of the slain civil rights leader.... Lewis is quietly afraid that a too-close identity with Atlanta's Black establishment will cost him valuable Black rank-and-file voters, who are not above showing their antipathy to the city's Black elite. And Abernathy's supporters contend the endorsements have limited value because of Abernathy's appeal to the city's Black ministers and Black low-income voters.... Abernathy emphasizes a similar theme in campaigning in the predominantly Black neighborhoods

in the southern portion of the Fifth District. It appears to go over well there, but Lewis and his backers are betting that it won't play on the predominantly white northside, where any Black candidate must garner at least 20 percent of the white vote to win a congressional race. Lewis, meanwhile, employs the "Andy Young strategy." He spends at least two-thirds of his time campaigning in Atlanta's Black districts and the other one-third pounding the streets and handing out brochures in the north-central, largely white area where Young picked up much of the white backing that helped to keep him in office since 1972.... Coverdell, a 38-year-old businessman, said he intends to take maximum advantage of his "base constituency"—northside whites and Republicans—to win enough votes to put him into the runoff. In the runoff, he said, he would "explode out"—campaigning all over the district, including the Black inner-city, to win the election. "My contention is that I will get a very substantial portion of the inner-city vote because I understand the inner-city, and I'm not a divisive candidate." For his part, Fowler said he is going to lean heavily on his city council record and his two years of service...as an aide to former Rep. Charles Weltner to get votes. Fowler, 36, said he expects to be in a runoff against Lewis. In any case, he said, he expects to be in the runoff and to win Young's seat. "My constituency is everywhere in the district," he said, apparently ignoring the fact that he has upset some Blacks by criticizing Maynard Jackson, Atlanta's Black mayor. "I have drawn substantial support from all corners every time I've run. I've never won a race where I didn't get at least 20 percent of the Black vote," he said. Fowler said he doesn't make the assumption "that all of the Black votes will go to a Black and all of the white votes will go to a white." If that were the case, he said, he wouldn't run. "That kind of victory would be meaningless," he said. "The person who would get that kind of a win wouldn't have the authority to govern a district as diverse as this."[20]

Fowler had cause for optimism, based on the results of a poll his campaign had commissioned. In a survey of 925 Fifth District voters conducted January 17 to 20, Fowler was found to have "good name recognition, a positive image, and sizeable support within all parts of the District.

He is the only candidate who has significant biracial support." Specifically, Fowler had 91 percent name recognition (versus 49 percent for Lewis and 55 percent for Coverdell), and 69 percent had a favorable opinion of his job performance versus 30 percent who held a negative view. Furthermore, though his performance marks were somewhat higher among white voters (74 percent positive, 18 percent negative), he received solid grades from African American voters as well (60 percent positive, 30 percent negative), belying claims that his clashes with the mayor had permanently damaged his position in the Black community. In the trial heat, Fowler easily led the field with 28 percent, with Lewis at 9 percent, 8 percent for Abernathy, and 6 percent for Coverdell. He held a large advantage among white voters (Fowler 36 percent, Coverdell 10 percent, Lewis 4 percent, Abernathy 2 percent, Other 16 percent, Undecided 32 percent) and was competitive among African American voters (Abernathy 19 percent, Lewis 19 percent, Fowler 15 percent, Coverdell 1 percent, Other 3 percent, Undecided 43 percent).

However, as the poll analysis reflected,

> some cautionary notes must be added in evaluating the figures. First, support for a candidate is in part a reflection of name recognition. Given his superior name identification, Fowler could be expected to do well against lesser known opponents. With sufficient money (for advertising) and/or organization, the other candidates could close the name recognition gap and in so doing improve their support. Secondly, there are a large number of undecided voters. Finally, the results of this poll would be most valid for an average or larger turnout (40 percent or more of the registered voters). Should there be a very low turnout (less than 25 percent) the actual results could be very different from those indicated in this poll. What the Fowler campaign needs, therefore, is an ability to maintain high visibility (to reach the undecideds and to produce a larger turnout) and to directly contact (by telephone, by letter or in person) those voters already inclined toward Fowler and to make sure that they make it to the polls to vote for him. As the actual campaigning starts, Fowler has the advantage of already having suffi-

cient support to make the runoff. The major task facing his campaign is to make sure that enough of those people are motivated to actually vote.

Based on the poll results, the Fowler campaign strategy for the March 15 election was threefold: identify existing Fowler supporters and motivate them to turn out to vote, reach out to undecided voters and persuade them to support Fowler, and lay the groundwork for victory in the anticipated runoff, given the large number of candidates and the potential viability of several of them. On this last point, as the campaign began in earnest, it was becoming apparent that Rev. Abernathy's campaign was falling behind in fundraising and organization, and thus the contest would be a three-way battle between Fowler, Coverdell, and Lewis for the two runoff spots.

Part one of the campaign strategy—identification and turnout of Fowler's supporters—was accomplished primarily through an extensive phone-bank effort in which campaign volunteers called registered voters to see if they supported Fowler. If they indicated they did, their names and contact information were noted, and they were scheduled for re-contact calls just before Election Day to remind them to vote as well as to offer them a ride to the polls if they needed it.

The campaign prioritized precincts for its direct voter contact efforts based on support for Fowler and turnout percentage in previous elections. The precincts that ranked highest in Fowler vote and turnout were called first. Additional calls were made from satellite offices in southwest Atlanta, Sandy Springs, and "neighborhood headquarters" in which homeowners in these areas performed a variety of campaign activities, including calling and canvassing in their immediate vicinity. All of the almost 11,000 supporting households were re-contacted between March 12 and Election Day, March 15.

A parallel canvassing program began on January 29 and continued up through March 15 distributing campaign brochures, leaflets, and, as the election approached, Election Day cards to targeted precincts. Another important part of the Fowler effort was the distribution of yard signs bearing the campaign's "We Want Wyche" slogan. Over the course of the campaign, 7,500 signs were placed in supporters' yards throughout the Fifth District.

None of these activities, which were at the heart of this as well as all other Fowler campaigns, past and future, would have been possible without the participation of hundreds of volunteers who gave of their time and energy to make the calls, hand out the literature, and put up the yard signs.

The second facet of the campaign strategy—voter persuasion—was accomplished via mass mailings, newspaper ads, and radio spots. A mass mailing of 7,500 "We Want Wyche for Congress" brochures was sent at the beginning of March primarily to areas north of the City of Atlanta, where Fowler was less well-known.

The newspaper effort was somewhat limited, consisting solely of January ads in the *The Northside Neighbor* and *North Fulton Today* (two weekly papers covering north Atlanta and north Fulton County), the *Atlanta Daily World* (an African American-owned daily), and the *Georgia State Signal* (a college campus newspaper), which solicited volunteers for the campaign ("We Want Wyche Workers").

The third component of Fowler's campaign strategy focused on positioning him for victory in the likely runoff and involved key elements from the first two strategy phases. The pro-Fowler voters reached by the telephone program served as the basis for re-contact phoning as well as the all-important get-out-the-vote effort. The ads were designed to appeal to supporters of the candidates who failed to make the runoff, particularly to those backing either Lewis or Coverdell. But it also involved how and where Fowler campaigned, and what issues he stressed.

The answer to the *how* and *where* was simple. By 1977, Fowler had already run three times (1969, 1972, and 1973) in most of the Fifth District, with a racially and economically diverse constituency. His natural inclinations as well as political necessity compelled him to develop a campaign style that was nonracial in tone and content, one that was as at home in a Southwest Atlanta Black Baptist church as in high-income northwest Atlanta neighborhoods. He had always sought support in both the Black and white communities and had always campaigned throughout the city (and in 1972 the entire Fifth District). 1977 would be no different.

The nature of this special election, however, posed new challenges. Even though Fowler had faced multi-candidate, multi-racial fields in his previous campaigns, most of those were in city elections, which were nonpartisan, with no party identification indicated on the ballot. The only exception was his one losing race, the 1972 Fifth District primary where his opposition had been limited to Democrats.

This time, there was another multi-candidate, multi-racial field, but one where the candidates were clearly identified as Democrats or Republicans (with one Socialist Workers Party contender as well). And his most likely opponents in the runoff represented polar opposites in many ways: John Lewis, a Democrat and African American with support centered in the heavily Democratic, overwhelmingly African American, and less affluent southern part of the district; or Paul Coverdell, a white Republican whose support was drawn primarily from largely Republican, economically well-to-do northwest Atlanta and north Fulton County constituents. For the Fowler campaign, the quandary was how to position him in the March race to be able to pivot in the runoff to go after the very different constituencies of Lewis or Coverdell, depending on which one was eliminated from contention.

Part of the positioning effort involved accentuating Fowler's unique credentials for representing Fifth District residents, Black and white, in Congress. He and his campaign pointed to his service as chief of staff to Charles Weltner, who had held this very seat, to his credibility with the news media and other opinion leaders on *national* issues, particularly foreign policy, and to his own representation and familiarity with most of the territory of the district. Fowler articulated some of these themes in a campaign brochure.

> I want to be your congressman for one reason: to put into action my firm belief that the federal government can be made to work for the individual—and specifically for you, the individual citizen of the Fifth District. Of course, to do so it takes someone who knows both the inner workings of Congress and the day-to-day needs of the people he represents.... I want to become what I call a "Front Yard" congressman—a representative able to draw on two main strengths: First, the ability to listen carefully to the people of our district; and second, the experience it takes to respond when you have a problem.

The same brochure expressed Fowler's views on the racial aspects of the campaign and his intention to focus first on local concerns, should he be elected. "I'm not going to try to fool anybody into thinking that the needs of, say, Roswell's neighborhoods are always going to be the same as Atlanta's inner city neighborhoods. But there is one overall destiny of this district—and it's up to your congressman to help solve an individual community's problem, while making sure the solution is compatible with the needs of the entire district."

On what is almost always the top concern to voters—the economy—the 1977 campaign document "Wyche Fowler on the Issues" stated that

> the biggest contribution that the federal government can make toward restoring prosperity is to pursue steady fiscal, monetary and budgetary policies. We must not follow the haphazard stop-and-go economic policies which were tried in the early 1970s. Steady, predictable economic policy from the federal government will do much to restore the confidence of the private sector. But the government has a responsibility toward those who are unemployed. There is too much work that needs to be done, in housing, in transportation, in energy development, to allow this forced idleness to continue. Therefore, in cooperation with the private sector, which is where most of the jobs are, the government must move to help create jobs. We must target these efforts toward the areas where the need is greatest.

The emphasis on the private sector and on steady fiscal policy would resonate with many Coverdell supporters while the focus on jobs and the federal government's responsibility toward the needy, as well as the implied criticism of the Nixon administration policies of the early 1970s, would find traction with Lewis voters.

The issue that Fowler placed particular emphasis on, however, was derived more from policy than political considerations. Energy policy had become a contentious issue in American politics after an oil embargo and price hikes were imposed by the Organization of Arab Petroleum Exporting Countries in 1973, which were meant to punish the United States and other nations for support they provided to Israel during the Yom Kippur War. The price controls and gasoline rationing that had occurred under the Nixon and Ford administrations, and the ongoing "stagflation" (stagnant economic growth accompanied by high inflation) that had been exacerbated (if not caused) by the oil embargo had produced major disruption in the American economy.

Fowler believed the issue cried out for more attention from the federal government, and during his 1977 campaign, he said, "The cornerstone of America's energy policy must be conservation. An effective national conservation policy would reduce our dependency on foreign oil and, in addition, would stretch out our current supplies of fossil fuels and allow us time to develop other practical, environmentally-sound sources of energy. Toward that end, we must direct much more of our research into developing solar energy and non-polluting coal." Fowler remained true to these convictions throughout his congressional career, and promoting energy conservation and the development of alternative energy sources became hallmarks of his record in the House and Senate.

The predominantly white northeastern Atlanta neighborhoods that were instrumental in Fowler's 1969 and 1973 victories also contributed to Andrew Young's win in the 1972 Democratic primary and were key battlegrounds where Fowler, Coverdell, and Lewis all sought support. Fowler built upon his 1973 pro-neighborhood pledge by calling for a revision in federal housing and transportation policies that had been harmful to in-town neighborhoods. Specifically, he called for greater emphasis on rehabilitation of existing housing, increased federal funding for mass transit, and strengthened mortgage disclosure laws to combat the practice of redlining (denying credit to residents of certain areas based on the racial or ethnic composition of those areas). Fowler also supported promotion of expanded open spaces and recreational areas for urban residents, including specific endorsement of Andrew Young's Chattahoochee River protection bill and the Great Park project alternative for the I-485/Stone Mountain right-of-way.

With regard to the Middle East, the only foreign policy issue to receive significant attention in the 1977 campaign, the Fowler campaign provided the following responses to a questionnaire submitted by the Atlanta Jewish community, which had supplied important volunteer and financial help to Fowler and other progressive candidates for some time.

> Any final settlement in the Middle East can only be achieved through direct negotiations between Israel and the surrounding

> Arab states. Mediation efforts by third parties can be useful in bringing the opposing sides to the conference table but no outside powers can or should impose a settlement. I totally support sufficient military and economic aid to insure that Israel can continue to defend itself against potential attackers and can be economically viable.... The PLO should not be permitted to participate in the Middle East negotiations until it eliminates terrorism in its ranks and amends its charter so as to recognize the right of Israel to exist as a Jewish state.... I am not in favor of supplying sophisticated weaponry to the Arab states. I am most concerned about the massive sales of arms to Saudi Arabia (including the projected sales of Maverick missiles and F-5E aircraft, both of which should be canceled). Additionally, the U.S. should exert pressure on the Soviets and the French to reduce their arms shipments to the Middle East.

These were Fowler's views in early 1977, and though his position evolved somewhat over the years, it must be borne in mind that the situation in Israel and the surrounding states has evolved too, and conditions were very different many years later when he became US Ambassador to Saudi Arabia.

One part of the Fowler platform attracted almost no attention in the 1977 campaign but was important to him then and remained so throughout his time in Washington. In response to a candidate questionnaire from the public interest group Common Cause, Fowler indicated support for the establishment of a single House intelligence oversight committee, but added, "In the past, Congress has not fulfilled its responsibility in overseeing the operations of the intelligence community. However, even under a new system with single House and Senate Intelligence Committees, the major problem will continue to be the overseers: Will the members of the oversight committees be diligent in carrying out their responsibility?" He would have much more to say (and do) on this topic in the years to come.

Racial considerations were even more prominent in the lead-up to the special election than they had been in the 1973 Atlanta runoff. Andrew Young reversed his earlier pledge of noninvolvement and endorsed John Lewis, stating, "It is important for Atlanta to have a Black congressman from the Fifth District, but we are not going to have a Black congressman unless we can develop a consensus around one person who we can support and trust and who also has support and trust in the white community." Abernathy made the point that there "should not be taxation without representation" for Georgia's African American community, which made up a third of the state's population but would have no one on the state's twelve-member congressional delegation after Young's departure. Hosea Williams, by then a member of the state House of Representatives, spearheaded the Coalition to Save Atlanta, a group of African American political leaders who sought to persuade the seven Black candidates in the race to unite behind a single candidate in order "to keep the seat."

Among the white candidates, the most prominent attempt to raise the question of race was an effort by the Coverdell campaign to link Fowler to a race-based strategy, which was reported in a March 9, 1977, article by Margaret Ballard in *The Northside Neighbor.*

> As election day draws nearer, the pressure has quickly accelerated among candidates fighting for the Fifth District congressional seat.... Fowler's feathers are ruffled over an article appearing in the March 5 issue of "The New Republic" magazine, a weekly political journal published in Washington, D.C. The magazine's political editor, Ken Bode, quoted in the story a source from the Coverdell campaign claiming that they "had intercepted a letter mailed to selected voters on behalf of the Fowler campaign." The alleged letter insists that a white Democrat can beat a Black Democrat in the runoff, but that a white Republican could not. Fowler hotly denied sending such a letter to "selected voters," and said no such letter existed. "The first thing we did was to go through all our letters sent out, from Roswell to the South Side," Fowler explained, "and we didn't find any evidence of this..." Fowler did say, however, that a personal letter had been sent by attorney Clifford Oxford to Bill Patterson, a vice president and a branch manager of Trust Company of Georgia's Buckhead branch. The letter outlines to Patterson, a Coverdell supporter, why Oxford is supporting Fowler instead of Coverdell.... The letter refers to Fowler as a "proven vote getter in the Black community" and points out that Fowler should

> pick up votes from Black voters who are "upset" over candidates in the race. But, Fowler points out, the letter is a personal communication and is not being sent to "selected voters." He further stressed he is not employing the strategy that a white Democrat can beat a Black Democrat in the runoff. [Coverdell campaign manager] Carter Clews acknowledged talking to Bode about the letter but denied saying it had been sent to selected voters in the Fifth District. "I talked to Bode about a number of things. And this [letter] was one of many. We had seen a copy of this letter and it does pretty well outline the strategy. I do want to stress that I didn't say it was being sent to selected voters." Clews said Bode could have misinterpreted his statement, and that he had apologized to Coverdell about the incident. But, he added, "the strategy is out there and we're picking it up, regardless who is sending it out. We're not saying that Wyche is sending it out. It may be coincidental, but we are picking up that message from our canvassing and our phone bank." Fowler was demanding an apology from Coverdell but Coverdell said he considers the incident dropped. Writer Bode is vacationing until March 18 and cannot be reached for comment.[21]

For the record, Oxford was never close to Fowler. He had opposed Fowler in the city council president race, in which he backed Wade Mitchell, and opposed him in all his subsequent runs for office.

In competing March 10 editorials, the major Atlanta dailies split their endorsements, with the *Constitution* backing Lewis while the *Journal* supported Fowler.

> The decision about which candidate to support for the Fifth District congressional seat was a difficult one. There are many qualified persons seeking the post vacated by Andrew Young, not the least being City Council President Wyche Fowler who has an outstanding record in politics and government. However, another candidate over the years has worked tirelessly to improve the status of Blacks and poor people by showing them that ballot power may be their most effective helper. He is John Lewis.... Lewis is an intelligent campaigner who has demonstrated he has a keen understanding of the problems and people of the Fifth District, white and Black,

> northsiders and central city residents. We believe he will be a worthy successor to Ambassador Young. The Constitution endorses John Lewis for election to the Fifth District seat in next Tuesday's special election.
>
> —*Atlanta Constitution*

> The Fifth Congressional seat vacated by Andrew Young is being warmly contested and has attracted some good people.... Of the candidates, we think WYCHE FOWLER will do the best job for us in Washington. He has been in the thick of it at City Hall as president of the city council where he has presided with wit and intelligence. He knows the politics of this area and its economic and social problems. There is nothing shy or anonymous about MR. FOWLER and we predict that if the Fifth District sends him to Washington that Washington will know in a very short while the needs of this district and exactly who represents it.
>
> —*Atlanta Journal*

On Tuesday, March 15, on a warm and sunny day, 75,400 Fifth District voters cast their ballots in the special election, representing a turnout of 33 percent of the 231,202 registered voters. The turnout rate was eight points higher among white voters (36 percent) than African Americans (28 percent), producing an electorate that was 66 percent white, 34 percent Black.

Wyche Fowler led the way with just under 40 percent of the total vote, followed by John Lewis, Paul Coverdell, and Ralph David Abernathy. Thus, Fowler and Lewis would be in the runoff three weeks later.

Wyche Fowler	29,898	39.65 percent
John Lewis	21,531	28.56 percent
Paul Coverdell	16,509	21.90 percent
Ralph David Abernathy	3,614	4.79 percent
Marge Thurman	1,626	2.16 percent
Billy McKinney	1,105	1.47 percent
Henrietta Canty	631	0.84 percent
Wyman Lowe	276	0.37 percent
James Harris	108	0.14 percent

Alma Johnson	37	0.05 percent
Harry Belfor	35	0.05 percent
Clennon King	30	0.04 percent

Fowler claimed the top position by having particularly strong showings in Northside Atlanta (63 percent in northeast Atlanta, 60 percent in the northwest, 56 percent in north-central Buckhead), but he also won clear majorities in the northern suburbs of Alpharetta (62 percent) and Roswell (52 percent). Only in the sprawling unincorporated Sandy Springs area just north of Atlanta did he run (slightly) behind Coverdell (48 percent Coverdell, 45 percent Fowler), who represented the area in the state senate.

John Lewis dominated the vote in Southside Atlanta, polling more than 70 percent in all but one of the city council districts there and finishing just under that mark in the other (69 percent in the Fourth Council District). Coverdell's strength was primarily north of the city of Atlanta, where he won more than 40 percent of the vote.

With the north/south divisions to a considerable extent corresponding to the racial composition of the district (predominantly white north, predominantly Black south), Fowler finished first among white voters, winning 57 percent of their votes, with Coverdell second (33 percent), and Lewis a distant third (6 percent). Among African American voters, Lewis (72 percent) ran far ahead of both Abernathy (13 percent) and Fowler (6 percent).

This represented a break in the frequent Fifth District pattern from both the past (with Weltner and Young both having won with significant biracial support) and the future (Fowler's later House and US Senate races). Numerous reasons have been cited for the greater racial polarization on this occasion. These included Fowler's disputes with Mayor Jackson, the large field of both Black and white candidates in a low turnout special election (which presumably would cause the campaigns to concentrate on turning out the vote in their strongest support bases), and the particular makeup of this field, which featured two viable Black candidates in Lewis and Abernathy and two viable white candidates in Fowler and Coverdell.

Fowler and Lewis, however, each made significant efforts in all parts of the district, and both would win significant biracial support in the future. The best explanation for the racial polarization in the 1977 election likely lies in a combination of the presence of attractive candidates—Fowler in the north and Lewis in the south, with Coverdell also winning many white votes north of the city and Abernathy appealing to a portion of African American voters—which left fewer voters available for all candidates beyond their bases and the nature of the time in which the special election took place.

In 1977, the city of Atlanta was still working through the changes in governmental structure and political power that had been ushered in with the 1973 elections and the new city charter, and Fowler had been most prominently reported on in the media on those limited number of occasions when he and Maynard Jackson differed on policy or procedure. Thus, his appeal was somewhat higher than before, or after, with less liberal whites and somewhat lower in the Black community at the time of the special election. Furthermore, for African Americans, the possibility of losing Georgia's only Black representative was a significant concern—especially considering that, at the start of the Ninety-Fifth Congress in January 1977, only three African Americans (including Andrew Young) represented Southern congressional districts, and only seventeen served in the entire US House of Representatives. Indeed, at the time of the 1977 special election, no African American member of the US House had been replaced by a white representative since the start of the twentieth century.

1977 Congressional Runoff

During the three-week runoff campaign, the Fowler team resumed its telephoning (undecided voters from previous calling contacted between March 16 and March 31, Fowler supporters re-contacted between April 2 and April 4) and canvassing programs. Two mass mailings were sent out on March 28 to three thousand African American households and 17,000 households in precincts where Coverdell had done best. The newspaper ad asking "What do Maynard Jackson, Andy Young and Wyche Fowler all have in common?" was placed in three newspapers whose principal audience was in the Black community (*Atlanta Voice* and *Atlanta Inquirer* on March 28, and *Atlanta Daily World* on April 1).

Fowler and Lewis took similar positions on most key issues, but there were some notable differences. Lewis took a more pro-organized labor stance and backed immediate adoption of comprehensive national health insurance while Fowler advocated first pilot testing such an approach in select localities.

In making their cases to voters at a joint question-and-answer appearance televised by WSB-TV on Monday, March 21, Lewis stressed that he was not a professional politician or lawyer, that he knew the people of the district and their problems, and that he would provide national representation for the underprivileged and the people of the Fifth District. Fowler, on the other hand, pointed to his experience in city government and as a congressional aide, his ability to represent a diverse district and local interests, and his capacity to work with and persuade others. When asked to cite the most urgent need facing the district, Lewis named unemployment whereas Fowler identified the need to relate national policy to local needs. Both candidates decried the racial polarization that had occurred in the campaign, though neither blamed the other for causing or contributing to the problem. Both men expressed the belief that good representation by the next congressman would help bring the people of the district together.

The *Journal* and *Constitution* reiterated their previous endorsements, with the former touting Fowler and the latter once again going for Lewis. In an April 5, 1977, editorial, *Constitution* editor Hal Gulliver praised both candidates.

> Fifth District voters in Atlanta and Fulton County have a rare chance today to choose between eminently well-qualified candidates for this district's congressional seat. This newspaper endorsed John Lewis.... Lewis has the potential for being one of the great congressmen of his generation, a Black American of exceptional talent and compassion, a man who in many ways represented the best of the American dream.... It would be an easier vote today if Lewis' opponent, City Council President Wyche Fowler, had not also compiled a record of both style and substance.... Fowler, perhaps more than any other white public figure in Georgia, has demonstrated that it is possible to run a positive campaign against a Black candidate without in any fashion appealing to racial prejudices. He

ran once against Andrew Young...and once against Rev.-Rep. Hosea Williams. Both Fowler campaigns were remarkable in that he managed to appeal to white and Black voters alike, without letting racial polarization set in.

Ralph Abernathy cited Fowler as a "good and able man" but endorsed Lewis in the runoff, as did Mayor Jackson. Paul Coverdell did not make an endorsement.

In his exceptional memoir *Walking with the Wind*, John Lewis recalled the 1977 campaign. "In Wyche Fowler I faced a formidable opponent.... [He] could charm a room full of college coeds, then turn around and pick up a guitar and sing hymns with a gathering of senior citizens."[22]

Two days into Passover, and five days before Easter, on April 5, 1977, a cloudy and chilly day, Wyche Fowler was elected to Congress by winning more than 62 percent of the 87,110 votes cast. The total vote represented an increase in turnout (to 38 percent) compared to the March 15 contest, with more of the additional votes coming from the Black community (African American turnout +6 vs. March 15 to 34 percent; white turnout +4 to 40 percent), resulting in an electorate that contained a slightly lower proportion of white voters than in the earlier contest (63 percent white, 37 percent African American).

Wyche Fowler	54,378	62.42 percent
John Lewis	32,732	37.58 percent

Once again, racial crossover voting was limited, with Fowler slightly increasing his vote share among African Americans to 8 percent while Lewis equaled his previous 6 percent vote in the white community. Geographically, Lewis won 92 percent of Southside votes, with Fowler taking 86 percent in northeast Atlanta, 93 percent in the north-central part of the city, and more than 96 percent in northwest Atlanta and north Fulton County.

After the votes were counted, Lewis complimented Fowler for running "a good race, a strong race, and a clean race," and Fowler, in turn, lauded his opponent: "[John Lewis] has grown considerably in stature, not only with me but with the people of the Fifth Congressional District for the kind of campaign he has waged. I know that he will be back. I hope it will not be against me!"

For both Lewis and Fowler, this would represent the last time either was unable to put together a biracial coalition in an election. Lewis was elected to the Atlanta City Council in 1981 and won the Fifth District seat in 1986 after Fowler vacated it to run for the US Senate. He was reelected to that position thereafter until his death in July of 2020.

Chapter 4

Ninety-Fifth Congress (1977–1978) and 1978 Election: Taming the Fly

After celebrating his victory well into the night of April 5, Fowler and a small group of staff and supporters took a 7:45 A.M. Delta flight the next day from Atlanta to Washington National Airport. Vowing to "hit the ground running," he was sworn in as the 434th (out of 435) member of the Ninety-Fifth Congress at 12:22 P.M. on April 6. (The vacant seat was that of former Washington state Rep. Brock Adams, who had been confirmed as President Carter's Secretary of Transportation. That seat was filled in a subsequent special election.) It was important for Fowler to make such a quick turnaround because the congressional Easter recess started the next day, and if he were not sworn in on the 6th, he would have to wait until the House reconvened on April 18. In that event, he would not have become an official member until then and would not have been entitled to office space or staff, thus depriving Fifth District constituents of representation during those two weeks. And, he always said, he would have missed two weeks of congressional salary!

The first order of business was to set up his offices in Washington and Atlanta. In the aftermath of the racially polarized special election, Fowler thought it important to move quickly to hire a biracial staff, and he was also looking for a mix of people familiar with the Fifth District and its needs, as well as those with some experience in working on Capitol Hill. He appointed English Bradshaw, an African American with previous congressional staff experience, as his first chief of staff in the Washington, DC, office, which would focus on legislative matters. Peggy Nielson, his campaign manager and a white woman, was selected to lead the Atlanta office, where the primary focus would be assisting district residents with federal bureaucracy issues, including Social Security and veterans' benefits.

In Washington, the Fowler office was located in the Longworth Building, but was split between the third and fourth floors. In Atlanta, the office was in the William-Oliver Building at 32 Peachtree Street, right at Five Points and across from Central City Park. On July 1, 1977, the Fowler Atlanta office launched the mobile office, a converted minibus that traveled throughout the district offering "office hours" to residents near their homes.

When he first moved to Washington after the special election, Fowler shared a small house in Georgetown with two friends, Spencer Oliver, staff director of the Helsinki Commission, and State Department spokesman Hodding Carter. After a short time, he bought a townhouse a few blocks southeast of the Capitol, behind the Library of Congress's Madison Building, and he would reside there for the remainder of his congressional service. Fowler friend Peter Paterson termed the dwelling "Chateau d'Espair" because of its unkempt appearance. Fowler traveled back to Atlanta on most weekends and during congressional recesses.

The newly arrived Atlanta congressman outlined some of the challenges facing him in a June 1977 interview.

> Your responsibilities all happen simultaneously.... Subcommittees meet at the same time that full committees are meeting. And both of them meet at the same time the House is in session, and you're supposed to be on the floor. You're supposed to be three different places, all at the same time.... You run back and forth or you send a staff member to cover your committee, and at the same time you also have to have some appointments with people from the District who need to see you. It's a fast pace...it's really the big league. It's tremendously different [from serving in local government].... It has been a tremendous emotional and psychological switch from City Hall to Washington.... The subject matter is of such broader scope...questions of national and international policy, rather than the day to day administration of the city. It's going to be an educational process for me, but also a psychological process.[23]

Fowler also spoke about the differences between the Congress he experienced as an aide to Representative Weltner in the 1960s and what he found as a new member:

"The first incredible impression is the way the younger members are encouraged to participate, to assert themselves," Fowler said. "It's just amazing to me how self-assertive the Congress is." He said that 53 percent of the members have been in Congress less than four years. The fabled seniority system that kept freshmen congressmen meekly in their place on the back benches "is not dead," Fowler said, but it would seem not exactly healthy either.... "There's a tremendous difference from when I was there last time [under Weltner]," he said. "The House used to go into session at 3 in the afternoon. We have been [starting], in the last month, at 10 in the morning, going to 5–7 at night. We are busy. Whether it is progress or not may be open to debate...." Fowler said he was struck by "the willingness [of congressmen] to question the system, as well as the country's priorities" in the budget bill and the Carter programs. The aggressiveness of many younger members may be linked to the fact that their political baptism came in opposing the Vietnam War, he said.[24]

International Relations and Energy

As the second least senior member of the House, Fowler's initial choices for committee assignments were limited, but he was able to secure appointment to the International Relations (known before and after as the Foreign Affairs Committee) and Small Business Committees. He played an active role in the work of the former, with highlights including his cosponsorship of the Nuclear Non-Proliferation Act of 1978 (Public Law 95-242), which was sought by President Carter and aimed to halt the spread of nuclear weapons by establishing controls on the export of nuclear materials and technology and encouraging all nations to ratify the Non-Proliferation Treaty, and his opposition to the president's proposed sale of seven advanced Airborne Warning and Control System (AWACS) aircraft to the Shah of Iran in 1977 because of concerns about the survivability of the Shah's government and the possibility that the aircraft might fall into the hands of an anti-American successor regime. After the House International Relations Committee voted to reject the sale by a 19 to 17 vote on July 28, 1977, the Carter administration modified the proposal by removing several pieces of the most advanced equipment and the committee removed its objection. However, the planes were never delivered because of the fall of the Shah and his government in 1979 and its replacement by the virulently anti-American regime of Ayatollah Khomeini.

Fowler also opposed the February 1978 Carter proposal to provide arms to Egypt and the Saudis. "It just violates common sense to arm all sides in the Middle East.... They always come to us for arms, and we have yet to say no, especially since that is our announced policy [to suppress global weapons trading].... What frightens me is the long-term question, that, if something happens to [Egyptian president] Sadat, we don't know who is going to be there after him.... If we want to help our new-found friends in Egypt...it should be done through aid that brings about economic stability, developmental aid in a very poor country."[25] Sadat was assassinated three years later, on October 6, 1981, Fowler's forty-first birthday.

On August 17, 1977, Fowler left on a three-week trip, sponsored by the American Council of Young Political Leaders and the State Department, to Nigeria, Liberia, Kenya, Tanzania, and the Sudan. He served as the leader of the delegation, which sought to assess the political and economic climate in the five countries and gauge the impact of US policy there. "I feel that these meetings with African leaders will be of great value to me as a member of the House Committee on International Relations in determining the proper direction for American foreign policy as Africa-related issues arise," Fowler said prior to departure.[26]

At the conclusion of the official visit, Fowler stayed over in Kenya to climb (successfully) the famed Mount Kilimanjaro. However, after drinking some homemade banana beer offered by a young entrepreneur following his descent, he developed an illness that persisted for some time. Upon his return to Washington, he sought the medical expertise at the Walter Reed Medical Center, but doctors there were puzzled. The disease, eventually determined to have been caused by the parasitic *shigella* bacteria, produced increasingly serious symptoms in Fowler, including significant weight loss, and proved resistant to a changing variety of "drug cocktails" recommended by the doctors. His stomach pain continued to worsen, and after having lost sixteen pounds, "I overheard a doctor in an adjoining room say 'I think we're going to lose him.'" Hearing his doctors "giving up on me," Fowler decided to "take matters into my own hands" and determined to "kill the parasite" by drinking several glasses of fifty-year-old Scotch whiskey given him by a lobbyist. Almost immediately after taking this "medicine," the stabbing pain stopped. He believed then (and still believes now) that he had cured himself, but whether from his own cure or not, the congressman made a full recovery.

In his first term in the House, Fowler took the first of many steps he would take through the years in support of solar and other renewable-energy technologies when he cosponsored the Solar Photovoltaic Energy Research, Development and Demonstration Act of 1978 (HR 12228). Although this proposal never became law, its passage by the House represented growing congressional interest in diversifying the nation's sources of energy.

Intelligence

In what would prove to be the most significant development with respect to Fowler's committee assignments, House Speaker Thomas "Tip" O'Neill selected him to serve as a charter member, and the only freshman, on the new House Permanent Select Committee on Intelligence, which was established on July 14, 1977. This committee replaced the temporary intelligence panel chaired by Otis Pike of New York, which had focused its efforts on investigating illegal activities by the CIA and FBI. The Permanent Select Committee was created to not only exercise oversight in order to prevent further illegal actions, but also to formulate policies to improve the performance of the intelligence community overall. It was an assignment that former army intelligence officer Fowler lobbied hard for, and for which he sought and received White House backing, including a call from the president to Speaker O'Neill. After the announcement of his appointment, Fowler spoke about his role on the new panel.

> It's a tremendous responsibility as well as a challenge to be one of only 13 to have this responsibility involving the utmost of national security matters. I believe the lack of oversight has allowed abuses to occur in the past which never should have happened. While recognizing that intelligence operations are essential to the internal and external security of the United States, we must do everything we can to minimize all abuse of power. The committee must strike a balance between the public's right to know almost everything about the operation of its government and the real security demands if true national security is to be maintained.[27]

He elaborated on his position supporting declassification of a large amount of the information held by US intelligence agencies in an October 1977 newspaper article.

> There are times when the public not only has a right to know what's going on, but it's in the national interest to see that the public does know about some things. If the public had known about [surveillance of civil rights figures in the 1960s], it would have been stopped overnight, but nobody knew about it, and those who did it made sure it remained secret. If you could only see the wealth of information that comes in and the things that they classify, you'd see there's a lot of information that people ought to know about, or at least I think so.[28]

Perhaps the most important undertaking of the House Intelligence Committee in its first two years was its work in concert with its Senate counterpart in developing the Foreign Intelligence Surveillance Act of 1978. This measure was signed into law by President Carter on October 25, 1978, as Public Law 95-511 in response to concerns about Nixon administration abuses in using federal resources to spy on political opponents in the United States. The Act, still in effect to this day, created procedures by which the Congress and the federal judiciary could provide effective oversight of the government's covert surveillance of foreign entities and individuals within the United States without compromising the secrecy of such operations. Fowler took an active role in the development of the law, and, prior to the bill's enactment, explained, "An agency that wants to use a domestic wiretap has to get a judge's order before the wiretap can go on, but we don't have that for foreign intelligence purposes, and the agencies have been able to do almost anything they want without a warrant."[29]

Local Projects

Most of Fowler's attention in his first term in the House, however, was directed at fulfilling his campaign pledge to focus on helping to resolve local problems. In his first speech on the House floor on May 10, 1977,

Fowler introduced an amendment to the Housing and Community Development Act to require local citizen input in the application and approval process for the new Urban Development Action Grant program created by the Act.

> One of the major problems we face in this country is how to relate national policy to local needs. Atlanta and the Fifth District have been one of the most successful areas in the nation in developing methods for citizen participation that go beyond federal requirements. We happen to believe that only through the active involvement of our citizens and neighborhoods can policies be developed which are responsive to public needs. But even in Atlanta we have had problems in insuring adequate citizen input at all stages of the policy process. A case in point is a current dispute in which a local neighborhood group was excluded from the planning and development of a Section 8 Rehabilitation grant application.... We have heard a great deal of talk on the floor today about experts and consultants. The consultants who matter are not those in HUD or other federal enclaves; they are not those who are found within city bureaucracies. The "consultants" who matter are the people who must live with the results of this program—my neighbors and your neighbors. This amendment requires such prior consultation with citizens. It requires citizen input and participation at the beginning of the process where it can make a difference.

The Fowler amendment won bipartisan support and was agreed to by the House and retained in the final version of the legislation that was signed into law by the president on October 12, 1977. Fowler told *Buckhead Atlanta*, "I hadn't planned on being so active legislatively initially, but it was an opportunity where, if I had not had my city experience, I would not have recognized the problem and known how to attempt to deal with it."[30]

The first significant bill Fowler introduced in the Ninety-Fifth Congress was designed to help resolve the long-standing issue of the proposed highway through northeast Atlanta neighborhoods. In June 1973, the Atlanta Board of Aldermen voted 15 to 2 to oppose the highway, and in December of that year they voted to shift $70 million in funds for the highway to Atlanta's MARTA rapid transit system. In 1975, Georgia Governor George Busbee instructed the state's highway department to remove the highway from its plans. Efforts to use the land that had already been taken for the highway for parks and other non-transportation purposes were stymied by a federal requirement that 90 percent of the funds advanced to a state for construction of an interstate highway that was not built had to be refunded unless used for approved transportation purposes. In this case, the amount was over $17 million, and the Georgia Department of Transportation used this as a basis for rejecting several proposals by the City of Atlanta and the affected neighborhoods for alternative use of the lands.

To break the deadlock, Fowler introduced HR 12918 on June 7, 1978. The bill directed that upon the withdrawal of approval of any portion of an interstate highway, refunds of any federal funds provided "shall not be required if the State applies such funds to an eligible transportation project or to a public conservation or recreation purpose" within ten years of the original provision of the funds. The measure, unofficially dubbed the "Great Park" bill because it would facilitate the development of such a project in Atlanta's Inman Park, Grant Park, and Druid Hills neighborhoods, also affected ten other states where plans for interstate highways had been abandoned. In slightly modified form, the Fowler bill was adopted as an amendment to the Surface Transportation Act of 1978, which became law on November 6, 1978. Passage of this legislation helped end the stalemate and eventually led to the creation of Sidney Marcus Park, John Howell Park, and Freedom Park in the affected neighborhoods.

The Chattahoochee River runs for 430 miles, beginning in the Blue Ridge Mountains in northeast Georgia and eventually merging with the Flint River in Lake Seminole on the Georgia-Florida border. The stretch of river between Lake Lanier and Atlanta had long been recognized for its potential to offer significant scenic, recreational, and other valuable resources. Congressman Andrew Young introduced legislation to create a federally protected recreation area by acquiring up to 6,300 acres of land along the forty-eight-mile section of the river between Buford Dam and Peachtree Creek. When Representative Young vacated his congressional seat, Rep. Elliott Levitas of Georgia's Fourth Congressional District (immediate neighbor to the east of the Fifth District) reintroduced the bill.

Once Wyche Fowler was sworn in, he signed onto the Chattahoochee legislation and worked hard to win its passage. His major contribution came when he was able to reach a compromise with Congressman Ed Jenkins, who represented northeast Georgia's Ninth Congressional District, which allayed the fears of Lake Lanier property owners (whom Jenkins represented) about the impact of the new recreation area on lake levels and lakeside property values. The Fowler-Jenkins compromise, which stated that the Chattahoochee protection bill was not intended "to require the manipulation or reduction of water levels in Lake Sidney Lanier," was attached to the bill and helped pave the way for its passage by a vote of 273 to 79 on February 14, 1978. Fowler called the House action "a valentine for future generations" and added, "The greatest thing about this bill is that kids who grow up in cities and think rivers are just open sewers...will be able to enjoy this in its natural state forever."[31] The Chattahoochee River National Recreation Area Act was signed into law by President Carter on August 15, 1978.

In March of 1978, Representative Fowler demanded an investigation by the US Bureau of Prisons into the eight murders that occurred during the previous sixteen months at the Atlanta Federal Penitentiary. The request asked for "an evaluation of responsible administrative personnel as well as a detailed review of procedures for protecting and isolating inmates within the prison." On April 2, the Bureau agreed to create a special five-member panel to investigate conditions at the prison. With a ninth murder having taken place in the interim, on May 10, Fowler released the Bureau's report, saying, "These recommendations are all-encompassing and must be considered in their entirety. They recognize the serious problems caused by overcrowding, but recommend steps that can and must be taken to improve the system within the next few months." The report called for a series of measures that included both security enhancements and personnel changes, and their adoption resulted in "significant improvements in prison security," according to the *Atlanta Constitution* and other observers.

The Bureau report also concluded that the age and design of the Atlanta facility, which opened in 1902, placed inherent limits on security improvements, and so recommended that it be closed down by September 1, 1984. On May 26, 1978, Fowler endorsed this position. However, in spite of further incidents at the prison, including riots in 1987 by Cuban refugees from the Mariel boatlift who had grown tired of their indefinite confinement and potential deportation back to Cuba, it has remained in operation, currently as a low-security federal prison.

During the Ninety-Fifth Congress, Fowler emerged as the member of the Georgia delegation most supportive of President Jimmy Carter's agenda. For example, he was the only member of the delegation to back the president's proposals for Election Day voter registration and the creation of an independent consumer protection agency, both of which were defeated. He was also generally the most sympathetic to Carter's call for a comprehensive national energy policy.

As was always true of Fowler's approach to representation, constituent service was a key component at the outset of his tenure in the House. A December 1977 article in the *Atlanta Journal* profiled the workings of his Atlanta office, which was the focal point for such work.

> [Fowler's] appointments [in the Atlanta office], most of them 15 or 30 minutes, are scheduled back-to-back for the entire time the congressman is in his office. During congressional sessions, that's three out of four weekends.... Fowler's Atlanta staff schedules meetings for him, beginning at 6:30 P.M. on Friday, when he usually arrives at his office. Appointments continue all day Saturday and sometimes into Saturday night. Since he was sworn in 10 months ago, Fowler has found that his district office is the last stop for constituents whose problems span the entire spectrum of human ills. Perplexed constituents have included little old ladies with Social Security problems, people who needed artificial limbs from the Veterans Administration, boys who want to get into military academies, poor people who don't have money to repair a falling ceiling, and armchair politicians who want to sit down with Fowler to talk about the Panama Canal or abortion.... Helping Fowler help people is his staff of eight, a team that mans the Atlanta office and helps herds of constituents through the bewildering red tape of governmental agencies on housing, passports, voter registration, program grants, labor relations, veterans benefits and education loans, to name a few.... The office gets some 2,000 calls a month and handles an average monthly "caseload" of 450 problems.... Fowler—or his office—are successful in 75–80 percent of the cases they receive,

boasts [office director] Peggy Nielson, who adds that success doesn't always mean the person got what he wanted. "We classify a successful case as one in which the person is satisfied with the outcome," she says. "It may not be to his benefit, but he is satisfied that whatever came back to him was fair."[32]

In September 1977, the *Atlanta Journal and Constitution*'s "Sunday Scene" named Fowler one of "Atlanta's 10 Most Eligible Bachelors":

> Congressman Wyche Fowler said he doesn't know why women are attracted to him. In fact, he argued they really aren't, that he gets along with everyone under 10 and over 60. He just has problems with the ones in between, both men and women. Then, as an afterthought, he added, "You know, I sort of look like Woody Allen." Maybe that's his secret, that charismatic Allen touch. Although he said he likes to "play hard," Fowler denied that he is the stereotypical bachelor. He said he avoids the social limelight and hasn't attended a diplomatic party in Washington, D.C., yet. The 36-year-old, divorced, former city council president, who spends almost every weekend in Atlanta, said he enjoys Braves games, walks in the rain, mountain climbing and sailing. "The more I talk, the more I sound like a jet-setter," he quipped. Like Woody Allen, Fowler enjoys humor and lists that as a requirement for women he dates. "I like people who have a fine sense of the absurd," he said.[33]

1978 Congressional Elections

Just sixteen months after his victory in the April 1977 runoff, Wyche Fowler was up for reelection to the US House, starting with the August 8, 1978, Democratic primary. In that contest, Fowler faced thirty-one-year-old Clint Deveaux, an African American state representative, and Harry Belfor, a white perennial candidate. During the primary, Fowler spoke of his approach to representing the Fifth District.

> I've got one of the five most diverse congressional districts in the country—racially, geographically and demographically, you know, from the inner city of Atlanta, the white suburbs of Sandy Springs, little independent towns and even rural areas. Well, that fits me.

> I'm not an ideologue. I think I have a healthy appreciation of what the public interest is about and of where it has to be paramount to certain special interests.[34]

One of the congressman's legendary tales—without doubt true, since witnessed in the television studio by his colleagues Ed Jenkins and Dawson Mathis—chronicled his live election-eve debate with Deveaux. Members of Congress to this day recall it with delight, as does Fowler.

> On the Saturday night before the debate—and three days before the election—I was shaking hands at Black nightclubs on Atlanta's west side. I was by myself, as usual when I campaigned. Suddenly I saw my opponent in the arms of Monica Kaufman, the noted TV journalist who was to be the sole anchor—and inquisitor—in tomorrow night's debate. What to do? Should I call the station and allege prejudice? Call off the debate unless Kaufman was replaced? I decided to let it go. The debate began. Monica began with a softball toss to Deveaux: "Sir, I understand you have a fascinating proposal to reform public education in Atlanta that will result in better quality results for our teachers. Please tell us about it." Deveaux went on, uninterrupted for several minutes, eating up time. Then to me: "Mr. Fowler, why did you vote for such-and-such amendment to such-and-such educational bill that would have decimated public education in Georgia?" This pattern continued: Deveaux as the friend of the people. Me as the obstructionist. Suddenly, I realized that time was running out and I had made no positive impression whatsoever. Wham! A huge deer fly slammed me on my forehead. "Did you see that fly?" I exclaimed. Monica: "Come on, Mr. Fowler, there are no flies in this studio, answer the question." Suddenly, the fly buzzed her head, causing her to wave her arms to ward it off. "I told you it was a big fly," I offered. Monica calmed down, but her rolling eyes remained distracted. Finally, our final one-minute statement. Deveaux went first, repeating his platitudes. I had my last minute, and as Ed Jenkins told our colleagues in the House, I had pointed my long index finger at him to refute his distortions of my record, when the fly *landed on my finger*! And settled. As the

camera dollied in to capture the moment, my last words were, "Ladies and Gentleman, I have *tamed* this fly!"

Congressman Fowler won an overwhelming victory in the primary.

Wyche Fowler	45,411	79.68 percent
Clint Deveaux	9,997	17.54 percent
Harry Belfor	1,582	2.78 percent

Fowler ran strongly among both Black (Fowler 66 percent, Deveaux 32 percent, Belfor 2 percent) and white voters (Fowler 90 percent, Deveaux 8 percent, Belfor 3 percent).[35]

By the late 1970s, the Fifth District had become thoroughly Democratic in its partisan orientation, as evidenced by the 68 percent won there by Jimmy Carter in the 1976 presidential contest. In the 1978 general election, Wyche Fowler easily defeated Republican nominee Thomas P. Bowles Jr.

Wyche Fowler	52,739	75.48 percent
Thomas P. Bowles Jr.	17,132	24.52 percent

Once again, Fowler won large majorities among both Black (Fowler 96 percent, Bowles 4 percent) and white voters (Fowler 64 percent, Bowles 36 percent).

After the election, Fowler went on a two-week visit to the People's Republic of China as part of a bicameral, bipartisan, 10-member congressional delegation headed by Sen. Edmund Muskie (D-ME). Fowler took his father with him on the trip and was constantly bemused by his Chinese hosts who, at every stop, assumed that his white-haired father was the congressman and seated him at the head table of dignitaries. The real Congressman Fowler said nothing and seated himself at the staff table.

A December 1978 article in the *Atlanta Journal* reported that four Georgia political figures were considering running against Sen. Herman Talmadge in 1980: US Reps. Dawson Mathis and Wyche Fowler, Mayor Maynard Jackson, and State Representative Bud Stumbaugh of Stone Mountain. The article was written in the wake of a decision by the Senate

Ethics Committee to launch a "full-blown probe" of allegations of financial misconduct by Talmadge.[36]

Chapter 5

Ninety-Sixth Congress (1979–1980) and 1980 Election: A Man of the House

As part of a series of profiles of Georgia's House delegation, Wyche Fowler was featured in a September 1979 article.

> It is a little-known fact that Wyche Fowler loathes electric toothbrushes, but if you listen long enough to the Atlanta congressman, you begin to perceive that there is a vigorously felt political philosophy behind this. It's kind of complicated to explain—but then so is Fowler. At times, he sounds like an emissary from an idealized past, when the swaddling closeness of family and community were fondly felt, when the bigness of government, business and labor were not so much upon us, and when the landscape was still sparkling and lovely. At other times, he appears more like an oracle sent into our midst to foretell a poetic future when the nation has emerged from its energy and economic crises and has learned to live comfortably within more realistic limits. But it is over the eerie, jangled, bewildering and changing present that Fowler most visibly suffers and struggles, pitting a mind that is roundly credited as "imaginative" and "challenging" against the frustrating circumstances in which he finds his country. That's where the electric toothbrush comes in.... Asked recently about the prospect of the 1980s, Fowler's brow wrinkled and, staring directly into his listener's eyes, he said, "It's scary because of its uncertainty. But I am very optimistic about the future, because I think that looking at ourselves, who we are as a people, where we want to get, whether we need all these electric toothbrushes, whether we need to be overly consuming, always demanding more and more, whether that's doing anything for our lives and values, is the healthy reexamination we can have in the future," he continued. "I think we are going to find that we'll save a lot of money and a lot of effort and redirect our attention to what kind of government we want and how do we save the

family, and the religious values that are so much more important than all the things that we have been consuming that have been distracting us," he added.[37]

Ways and Means Committee

The House Committee on Ways and Means is the oldest committee of the US Congress and considered one of the most powerful. Under the Constitution, "all Bills for raising Revenue shall originate in the House of Representatives," and Ways and Means has fulfilled that responsibility since its beginning in the late eighteenth century. However, the committee's reach is much broader than taxes, and over the last 150 years, it has gained jurisdiction over trade and tariffs, Social Security, Medicare, and various social services programs.

A seat on Ways and Means is coveted by many, if not most, members of the House, and after his reelection in November 1978, Wyche Fowler sought to be selected. Committee assignments are handled separately by the two parties. Much like today, in 1979 the assignment of Democratic members was a two-part process, with the Democratic leadership-controlled Steering and Policy Committee receiving applications from members and then developing its slate of nominees. The work of the Steering Committee was then subjected to final confirmation by vote of the entire Democratic membership in the House (the Democratic Caucus). Almost always, this second step had been pro forma, as the rank-and-file membership did not wish to antagonize the leadership.

On January 16, 1979, the Steering and Policy Committee nominated Democratic Reps. Thomas Downey of New York, James Shannon of Massachusetts, Frank Guarini of New Jersey, Cecil Heftel of Hawaii, and Sam Hall of Texas for the Ways and Means vacancies. Fowler's attempt to gain nomination by the Steering Committee had failed for several reasons. First, the leadership had already provided recognition to the not-even-one-full-term congressman by naming him to the Permanent Select Committee on Intelligence. Second, Georgia already had a representative on the Ways and Means Committee in Ed Jenkins. Finally, members of the Democratic leadership and the Steering Committee had their own personal favorites for the coveted slots on the powerful committee.

Fowler said the outcome was a "big disappointment" to him and called attention to the fact that none of the nominees represented the southeast. He indicated he intended to meet with other southeastern Democratic members to determine who among them would be the strongest candidate in the subsequent caucus election. "If it's me, I'm up for the run. If it's someone else, we'll support them."[38] The attempt to arrive at a regional consensus candidate was unsuccessful, and Fowler and two other candidates challenged the five Steering Committee nominations.

On January 23, 1979, Wyche Fowler led all eight candidates in the Democratic Caucus vote for Ways and Means assignments. Four of the five Steering Committee nominees followed in the balloting, with Representative Hall placing sixth. Until the Fowler victory, no committee recommendations by the Steering Committee had been overturned by the caucus in the six years since the committee selection process had been opened up. The January 24, 1979, edition of the *Atlanta Journal* analyzed the outcome.

> Capitol Hill insiders say Hall's conservatism hurt him, while Fowler's image as a middle-of-the-roader helped him. In addition, Fowler argued, apparently successfully, that the southeast was underrepresented on the influential committee.... Mainly, Fowler worked hard to get the seat. After deciding late Thursday to make the try despite his failure to be nominated, he and his staff spent all day and much of the night Friday, Saturday and Monday trying to round up votes. Fowler said that by the time the caucus gathered Tuesday he had personally contacted about 260 of the 275 House Democrats and cornered the rest on the floor of the House.[39] [

The same paper editorialized about the Fowler triumph the following day.

> We congratulate Atlanta's Rep. Wyche Fowler for getting himself elected as a member of the powerful House Ways and Means Committee. His 5th Congressional District will benefit from the important influence he will gain through a seat on the committee which initiates the process of writing the nation's tax laws. Fowler did it the hard way, too—the House leadership had turned down his request to be recommended for the committee, but Fowler was elected to it when he appealed to rank-and-file Democratic House

> members. Some said the House leadership originally turned down Fowler because another Georgian, Rep. Ed Jenkins, already is on the committee. But Fowler's election despite this shows he stands high in the estimation of his colleagues at large.[40]

It was a major upset and a mark of considerable personal accomplishment for the young congressman. In the process, he had denied a seat to the odd man out, Representative Hall of Texas, who had been sponsored by his fellow Texan, the powerful House Majority Leader Jim Wright. After the vote, with his local media back in Texas reporting that Fowler's win was a personal rebuke for Wright, the majority leader asked Fowler to speak to the reporters and make clear this was *not* the case. Fowler was happy to oblige.

The central policy-making role played by the Ways and Means Committee was demonstrated right off the bat for Fowler, who was to play a key part in developing and winning support for three major policy initiatives backed by the Carter administration in 1979: a windfall profits tax on the oil companies, welfare reform, and containment of rising health care costs.

The Crude Oil Windfall Profit Tax Act was introduced in the House in May 1979 and referred to the Ways and Means Committee. The Carter administration and supporters of the proposal—including Wyche Fowler—wanted to recapture some of the substantial "windfall profits" that were expected to accrue to the US oil industry as a result of the massive increase in global oil prices produced by the 1973 oil embargo. The high oil prices coincided with the gradual end of the federal controls on domestic oil prices that had been originally imposed by the Nixon administration in 1971. The rationale for price decontrol was to allow US oil prices to reset to the world level and thereby increase the incentives for energy conservation and alternative energy production. In addition, supporters of the tax saw it as an important source of revenue at a time when the federal deficit was worsening.

As an advocate of a comprehensive energy policy, Fowler supported the original Carter proposal for utilization of the new tax's revenues. In his January 21, 1980, State of the Union address, the president said, "It is essential that these revenues be invested on behalf of all Americans to help us become an energy secure nation. The revenues from the tax will be used to support key national energy goals: low-income energy assistance, improved and expanded mass transit and energy supply and conservation programs." Four days later, Fowler wrote to President Carter.

> I am deeply concerned that, unless you and others who are committed to a comprehensive national energy policy clearly and firmly reaffirm your strong support for significant energy investments from the windfall profits tax proceeds, we will lose the opportunity to accomplish this vitally important objective.... At the present time, it appears that the Conference Committee [meeting to reconcile the different versions of the legislation approved by the House and Senate] will not set aside any funds for mass transit and will substantially reduce the energy production and conservation tax credits included in the Senate bill. Thus, we may well see the windfall profits tax measure, which was designed and has been proclaimed to be a comprehensive energy bill, turned into a general tax bill.

After undergoing consideration and amendment in the House and Senate throughout 1979, a final version was approved by both chambers and signed into law by the president on April 2, 1980. The law imposed a temporary excise tax (to be phased out by 1991) on the difference between the market price of oil and a specified 1979 base price, though one-third of domestic production was exempted and the taxes paid by the oil companies were made deductible against their income tax liabilities. In the use of the proceeds, Fowler's fears did partially materialize because the final proposal set aside 60 percent of the funds for income tax reductions. It did, however, reserve 25 percent for a grant program to provide assistance to low-income households in meeting rising energy costs, and 15 percent for alternative energy supply and conservation tax incentives. No funding was provided for mass transit. After the 1980 election of Ronald Reagan, who opposed the Windfall Profit Act, the law's tax rates were reduced, and with lower oil prices in the late 1980s and minimal revenue being generated by that point, it was repealed in 1988.

A perennial "hot potato" for any public official to take on was welfare, a system no one was happy with and yet where few effective remedies had been found. As a member of the Ways and Means Committee, Wyche

Fowler entered this fray, which offered him little political reward but considerable risk.

The Carter administration had proposed a comprehensive reform of the nation's welfare system in 1977, but it garnered limited support and never came up for a vote in either the House or Senate. A somewhat scaled-back version, the Social Welfare Reform Amendments of 1979, was introduced in the House in July 1979 and referred to the Ways and Means Subcommittee on Public Assistance, to which Fowler had been assigned. The legislation

- established a minimum national benefit floor under which states would be required to provide cash and food stamp benefits worth at least 65 percent of the poverty level for eligible families with dependent children;
- made eligibility and benefit standards more uniform across the states;
- provided $900 million in increased assistance to the states to cover increased costs;
- reduced administrative costs; and
- provided tax credits to private employers and job training and job search assistance to help welfare recipients get jobs and off welfare rolls.

Fowler took on the task of trying to line up Southern support for the proposal, which aimed to reduce welfare dependency by ensuring that an individual would always be better off by earning wages, and by eliminating the welfare system's incentives for the break-up of families. The legislation was very controversial, especially in the South, because it would have increased some welfare benefits. During floor debate on November 7, 1979, Fowler set forth his reasons for supporting the measure.

> The bill now before us...is not a comprehensive rewrite of our welfare laws. It is not a final, decisive battle in the war on poverty. It is an exercise in the art of the possible. It is a carefully crafted package consisting of some increase in benefits, a tightening of program administration, and fiscal relief for State and local governments.... Despite the fact that the incidence of poverty is disproportionately

> higher in Southern and rural areas, fewer of the poor in those areas receive aid from public assistance programs and those who do receive some aid generally are given lower benefits. I think it is fair to say that the current welfare system is highly discriminatory against the southern working poor.... The bill before us today is very clearly pro-work. By providing for a more gradual phase-out of eligibility and benefits as earnings increase, [this bill] ensures that a person will always be better off by earning an extra dollar.

Even though most governors supported the legislation, Fowler's efforts, which helped secure House passage by a vote of 222 to 184, won him little praise, and the legislation was subsequently killed in the Senate. Significant welfare reform would have to wait another seventeen years, when President Bill Clinton struck a deal with congressional Republicans that resulted in enactment of the Personal Responsibility and Work Opportunity Act of 1996, a measure somewhat similar to the Carter proposal, but one that contained fewer "carrots" and more "sticks."

Inflation was a serious national problem in 1979, but health care expenses—especially the hospital component of those costs—were especially problematic, with hospital price increases being double the overall inflation rate and reaching 12.8 percent in 1978. The Carter administration's Hospital Cost Containment Act proposed a system of voluntary price controls for hospitals. Those institutions failing to operate within the limits set under the voluntary program would be subjected to a mandatory federal cost-containment program. Fowler played an active role in the committee's development of the legislation, winning approval of his amendments to provide for automatic expiration of the cost-control program after five years, require the administration to report to Congress on alternative cost control measures, award performance bonuses to efficient hospitals, and provide grants to states to help defray the costs of their cost-control programs.

When the bill was brought to the House floor on November 15, 1979, an effort was made to eliminate the cost-control programs and to substitute a national commission to study the problem of hospital expense increases and make recommendations to Congress as to how those increases could be curbed. Representative Fowler spoke against the substitute and in favor of retaining the cost-control programs.

> The hospital industry needs to address the problem of third-party payments. The hospitals and medical profession need to re-examine the doctor-hospital referral system and its impact on costs. And all of us need to have an answer to the question of whether every hospital needs to duplicate every other hospital in purchasing every new piece of modern technology.... All of these questions are being studied. They are being studied by the Government. They are being studied by the hospitals. They are being studied by the doctors' organizations, and all of us are thankful that that research is going on.... This legislation allows all this research to go on but does not impose mandatory controls of any kind unless a hospital fails [to meet any of the voluntary limits], all of which are very tough to fail.... The last thing in the world we need to say to the American people on either side of this debate is: "What are we going to give you to stem such escalating costs? We are going to give you another Commission. We are going to give you another study."

In the end, the House did vote to replace the cost-containment effort with a study commission. With the teeth removed from the bill, there was little impetus for further action, and it was not acted upon in the Senate. Health care and hospital costs continued to be a significant problem in the years that followed (rising, for example, by 13.4 percent in 1979) and were not seriously addressed until the enactment of the Obama administration's Affordable Care Act of 2009, with the jury still out on the effectiveness of its cost-control provisions.

Energy Policy

Fowler's service on the Ways and Means Committee also offered him a position from which to advance the cause of alternative energy sources, long a personal priority, by sponsoring legislation to provide tax credits for such sources. In August 1979, he introduced the Solar Energy Incentives Tax Act, which sought to encourage the purchase and installation of solar equipment by proposing four changes in the tax code:

- increase the investment tax credit for solar energy to 40 percent;
- shorten the depreciation deduction period for solar equipment to 36 months;
- make lessors of solar property eligible for the residential and investment tax credits for solar energy; and
- make passive solar energy systems eligible for the residential solar credit.

Although the House did not consider the Fowler bill, the final version of the Windfall Profit Tax legislation included some related provisions, increasing the investment tax credit for solar, wind, and geothermal energy to 15 percent and raising the residential renewable energy property tax credit to 40 percent of the first $10,000 of expenditures.

After the enactment of that legislation, Fowler concentrated his efforts on the promotion of passive solar energy building design, which relies on energy-efficient architectural techniques and the use of special building materials to capture solar energy, and which can reduce residential energy requirements by up to 80 percent.

On June 27, 1980, Fowler introduced a bill to provide homebuilders with up to a $2,000 tax credit for constructing residences incorporating a passive solar energy system. The credit would be available based on the system's effectiveness in reducing a home's heating and cooling load. At a September 5, 1980, press conference, Fowler said,

> For both economic and national security reasons, we cannot afford to let nature take its course in moving our country toward a more energy-efficient future, but we must pursue public policies to speed this transition. In my opinion, the passive solar tax credit, which would utilize the private sector rather than governmental bureaucracy, represents one of the most cost-effective ways of achieving energy self-sufficiency.

Though no further action was taken on the measure after its introduction, Fowler was able to increase awareness of the issue and build support for the future by obtaining the cosponsorship of 145 House members.

Fowler laid out his overall vision for a national energy policy in a December 28, 1979, speech.

> Our reliance on ever increasingly expensive and undependable foreign oil has meant: a much higher level of inflation than we would otherwise have experienced; substantial trade deficits; strategic vulnerability of our energy supply in the event of war; and a severe drain on the rest of the economy because of the diversion of a larger share of national investment to energy production and consumption.... Ladies and gentlemen, the energy crisis is real. It is a more serious threat to our nation's security and well-being than any foreign weapon. The era of cheap and abundant fossil fuels is over and will never return.... Today, I want to present you with my approach to a comprehensive energy policy. The first part of this program has already been acted on by the Carter Administration: to allow oil and natural gas prices to reflect their true replacement costs and to redirect some of the additional revenues that would have been received by the oil companies because of price de-control to more cost-effective energy investments.

Fowler called for making conservation "the top priority" in the nation's energy policy by providing federal assistance for the purchase and installation of energy-saving equipment for residential, commercial, and industrial users, and of certified automobile fuel-efficiency devices. He also reiterated his support for renewable energy in the form of the solar energy proposals he had authored, and endorsed the creation of an investment tax credit for the installation of hydroelectric facilities on existing small-scale dams. Finally, he voiced support for greater use of coal by requiring conversion of certain oil- and gas-fired power plants to coal supplemented by federal assistance for the purchase of the pollution-control equipment necessary to allow coal plants to meet air and water quality standards.

The *Atlanta Journal* offered support for the Fowler presentation in a January 2, 1980, editorial.

> In a speech to the West End Rotary Club the other day, Rep. Fowler stated plainly that the emphasis for the next few years must

> be placed on reducing current consumption...and on coming up with renewable energy resources.... The performance of Congress on energy to date hasn't been very heartening. Both chambers have fallen victim to provincial interests at the cost of national interests.... Perhaps Congressman Fowler's speech is an indication that there is at last a recognition of the genuine depth of the problem and of the proper ways to go about solving it. We commend him for his stand, and urge his compatriots in the House and Senate to take a close look at what he has to say. It is worth heeding.[41]

Other than its support for coal—which subsequent concerns about global warming, as well as the never realized objective of "clean coal," rendered as an increasingly undesirable energy-production resource—this 1980 policy statement remained an accurate outline of Fowler's energy priorities for the remainder of his time in the Congress.

ABSCAM

Under House Democratic Caucus rules, Fowler's placement on the Ways and Means Committee required him to relinquish both the International Affairs and Small Business Committee assignments, though he was able to retain his slot on the Intelligence Committee. In a further mark of the high regard in which the second-term Atlanta congressman was held by his peers in the House, Fowler was given another special committee assignment in February 1980: temporary service on the House Committee on Standards of Official Conduct (generally referred to as the Ethics Committee) in order to participate in the committee's investigation of potential wrongdoing by House members in the so-called ABSCAM case.

ABSCAM, short for "Abdul scam," was an FBI "sting" investigation of corruption by public officials that began in 1978. In February 1980, it was publicly reported that the investigation included members of Congress. Thirty-one individuals were targeted, including state, local, and other federal officials, in addition to the congressional members. Ultimately, one senator and five members of the House were convicted of bribery and conspiracy in separate trials that ended in 1981. Independent of these judicial proceedings, the House and Senate had to determine what disciplinary action to take against these individuals.

An *Atlanta Journal* article reporting on the ABSCAM investigation provided some insights into the challenges faced by the Ethics Committee and Fowler's approach to passing judgment on his colleagues.

> Ethics Committee members face a problem getting the evidence against the seven congressmen, reportedly videotaped while an FBI undercover agent posing as an Arab sheik proffered gifts of cash to obtain special legislation.... The committee would like copies of the videotapes. But the Justice Department will not turn them over for fear of jeopardizing subsequent prosecutions. Fowler tried to force the issue in a committee meeting last week, but lost when he offered a motion to subpoena the films. He is not sympathetic to the Justice Department's denial of essential evidence, since what is publicly known resulted from a presumed Justice Department leak. "The bind was created by Justice in its own leak. Their sensitivity about the criminal process is a hole they dug for themselves," Fowler said.... The possible defense of entrapment, which may be raised by some congressmen netted during ABSCAM, will not play well on the Hill. "If you plead entrapment, you're saying, 'I did it, but you caught me unfairly.' No congressman could make that defense before Congress without admitting he violated his oath of office [to uphold the laws of the United States]," Fowler said.... To Fowler, being expelled from Congress, the most drastic action the committee could recommend, is harsher punishment than a short jail sentence. "The recent history of congressional cases in court resulted in slaps on the wrist, minor fines, six-month confinements in country club prisons. But a person expelled from the highest legislative body by his colleagues...that shame and stigma is an awful punishment," he argued.[42]

Four of the House members resigned before any such action could be taken against them. The one senator (Harrison Williams, D-NJ) and one of the House members (Michael "Ozzie" Myers, D-PA) did not resign initially, though Williams eventually did so prior to a scheduled vote on his expulsion. It was left to the House Ethics Committee, including Wyche Fowler, to determine the punishment for Representative Myers. On October 2, 1980, the House voted 376 to 30 to accept the Ethics

Committee's recommendation that Myers be expelled from the House. Just prior to that vote, Representative Fowler spoke on the House floor.

> There are three issues that no one can decide but each of us here. They all have to do with justice.... The first question is whether or not justice has been accorded Mr. Myers. For the committee, a large majority would submit that in every way possible that we could, we believe justice has been accorded. Mr. Myers was given every opportunity to present every defense, every witness. Second is the question of justice to this institution, because we are all on trial and we all have to make the decision as to whether or not the integrity of this institution has been violated, if you find that the allegations brought by this committee to you are so heinous that only expulsion can uphold the integrity of the institution. Lastly, I suppose, is the question of justice to the people we represent, and in that, as Learned Hand said, "Justice delayed is justice denied." We are all stewards of this trust and if the [offense] is so heinous that this body must deal with the sanction, the ultimate sanction [of expulsion], then the only fulfillment of all of our contracts to the people that we represent is to perform this sad duty.

Ironically, Fowler's name itself had come up during the course of ABSCAM when one of the public officials under investigation implicated him to an FBI undercover agent. Investigations by both the Justice Department and the special counsel employed by the House Ethics Committee totally exonerated Fowler from any involvement.[43]

Foreign Policy

Fowler continued to be a "frequent international traveler" in the Ninety-Sixth Congress, primarily in furtherance of his role on the Intelligence Committee, which tended to focus his visits on trouble spots around the globe. He was occasionally criticized for such trips, culminating in an attack ad aired by his opponent, Sen. Mack Mattingly, in the 1986 Senate race, but he always felt that these fact-finding missions were essential in fulfilling his duties.

In January 1980, Fowler was part of a twelve-member bipartisan congressional delegation sent to Saudi Arabia, Nigeria, South Africa, and

Rhodesia (now Zimbabwe). The ostensible purpose of the mission was to explore energy policy, and, indeed, as reported in a January 1980 story in the *Atlanta Journal*, Fowler indicated, "I've realized how fragile our industrial state is because of our dependence on two countries like Saudi Arabia and Nigeria, which are in two of the most troubled areas of the world. The Nigerians and the Saudis are saying this can't go on. Not only is the oil supply dwindling, but the competition has become so great for it."

The journey also afforded the Atlanta congressman invaluable insights into the political situation in the Middle East and southern Africa, and he later said that of all of his congressional trips, this one left the deepest impression on him. The *Journal* article included Fowler's assessment of Saudi Arabia during his first visit to the kingdom.

> "They [the Saudi royal family] feel very nervous because of the Soviets." After meeting earlier this week in Riyadh with King Khalid, Crown Prince Fahd, Defense Minister Sultan and Oil Minister Yamani, Fowler learned that the Saudis are keenly concerned with a $120 million U.S. arms sales now pending in Congress. "They are terrified over the Soviet incursion into Afghanistan and feel like they have been warning against it for several years." The Soviets, they feel, have been marching steadily toward the water on the Persian Gulf. This is not only a historical wish that the Soviets are beginning to implement, Fowler's hosts related, but considered a direct attack on Islam. The fear also spills into unstable Iran, to the east, and Soviet-influenced Ethiopia, to the west. "They're very nervous about Iran," Fowler said, "because they fear a pincer movement, designed to encircle the countries on the water, allowing the Soviets to go after the oil fields." Fowler, who voted against an arms sale to Saudi Arabia last year, said he will reconsider this year because of Soviet military action, but will do so only after carefully considering any possible threat the weapons could pose to Israel and overall peace in the Middle East. The Saudis, Fowler said, generally believe the Camp David accords worked against a comprehensive peace, while the Americans feel it was the first step toward that goal. However, as a result of his meetings, Fowler learned that the Saudis are not going to say publicly that they are going to have Israel included for peace. But, Fowler said, "They talked around the

question enough to satisfy me that they realize you cannot have a stable peace in the Middle East unless Israel is somehow included." By contrast, Saudi support for President Carter's action in Iran is much greater.[44]

Another article recounted Fowler's experiences on the African portion of his trip.

While Nigeria did not have the problem of a ruling white minority after colonial rule ended, the 18 percent South African white population is subjecting the Black majority to much greater control, Fowler says, than he expected. It was enough to prompt him and Rep. William Gray (D-PA) to take a separate trip, without authorization, to the Black township of Soweto, outside of Johannesburg, and meet with the Council of Ten, the top Black leaders in Soweto. There, Fowler and Gray got a "firsthand account of what racial categorization" means in the daily life of non-whites in South Africa. "We saw official documentation that classified individuals as either a white, Black or colored, which determines what jobs you can have, which schools you can go to, where you can live for your entire life," Fowler said. However, what shocked Fowler and Gray equally as much was that the Soweto Blacks, from whose ranks Black leaders may be selected as future government leaders, were not "more militant." Instead, they are seeking accommodation. "They want to talk and negotiate, and not riot," Fowler said. By contrast, the Rhodesian settlement and upcoming majority rule elections showed the end of the grip of the 4 percent white minority on the Black Rhodesian majority. Fowler said the current situation is very fragile, but he picked up encouraging, if not startling, news. Fowler said he learned that former Prime Minister Ian Smith may be ready to abandon his support for the "internal settlement" coalition with Bishop Muzorewa, whom Fowler met with, and set up an alliance with the likely winner of the upcoming elections, Joshua Nkomo, co-leader of the Patriotic Front. "Informed sources hinted strongly that Ian Smith might be backing Nkomo," Fowler said, explaining that "Smith has probably realized he is not going to have a country unless the Patriotic Front is given a piece of the action."[45]

One final international trip during this time produced a Fowler recollection of the "honey incident."

> One of my earliest interests, undoubtedly stemming from my Sunday school days of studying Old Testament maps of Israel and the Middle East, was what is now known as biblical archeology—excavations at sites mentioned in the Bible as major towns during and before the time of Jesus. That interest matured into fascination with ancient Greek and Roman ruins, and I remained alert for any new reported discovery.
>
> Over the Easter congressional break in 1979, eight of us, four Democrats and four Republicans, traveled to the Middle East, ending with a free weekend in Athens, Greece, not for rest, but, alas, for shopping. We had our own Air Force plane and pilots, and our return to Washington was set at 6 P.M. Easter evening. I had noted several weeks earlier the announcement of an archeological dig some 70 or so miles north of Athens, and wanted to visit it. Asking permission from delegation leader Dante Fascell (D-FL), as well as the use of his car and driver, I knew was bold, but I did it, and because he trusted me to return on time, he acquiesced.
>
> We left at 4 A.M. on Easter Sunday morning and had an unremarkable drive, arriving at the site at sunrise around 7 A.M. The archeologists, once they got over the shock of an American congressman wanting to see their discoveries, treated me like royalty, detailed the ancient history of the site and showed me the artifacts that they were convinced would lead to the revelation of a temple. (Unfortunately, it didn't, I later learned.)
>
> Toward mid-morning I began to make my apologies to leave, but they insisted that we have a meal together, and a goat smelled roasting on a near-by spit was produced and devoured. Lastly, fresh bread and honey was laid before us. The honey was unique, both sweet and tart, like a fine wine, and my hosts described that the bees made it from two flowers, unique to this region, growing in the spring only on the "dark side" of this mountain. "I must go," I repeatedly urged, explaining that I could not miss my plane. Finding about thirty dollars-worth of Greek drachmas in my pocket, I asked

if I could purchase a jar of their honey to take home with me. Pushing my money aside they headed to a rickety wooden shed secured by a rusty old Yale lock. Where was the man with the key? As luck—or fate—would have it, he was visiting his parents for Easter on "the other side of the mountain." Scratching out my address, I leapt into the car, with promises of sending me honey ringing in my ear.

A small historical perspective: My mother's oldest sibling, my aunt Pauline, who at the time was about 88 years old, had lost her eyesight some five years earlier, and had come to live with us in Atlanta. She was a tiny woman, with a sharp mind and an extraordinary memory. Weighing well under 100 pounds, she ate little, but loved honey. Her breakfast was always twice-baked toast with honey and black coffee. She delighted when I traveled abroad, knowing that I would return with tiny samples of honey from every country I visited, often six or eight originals at a time. I was hoping that my new friends would not forget to send a sample for Polly.

The roads back were jammed with Easter travelers returning home, something I should have anticipated, but didn't. We had plenty of time, I assured myself, having six hours to make it to the airport by flight time. Suddenly, we rounded a bend and stopped dead still. The bridge across the main river was out! For the first time I felt panic and urged the driver to find an alternate route. He did, knowing the region very well, but by the time we had woven our way north on meandering back lanes to an alternative bridge, we had sacrificed precious hours. More traffic awaited, and when we finally dashed into the airport at 6:30 P.M., my colleagues had just taken off. I was crushed, and as these were the days before cell phones, I had no way of letting Fascell know of my plight—or sorrow.

Then came the next blow. Pan Am non-stop to JFK left at 8 P.M. I reluctantly handed the agent my credit card for the flight, then headed for the bar for a strong martini to ease my pain. I headed to the gate when my boarding announcement was called. Suddenly, I heard a familiar rattle behind me on the concourse. It was a rattle I remembered from my high school days working at the local grocery store after school: shopping carts on a hard surface.

Turning, I saw the two chief archeologists (actually brothers) steering two shopping carts bound together and loaded with a huge wooden barrel of what turned out to be honey! My only thought was the cost of transporting the barrel, which must have weighed at least two hundred pounds. I couldn't afford it. After embracing them and thanking them profusely, reluctantly we reached the ticket man. Unbelievably, he was a friend from their village. After tagging the barrel and giving me the stub, he welcomed me on board. No charge.

Settling into my seat, exhausted yet thankful I would be back in time for the congressional session the next day, I heard the captain's voice come over the intercom. "Welcome to Pan Am's flight 386, now non-stop to New York's John F. Kennedy airport. We are on our way through 17,000 feet to our cruising..." BAM!!! A loud explosion caused the airplane to drop so precipitously that three stewards standing in the aisle hit the roof. Fortunately, none was seriously injured. For what seemed like an eternity, my fellow passengers and I waited for the crash. Finally, the captain came back over the air: "Ladies and Gentlemen, my apologies. I have been flying for Pan Am 27 years and have never encountered such an air pocket. I have now checked all systems and all are normal. Free drinks for all for the rest of the flight. I expect smooth weather and no more incidents." I ordered a double martini, downed it in a gulp, and slept the rest of the journey.

After disembarking at Kennedy airport and wandering to the baggage claim area, we were met by an airline employee who asked all passengers on PA 386 to follow him. We did, through innumerable underground tunnels, before emerging into the brilliant sunlight of a New York morning on the airport's tarmac. There, the shocking sight left us speechless. Spread out on the tarmac were hundreds of pieces of our luggage covered with an inch of viscous honey. The honey bomber had struck! The first honey *terrorist* had struck!!! As I stared, frozen, I found myself literally eating my claim check, destroying the evidence of my "luggage." No one moved. Our luggage was destroyed.

Dazed, I found myself in a cab going into the city, where I wandered the streets trying to reclaim my senses. A day later I made it back to Washington. I don't remember how.

I never told this story to anyone for over seven years, fearing that until the statute of limitations had run out, I could be found culpable. Two years after the incident, Pan Am filed for bankruptcy. Was I a contributing cause? Was I *the* cause? I'll never know. Although I tried, my aunt Pauline never got her special Greek honey.

Local Projects

Fowler's growing involvement in national and international affairs did not mean that he slackened his efforts on behalf of more localized needs. One of these was his fight to block a plan by the Carter administration that would have discontinued Atlanta's only long-distance passenger train, the *Southern Crescent,* which operated between New Orleans and Washington, DC, via Atlanta.

In late January 1979, the US Department of Transportation presented Congress with a proposal that called for reducing the size of the nation's Amtrak passenger rail network by 43 percent, from 27,500 miles down to 15,500 miles. The DOT plan, which was to take effect unless explicitly rejected by Congress, would have eliminated the *Crescent,* along with a number of other routes. Fowler's interest in the issue went beyond simply saving the *Crescent,* however, and on March 29, 1979, he introduced a resolution to disapprove the DOT recommendations for reductions in the Amtrak system. He presented his rationale in his introductory statement.

> The DOT recommendations seem to have been developed without any recognition of the enormous energy conservation potential of modern passenger rail service. A filled passenger train is six times as energy efficient as the automobile, twice as efficient as a bus, and as much as seven times as efficient as a 747 jumbo aircraft.... Missing from the [DOT] report is any discussion of the impact of the Airline Deregulation Act of 1978. By the first week of February 1979, 184 communities had experienced decreases in the frequency of flights since February of 1978. In the past month and a half, the increasing cost and spot-shortages of jet fuel have led to additional

> cutbacks. The DOT report fails to consider the hardships caused by this reduction of public transportation, which would be further compounded by the elimination of rail service. The Congress must not endorse the DOT's lack of attention to the critical problem of preserving mobility for the Nation's citizens.

The House considered the DOT Amtrak plan in July 1979. On July 24, Fowler, along with Rep. (and future vice president) Al Gore (D-TN), offered an amendment to place a one-year moratorium on any cuts in the Amtrak system to allow for detailed evaluation of the impact on train ridership of increased gasoline prices and reductions in air service caused by the Airline Deregulation Act. The Fowler-Gore amendment was narrowly defeated (197–214), but the support it generated led the House to adopt, by voice vote, another amendment that reduced the cutbacks in service to just 5,500 miles (to a 22,000-mile network) and preserved the *Crescent* and a number of other passenger routes. In response to the congressional action, on August 29, 1979, the Amtrak Board of Directors cut six passenger lines (including the Chicago to Miami *Floridian*, which had stops in Valdosta and Waycross, Georgia). However, the *Crescent* was spared and continues in service to this day, while Amtrak still operates a 21,000-mile rail network.

Another local transportation issue occupied Fowler's attention throughout his career in the House and Senate: the development of the Metropolitan Atlanta Rapid Transit Authority (MARTA) subway system in Fulton and DeKalb Counties. By the end of 1979, the East-West line between the Avondale and Hightower Road Stations had opened, but further expansion was in some doubt because of uncertain federal financial commitments. To bolster MARTA's case, in late 1979 Fowler convened a meeting between the Georgia congressional delegation and MARTA officials to discuss strategy. This led to a further meeting in early 1980 in which Fowler obtained a commitment from the head of the federal Urban Mass Transit administration to issue a letter of intent promising $105.9 million in federal funds to allow MARTA to begin construction of two and a half miles of rail and three stations on the North-South Line.

The School of Medicine at Morehouse College in Atlanta was founded in 1975 as a two-year medical program, with the first students admitted in 1978. Under the leadership of dean Dr. Louis Sullivan, the school sought to obtain $1 million in federal funding to allow it to expand its program and become a full, four-year medical-degree-offering institution. Because of tight budgets, the Carter administration initially cut the grant award by almost half. However, congressional efforts led by Wyche Fowler resulted in the August 13, 1980, announcement that the entire $1 million grant would be provided. This allowed the Morehouse school, which became the first medical college founded by a predominantly African American institution since the nineteenth century, to proceed with its plan to provide a primary care medical education program training doctors to serve minority and other underserved communities. As Fowler said, "This money will go a long way toward improving the distribution of health care professionals in areas suffering critical health care shortages. It will also help fulfill national equal opportunity goals by training minorities for highly skilled health care positions." The next year the congressman was awarded an honorary doctorate from Morehouse College.

Representative Fowler was a cosponsor of the legislation to create the Martin Luther King Jr. Historic Site near downtown Atlanta, and he worked hard for its enactment. The bill passed the House in September 1980 and was signed into law by President Carter the following month. Fowler would continue to support the site by seeking funding for its development and maintenance throughout his career in the House and Senate.

Baseball

Fowler's lifelong love of the game of baseball led to a memorable experience in the fall of 1979.

> The Atlanta Crackers were known as the "winningest team in the minors," having amassed 19 minor league championships by the early 1950s. I followed them assiduously, memorizing the stats of all the regulars and listening to road games on my crystal set, usually hiding under the covers way past my bedtime. The games were "broadcast" by "wire recreation," which meant that the announcer was not at the park where the game was being played, but in an Atlanta studio reading ticker tape as it came across the wire and "recreating" the play-by-play for the listening audience. Jim Woods was his name, and I longed to someday meet him. The tape would

simply say Ball One, but Woods would report, "Frankie takes one high and tight for ball one." When the tape said "single to left," Woods excitedly called, "Jeff lashes one down the line out of the reach of the third basement for his second single of the game." And so it went—a thrilling recreation in real time.

My Daddy took me to several games every summer at Ponce de Leon ballpark on North Avenue, where I saw Jackie Robinson play in an exhibition game against the Crackers on his way to the majors. The crowd treated him respectfully for the most part, although a few hecklers shouted their racial bias.

When I arrived at the Capitol to work for Charles Weltner, I quickly made friends with the staff of the Speaker of the House, Thomas P. "Tip" O'Neill, and was often invited to come by his office after hours to hear the legendary storyteller regale us with tales, true and "truish." I was fascinated, especially by his baseball stories. Ronald Reagan, another Irishman with whom I served for his two terms, was also a riveting raconteur, but I always thought Tip's tales superior. (Tip's nickname, he told us, came from that of Edward O'Neill, a star of the old St. Louis Browns. In 1887, O'Neill finished the season with an astonishing batting average of .492. Walks were counted as base hits then, so today's record books calculate his average as .435, still the second highest in the history of the game. O'Neill was a genius at drawing walks, fouling off pitch after pitch until the frustrated pitcher deliberately threw the pitch out of the strike zone. Because of his hundreds of foul tips, Edward became known as Tip O'Neill.)

When I was elected to the House in April 1977, I was met by the beaming Speaker, genuinely pleased that I had fought back a field of twelve to win the seat. After a huge bear hug, he said: "Wyche, wouldn't it be wonderful if the Boston Braves and the Boston Red Sox meet in the World Series this year!" Long a Red Sox fan, he knew that the Atlanta Braves were the old Boston Braves by way of Milwaukee. I agreed, and was escorted by the Speaker himself to my new congressional office.

As it turned out, my positions on congressional initiatives largely mirrored his, and I quickly became a loyal follower of his leadership. I was rewarded in 1977, only months after my election, when Tip chose me over some 200 applying Democrats to serve on the new House Select Committee on Intelligence. I was the only freshman on the charter committee, and it marked me as one of the Speaker's favorites.

In October 1979, the Pittsburgh Pirates and Baltimore Orioles met in the World Series. The series was tied at three apiece when the seventh game was to be played in Baltimore. The weather had been atrocious in both cities during the week, resulting in several postponements. But the weather was forecast as favorable for the decisive game.

I was in Tip's office alone [with him], I don't remember why, when he received a call from President Carter. The president was inviting him to the final game. Leaping from my chair and dancing like a madman, I implored the Speaker, silently, to invite me along. I can still hear Tip's voice: "Mr. President, I'd love to go, but in my office with me is Congressman Fowler, a great baseball fan, and your best supporter in the Georgia delegation. Could we bring him along?" The president said yes. We were to meet at the White House at 8 P.M., and along with us would be Dan Rostenkowski, my chairman on the Ways and Means committee. Only while driving myself to the White House did it occur to me: How are we going to get to Baltimore by the 8:30 game time?

Bo Ginn, my colleague representing Georgia's coastal counties, had been searching for tickets for this game all week. His young son wanted to go, and Bo had called lobbyists and corporate executives before finally getting two tickets on the very back row in the left field stands. I could not bring myself to tell him of my good fortune.

Bo tells the story from here on: "After crawling in rain-lashed traffic for almost five hours, Bo-Bo and I managed to get one of the last spots in a parking lot almost a mile's walk to the stadium. Arriving at our seats we grabbed two soggy hot dogs as the rain finally abated and I got out my binoculars to try and find the field. Suddenly, a familiar thud-thud-thud sound overhead announced the approach of a helicopter. The copter hovered briefly over the field before landing on the mound. As I watched in disbelief, out came the president of the United States, the Speaker of the House, the chairman of the Ways and Means committee, and... *Wyche Fowler*! All now strolling twenty yards to a reserved field-level box. I have never felt so cold and miserable in my life. How did the son of a bitch do it???"

The game was close and tense through the 9th inning when the Pirates added two runs to win 4–1. Jerry Rafshoon, a senior Carter media advisor, began late in the game to convince the president that he should go to both locker rooms and greet the players. I advised the president against it for several reasons, but the president wanted to go. The mother of Chuck Tanner, the Pirates manager, had died the day before. We headed first to the losers' locker room, where Earl Weaver, the Orioles manager, intercepted us before we got to the solemn and despondent team. "I'm so sorry to hear about your mother," the president said to Earl. "Not me, it's the other guy's mother, Mr. President," Earl responded.

1980 Senate Race

Along with his congressional workload, between August and late December of 1979 Fowler undertook a "testing of the waters" for a potential Senate bid against Herman Talmadge in 1980. This effort brought him to many communities across the state, including Albany, Americus, Athens, Augusta, Cartersville, Columbus, Cordele, Dalton, Decatur, Gainesville, Griffin, Jonesboro, Lakeland, Louisville, Macon, Marietta, Newnan, Rome, St. Simons, Savannah, Snellville, Thomaston, Thomasville, Tifton, Toccoa, and Valdosta.

Back in February 1979, the Fowler campaign conducted a statewide survey to gauge the congressman's standing among Georgia voters at that point. The poll showed that he was quite well-known (82 percent name recognition) and generally well-regarded (55 percent positive, 27 percent negative) in the metro Atlanta area (including Fulton, DeKalb, Cobb, Clayton, Gwinnett, Douglas, Henry, Paulding, and Rockdale Counties), and that he fared relatively well in the rest of north Georgia (65 percent recognition; 41 percent positive, 25 percent negative), which was almost entirely within the reach of Atlanta television. On the other hand, and not surprisingly, there was much less awareness of the Atlanta congressman in both middle (40 percent recognition) and south Georgia (34 percent recognition).

When matched against a multi-candidate field of potential Senate candidates, Fowler placed third (at 12.8 percent), trailing incumbent Herman Talmadge (24.4 percent) and Lt. Gov. Zell Miller (20.3 percent), with 21 percent undecided and the remainder divided among other contenders. With Miller, who at that time had not decided whether he was going to enter the race, not included, Fowler came in second (19.4 percent to Talmadge's 31 percent). On October 29, 1979, Miller announced his candidacy.

In an August 1979 article, *Atlanta Journal and Constitution* reporter Henry Eason commented on one of Fowler's early statewide forays.

> Fowler's keenly felt dilemma is whether to seek reelection to the House seat he won in 1977, whether to pursue an already promising career with his newly won seat on the potent Ways and Means Committee, or whether to abandon what he has earned and plunge into a fierce Senate race. This fence-sitting posture had overshadowed his speeches in Dalton and Cartersville the day before to the extent that his remarks came across fuzzy and indecisive. He rambled on vaguely before audiences there about economic and energy problems, and uncomfortably dodged questions about his plans. But that day in Gainesville, Fowler could no longer suppress something inside him that made him want to give the mildly curious Kiwanians something to think about.... He fairly shouted out that there is no longer a place in Georgia politics for "any gallus-snapping perception of the past pitting rural against urban, small towns against Atlanta, the north against the south." "Gallus-snapping," a reference to Gene and Herman Talmadge's habit of stripping off their coats and proudly snapping their red suspenders against their chests, suddenly became Fowler's code word for Talmadge.... And, in the speech that he would use again and again, he put his audiences in mind of the fact that they deserved the quality of leadership (read Talmadge) they got. "The fault, dear Brutus, is not in the stars but in ourselves," he quoted Shakespeare. "If you tolerate apathy, you get apathetic leaders. If you tolerate men of questionable integrity, that's what you're going to get," Fowler declared. Fowler, looking very much a part of the young generation of the 1980s and 1990s of whom he spoke, talked movingly about uniting Georgia's

> ancient divisions, of pulling rural and urban areas together as a whole state, where Atlantans and farmers joined in common cause. After a few days a perceptible enthusiasm about his August mission emerged that was lacking in the beginning. After his speeches, more and more of his audiences began approaching him with encouragement. He carefully filed away their names and addresses and began to invite those he saw to write him.[46]

On November 1, 1979, Fowler announced he had hired South Carolina political consultant Marvin Chernoff to assist in preparation for a potential Senate bid, and stated, "I am actively exploring the possibility of running for the Senate." However, he told a reporter in early December that "the decision is personal."

> He says it turns on whether he wants to be in the Senate instead of the House and whether he can do more for Georgia from that post than his present one. "The only decision is whether or not I should leave my seat at this time. I like my work. I've got the best committees [Ways and Means and Intelligence] and the [House] leadership is good to me," said Fowler in an interview.... The Senate is different. It is clubby, more reliant on staff and a much tougher place for a junior member to have an impact, Fowler noted. "I don't know if I want the life in the Senate. You take the risk of going to the Senate and being put on the Water Committee. I like to be where I have the most influence," he said.[47]

The perils of Fowler's "testing the waters" far from where he was well-known was highlighted by Ron Hudspeth in an October 29, 1979, snippet in the *Atlanta Journal.*

> Recently Fowler, who is rumored ready to run for Herman Talmadge's job, was in Waycross campaigning and feeling a bit sorry for himself that not a soul recognized him. Finally, a young south Georgia miss excitedly approached Fowler on the street and began screaming: "I know who you are! I know who you are!" "Well, say it," grinned Fowler, tickled pink someone had recog-

nized him. "Say my name out loud!" "You're...you're...Art Garfunkel," she said dreamily. "I couldn't disappoint her," Fowler said. "I signed an autograph: To Joanie, From Art."

On February 18, 1980, Fowler announced his decision not to seek the Senate seat that year.

> Today marks the end of a lot of hard thinking. As you know, I have wanted to make the race for the Senate for at least two reasons, strongly felt: 1) I am intensely committed to bringing some sense to our energy problems and our foreign policy. 2) I reject the notion that people who live in different parts of Georgia have different hopes and ambitions for themselves and their families simply because they live in different communities or are of different races. This is a myth that divides us, and that blocks our progress as a state. But because of recent events, I have decided that I can do a better job for now by asking my constituents to return me to the House. In the last 18 years, the people of Atlanta and Fulton County have had no congressman serve beyond two terms. None was defeated. Each one voluntarily chose other paths. And though I think that periodic change is often good, I also believe that in tough times for our country, people deserve a representative who will see the job through for them—and with them. It is always easier to campaign than to serve. It is easy to promise, but hard to deliver. Simply put: My work in the House is not yet finished.... As for the Senate, I am not immune to the idea of serving all the people of Georgia. But that must await the future. I am a young man. There will be another day.

1980 Congressional Elections

Although John Lewis considered making a run for the Fifth District seat following his resignation as head of the federal VISTA program, especially when it appeared that the incumbent might opt for the US Senate race, Fowler faced limited opposition in the 1980 Democratic primary and general elections. As of October 1980, the Fifth District had a total of 248,686 registered voters, 60.6 percent of whom were white and 39.4

percent of whom were African American. This represented a 25,000 increase in voter registration and a slight rise in the white proportion of registered voters compared to 1978.

In the August 5 Democratic primary, Fowler overwhelmingly defeated Doug Steele, a white thirty-two-year-old real estate broker.

Wyche Fowler	52,547	85.71 percent
Doug Steele	8,760	14.29 percent

In November, Sandy Springs physician and Republican Party activist F. William Dowda was the opponent. Fowler again prevailed, and by a similar margin as in the 1978 general election.

Wyche Fowler	101,646	74.04 percent
F. William Dowda	35,640	25.96 percent

Chapter 6

Ninety-Seventh Congress (1981–1982) and 1982 Election: Contesting the Reagan Revolution

Reagan Policies

On the same day Wyche Fowler was overwhelmingly reelected to a third term in the US House of Representatives, a major shift in the direction of American politics and government took place. Though he was able to carry his native Georgia, President Jimmy Carter was decisively defeated by former California Governor Ronald Reagan, who won the national popular vote by 51 percent to 41 percent, and the Electoral College by 489 to 49. At the same time, the GOP picked up twelve seats in the Senate, taking control of that body for the first time since 1952. (One of the defeated Democratic senators was Herman Talmadge, who lost to Republican challenger Mack Mattingly.) The Democrats retained control of the House but lost thirty-four seats.

For Wyche Fowler, the election of Ronald Reagan represented a significant change in how he viewed his role in national policymaking. During the Carter presidency, Fowler had generally found himself in agreement with the president's initiatives, from arms control and the Camp David accords to energy policy, hospital cost containment, and welfare reform, among others, and he had played a supportive role on these national issues while devoting much of his own time and effort to more local concerns. But Reagan was on the other side on almost all of these policies. Furthermore, in sharp contrast to Fowler's belief that government had an obligation, in the words of the preamble to the US Constitution, not only "to provide for the common defense" (a premise which the new president seemed to share), but also to "establish justice, insure domestic tranquility...promote the general welfare, and secure the blessings of liberty to ourselves and our posterity," Ronald Reagan came into office expressing great reservations about the government's role.

In an article written shortly after President Reagan's inauguration in January 1981, Fowler outlined his concerns.

> I was impressed by much of our new President's Inaugural Address, especially his sense of optimism, his expression of commitment to a growing and non-discriminatory economy, and his call for equitable sacrifices and solutions to the problems we face. President Reagan deserves, and will get, a chance to move against our economic and other problems backed by a spirit of national unity and bipartisanship. But one theme clearly spoken in the President's speech disturbed me. That was his assertion, which he has made many times before, that "in this current crisis, government is not the solution, it is the problem." I would absolutely agree that individual policies of the federal government have definitely contributed to many difficulties now facing our country. But I cannot accept the criticism that government is the problem. In a Constitutional republic governed by democratic rules, this idea is not only wrong, it is dangerous. Not only Communist tyrannies but also our democratic friends listen with amazement to this assault on the government, especially since Mr. Reagan later in his speech praised our government as being uniquely "of, by and for the people." Government is certainly not the answer to all our problems, but neither is it the cause of them all. The protections of the Constitution and the ballot box offer us the means to correct government abuses when they occur and to set the government in the direction that we the people determine.

Over the next several years, Fowler found himself fully engaged in the national debates on the federal role across a wide range of issues, including the federal budget, national defense, intelligence, and foreign policy. It was his belief that it was not enough to simply criticize what the president was proposing, but rather he had an obligation to his constituents and the country to articulate his own vision on these critical concerns. It is worth pointing out that even though Fowler was often criticized for being out of step with his state and the rest of the Georgia congressional delegation in his opposition to much of the president's agenda, Reagan lost Georgia by a substantial 56 percent to 41 percent margin and trailed even further behind in Fowler's Fifth District (losing 60 percent to 35 percent there).

In the 1980 campaign, Ronald Reagan had stressed three key policy positions: 1) tax cuts; 2) increased defense spending; and 3) reductions in nondefense spending. By August 1981, he was able to achieve most of what he had requested on all three counts, in part by winning sufficient support from Democrats, who still held a substantial majority in the House. The Economic Recovery Tax Act of 1981 cut taxes by $38 billion in fiscal year (FY) 1982 and by more than $747 billion over a five-year period. Among its main features was a phased-in cut of 25 percent in individual tax rates over three years, resulting in the top rate falling from 70 percent to 50 percent and the bottom rate dropping from 14 percent to 11 percent.

The second major legislation enacting the Reagan fiscal plan was the Omnibus Budget Reconciliation Act of 1981 (Public Law 97-35), which cut nondefense programs by $35 billion in FY 1982. Included were reductions in the food stamp, subsidized housing, school lunch, student loan, and Medicaid programs and the elimination of the Social Security minimum benefit.

Finally, the appropriations process provided for a $31 billion increase in defense spending in FY 1982.

Fowler had supported the tax-cut bill reported out by his Ways and Means Committee that differed most prominently from the Reagan plan by providing a 15 percent cut in average individual income tax rates phased in over two years, with the cuts skewed to those making under $50,000 a year. When the matter reached the House floor on July 29, 1981, he voted against the Reagan-backed substitute, which was nonetheless approved by a 238 to 195 margin, with forty-eight Democrats supporting the president. (Fowler's fellow Ways and Means member Ed Jenkins was the only other "no" vote within the Georgia delegation.) Even though he retained serious misgivings about the size and distribution of the Reagan tax cut, Fowler joined in the overwhelming subsequent 323 to 107 vote in favor of final passage of the amended bill because of his belief that some type of tax relief was urgently needed.

On the reconciliation bill, Fowler backed the Democratic proposal calling for $38 billion in spending reductions in FY 1982 but voted against the Reagan alternative that would cut an additional $20 billion over three years. Once again, the president's position prevailed, this time by a margin of 217 to 211, on June 26, 1981, with twenty-nine Democrats in support. On that vote, Fowler was joined by four other Georgia Democrats in voting "no" and was one of four Georgians to vote against final passage of the amended bill, which was approved 232 to 193 on the same day.

Fowler expressed his concerns about the final versions of the tax and spending bills in his winter 1982 newsletter to his Fifth District constituents.

> While I supported and still support the president's overall goals of spending restraint, tax relief, and improved defense readiness, I could not support the specific means he chose for achieving these ends. In particular, I objected to some of the Administration's spending priorities (which cut education, job training, scientific research, and nutrition programs but largely left untouched such "sacred cows" as water projects and nuclear energy) and to the distribution of the tax cuts (which were more heavily weighted toward individuals in the highest income brackets and to larger businesses). Finally, I was concerned that the large tax cuts could produce unacceptably high deficits, especially if interest rates remained high and the economy spun into recession.

In point of fact, the deficit did climb (from 2.6 percent of gross domestic product in 1981 to 4 percent in 1982 and 6 percent in 1983), interest rates skyrocketed (from 11 percent in 1979 to 20 percent by June 1981 and 21.5 percent in June 1982), and the country spun into recession, with unemployment rising from 7.5 percent at the end of 1981 to 10.8 percent in November and December of 1982, which remained the highest level reached since the Great Depression of the 1930s until the COVID-inspired economic lockdown in the spring of 2020.

Fowler Budget and Tax Alternatives

Throughout 1981 and 1982, Fowler worked to develop alternatives to Reagan's tax and spending plans. On the former, he played his part in developing the Ways and Means tax-cut bill, which included the Fowler language to provide homebuilders with up to a $2,000 performance-based tax credit for construction of homes with passive solar energy systems. However, the Reagan-backed, House-passed substitute did not contain this provision. Fowler's efforts, though, were recognized by the Solar Energy Industries Association, which presented him with its 1982 Solar Man of the Year Award.

Fowler also produced his own comprehensive budget proposal, which was released in December 1981 and included

- a three-month delay in the scheduled 1982 and 1983 tax cuts and cost-of-living adjustments for all federal entitlement programs, including Social Security;
- cancellation of the Clinch River Breeder Reactor for nuclear fuel;
- implementation of a hospital cost-containment plan to restrain health care cost increases;
- cuts in federal spending for water projects;
- cuts in foreign military sales credits; and
- cancellation of the B-1 bomber and MX missile programs.

Another important feature of the Fowler plan was its call for a fourteen-cents per gallon increase in the gasoline tax, indexed for inflation, with a portion used to pay for increased investments in highway and mass transit infrastructure and a part used for deficit reduction. This was in keeping with his consistent support for higher gasoline taxes, where he cast votes for such taxes in both the House and Senate, in spite of survey after survey indicating that this was one of the most unpopular of all taxes. His reasoning was that at a time when federal spending continued to run far in excess of federal revenues, gasoline taxes offered a relatively simple-to-administer method to close the deficit, promote energy conservation and reduced air pollution, and fund badly needed infrastructure investments. In 1982, the tax was raised for the first time since 1959, and funding for mass transit was finally included as one of the uses of the proceeds.

None of the major Fowler proposals were adopted at the time, and his efforts attracted relatively little attention from the news media. Yet he felt it was important to set forth in detail an alternative to the Reagan approach that was more equitable, fiscally sound, and geared to the country's long-term future.

Even before 1981 ended, there was recognition both at the White House and on Capitol Hill that the tax and spending decisions earlier in the year had produced an unacceptably large increase in the federal deficit. Thus, in September, President Reagan indicated that in the coming year he would be requesting a $22 billion increase in taxes for fiscal years 1982 to 1984 through the elimination of unspecified business and individual tax preferences, and another $980 million in higher user fees on yachts, private airplanes, and other cases where the owners benefitted from specific federal services. Furthermore, he asked for additional cuts in nondefense spending to take effect immediately, and in December, the president signed into law an appropriations bill that contained $6 billion more in spending reductions. Thus, the stage was set for another round of tax and budget battles in 1982.

On the tax side, the Tax Equity and Fiscal Responsibility Act of 1982 was passed by the House and Senate on August 19, 1982, (with Fowler being the only member of the Georgia House or Senate delegations to vote for the bill) and signed into law by President Reagan on September 3. The new law preserved the reduced tax rates adopted the year before but raised an additional $98 billion in revenues over the following three years by repealing some of the provisions of the 1981 tax law (primarily the changes in the business depreciation system), instituting income tax withholding on dividend and interest payments, broadening the wage base and increasing the tax rate on federal unemployment taxes, and temporarily increasing excise taxes on cigarettes and telephone service.

Another Omnibus Budget Reconciliation Act was adopted by Congress and signed into law by the president on September 8. This measure, which Wyche Fowler supported, cut spending on entitlement programs (primarily food stamps and farm price supports) by an estimated $13.3 billion over the following three years.

As the budget was working its way through Congress in 1982, Fowler renewed his efforts to reshape spending priorities. To do so, he developed three amendments to the House budget resolution. He explained his purpose in testimony before the House Committee on Rules.

> We have finally reached the point where the general public and those in government realize that taxpayer dollars are not limitless and that federal programs will never again be allowed virtually

open-ended growth. In this new world, hard choices between worthy, and not-so-worthy, competing claims must and will be made. My concern is that we make these choices consciously and in full public view rather than by default or bureaucratic dictate. It is essential not only to reduce the deficit but to do so in a way that will fulfill national objectives, and promote economic growth. It is important to be concerned not only with the bottom line but with what goes in to making that bottom line.

The three amendments, each of which was revenue-neutral—that is, proposed additions in spending were matched by an equal number of cuts in other areas—were as follows:

1. *Adjust national security priorities* by canceling both the flawed MX missile program, which would inadvertently destabilize existing nuclear stability, and the Clinch River Breeder Reactor, which prematurely subsidized reactor production. The resulting $2 billion in savings would be reallocated to energy conservation, renewable energy research and development, the Strategic Petroleum Reserve, and job-training programs.

2. *Invest in the future* by reducing funding for the least cost-effective federally financed water projects, imposing additional user fees on beneficiaries of federal resources (including livestock grazing, ocean dumping, hard-rock mineral production, irrigation, and deep-draft port usage), and gradually reducing dairy price supports and transferring the savings to scientific research, national parks, historic preservation, environmental protection, and agricultural research and education.

3. *Maintain national infrastructure and promote workable federalism* by returning program responsibilities and revenues for highway programs to the states, accompanied by a ten-cent per gallon national motor fuels tax; establishing block grants for water resources, multifamily rental housing, and mass transit; and transferring the resulting federal savings to airport modernization, the Coast Guard, and providing law enforcement grants for state and local governments.

Because of the large number of amendments that were offered to the budget resolution, Fowler was asked to put forward only one of his proposals. On May 27, 1982, he proposed the first (dealing with national security) on the House floor. The amendment was opposed by the leadership of both parties and defeated by voice vote. However, the Clinch River project was terminated just a year later, in October 1983, because of rising costs and nuclear proliferation concerns. As for the MX, in July 1985, Congress limited MX deployment to fifty missiles because of the lack of a survivable basing mode, and those missiles were deactivated between 2003 and 2005, after the demise of the Soviet Union.

Fowler Defense Alternatives

Alongside his work on the budget proposals relating to national security, Wyche Fowler became actively involved in the debate on defense policy that emerged after President Reagan's inauguration. He laid out his perspective on the Reagan defense program in a November 18, 1981, statement on the floor of the US House during debate on the FY 1982 Department of Defense Appropriations bill.

> I rise in support of 98 percent of the appropriations contained in [this] bill but in opposition to the roughly $4 billion it provides for the B-1 bomber and the MX missile.... My reason for opposing the B-1 program is simple: I do not believe that the marginal improvements it offers as a penetrator or cruise missile carrier are sufficient to justify the $28 billion to $39.8 billion price tag. The [existing] B-52 will be capable of serving as a penetrating bomber through the mid- to late 1980s. The B-1 will be deployed between 1986 and 1988 and it is expected to be able to penetrate Soviet air defenses until the early to mid-1990s.... A similar story emerges when one looks at the cruise missile carrier mission. The B-52 will be effective in this role until the end of the century while the B-1 will be able to perform this function for an indeterminable amount of time beyond that date. In my judgment, the few years that we would gain in the penetrator mission are more than offset by the cost of the B-1. With such an expenditure we run a grave risk of stretching out or curtailing both the ALCM [AGM-86 Air-Launched Cruise Mis-

sile] program, which will be the major contributor to improved survivability of our air-breathing strategic forces whether the carrier is the B-1, the B-52 or some other aircraft, and the advanced technology (or Stealth) bomber program, which the Reagan Administration acknowledges to be an essential element of U.S. strategic forces in the 1990s....

My opposition to the proposed MX system is not based primarily on cost but rather on its strategic implications.... The primary mission of our strategic nuclear forces is to deter aggression against ourselves, our interests, and our allies.... The problems that do or will exist in the triad stem not from insufficient numbers of warheads or too little firepower but from the perceived survivability of our missiles and bombers—that is, their ability to ride out potential attack and to inflict unacceptable damage to any aggressor. The major reason that defense planners have pushed for an MX program has been to improve the survivability of U.S. land-based missiles against potential Soviet attack.... The president's MX decision makes even less sense to me than earlier proposals. Essentially, it postpones a final decision on the proper basing of the new missile by calling for the deployment of the first 36 MX missiles off the production line into fixed silos that now house our aging Titan missile forces.... This short-term solution is most unsatisfactory because the MX missiles in the fixed silos will be as vulnerable as our current land-based forces. In fact, they must probably be judged to be more vulnerable because, with their improved accuracy and larger number of warheads, they represent a greater threat to Soviet forces and are thus a more urgent target for attack.

Fowler's efforts to halt the MX program were undertaken through his budget proposals. He addressed the B-1 program in a floor amendment that he offered to the FY 1982 Department of Defense Authorization bill on July 9, 1981. On that occasion, the congressman sought to overturn a directive contained in the committee-passed bill that "the Secretary of Defense shall complete full-scale engineering development and shall begin initial procurement of the B-1 manned strategic bomber aircraft in a manner that will achieve an initial operational capability for such aircraft not later than July 1, 1987." President Reagan publicly indicated that he opposed this language as an unnecessary restriction on his congressionally mandated responsibility to recommend a multirole strategic bomber for the late 1980s and beyond.

Fowler's amendment, which was offered at the last minute because he anticipated that a Republican member would be offering such a measure in support of the president's position, would have replaced the committee language and provide instead that "amounts appropriated...for aircraft procurement that are available for the B-1 bomber aircraft shall be available for research, development, test, and evaluation of an advanced technology bomber aircraft." In effect, the Fowler proposal would have preserved the president's right to recommend the development of an advanced technology bomber (later to be called the B-2) instead of the B-1, as mandated by the House Armed Services Committee. The amendment was defeated on a vote of 153 to 254. Though the Fowler proposal was in keeping with the president's stated position, House Republicans overwhelmingly voted against it—for: 26, against: 155.

President Reagan ultimately decided to proceed with both the B-1 and the Advanced Technology Bomber. A total of one hundred B-1s were produced between 1984 and 1988, but even before the final B-1 was delivered, the Air Force had determined that the aircraft was vulnerable to Soviet air defenses, and its role was shifted from strategic to conventional bombing missions.

In March 1982, Representative Fowler presented his "National Security Budget for the Eighties" as an alternative to the president's defense plans. After supporting the $35 billion increase in FY 1982 defense spending approved by the Congress, Fowler proposed that, in order to hold down the deficit without compromising our defense posture, the FY 1983 increase should be held to 4 percent by cutting a net of $25 billion (9.5 percent) from the $263 billion Reagan recommendation. He also identified precisely where he would make the reductions.

With regard to arms control, Fowler staked out another position that was at odds with the president when he cosponsored, and voted for, the so-called Nuclear Freeze Resolution that called for US ratification of the SALT (Strategic Arms Limitations Talks) II agreement and further negotiations with the Soviet Union that would produce a mutual and verifiable freeze on nuclear weapons, followed by reductions in such weapons. On

August 5, 1982, the resolution reached the House floor, and Fowler participated in the debate.

> We are not currently at a disadvantage in strategic forces. A freeze of strategic forces at current levels would preserve U.S. advantages in the following areas: number of warheads; missile accuracy and reliability; bomber forces; cruise missiles; and survivable submarine forces. Of course, the freeze would preserve Soviet advantages in other areas but no country, including the United States, could agree to an arms control arrangement that gave all the advantages to one party. A freeze would merely maintain the balance that currently exists between United States and Soviet strategic forces.... Approval of the SALT II Treaty, which would require the Soviets to reduce their operational strategic bombers or missiles by at least 250 units while imposing no such reduction on U.S. forces, followed by "a mutual and verifiable freeze" on nuclear warheads and delivery systems would be in the best interests of the United States as preparatory steps toward the major, mutual reductions advocated by both President Reagan and [this resolution].... [The resolution] does not unilaterally commit the United States to observe a nuclear freeze; rather, it commits us to seek these goals in the context of an agreement that is mutual and verifiable.

The resolution was modified on the House floor by removing the reference to approval of SALT II and applying the notion of a freeze to the reduced level of weapons to be achieved in the future Strategic Arms Reduction Talks (START) advocated by the Reagan administration. Fowler felt the original resolution was stronger and he was the only member of the Georgia House delegation to vote against the substitute, which prevailed by the narrow margin of 204 to 202. However, he did vote for the modified version on final passage, and it was adopted by a vote of 273 to 125. President Reagan proposed the START talks in May 1982, but the negotiations were delayed several times during the rest of the decade, resulting in a new and large arms race between the two countries. The treaty, which Fowler fully supported, was finally signed in July of 1991 and entered into force in December 1994.

Other Legislation

Congressman Fowler's service on the Ways and Means Committee and, as of 1981 on its Social Security subcommittee, also placed him in the midst of another major dispute between House Democrats and President Reagan. In May of 1981, the Reagan administration announced proposals that represented the first major reduction in Social Security benefits since the program was created in 1935. There was bipartisan recognition that something had to be done to preserve the ability of the system to meet its benefit obligations both in the short and long terms. The most controversial element of the administration plan was a sharp reduction in benefits for those who retired before the age of sixty-five, though initial benefits would also have been reduced for those retiring at age sixty-five or later. These changes were rejected by both houses of Congress, but the Omnibus Budget Reconciliation Act of 1981 included some other Reagan Social Security cuts, including elimination of the minimum benefit, phasing out benefits for most postsecondary students, and tightening eligibility for the lump-sum death benefit payment.

In his summer 1981 newsletter to constituents, Fowler reported,

> The president's program is designed not only to restore the financial integrity of the Social Security Trust Fund, but to allow for payroll tax reductions in future years. It would reduce the size of the current Social Security system by 25 percent. The system does face some serious long- and short-term financial difficulties, but I believe the president's proposal goes beyond what is necessary to maintain a satisfactory reserve fund.... I realize that some changes in the system are inevitable, but I do not think that it would be fair to make substantial reductions in benefits for people who have already retired or are just about to retire.

Fowler also opposed the 1981 Reagan administration plan to sell five airborne warning and control aircraft (AWACS) and sixty-two F-15 fighter aircraft to Saudi Arabia, writing to constituents

> I do not believe that the AWACS and the other advanced equipment are an appropriate or effective response to the real defense

> needs of the government of Saudi Arabia. These systems would be far in excess of what would be required to defend the Saudi oilfields against small-scale attacks, yet would be inadequate unless greatly supplemented by United States air power to repel massive, Soviet-led attacks.... The greatest threat to the stability of regimes in the Middle East, whether in Iran or more recently in Egypt, has come from internal forces. The AWACS could not have saved the Shah of Iran or President Sadat.

Although the House voted to disapprove the sale by a 301 to 111 margin, the Senate rejected the disapproval resolution, and it went through as proposed. Years later, when he was nominated to be ambassador to Saudi Arabia and was meeting with Prince Bandar, the Saudi ambassador to the United States, Fowler recalled, "We first met back when you were lobbying for the AWACS sale." To which Bandar replied, "You voted for that, so you're in!" "No, I voted against it, but that was early in my career and I didn't know any better."

As a member of the Ways and Means Committee, Congressman Fowler became embroiled in another controversy involving the always politically unpopular welfare program. On this occasion, in May 1981, the House Ways and Means and Senate Finance Committees engaged in a "bidding war" to determine whose states (and which low-income beneficiaries) would bear the brunt of cuts in spending for the Medicaid and Aid to Families with Dependent Children (AFDC) programs. A June 3, 1981, *New York Times* article reported that both sets of cuts "seem to go beyond the Reagan administration's spending cutbacks in long-term effect, [and] have stirred alarm among state governors and strong criticisms from social scientists. Southern governors in particular were described as 'furious' and 'up in arms' over the proposals." The Senate finance plan would have made additional cuts by reducing the minimum federal matching rate for Medicaid, and would mainly have adversely affected states (and individuals) in the Northeast and on the West Coast. On the other hand, the Ways and Means measure would have achieved the savings by reducing the maximum federal match in the AFDC program, with the impact limited largely to Southern and New England states (and their low-income families). Though with little publicly expressed support for his efforts, Fowler took the lead in successfully opposing the proposed

AFDC change in the Ways and Means Committee. (His actions did earn him the very first Sunbelt Annual Award presented by the Southern Governors' Association, the Congressional Sunbelt Council, and the Southern Growth Policies Board "for distinguished and outstanding service to the people of the Sunbelt States.")

Missing and Murdered Children and Other Local Issues

Although he was increasingly involved in national policies, Fowler continued to attend to local concerns. The most serious of these was what came to be called the "missing and murdered children case," in which a minimum of twenty-eight African American children, teens, and young adults (mostly between the ages of nine and fifteen) were killed during the period from July 1979 through March 1981. At the outset, Atlanta police handled the investigations, and by the time a special task force was created in July 1980, the effort had become the most intense crime-solving operation in the city's history. The local effort was supplemented by $200,000 appropriated by the State of Georgia to assist the investigation.

In October 1980, federal public and mental health agencies began to provide assistance to their local counterparts, and the FBI joined the investigation in November 1980. A federal task force comprised of officials from the Departments of Justice, Education, and Health and Human Services, was established in February 1981 to help the city through community assistance, health service programs, and technical assistance for the criminal investigation. On March 5, 1981, President Reagan announced a $979,000 grant for programs requested by Mayor Maynard Jackson, and on March 13, an additional $1.5 million in federal funds was made available.

Congressman Fowler actively sought to expedite and expand federal assistance for the investigation of the murders and for the protection of the mental and physical health of the Atlanta children most at risk. As part of that effort, he organized a special session on the House floor on March 31, 1981.

> The federal response under Presidents Carter and Reagan has been appreciated and put to good use. I especially want to extend my

thanks to President Reagan and Vice President Bush for their interest in and attention to the needs of my constituents in Atlanta.... What more is to be done? First of all, I would hope that the Congress will act swiftly and favorably on Congressman Clay's bill to provide explicit authorization for federal financial aid for the full range of investigatory activities concerned with the deaths and disappearances of the Atlanta children.... Second, the prayers and demonstrations of concern of all Americans can be a major source of comfort and inspiration in helping the people of Atlanta to get through the crisis and then to recover.... The children of Atlanta and their families, and for that matter the children and families of America, need to know the real dangers facing them, to be neither shielded from the truth nor terrified into fearing every shadow. Third, we must all pull together. All of us, wherever we live, whatever our station in life, have a stake in seeing the killer or killers apprehended and the murders stopped.... Fourth, and most importantly, we must commit ourselves to the creation of a society and communities where such tragedies will not occur in the future. In this, I do not mean primarily a governmental response. It is in our individual roles as mothers and fathers, neighbors, and concerned citizens that we can do the most to make sure that the deaths in Atlanta are not forgotten, or repeated. Finally, we must unite as a country to reevaluate the status of child welfare in the United States. The horrible crimes in Atlanta are shocking; it is likewise shocking that more than 17 million children live in debilitating poverty according to a 1980 report by the U.S. National Commission on the International Year of the Child. According to the same report, one million youth are victims of child abuse and neglect; 10 million children have no regular source of medical care; and 13 percent of all 17-year-olds are functionally illiterate. No nation is secure unless its most vulnerable population, its children, are safe and well-cared for. As concerned parents and citizens, we must make the welfare of our children our first priority, by providing adequate health and educational systems, juvenile justice, nutrition and housing. Only in this way can we ensure the security of our children and nation.

On June 21, Atlanta police arrested Wayne B. Williams, a twenty-three-year-old African American, and charged him with two of the murders, though there was strong suspicion at the time (and since) that he was involved in many, if not all, of the remainder. The trial began on January 6, 1982, and Williams was convicted on both counts on February 27 and sentenced to life in prison. He has maintained his innocence throughout, and there have been speculations over the years that others may have been involved. Nonetheless, there were no more murders linked to the case after the arrest of Williams.

Though not in his district, Cumberland Island, located off the Georgia coast, had long been an interest of Fowler's. He first visited there in the late 1960s and met Bobby Richarde, a New Orleans native, descendant of slaves, and retired baggage handler for Eastern Airlines who owned a small, two-room house on the island. The two hit it off at once, and over the next several years, Fowler made a number of return visits, which featured net fishing for mullet in Christmas Creek followed by Richarde's frying the catch, with bourbon the preferred beverage at the ensuing meal. In addition to being awed by its natural splendor, Fowler learned about the history of the island from the five-foot-four Richarde, who wanted the National Park Service to take over management of the island in order to preserve it for future generations. Fowler discussed the matter with then-Governor Jimmy Carter, who also befriended Richarde and became involved in Cumberland preservation efforts. When Carter became president, Fowler suggested their mutual friend might greatly enjoy a visit to the White House, and the president indeed hosted Bobby and Adele Richarde, who brought buckets of shrimp and spent the night there. Upon his death, Richarde bequeathed his Cumberland property to Fowler, who subsequently donated it to the Park Service in furtherance of his friend's desire that the island be protected.

In the Ninety-Seventh Congress, Fowler cosponsored Rep. Bo Ginn's (D-GA) bill to designate more than eight thousand acres on the island as a national wilderness area. The measure was approved in the House in December 1981 and attached to another wilderness bill that was passed by the Senate in August 1982 and signed into law by the president in September 1982.

1982 Redistricting

The 1980 Census revealed that the Fifth District lost population over the preceding ten years, dropping from 460,589 in 1970 to 420,774 ten years later (with the African American share of the total rising from 44 percent to 50.3 percent). This population loss left the district far short of the 546,000 average for Georgia congressional districts necessary to comply with the one-person, one-vote Supreme Court mandate. Thus, when the Georgia General Assembly met in special session starting in August of 1981 to carry out the required post-Census redistricting of congressional and state legislative districts to make adjustments based on population shifts, it was certain that Fifth District boundaries would have to be changed to bring in more people. In addition to equalizing the populations of these districts as nearly as practicable, Georgia—along with other states—was required to satisfy the provisions of the Voting Rights Act. Once again, the composition of the Fifth District was to play a major role in shaping US electoral law.

The Voting Rights Act of 1965, enacted in the aftermath of the beatings of John Lewis and others on the Edmund Pettus Bridge in Selma, Alabama, has proven to be one of the most important and effective pieces of legislation to emerge out of the civil rights movement. The legislation prohibits state and local governments from adopting any laws, practices, or procedures that would deny or abridge the right of any United States citizen to vote based on race. Among the practices that were explicitly banned were poll taxes and so-called literacy tests. In addition, it required states with a history of discriminatory voting practices to obtain the approval of the US Justice Department before changes affecting voting could be adopted. This latter "preclearance" requirement was applied primarily to Southern states, including Georgia. The Voting Rights Act was amended and extended in 1970, 1975, 1982, and 2006, but Supreme Court decisions in 2013 (*Shelby County v. Holder*, which gutted enforcement of its preclearance provisions) and 2021 (*Brnovich v. Democratic National Committee*, which made it harder to challenge discriminatory voting restrictions) have rendered the law less effective in recent years.

Wyche Fowler was (and is) a strong supporter of the Voting Rights Act. In his fall 1981 newsletter to constituents, he hailed the law and its impact in Georgia in increasing the voter registration of voting-age African Americans from 29.3 percent in 1960 to 51.9 percent in 1980, and called the Act "the most effective piece of civil rights legislation in American history." In a speech on the House floor prior to the House's October 5, 1981, adoption of the bill extending the Voting Rights Act, Fowler reiterated his support.

> We as a nation have made great strides in increased minority participation in our democratic process. Much of this progress can be directly attributable to the enactment and enforcement of the Voting Rights Act of 1965. Seven states were originally covered by the Act and Black registration more than doubled in these states in the decade following the adoption of the Act. In Mississippi, the percentage of Blacks registered to vote increased from a remarkable 6.7 percent to an equally remarkable 59.8 percent in just two years.... You and I know that voting power is real power in this country. Voting strength for minorities, in the practical world of politics and government, means improved public services, fairer location of public parks and cultural facilities, improved transportation routes, participation in public employment—in short, responsive government. Assured of this first step, Blacks and Hispanics by the millions have taken the additional steps toward full participation in all phases of society. They have built upon the cornerstone of their vote a solid foundation in our economic and political life. With this bill, we in the Congress have the opportunity, and the moral obligation, to ensure that the right to vote is not abridged, and that no citizen is ever discriminated against, directly or indirectly, when registering, voting, or running for public office. To deny one citizen that right is to undermine our entire democratic system.

On September 17, 1981, the Georgia General Assembly approved a redistricting plan for Georgia's ten congressional districts in which the Fifth District's population was increased to 542,592 to satisfy one-person, one-vote requirements, and the African American share of the electorate was increased from 50.33 percent to 57.28 percent. As required by the Voting Rights Act, the State sought preclearance of the plan from the Justice Department, but the request was rejected when the attorney-general found that the Fourth and Fifth Districts created by the General Assembly violated the Voting Rights Act. The State then sought a declaratory judgment from the US District Court of the District of Columbia that its redistricting plan "does not have the purpose and will not have the effect of denying or abridging the right to vote on account of race" to enable it to proceed with implementation of the plan.

At that time, the principal Supreme Court decision that was relevant to the Georgia case was the court's 1975 ruling in *Beer v. United States.* The 1965 law provided that proposed voting changes could be rejected based on either their "purpose" or "effect of denying or abridging the right to vote on account of race or color." The *Beer* ruling clarified the court's interpretation of each concept, finding that the "effect" standard applied only in instances of voting changes that would "retrogress" (lessen) minority voting strength, and thus "a legislative reapportionment that enhances the position of racial minorities with respect to their effective exercise of the electoral franchise can hardly have the 'effect' of diluting or abridging the right to vote on account of race within the meaning of [Section 5 of the Voting Rights Act]." On the other hand, the court indicated that even an "ameliorative" redistricting plan could be rejected on the basis of intent "if the new apportionment itself so discriminates on the basis of race or color as to violate the Constitution."

Since Georgia's proposed redistricting plan did not reduce (and indeed increased) the Black population percentage in the Fifth District, whose composition was the only real point of contention with little attention devoted to the other nine districts, the proceedings before the US District Court centered on the question of the intent of the Georgia state government in adopting the Fifth District plan.

The trial of the case known as *Busbee* (Georgia Governor George Busbee) *v. Smith* (US attorney general William French Smith) was held before a three-judge panel (Judges Harry Edwards, Aubrey Robinson, and June Green) of the US District Court in Washington, DC, from June 28 through July 1, 1982.

> In testimony elicited by the court, it was indicated that at the outset of their deliberations on congressional reapportionment, the Georgia House and Senate reapportionment committees met with Justice Department officials and were informed that to comply with

the Voting Rights Act, a reapportionment plan could have neither the purpose nor the effect of discriminating on account of race. Specifically, the legislators were instructed that a plan could not cause retrogression (a reduction in the percentage of Black voters in a particular district) and that the legislators should not split concentrations of Black population. The legislators were further informed that because a larger percentage of whites vote than do Blacks, for Blacks to cast a majority of votes in a given election, at least 65 percent of the population in a district would have to be Black.

Wyche Fowler was called to testify before the court panel on June 30. In response to questions from Joseph Dorn, a special assistant attorney general for the State of Georgia, the congressman spoke about his role in the redistricting process.

Dorn: Did anyone solicit your views at the time the General Assembly was considering redrawing of congressional districts?
Fowler: They did. Well, maybe informally. I mean I am the Representative. But I believe it was—and I think my office has provided you [with a copy]—Senator Hudson, as chairman of the Reapportionment Committee in the Senate, [who] wrote to all the Georgia congressional delegation, formally asked for our views, to which I responded.
Dorn: What was your response?
Fowler: I don't have the letter in front of me. But it was basically not to endorse any plan but to set out the criteria which I hoped that the legislature would follow in any plan that they drew, which is, number one, to keep the city of Atlanta together, for a lot of reasons that I have—well, because of the, as I mentioned before, you do not have progress, whatever that means to different people, unless you have local and state, and Federal officials closely cooperating and working together. If you divide up a municipality, certainly one like the city of Atlanta with its diversity, into five or six different districts, then it becomes very hard to coordinate the policy approach. And that is just not my view. Mayor Maynard Jack-

son wrote to the General Assembly, pleading with them not to divide the city along the lines Senator Bond and Senator Coverdell proposed. Central Atlanta Progress, the Atlanta Chamber of Commerce, almost all the private business organizations, many of the political subdivisions [also supported this position]. So that was criterion number one.... Secondly, to the best of their ability, to respect existing congressional district lines and county and municipal lines to the greatest extent possible. As a result of the Census, the Fifth Congressional District had to pick up 120,000 new people from somewhere. And it would have been very easy to do it by building on—to keep the Fifth District as it was and to build from that base to pick up those extra 120,000. And the reason for that also ought to be obvious, I would assume, to everybody. And that is, we have enough citizen confusion now as to who their Representatives are, who their Congressmen are. You keep changing those lines every time you have a chance and cross different jurisdictions, split local lines, go into other counties.... So that whenever possible, and it is possible, in these lines, you should try to not disrupt existing boundaries to the greatest extent possible. And I so stated in my letter. The third thing was, in the letter, was...to maximize, as we all appreciated had to be done...minority participation in the Fifth Congressional District.

Fowler's testimony continued with an exchange with Laughlin McDonald of the ACLU, who was representing those in support of the Justice Department's rejection of the Georgia congressional redistricting plan.

McDonald: Did you want to see the Fifth District retain its preexisting racial percentages?
Fowler: I wanted to see, still want to see, the Fifth District continue the biracial diversity that has made it the strong congressional district that it is today, with the evidence to date to back up that biracial diversity. And I do not want to see it polarized or re-segregated, re-segregated along racial lines.
McDonald: Is that yes to my question?

Fowler: I think your question needed some elaboration, so I elaborated.
McDonald: Well, it's a very simple question, with all due respect.
Fowler: Well, ask it again. I'll try to do that.
McDonald: Yes, sir. Did you want to see the pre-existing racial percentages maintained—
Fowler: No.
McDonald:—in the Fifth Congressional District?
Fowler: No.
McDonald: Did you want to see the Black percentage increased?
Fowler: Yes.
McDonald: To what percent, sir?
Fowler: I have not supported any plan. I want to see that the Voting Rights Act is fully implemented as it applies to the Fifth Congressional District of Georgia and wherever in the country. And that requires a review under my understanding of the law. After this last Census, in order to ensure that Black citizens have the opportunity to run and be elected—where this thing is off track, if the court will forgive an aside, in trying to answer the question, is that there has been no evidence in the Fifth Congressional District that Black citizens did not have that full opportunity under the present system. That does not mean it should not be changed in the future. It's just perfectly obvious that when you have a Black man, Andrew Young, elected in a majority white district three times and a white man, Wyche Fowler, elected in a majority Black district three times, neither of which could have been elected without substantial votes from the other race, I don't see how there has been—I think that speaks for itself. That is the history of our district.
McDonald: I would proffer to strike that as not responsive, Your Honor. Do you have any opinion whether or not you would win in a 69 percent Black congressional district?
Fowler: Well, I don't believe, sir, in all due respect, that race is the primary criterion for the determination of whether or not a man or woman is selected by the voters of a congressional district to represent them...
McDonald: Can I get an answer to my question, sir?

Fowler: I'm doing my best. You asked whether or not I thought I could be elected in a 69 percent Black district. My answer is that that is not a proper question. It is not my opinion. It speaks to the heart of our system. It is for the voters in a congressional district, in the Fifth Congressional district, to determine who they want to represent them. I don't believe they look to race as the primary qualification for their representatives. If the court wants me to continue, I'll try to explain why.

McDonald: You have no opinion whether or not you could get elected in a 69 percent Black Fifth Congressional District, is that correct?

Fowler: I have announced for reelection. I have said in that announcement that I will be a candidate for the United States Congress from the Fifth Congressional District wherever these lines are drawn, whether it is a 69 percent district, a 80 percent district, or a 100 percent district. And I have made that statement because of my firm belief that color should not be the criteria of anything. And that the people of Atlanta, Georgia, that I am privileged to represent will not use race as the primary determination as to whom they elect in 1982 to come back to Washington. And if that is my principle, as Margaret Thatcher said, there ain't no point in having principles unless you stand on them every once in a while. So I will be in the race and whatever the voters determine, whether it's 69 percent or a hundred percent, I'm perfectly willing to abide by that decision.

McDonald: With all due respect, that is not responsive to my question. Do you have an opinion whether or not you could get elected in a 69 percent Black Fifth—

Judge Robinson: He's running. He has an opinion.

Fowler: If that doesn't answer your question, sir, I can't do it. I'm not running as the sacrificial lamb. Obviously, I believe I am going to win.

When McDonald continued his questioning along the same lines, Judge Robinson gave a strong indication of his views of the case.

McDonald: Do you have an opinion as to what percent the Fifth District would have to be Black for it to be unlikely that you would win?
Fowler: I reject the total philosophy behind your question.
McDonald: I would appreciate it if you would answer my question, Congressman. Then you can make your speech.
Fowler: I cannot answer a question when I have just told you that race is not the criterion for selecting men and women to the United States Congress from the Fifth Congressional District.
Judge Robinson: Mr. Congressman, if that were so, there would be no Voting Rights Act legislation, which has been extended for 25 years by the president's signature yesterday. Now, we're living in a world of reality. This case does not deal with political idealism at all. It deals with the reality of the political scene in 1982, particularly in the State of Georgia. That is why we're here. Now we can appreciate what we would all like. I'd like to sit in a court and not have to be called a nigger. But this is 1982, not 1992 or 2002. That is what we're dealing with. If you can answer the question counsel asked, and it is relevant to this litigation, answer it. If you cannot, we will accept your answer that you cannot.
Fowler: Counselor, I have no opinion on that matter. The facts in the Fifth Congressional District speak for themselves. That is, a Black man has been elected and a white man has been elected by biracial majorities. I expect that to continue because of the history of the voting patterns.

Whatever the judges thought of the exchanges with Congressman Fowler—who had been representing the Fifth District, which was at the heart of the matter, for more than five years—this evidently played no part in their evaluation of the facts and circumstances of the case because they were not cited in any of the court's 125 findings of fact nor in its twenty-five conclusions of law.

The district court panel issued its ruling on July 22, 1982.

Overt racial statements, the conscious minimizing of Black voting strength, historical discrimination and the absence of a legitimate non-racial reason for adoption of the plan at issue mandates the

> conclusion that [the Georgia redistricting plan] as it pertains to the Fourth and Fifth Congressional districts has a discriminatory purpose in violation of Section 5 [of the Voting Rights Act].... In concluding that Plaintiffs [the State of Georgia] have failed to demonstrate that the manner in which the Fourth and Fifth Districts of [the redistricting plan] were drawn is not the product of purposeful racial discrimination, the court expresses no view as to which plan the General Assembly should have adopted. The plan drawing process is a legislative responsibility, but the Voting Rights Act requires that it be carried out without racial discrimination. The record clearly reveals that if the "gross racial slurs" had been eliminated from the reapportionment process, the boundary between Districts Five and Four would have been drawn differently; it is not possible for the court to conclude which plan might have resulted since such a result would be determined by the nondiscriminatory functioning of the political process. In this case, however, the political process did not function in a nondiscriminatory manner. Blacks, solely because of their race, were excluded from the final decision-making process, (i.e., the Conference Committee); and whites who, for racially discriminatory reasons, opposed the creation of a district which might allow Black voters an opportunity to elect a candidate of their choice were entrusted with the decision-making responsibility. The Court's decision does not require the State of Georgia to maximize minority voting strength in the Atlanta area. The State is free to draw the districts pursuant to whatever criteria it deems appropriate so long as the effect is not racially discriminatory and so long as racially discriminatory purpose is absent from the process. [The Georgia redistricting plan] is being denied Section 5 preclearance because State officials successfully implemented a scheme designed to minimize Black voting strength to the extent possible; the plan drawing process was not free of racially discriminatory purpose.[48]

There were some curious findings of fact made by the court in support of its ruling. First, it briefly addressed the historical fact that African American voters in the Fifth District itself had already on three occasions

(1972, 1974, and 1976) participated in the election of an African American (Andrew Young) at a time when they constituted a minority of the district's population and an even smaller minority of its registered voters. Under these circumstances, presumably African Americans had been enabled even then to "have an opportunity to elect a candidate of their choice." Furthermore, the court found "the evidence indicates that racial polarization has increased since that time."

One of the authorities cited in that finding was Professor Charles Bullock of the University of Georgia, a recognized authority on racial voting patterns in the South. Yet, in an article in the February 1984 academic publication *Journal of Politics*, Bullock reported that his research, which examined "fifty-two Atlanta area elections in which Black and white candidates opposed each other," indicated the opposite was true.

> To determine whether racial bloc voting has changed over time, the period under study was trichotomized into 1970–73, 1974–78 and 1979–82. Although white crossover voting is always greater than Black, there have been increases for both races.... White incumbents average 39 percent of the Black vote compared to 7 percent for white challengers and 11 percent for whites seeking open positions. Black incumbents poll almost half the white vote (47.6 percent) while Black challengers and contestants for open seats average 18.5 percent white crossovers.... Crossover voting has enabled candidates to win when their race was in the minority. Andrew Young won a seat in Congress when Blacks constituted less than 40 percent of registered voters.... In some southern communities prejudice among whites and the desire for self-preservation by Blacks produce almost total racial polarization at the ballot box. In Atlanta, the race of the candidate, while important, is not the only consideration.... Crossover voting is critical in the outcome of Atlanta elections.[49]

The court also appeared to give little consideration to factors other than race that traditionally have loomed large in the redistricting process. For example, though there has been widespread agreement over many years that partisan considerations are almost always crucial in the redistricting process, the district court found that

> the Lieutenant Governor's [Zell Miller's] reason for opposing the configuration of the Fourth District, i.e., it created a Republican district, is...suspect. According to [state] Senator [Julian] Bond, no Senator argued at the time of reapportionment that the Bond Amendment [which passed the state senate and would have created a Fifth District with a Black population of 69 percent] would result in the creation of a Republican congressional district. [State] Senator Paul Coverdell, a Republican who is minority leader in the Senate, agreed that the issue of creating a Republican district was not raised in reference to the Bond Amendment during the entire process. He stated: "This was not a Republican matter. The entire issue that was being debated was what the minority percentage would be in the Fifth District, pure and simple. There were many instances one might note that would indicate ample opportunity to indicate that this was a Republican-Democrat matter. In fact this was not. The question was minority representation in that district."[50]

The Court appears to have taken Senator Coverdell's word for it because it essentially dismissed the notion that the 1982 redistricting actions by the overwhelmingly Democratic Georgia General Assembly had any partisan intent. Yet Professor Bullock, who had participated in the district court proceedings in 1982, wrote in his November 2005 article "Changing Standards for Legislative Redistricting and their Consequences,"

> few Republicans recognized in 1982 the potential benefit to their party that might flow from promoting minority attacks on districting arrangements. One of the first to see how his party could benefit was Paul Coverdell, a Republican in the Georgia Senate. In 1982, Coverdell joined Sen. Julian Bond...to push a Congressional districting plan that increased the Black percentage in an Atlanta district to almost 70 percent while simultaneously dropping the Black percentage in the neighboring [Fourth] district to about 10 percent. After the Department of Justice forced the adoption of a plan similar to the Coverdell-Bond proposal, a Republican won the "bleached" district in 1984.[51]

And Julian Bond made no secret of his collaboration with Republicans in seeking to maximize the Fifth District's Black population. In a 1994 speech to a Voting Rights Conference at American University, he outlined his 1981 to 1982 work with Senator Coverdell.

> [After the Georgia General Assembly adopted its redistricting plan with a 57 percent Black population Fifth District,] with the assistance of Georgia's then-Republican Senator Mack Mattingly, I sought a meeting with William Bradford Reynolds, the Assistant Attorney General for Civil Rights. When Senator Mattingly was unable to arrange a meeting, I turned to State Senator Paul Coverdell, the Minority Leader of the Senate. He secured a meeting with Reynolds, and he and I flew to Washington. Reynolds received us graciously, heard our arguments, and imposed a Section 5 objection against the Georgia plan. Georgia sought a judgment against his decision in the federal court here in Washington. With a number of other legislators, I intervened, and *Busbee v. Smith* was joined.... Coverdell and the Republicans were accused in the media of trying to move Blacks from the Fourth to the Fifth, solidifying the already Democratic strength of the Fifth, while increasing Republican hopes in the Fourth. Of course, Republicans, then and now, were willing to help Black legislators, all of us Democrats, create a "Blacker" Fifth. We Blacks were eager to accept whatever assistance was offered and little was forthcoming from members of our own party.[52]

The 1982 redistricting of Georgia's Fifth Congressional District thus represented one of the early uses of the strategy of racial "packing," under which electoral districts are drawn to consolidate the population of people of color into a small number of districts, thus diminishing their share of the vote in the many surrounding districts. This has become a major tenet of Republican partisan gerrymandering efforts ever since.

1982 Congressional Elections

After the district court's rejection, the Georgia General Assembly proceeded to adopt a new plan that created a 65 percent Black Fifth District, with a 60 percent African American voting-age population. This plan was submitted to the court on August 9 and was approved on August 13, along with a revised schedule (which called for a special primary on August 31 with the general election held on the regularly scheduled date of November 2) for holding congressional elections in all districts except the Fourth and Fifth. After rejecting the State's initial plan for using the same election schedule in those districts, the district court also rejected a second proposal from Georgia to hold special primaries in those districts on September 14, which again would have allowed use of the regular November 2 date for the general election, finding that the "state made no attempt whatsoever to demonstrate that the proposed schedule had neither a discriminatory purpose nor a discriminatory effect." At a hearing on August 24, the State requested that the court itself determine an acceptable election schedule, and the court did so, setting special primaries for the Fourth and Fifth Districts on November 2, which would coincide with the general election date in all other races, with any necessary runoffs to be held November 9, and a special general election on November 30, the Tuesday after Thanksgiving.

The new Fifth District stretched from portions of Roswell and Sandy Springs in north Fulton County through most of the city of Atlanta to East Point, Hapeville, and other portions of south Fulton County in the south, and southwest DeKalb County in the east. In the 1982 elections, there were 251,097 registered voters, of whom 141,013 (56.2 percent) were Black and 110,084 (43.8 percent) were white, compared to a 61 percent white electorate in 1980.

In spite of much speculation at the time, Julian Bond declined to run. Indeed, Fowler was unopposed in the Democratic primary, with three candidates vying for the Republican nomination: Paul Jones, Doug Steele, and Jack Hester. (Steele had switched parties after his loss to Fowler in the 1980 Democratic primary.)

Turnout in the two primaries combined was 64,592, or 25.7 percent of registered voters. Fowler won more than 80 percent of the total votes cast in the two primaries on November 2. African American Paul Jones led the Republican field but fell short of the 50 percent mark and was forced into a November 9 runoff in which only 1,628 individuals voted.

Democratic Primary		
Wyche Fowler	53,440	100.00 percent
Republican Primary		
Paul Jones	4,365	39.14 percent
Doug Steele	3,750	33.63 percent
Jack Hester	3,037	27.23 percent
Republican Runoff		
Paul Jones	950	58.35 percent
Doug Steele	678	41.65 percent

The general election followed four weeks later, just after Thanksgiving. African American state Representative Billy McKinney (who had also run in the 1977 special election) qualified to appear on the ballot as an Independent.

A total of 65,946 voters turned out for the post-Thanksgiving special general election on November 30, representing a slightly higher percentage (26.3 percent) than in the November 2 special primaries. Fowler received his highest general election voting percentage to date, winning with more than 80 percent of the total votes cast.

Wyche Fowler	53,264	80.77 percent
J. E. ("Billy") McKinney	9,049	13.72 percent
Paul Jones	3,633	5.51 percent

Turnout was higher in the Fulton County portions of the Fifth (28 percent) than in the DeKalb County parts (16.8 percent), and Fowler ran slightly better in the former (81.2 percent in Fulton, 75.2 percent in DeKalb) in winning an estimated 69 percent of the African American vote.

At the time of the 1982 election and afterward, there was rumor of a "deal" Fowler had supposedly made with certain Black leaders to the effect that no major African American candidate would run against Fowler if he agreed to vacate the seat to run for the Senate in 1986. Fowler has stated repeatedly and unequivocally that there was no such deal, formal or otherwise, and that he was never approached by a single African American leader—then or at any other time, before or after—urging him to drop out of the Fifth District race. Moreover, few potential challengers would likely defer their ambitions for four years without knowing what the situation would be in 1986. Further, Fowler had made no secret of his interest in the US Senate and had given a clear indication of that interest in his February 1980 speech announcing he would not seek the Senate that year. With Georgia's very popular (and fellow Democrat) Senator Sam Nunn up for reelection in 1984, the odds were high that Fowler was going to seriously consider a 1986 race against freshman Republican Mack Mattingly (whom Fowler perceived to be very vulnerable) regardless of the outcome of the 1982 redistricting battle.

Chapter 7

Ninety-Eighth Congress (1983–1984) and 1984 Election: Intelligence

Wyche Fowler was involved in the usual wide array of national and local issues in the Ninety-Eighth Congress, including such important matters as Social Security reform and economic and budgetary policy that were of major concern to the news media and to his constituents back home. However, it was his work on the Intelligence Committee, and his elevation to chairman of its key oversight subcommittee, that took more of his time and energy than any other assignment in 1983 and 1984.

Service on the House and Senate Intelligence Committees is unique because, first of all, most of the work must necessarily remain secret, so little political credit is ever possible. Second, and again because of security concerns, the member's personal staff is, for the most part, precluded from assisting, so the representative or senator is largely left on their own (though aided by committee staff) in fulfilling the assignment.

Throughout his almost eight years on the intelligence panel, Representative Fowler took an active role in supporting efforts to upgrade American intelligence capabilities, in his vigorous questioning of intelligence activities undertaken by both the Carter and Reagan administrations, and in visiting a number of CIA station chiefs in out-of-the-way trouble spots around the globe. At the conclusion of his service on the committee (mandated by House rules that placed a four-term limit on Intelligence Committee membership), he was honored to receive the CIA Seal Medallion "for distinguished service in overseeing our nation's intelligence activities," and the National Security Agency Seal "for outstanding contributions to our national security through service on the House Select Committee on Intelligence as a charter member."

Nicaragua and the Contras

During his time on the Intelligence Committee, Congressman Fowler usually supported the clandestine policy initiatives of Presidents Carter and Reagan. In fact, the only major disagreement in the eight years was over the policy that became all too public: the Reagan program of attempting to overthrow the Sandinista government of Nicaragua by backing the "contras."

The Sandinista National Liberation Front ousted the longtime Nicaraguan dictator Anastasio Somoza in 1979 and at first ruled as part of a broad-based coalition. However, after centrist members resigned from the government in protest of the increasingly authoritarian policies of the Sandinistas, the latter seized complete power in March 1981. Among its policies that were most objectionable to the United States and other governments was its provision of arms to the guerillas in neighboring El Salvador who were seeking to topple the US-backed military junta there. Shortly after the Sandinista seizure of control, an opposition militia called the contras was formed with the aim of removing the Sandinista government.

From almost the very beginning, the United States—mainly through the CIA and under the express authorization of President Reagan—provided money, equipment, and operational support for the contras. Given that this was a covert operation, the House and Senate Intelligence Committees were responsible for providing congressional oversight. Initially, the Reagan administration claimed that the aim of the program was to force the Sandinistas to stop arming the Salvadoran rebels, but many suspected, then and later, that the goal was always regime change in Nicaragua, especially after the proclamation of the Reagan Doctrine in 1982, which called for US support for democratic reform or revolution around the world.

Because members of the Intelligence Committees were sworn to secrecy with respect to clandestine operations of the American government, Congressman Fowler was not able to make any public statements about the contra program in 1981 and 1982. However, as the contra attacks increased and began to be reported by the news media, US support for the contras became widely known, including through public proclamations by the contras themselves, and some members of Congress started to publicly question and criticize that policy. It was later revealed that the Intelligence Committees had sought to limit the covert US aid to funding for arms interdiction efforts aimed at halting the flow of weapons from the Sandinistas to the Salvadoran rebels. When this proved ineffective, and amid growing calls from non-Intelligence Committee members to end American support for the contras, on December 8, 1982, the chairman of the House Intelligence Committee, Edward Boland (D-MA), offered the following successful amendment (approved by a vote of 411 to 0) to the FY 1983 Department of Defense Appropriations bill: "None of the funds provided in this Act may be used by the Central Intelligence Agency or the Department of Defense to furnish military equipment, military training or advice, or other support for military activities, to any group or individual, not part of a country's armed forces, for the purpose of overthrowing the Government of Nicaragua or provoking a military exchange between Nicaragua and Honduras."

The same language had been previously adopted, secretly, as part of the classified annex to the FY 1983 intelligence authorization bill. Wyche Fowler helped draft the language of both of these provisions, as well as the subsequent versions adopted up through 1985.[53]

The Boland Amendment represented a compromise between those seeking to end all aid to the contras and supporters of preventing the flow of arms to the Salvadoran rebels. The language became part of the catch-all Further Continuing Appropriations Act of 1982 that funded much of the federal government and was signed into law by President Reagan on December 21, 1982. However, contra attacks continued to grow in number and intensity even after the enactment of the Boland Amendment, and in early April 1983, House Intelligence Oversight Subcommittee chairman Fowler went on a 6-day trip to Panama, Nicaragua, and El Salvador to see for himself what was going on.

While Fowler was, from the beginning, critical of the Sandinista dictatorship and supported all efforts to prevent that regime's attempts to export its revolution to neighboring countries (including El Salvador), he became increasingly concerned that, in pursuing a secret war to achieve our national objectives, we were both precluding any chance of success for the numerous attempts to reach a negotiated end to the Nicaragua civil war and compromising our intelligence agencies by having them take the lead in what was primarily a military operation.

On April 7, 1983, Fowler held a press conference in Washington upon his return from the Central America trip, choosing his words carefully to avoid compromising the classified information he was privy to.

> I found much to be troubled about in Nicaragua. There were definite signs, from the churches, the universities, the private sector, opposition political parties, and elsewhere, of a reduction in the human rights respected by the Nicaraguan government. Censorship and harassment of the opposition forces seem to be growing steadily. Also, Nicaragua's neighbors expressed genuine concern about the future capabilities and goals of the large Sandinista army. On the other hand, the Sandinistas point to the counter-revolutionary threat [represented by the contras], which they attribute primarily to the United States, as the cause of whatever internal crackdown they have made and of their military build-up. As to the actual role of the United States in Nicaragua, I have been forced to conclude, by publicly available information and my unclassified discussions with individuals in Washington, Managua and elsewhere, that the law of the land as embodied in the Boland Amendment is not being fully adhered to. No branch of our government may pick and choose which statutes it will obey. If the law is being violated the Congress has a clear responsibility to bring our government into compliance.

The press conference received national attention. Perhaps the most incisive report appeared in the April 8 edition of the *Miami Herald.*

> A key House Intelligence Committee member Thursday joined mounting opposition to U.S. covert activities in Central America, accusing the Reagan Administration of ignoring Congressional restrictions that prohibit efforts directed at the overthrow of Nicaragua's Sandinista government.... Earlier in the week, Sens. Daniel Patrick Moynihan (D-NY) and Patrick Leahy (D-VT), members of the Senate Intelligence Committee, told fellow senators that they feared U.S. activities had gotten out of hand. Fowler's criticism, however, was the strongest yet heard.... Intelligence Committee

> sources said Fowler's decision to go public with his concerns reflected the gravity of the situation as he sees it. There are indications as well of growing concern and some opposition to the covert activities within the Reagan Administration itself, particularly among middle-level State Department officials involved in Latin American affairs. They are said to have expressed their reservations both to influential legislators and to the White House.... Fowler said he and other committee members had had misgivings about the Nicaragua operation since they were first briefed on it by CIA Director William Colby and other administration officials. But, he said, the Intelligence panels went along because they received assurances that the principal goal was to stop the arms flow to Salvadoran guerillas and not to undermine or overthrow the Sandinista government.... Now, Fowler said, he is convinced that the anti-Sandinista forces financed by the United States are not interested in interdicting weapons, but in ousting the Sandinistas.[54]

On April 27, 1983, President Reagan addressed a joint session of Congress about US policy in Central America. Although much of the speech was devoted to attacks on the Sandinista regime, Reagan told the Congress, "We do not seek [that government's] overthrow. Our interest is to ensure that it does not infect its neighbors through the export of subversion and violence." Several Congressmen, including Wyche Fowler, participated in a discussion on the House floor following the president's speech. Fowler reiterated his concerns about administration policies and offered his suggestions for improving upon them.

> I have no quarrel with the publicly stated goals of the President concerning our policy in Central America. I, too, believe that the United States has legitimate interests in the Caribbean Basin, including the promotion of stability, the pursuit of human rights, and the prevention of hostile military influences within the area.... However, I have serious reservations about the success of the methods the administration has chosen for achieving its policy....
>
> It is my opinion, and one shared by the distinguished panel of American and Central American political and economic leaders who recently issued the "Report of the Inter-American Dialog,"

that the principal problems in Central America are economic and political rather than military, and are primarily domestic in origin rather than foreign dominated. I am pleased that the President has at least rhetorically acknowledged there is truth to these propositions. But the administration's primary reliance on military solutions to the turmoil in the region has risked widening the conflict and made it more difficult for the United States to be credible in its support of regional negotiations...

The arms flow to the rebel forces in El Salvador appears to have not been seriously impeded. The hold of the Sandinistas on the major cities and institutions of Nicaragua appears to have become more entrenched.... The economies in the region have been seriously damaged. Finally, and fundamentally, the level of violence in the area has not abated. It is this last point, more than anything else, that threatens the democratic process, undermines economic reforms, diminishes human rights, and spreads instability....

I urge the president...to take a fresh, pragmatic look at the effectiveness of his policies, and to reach out for other viewpoints...in order to forge a national consensus on our policy in Central America. None of this would require him to abandon his publicly stated goals, which are, in my opinion, widely shared. However, I am asking him to reconsider his methods. In that spirit, I offer the following recommendations:

First, the United States should openly, and unequivocally, endorse and encourage the regional peace initiative undertaken by the Contadora Group of Mexico, Venezuela, Colombia and Panama. These allies of the United States have urged "all countries of Central America to use dialog and negotiations to reduce tensions and to establish the basis for a permanent climate of peaceful coexistence and mutual respect." While we have offered vague encouragement to regional peace initiatives...we have effectively opposed the Contadora effort by our continued opposition to bilateral dialogs between Nicaragua and its neighbors and to unconditional discussions within El Salvador and Nicaragua between the governments and the opposition....

Second, I would ask the consideration of the president to "go to the source" by engaging in bilateral discussions with Cuba.... Many

> of the administration's legitimate concerns about Central America center on Cuba's role in that region. While bilateral talks are certainly no guarantee of a successful resolution of our problems with the Cubans, an absence of direct dialog substantially reduces the chances for peaceful solutions....
>
> Third, in order to reduce domestic and international skepticism about American willingness to support negotiations, I would urge the president to follow through on his intention to appoint a special, independent, high-level envoy to coordinate our negotiations effort in Central America....
>
> The goal of these suggestions is to place the United States squarely on the side of transferring conflicts from the battlefield to the conference table. It is my contention that only in this way can any of our legitimate objectives in Central America, including those enunciated by the administration, be achieved.

On April 28, the president did appoint former Senator Dick Stone (D-FL) as an ambassador-at-large charged with promoting negotiations in Central America. However, the military conflict in Nicaragua only continued to grow. With CIA assistance, the contra forces continued to increase in numbers (to approximately 10,000), and by mid-1983, they began to conduct air strikes. The CIA itself carried out covert actions inside Nicaragua, including blowing up fuel tanks. In response, the Sandinistas turned more and more to the Cubans and the Soviet Union for military support. As later reported, Reagan officials justified the continuation of the policy on the grounds that, since the US itself was not intending to overthrow the Sandinistas, it could provide support for the contras, even if they did have such an intention.

With the war in Nicaragua continuing to expand, the chairmen of the House Intelligence and Foreign Affairs Committees, Edward Boland and Clement Zablocki (D-WI), introduced legislation the same day that the president addressed the nation. Their proposal sought to close all loopholes by prohibiting any entity of the US government from providing support for military or paramilitary operations in Nicaragua. In addition, however, their measure explicitly authorized open US aid ($30 million in FY 1983 and $50 million in FY 1984) to friendly governments in Central America for the purpose of interdicting the supply of military equipment from Nicaragua and Cuba aimed at overthrowing any other government in the region. That measure was cleared by the House Intelligence panel (with Fowler's active involvement and support) on May 3, 1983, and the House Foreign Affairs Committee did likewise a month later. When the Boland-Zablocki bill reached the House floor at the end of July, a major debate was joined by supporters and opponents of the legislation.

The House deliberation on the Boland-Zablocki measure represented the first time the Reagan administration's Central American policies were fully debated in either the House or Senate. It was kicked off by a highly unusual closed session on July 19. According to press accounts, Boland and Fowler led the presentation on behalf of the legislation, pointing out that the Intelligence Committee had, in 1981 and 1982, already insisted that any covert activity in Nicaragua be limited to arms interdiction. However, the administration had violated those restrictions by expanding the operation into full-scale support of the contras and their widening military activities. Therefore, additional restrictions were both justified and necessary.

Fowler subsequently spoke in open session on the House floor on July 21, 1983.

> The July 17 declaration by the Contadora presidents [of Colombia, Mexico, Panama and Venezuela] stated: "The use of force as an alternative solution does not solve but worsens the underlying tensions. Central American peace will only become a reality to the degree that the fundamental principles for peaceful co-existence between nations are respected: nonintervention, self-determination, the sovereign equality of states, cooperation for social and economic development, peaceful solution to controversies, as well as free and authentic expression of the people's will." Nicaragua has itself violated many of these guidelines, but it is equally true that U.S. policy in support of the contras is diametrically opposed to the Contadora principles.... On the other hand, the legislation now before the House is fully consistent with the Contadora Initiative. The Boland-Zablocki bill specifically addresses the arms trafficking and Nicaraguan-Honduran border problems identified by the Contadora Group as the most immediate and dangerous sources of tension in the region. It fully respects the principles of nonintervention

and the use of peaceful means to resolve conflicts. It enhances the ability of our regional allies to protect their own sovereignty and territorial integrity.

After several days of debate, and the adoption of a limited number of amendments that augmented, but did not alter, the essential components of the bill, the Boland-Zablocki legislation was approved by the House on July 28, 1983, by a vote of 228 to 195 (Democrats: 210 Yes, 50 No; Republicans: 18 Yes, 145 No), with Fowler the only member of the Georgia delegation to vote for the measure, but the Senate took no action. The House considered the issue again on October 20 when the Boland-Zablocki language was attached to the FY 1984 Intelligence Authorization Bill by a margin of 227 to 194 (Democrats: 209 Yes, 48 No; Republicans: 18 Yes, 146 No), Fowler again being the lone supporter in the Georgia delegation. The Republican-led Senate resisted once more, and in the conference committee that met to reconcile the House and Senate versions of the intelligence authorization (of which Fowler was a member), the insistence of the Senate conferees succeeded in modifying the bill's language to provide a dollar limitation ($24 million)—but not a prohibition—on the amount of covert assistance that could be provided for operations in Nicaragua.

Thus, as 1983 ended, the original Boland Amendment was still on the books but was generally ignored by the Reagan administration, and the Republican-controlled Senate was unwilling to place any further limitations on the contra aid program. But events in early 1984 ultimately led to a change in congressional policy, if not, ultimately, in the administration's approach. On January 7, 1984, and again on February 29, the CIA mined harbors in Nicaragua, resulting in the sinking of several Nicaraguan boats and damage to a number of foreign-owned ships. The contras initially claimed responsibility, and the administration's required advance reports to the House and Senate Intelligence Committee were not clear on that point. Indeed, Republican Senator Barry Goldwater, chairman of the Senate Intelligence Committee, stated emphatically that the administration had not provided advance notice to his committee, as required by law. Boland indicated that the House committee had received initial notice on January 31 that the mining had occurred but was not given a full briefing until March 27. On April 6, 1984, the *Wall Street*

Journal broke the news that the US was directly responsible for the mining operation, reigniting the public and congressional debate over the contra program.

On April 26, Congressman Fowler embarked on a six-day trip to Latin America as part of a three-member, bipartisan delegation along with Reps. Bill Alexander (D-AR) and Ralph Regula (R-OH). When the delegation arrived at its hotel in the Honduran capital of Tegucigalpa, Fowler was confronted by a group of contras, including Adolfo Calero, a contra leader and former Coca-Cola executive whom he had met on several occasions back in Washington. The group demanded that Fowler reconsider his opposition to the contra aid program, but after a brief exchange of words, the situation was defused and the contras departed.

Fowler presented his findings at a May 2 press conference in the US Capitol.

> Our trip to Honduras, Panama and Colombia focused on the U.S. military presence in Honduras, and the current status of the Contadora peace process.... We found that the United States is committed to an enhanced, if not permanent, military presence in Honduras. We also found that while our friends in Central America disagree over many things with regard to U.S. policy in Central America, they agree with virtual unanimity that they are extremely unsure of the U.S. commitment to a negotiated settlement.... If we continue our present course, we run substantial risk of regional war, with or without direct U.S. combat participation. An alternative is the advancement of our national interests through the negotiation process. Negotiations may not give us everything we as a nation would prefer, but in my opinion the military options produce fewer benefits at a much higher cost. As the foreign minister from one of our Central American allies said to us, the military option is not working for anyone. In the short time that we were in Central America, we saw 14-year-olds being trained in combat tactics. We heard requests for more military aid from countries whose standards of living are among the lowest in the Western Hemisphere. We received reports of military stalemate, arms build-ups and increasing violence. We did encounter a number of encouraging signs within the region of a willingness to peacefully resolve internal and

> external differences. Some of the Contadora foreign ministers expressed guarded optimism about the possibility of their producing a comprehensive and verifiable regional peace treaty. But we have heard such indications before, and they have always evaporated before a new military action. The hour is late, and though in the past we have had serious differences with the Administration, it is not too late to commit our full support to the Contadora process and to re-examine the policy ramifications of our nation's present course in Central America.

In response to a protest filed by the Nicaraguan government, on May 10 the International Court of Justice (the World Court) issued a preliminary ruling that condemned the CIA's involvement in the mining of Nicaraguan harbors and called on the US to "immediately cease and refrain" from such operations. The Reagan administration had previously stated that it did not recognize the court's authority with respect to US actions in Central America and subsequently announced that it would boycott any further proceedings on the matter.

The revelation of growing direct American involvement in the Nicaragua conflict, added to a feeling that the Reagan administration was not forthcoming in its reporting to Congress on its Central America policies, led first to denial of administration requests for additional FY 1984 funding for aid to the contras, and then to the adoption of a second Boland Amendment as part of the catch-all FY 1985 Continuing Appropriations Bill. In its final form, signed into law by the president on October 12, 1984, it provided that "during fiscal year 1985, no funds available to the Central Intelligence Agency, the Department of Defense, or any other agency or entity of the United States involved in intelligence activities may be obligated or expended for the purpose or which would have the effect of supporting, directly or indirectly, military or paramilitary operations in Nicaragua by any nation, group, organization, movement, or individual."

Thanks to the Senate's insistence, the administration obtained language allowing the president to spend $14 million on contra aid after February 28, 1985, provided he certified to Congress that such funds were needed to combat Nicaraguan expansionism and both houses of Congress approved the request. Thus, in effect, the House would have a veto over continuation of the Nicaraguan operation.

In spite of the tightened restrictions, the Reagan administration continued to look for ways to fund the contras. It was later discovered that two primary methods were used to circumvent the Boland language: 1) soliciting funds for the contras from other countries and private US citizens, since these were not explicitly banned by the law, and 2) directing the US government's contra support program through the National Security Council, which was not named in the Boland Amendment and, the administration rationalized, was a policy-making rather than intelligence agency. Thus, the US-backed contra war against the Sandinistas continued.

Intelligence Oversight

Partly as a result of his long-standing interest in the subject, and partly based on his experiences in the Nicaragua case, in the Ninety-Eighth Congress, Wyche Fowler took up a cause that had few vocal supporters: reform of the system of congressional oversight of intelligence activities. In the Congress itself, as with much of the public, a desire to avoid any chance of a security breach as well as a general willingness to defer to the president in matters of foreign policy tended to dissuade would-be reformers from tackling the issue. However, Fowler felt that legislative changes were needed to clarify the decision-making process governing covert operations in order to restore the bipartisan national consensus for improved US intelligence capabilities that had been jeopardized by certain abuses disclosed in the 1970s and early 1980s, and by the contentious contra operations of the Reagan administration.

On April 27, 1983, and shortly after his return from his trip to Central America, Congressman Fowler introduced the Intelligence Activities Oversight Improvement Act, which included the following major provisions:

- Prior to the initiation of a covert action, the president must submit a written report to the House and Senate Intelligence Committees finding that the activity is: essential to the national defense or foreign policy of the United States; consistent with, and in support of, publicly avowed US foreign policy; likely to produce benefits that justify the anticipated risks and consequences of disclosure; necessary because other means could not achieve the intended objectives; and required by circumstances that necessitate the use of extraordinary means.

- After receiving the written finding, the Intelligence Committees would have fifteen days in which to jointly disapprove and prohibit the activity.
- In emergencies, the president could limit the provision of prior notice of major covert activities to the chairmen and ranking minority members of the Intelligence Committees.
- All wartime intelligence operations would be exempt from the provisions of the bill.

In his introductory statement, Fowler outlined the reasoning behind his proposal.

> The absence of clear and permanent standards to govern the conduct of covert activities has been, in my opinion, harmful to both our overt and covert foreign policies. Suspicions abroad and here at home about "uncontrolled" covert actions have reduced confidence in the intelligence community and undermined our efforts to rebuild the national consensus in favor of necessary intelligence activities that was damaged by the revelations in the early 1970s.... Over the years the Congress has shown great reluctance to become involved in intelligence activities. In part this stemmed from deference to the president as the architect of American foreign policy and in part it resulted from uneasiness about potential security breaches if Congress thoroughly reviewed intelligence programs. However, I would say that the very nature of intelligence activities, which cannot be subjected to the crucible of full public scrutiny, cries out for the involvement of the people's branch of government, the Congress, in passing judgment on these activities. Such outside scrutiny can also serve to sharpen the internal review process within the intelligence community and the executive branch.... The current arrangement with respect to covert actions is less than totally satisfactory. It is ambiguous. It confuses the line between power and responsibility. The "plausible deniability" that the Congress created for itself in the area of covert activities does not lend well to full accountability for either the executive or legislative branches. The

Intelligence Activities Oversight Improvement Act seeks to remedy these problems by establishing a clear role for the Congress in the conduct of covert actions.

The *Atlanta Constitution* offered a generally positive assessment of the Fowler bill.

> Under present law, the executive branch must tell members of the House and Senate committees on intelligence about clandestine operations, contemplated or just underway. Specially selected by Congress' leadership for their maturity, judgment and willingness to abide by secrecy rules and to accept this fearsome responsibility, these members can only review each operation; they are not empowered to approve or reject. Fowler's proposal would give the congressmen a negative option: If a majority of the members of both committees, upon consideration of a proposed mission, decided to disapprove, it would be scotched. One of the best features of Fowler's bill is the clarity of the standards it sets for determining the worth of each mission: Is it essential to national security? Is it consistent with avowed foreign policy? Do its benefits outweigh its risks? Is it necessary because less sensitive, overt measures would not produce the desired objective?... The only nagging doubt about the Fowler bill concerns the politics of the negative option—the remote danger that committee members might block an important operation for fear of voter retaliation if it went sour. Nothing in the six-year history of the committees suggests that their members would run for cover.... Still, it is a worry, an issue that should be thoroughly aired as Congress debates the bill. The rest of the bill is unquestionably sound; Fowler has made it plain he is not out to prohibit covert activities, but to strengthen the process by which they are undertaken. The administration should welcome the thoughtful participation of qualified members of Congress and their willingness to share the burden in making these ultrasensitive decisions.[55]

Fowler introduced a second bill designed to improve congressional oversight of intelligence operations: the Intelligence Expenditures Oversight Act. This measure aimed at enhancing the House and Senate Intelligence Committees' ability to monitor CIA activities that are financed through the agency's contingency fund or by transfer of funds from another agency. Specifically, the Fowler bill required the two Intelligence Committees to give explicit approval before funds could be released from the contingency fund or transferred from another agency when the sums involved exceeded $2 million during a fiscal year or were to be used for a covert military or paramilitary operation. Fowler explained, "At the moment, the power of the purse is supposed to be the prime means for Congressional control of covert operations. However, the use of contingency funds and transfer authority has severely weakened this power in practice. Thus, [this bill] seeks to make the <u>current</u> oversight system function properly and therefore can be considered apart from the more far-reaching proposals made in my other legislation."

In June of 1983, the US Supreme Court issued a decision in the case *INS v. Chadha* that raised serious questions about the constitutionality of legislative vetoes, like the one contained in the original version of the Intelligence Activities Oversight Improvement Act. In response, Fowler developed a second version of that bill, which he introduced on September 13, 1983. The revised bill removed the committee veto provisions and substituted a requirement for an explicit authorization for any clandestine military or paramilitary operation that could be waived provided the president determined that covert aid to a country "invaded, attacked or occupied by the armed forces of another country...is essential in order to meet extraordinary circumstances affecting the vital interests of the United States." In addition, the new measure imposed more specific reporting requirements on the executive branch prior to the initiation of a covert action.

From September 20 to 22, 1983, the House Intelligence Committee held hearings on the Fowler proposals.

> Rep. Wyche Fowler, Jr. (D-GA) summoned some of America's most knowledgeable former spies and spy watchers to conduct a rare public debate about intelligence legislation, specifically his proposal to require prior congressional approval of any CIA military or paramilitary operations.... At present, the intelligence committees are informed "in a timely fashion"—in practice, within 24 hours—of the start of covert operations, and committee members have a right to object. They frequently do. But the CIA does not have to

> listen. It has a huge, secret "contingency reserve fund." The intelligence committees clear it in advance and in total every fiscal year as part of the intelligence authorization act. The agency then uses the fund to keep operations going and growing, when the White House wants them to, no matter what intelligence committee members think.... "Once an operation starts, it's almost impossible to stop. The ground changes," Fowler said. As the program begins to have some impact, it inevitably becomes public. Backers then argue that people have committed their lives and need increased U.S. aid to avoid a retaliatory bloodbath. "The word and prestige of the United States are on the line.... It's a totally different scenario," Fowler said.... After three days of...testimony, Fowler's proposal appeared moribund. Most of the Democrats seemed convinced that foreign policy requires what one member called "wriggle room," presidential authority to learn secrets, spend secret money and take secret action to advance U.S. goals without prior congressional clearance.... The possibility remains that, messy as it is, the current process works just fine for Congress in providing what the intelligence world calls "deniability" when foreign efforts go awry.[56]

This report proved accurate in assessing the dim prospects for the Fowler intelligence oversight proposals, as no further action on any of them occurred after the September hearings. But Fowler considered this as unfinished business and would return to the same subject in future years.

The CIA Seal Medallion awarded to Wyche Fowler upon completion of his service on the House Intelligence Committee at the beginning of 1985 provided details on the agency's assessment of Fowler's role.

> WYCHE FOWLER is hereby awarded the AGENCY SEAL MEDALLION in recognition of his outstanding accomplishments as a member of the House Permanent Select Committee on Intelligence from July 1977 to January 1985. He was a leader in establishing the oversight of intelligence which was and is today in the finest spirit of bipartisan government. Consistently adhering to the highest standards of personal and professional integrity in furtherance of the national security of the United States, Congressman Fowler clearly demonstrated that effective oversight of intelligence can be realized in a

democratic nation without risk to the intelligence process. Serving with full knowledge that his achievements would never receive public recognition, he chose to align himself with the thousands of men and women who have devoted their lives to support the intelligence needs of our country. Congressman Fowler's extraordinary contributions and exemplary dedication while serving on the House Permanent Select Committee on Intelligence reflect great credit on himself and the Congress of the United States.

Social Security

Though there was a gradually growing concern about US policy in Central America, the biggest issue to face the Ninety-Eighth Congress when it convened in January 1983 was the fate of the Social Security system. By 1981, it was recognized that Social Security faced an approaching financial crisis, and after the widespread opposition to his initial proposed benefit cuts, late in that year President Reagan announced the creation of a bipartisan national commission on Social Security reform. Members were appointed by the president, Senate Republican Majority Leader Howard Baker, and Democratic Speaker of the House Tip O'Neill. The commission began its work in February 1982, and on January 20, 1983, presented to Congress a package of revenue increases and benefit cuts to address the system's problems. Without further action, it was estimated that the Social Security trust fund would begin to run a deficit by midsummer, resulting in a disruption in the distribution of benefits, and that there was a need of an additional $150 to $200 billion in tax increases and/or benefit reductions if Social Security was to remain solvent for the remainder of the decade.

Moving with unaccustomed swiftness, the Congress adopted most of the commission's recommendations, attached additional provisions to improve the longer-term financial picture for Social Security and Medicare, and completed action on what became the Social Security Amendments of 1983 by late March. The measure was signed into law by President Reagan on April 20, 1983 (PL 98-21). In its final form, the total package consisted of $168 billion in new revenues and reduced benefits, including the following major provisions:

- moved the annual Social Security cost-of-living-adjustments from July to January of each year (resulting in a six-month delay in 1983 only);
- accelerated the implementation of scheduled payroll tax increases;
- increased the payroll tax rate for the self-employed;
- gradually raised the full benefit retirement age from sixty-five to sixty-seven early in the twenty-first century;
- made up to one half of the benefits received by high-income recipients subject to federal income taxes; and
- put newly hired federal workers and all nonprofit organization workers into the Social Security system as of January 1, 1984.

The new law solved the short- and middle-term financing problems and substantially improved the Social Security system's long-term outlook. Furthermore, it represented an example of bipartisan compromise to address a serious national problem. In the words of President Reagan, "Each of us had to compromise one way or another. But the essence of bipartisanship is to give up a little in order to get a lot. And, my fellow Americans, I think we've gotten a very great deal."

As a member of the Ways and Means Subcommittee on Social Security, Wyche Fowler was involved in the development of the legislation from the start. On March 9, he spoke on the House floor in support of the proposal.

> The Social Security system is in serious trouble, and we have only two alternatives from which to choose. We can approve this bi-partisan compromise before us today, or we can put off yet another time the difficult decision that faces us, and continue the fears of so many about the future of the Social Security system.... What would happen if this body were to shirk its duty and defeat this package which carries the endorsement of people across the political spectrum, including President Reagan [and] the House and Senate leadership? This is what would happen. The 36 million beneficiaries and the 115 million workers covered by Social Security would face additional months of uncertainty about the future of the system. Beneficiaries and workers alike would lose faith in our greatest and

most popular social program. Younger workers, concerned that Social Security would be broke by the time of their retirement, could push for the elimination of the system. People in and near retirement would grow more uncertain of the system's future. We cannot allow this intergenerational strife to occur. No one favors every element in this package. Yet, given the widely varied interests represented in this chamber, we have achieved as perfect a package as is politically possible. The sacrifices called for in this compromise are as broadly distributed and equitable as possible. In both the short-term and long-term, beneficiaries and workers alike contribute to shoring up Social Security.... In the depths of the Great Depression, amid widespread poverty among our nation's elderly, the United States Congress enacted the Social Security Act of 1935. At that time, over half of our elderly population subsisted on incomes below the poverty line. Over Social Security's 48-year history, the system has drastically reduced poverty among the elderly by 75 percent and become America's most popular and successful social program. We cannot abdicate our responsibility to workers and beneficiaries. We must deal decisively with this issue and restore faith to all Americans of Congress' commitment to Social Security.

Deficit Reduction and Fowler Mega Cap Proposal

Although a modest economic recovery began in 1983, the Ninety-Eighth Congress and the Reagan administration still faced a growing deficit problem caused by the 1981 tax cuts and the large 1981 and 1982 increases in defense spending, exacerbated by the recession. The 1982 budget reconciliation and tax acts alleviated the problem somewhat, as had the Omnibus Budget Reconciliation Act of 1983, which cut spending by $8.2 billion over four years through changes in federal employee pay and pension formulas, but in February 1984, the Congressional Budget Office was still forecasting an ongoing rise in the federal deficit, from $195 billion in FY 1983 to $326 billion by FY 1989, unless further action was taken.

In recognition of these facts, the House Ways and Means Committee began developing additional deficit-reduction measures in 1983. In their respective budget resolutions, the House proposed $30 billion in revenue increases in FY 1984, tacitly endorsing the repeal of the third year of the 1981 tax-cut law, whereas the Senate called for approximately $10 billion in additional revenue. During the committee's consideration of various tax-reform proposals, Representative Fowler offered his alternative, the Bracket-Flattening/Mega Cap tax proposal, which he had been working on for several years. Though never introduced as a freestanding bill, Fowler presented his plan in the June 14, 1983, *Congressional Record.*

> The prospect of ever-growing deficits surpassing $300 billion a year by the end of this decade is frightening. The deficit problem is compounded by the growing incomprehensibility and inequity of the federal tax system, which in turn is driving more and more taxpayers to evade their income taxes.... Many of us are concerned [about proposals to repeal the third year of the tax cut] because, although we recognize that the gap between spending and revenues cannot be narrowed by spending cuts alone, the increased tax burden caused by repeal of the third year of the tax cut would fall most heavily on those least able to bear the additional burden—lower and middle income taxpayers. These same people are also the ones who benefitted the least from the earlier stages of the tax cut.... What I propose to do is to split the difference between the House and Senate revenue targets with my own proposal for tax reform. The Fowler bracket-flattening/itemized deduction mega cap proposal would move our complicated tax code toward a flatter income tax system by reducing the number of marginal tax brackets. At the same time, it would broaden the income tax base without requiring repeal of any specific tax preferences. It would accomplish these goals equitably while raising some additional revenues.

Specifically, the Fowler proposal would have repealed the third year of the 1981 tax cut, replacing it with fewer but broader income tax brackets and placing a cap on taxpayers' total itemized deductions, limiting them to no more than 40 percent of adjusted gross income in any year. It would have raised an additional $19.5 billion in revenues in FY 1984, and larger amounts in later years, with most of the burden falling on households earning more than $100,000, who had been the major beneficiaries of the 1981 tax cuts.

The Fowler plan represented a major change in the income tax code that the Congress was not yet ready to consider (although the notion of "flattened" brackets and an expanded tax base were to be fundamental to the landmark Tax Reform Act of 1986). Instead, the Deficit Reduction Act of 1984 that was ultimately enacted (signed into law by President Reagan on July 18, 1984) contained a number of relatively small changes that produced an extra $1.1 billion in revenues in FY 1984, $10.6 billion in FY 1985, and a total of $50.7 billion over a four-year period. While the Fowler cap on itemized deductions was never adopted in the form he proposed, a different, and more limited, version was enacted in the Omnibus Budget Reconciliation Act of 1990, and President Obama consistently proposed limiting the value of itemized deductions to no more than 28 percent of income, though this, too, has never been adopted by the Congress.

In all, the 1983 budget reconciliation law, the 1984 Deficit Reduction Act, and cuts in farm programs and in various appropriations bills resulted in a $90 billion reduction in the FY 1984 budget deficit, from $262 billion to $172 billion.

Energy and Space

Fowler continued to seek support for renewable energy by authoring legislation to provide tax incentives for such technologies. In the Ninety-Eighth Congress, he once again introduced the passive solar tax credit bill (this time raising the credit to $2,500). He also sponsored legislation to extend the existing business and residential tax credits for solar energy installations through 1990.

In the face of an administration seemingly indifferent to renewable energy sources and a Congress that needed to raise additional revenues, neither of the Fowler energy proposals received further action.

In 1983, Wyche Fowler joined the Congressional Space Caucus and was named chairman of its Task Force on Space Science, a position he held for the remainder of his service in the House of Representatives. In his winter 1983 newsletter, Fowler reported to constituents on his initiatives in this field.

> It is estimated that the current NASA budget has only about 40 percent of the purchasing power of the 1966 budget. The results of these cutbacks have been predictable. The U.S. averaged 47 space launches a year during the 1960s, but only 16 launches a year in

> the 1980s. No American flew in space between July 1975 and April 1981. No American planetary mission has been launched since 1977. Our once unquestioned leadership in virtually every field of space exploration is now being challenged by many nations, including the Soviet Union. In response, I have introduced two resolutions [on October 15, 1983] which are intended to ensure a balanced and affordable civilian space program.... My proposals would make long-range national commitments to NASA's space science programs. The two resolutions outline specific priorities, programs and funding levels for astronomy, astrophysics, and solar system exploration. These proposals were taken from the reports of two distinguished panels: the Astronomy Survey Committee of the National Academy of Sciences and the Solar System Exploration Committee of NASA. Among the programs endorsed by my resolutions are the Venus Radar Mapper, a mission to a comet and the asteroid belt, a mission to Saturn's moon Titan, an orbital X-ray telescope, a Very-Long-Baseline Array of radio telescopes, and an astronomical search for extraterrestrial intelligence. The future of our space program, and of U.S. leadership in this prestigious and technology-expanding field, is in our own hands. [**block quote**]

Though no formal action was taken on the Fowler resolutions, they did help to focus attention on the space science program and won for Fowler a May 1984 award from the American Space Foundation. These efforts represented only the first of many that he would undertake on behalf of space science while serving in the US Congress.

Local Projects and Honors

As usual, Fowler was actively involved in a number of initiatives having particular relevance to the Fifth District.

- He was a cosponsor and strong supporter of legislation to make the birthday of Dr. Martin Luther King Jr. a national holiday, a measure that was signed into law on November 2, 1983.
- He cosponsored successful legislation to expand the boundaries of the Chattahoochee River National Recreation Area.

• He helped obtain $1.388 million in federal funding for the further development of the Martin Luther King Jr. National Historic Site in Atlanta.
• He worked to persuade officials in the Department of Housing and Urban Development to award the City of Atlanta $10 million for the redevelopment of Underground Atlanta.

Fowler received additional recognition for his work in the Congress by being named, in September 1983, to the Democratic Steering and Policy Committee, the executive panel for House Democrats that set party policy and recommended committee assignments. He was also picked in 1983 to serve on the Democratic Party's Commission on Voting Rights and Voter Participation. Closer to home, he was given the 1983 Clarence A. Bacote Award by the Morehouse College State Committee on the Life and History of Black Georgians "for exemplary courage in the cause of human rights."

A further honor was Fowler's selection to deliver the Democratic response to President Reagan's 1983 Christmas Eve national radio address.

> Mr. President, my fellow citizens, on this Christmas Eve we speak not as partisans but as Americans, proud that our national heritage was built on a firm foundation of faith. Christmas is the season for remembering the joys of the past, and for savoring the blessings of the present. But most of all, Christmas is the season of hope. And in the midst of all the danger and turmoil of 1983, there can yet be seen, for those with eyes to see, green shoots of hope springing from many corners of a weary world: the spirit of Solidarity in Eastern Europe; consolidation of democracy in Spain and Nigeria; the return of democratic institutions in Argentina, and perhaps soon, in Brazil; the prospect of continuing reconciliation and cooperation among the great religions of the world; freer passage of people and ideas across international borders. But hope is a fragile thing—as fragile as a newborn babe—and if it is to grow into strength and power it must be rooted firmly in the soil of truth; and it must be nurtured from a spirit of righteousness. For as the prophets remind us, a nation's true strength lies in righteousness....

Christmas is the season for recalling the blessings which a bountiful Providence has heaped upon us—blessing upon blessing—in a world in which, every day, millions of families move closer to starvation. Should we not recall that in the measure which God has blessed us, in the same measure does God require of us a stewardship of our wealth—for the hungry, the sick, the wretched of the earth?

Most of all Christmas is a season for resolve. Resolve that we shall not abandon the hope born into the world at Bethlehem 2,000 years ago. Resolve that we shall not trample that hope in a rush to wealth and power and arms. Resolve that, in our national life and in our national stewardship, we shall not forget the weakness of the little child whose birth we celebrate, and the power and strength of the man He became. Resolve that we shall remember these words, which He gave to us and to men and women of every generation: "Blessed are they which do hunger and thirst after righteousness: for they shall be filled. Blessed are the merciful: for they shall obtain mercy. Blessed are the peacemakers: for they shall be called the children of God." Merry Christmas and God bless us each and every one.

Although his policy work in Washington attracted the most media attention (and there was considerably more such coverage in the 1970s and early 1980s than afterward, as local media outlets drastically reduced their coverage of national affairs), for most constituents, the most likely source of any interaction with Congressman Fowler was through his district office in Atlanta, which provided information and help in cutting through bureaucratic red tape for those who had problems associated with the federal government. By mid-1984, that office had handled more than 28,000 constituent requests, with Social Security, Medicare, veteran's benefits, and immigration matters being among the most frequent; staffed thirty-six mass meetings open to Fifth District residents; and operated the mobile office (a modified van) for a total of 136 stops at locations throughout the district.

1984 Congressional Elections

In many ways, Fowler's 1984 campaign promised to be the most challenging since his first election to Congress back in 1977. He would be running in the district created just before the 1982 special elections, but those contests were brief and attracted only relatively minor opposition. This time, would-be opponents would have the entire regular two-year House election cycle in which to prepare.

On October 1, 1983, Fowler delivered a speech to the DeKalb County Community Relations Commission that addressed, among other topics, the question of coalition-building, a subject that would be crucial to success in the new Fifth District, in which 59 percent of registered voters were Black and 41 percent were white.

> I am a product of coalition politics. I could not have been elected to the City Council, nor to the position of City Council President, nor to the Congress without substantial bi-racial support. And I am certainly not the only beneficiary of such support. William Hartsfield, Maynard Jackson, Ivan Allen, Michael Lomax, Charles Weltner, Marvin Arrington are but some of our local elected officials who have been coalition-builders. But I do not advocate coalition politics merely as a matter of political strategy and convenience. I am a true believer that in the long run it is only by building bridges, by forging sturdy links of cooperation and consultation, and by binding ourselves together into one community that we can solve the problems that ultimately face us all. To quote President Kennedy, "In the final analysis, our most basic common link is that we all inhabit this small planet. We all breathe the same air. We all cherish our children's future. And we are all mortal."
>
> Unquestionably, coalition-building is difficult for there are indeed many factors of history and circumstance that divide us: along economic lines, along racial lines, along age lines. And unfortunately, it always seems that it is easier to destroy than to build. But in the end polarization and division never solve anything. It is the genius of coalition politics that allows those who may be a political minority to join together with individuals of different backgrounds

in order to forge a broad-based majority capable of getting things done.

Those in the American Jewish community could never have succeeded in obtaining strong U.S. support for the State of Israel without building a coalition with non-Jews in the country and in the Congress. American farmers could not have gotten their price support legislation through the Congress without first joining with urban representatives who were seeking support for the Food Stamp program. Those of us who represent areas needing federal assistance for the mass transit program could not have been successful without reaching out to rural and suburban representatives.... Civil rights groups could not have won passage of the Civil Rights Act of 1964 and the Voting Rights Act of 1965 without the support of legislators like Senator Hubert Humphrey and Atlanta Congressman Charles Weltner. I think the lesson is clear: you can't go it alone. You need allies to accomplish your objectives. And often it is the ally, from outside the group, who can lend more credibility and help build a broader base of support.

There were a total of 272,011 registered voters for the 1984 primary elections, 160,700 of whom were Black (59.1 percent), with 111,311 white registered voters (40.9 percent). This represented a further increase in the African American share of the Fifth District electorate (up from 56 percent in 1982).

In December 1983, the Fowler campaign commissioned a poll of three hundred Fifth District Democratic primary voters, with an error margin of plus or minus 6 percent. Fowler's job performance was highly rated by these voters—76 percent positive, 18 percent negative, 6 percent not sure—and, in a hypothetical matchup against Julian Bond and Public Safety commissioner Reginald Eaves, Fowler enjoyed a commanding lead (Fowler 66 percent, Bond 11 percent, Eaves 9 percent, Other/Undecided 14 percent).

Although there were reports that Bond, Eaves, or John Lewis might run, none of them did, but four other African American candidates qualified to challenge Fowler in the Democratic primary: Alveda King Beal, former state representative and niece of Dr. Martin Luther King Jr.; Henrietta Canty, former state representative and 1977 candidate for the Fifth

District seat; Robert Waymer, later a member of the Atlanta Board of Education; and Hosea Williams, civil rights leader and then a member of the Georgia House of Representatives. Of the four, Williams, who had faced Fowler in the 1973 race for city council president, was considered the most formidable, a fact underscored by the endorsements he received in a July 1984 fundraising appeal made by Andrew Young, Julian Bond, and the president of the Southern Christian Leadership Council, Joseph Lowery: "Please join us in support of Hosea. We know better than most the debt we owe—and all Americans owe—to this valiant warrior for racial justice and human dignity.... No one has given more to the [Civil Rights] Movement than Hosea Williams, and if anyone can make Congress and the nation more responsive to the needs of Black people, surely it is Hosea."

A total of 78,230 Fifth District voters went to the polls on Tuesday, August 14, representing a turnout of just under 29 percent of registered voters, which was slightly above participation rates in the 1982 contests. White voters turned out at a slightly higher rate (approximately 27 percent for African Americans, 31 percent for whites), producing an electorate that was approximately 56 percent Black, 44 percent white.

Wyche Fowler won nearly two-thirds of the vote, exceeding his vote percentage in the 1977 runoff against John Lewis when the electorate was 63 percent white. Hosea Williams was a distant second, and the other candidates trailed far back.

Wyche Fowler	49,962	63.87%
Hosea Williams	22,293	28.50%
Alveda King Beal	3,090	3.95%
Henrietta Canty	2,151	2.75%
Robert Waymer	751	0.96%

Williams ran slightly ahead of the incumbent in the predominantly African American DeKalb County portion of the district (Williams 46.9 percent, Fowler 42.7 percent), but Fowler dominated in the much larger Fulton part, which featured 89 percent of the votes cast (Fowler 66.6 percent, Williams 26.1 percent). Fowler won 95 percent of white votes and split the African American vote with Williams at approximately 44 percent each, with the other candidates drawing the remaining 12 percent.

Running unopposed, Fowler received 151,233 votes in the November general election.

The 1986 *Almanac of American Politics* gave its take on Fowler's situation as of the end of the 1984 elections.

> [The Fifth District's] current boundaries were set by a federal court, which decided that the Georgia legislature's district did not contain enough Blacks to satisfy the Voting Rights Act.... The result was ironic. A 5th District with a white majority elected Andrew Young congressman in 1972; ten years later a 5th District with a court-augmented Black majority has elected and reelected Wyche Fowler, who is white. He has won for the most sensible of reasons: most of the voters in the district thought he'd do a better job than his opponents. Fowler has been representing Black voters for many years; he was president of the City Council before his election to Congress in 1977.... In 1982, even though Atlanta is full of talented and well-known Black politicians, none so much as filed to run against Fowler. In 1984, Fowler did draw a strong opponent, former civil rights leader Hosea Williams. But in the Democratic Primary, tantamount to election in this most Democratic of Georgia's districts, Fowler won 64 percent of the votes to Williams's 28 percent. There is a kind of informal understanding in Atlanta that Fowler is going to run for the Senate in 1986.... In the Senate race, Fowler could prove a formidable candidate. His strength with Black voters could give him a large base, and yet neither that nor, as the differences between Atlanta and the rest of the state diminish, his Atlanta base are likely to make him unacceptable to the rest of the electorate.[57]

Chapter 8

Ninety-Ninth Congress (1985–1986): Challenger

The Ninety-Ninth Congress presented Wyche Fowler Jr. with perhaps the greatest set of challenges he faced in his public career. While seeking a seat in the United States Senate for the largest state east of the Mississippi, facing opposition in the primary and a well-funded incumbent in the general election, he also continued to represent the Fifth District and the City of Atlanta in the US House. The degree of difficulty was only compounded when taking into account the fact that no Atlanta-based candidate had ever been elected to represent Georgia in the US Senate.

The Federal Deficit and the Tax Reform Act of 1986

In his role as Fifth District congressman, Fowler continued to address a wide range of national and local concerns, and his position on the Ways and Means Committee placed him in the midst of the two biggest issues of the session: the deficit and tax reform. Though the tax and entitlement savings measures adopted in 1982 and 1983 had managed to slightly reduce the federal deficit (from $207.8 billion in FY 1983 to $185.4 billion in FY 1984), the full phasing in of the 1981 tax cuts and the sustained defense buildup had driven it back up again to record peace-time highs ($212.3 billion in FY 1985 and $221.2 billion in FY 1986). This turn of events led the Ninety-Ninth Congress to take additional action to curb the red ink.

In December 1985, the Balanced Budget and Emergency Deficit Control Act was signed into law. This legislation, also known as the Gramm-Rudman-Hollings Act after its three chief sponsors in the Senate, required that budget deficits must be decreased annually until a balanced budget was achieved in FY 1991. If the annual deficit target was not met, the law provided for automatic across-the-board cuts to achieve the target, exempting only Social Security and a few other programs. Though this "sequestration" system was replaced in 1990 by the Budget Enforcement Act, it was revived in slightly different form in 2011.

The final version of Gramm-Rudman-Hollings passed the House by a vote of 271 to 154, but a majority of Democrats (130 of 248) had opposed it. Fowler, along with all other members of the Georgia delegation, voted in support, and he outlined his reasons in his December 1985 newsletter to his Fifth District constituents.

> While the Deficit Control Act is not as comprehensive as other deficit reduction measures I have supported in the past, such as the budget freeze and a "pay as you go" requirement, I voted for it as at least a first step in the right direction. We have seen the harmful effects of record-high deficits in high real interest rates, which have produced an over-valued dollar. This in turn has led to the worst international trade balance in 50 years. It has also led to a massive inflow of foreign capital, which in 1985 will make the United States an international debtor for the first time in 67 years. Finally, the deficits have produced a doubling in the share of total national savings absorbed by federal debt service. If we fail to reverse these trends, all Americans but especially our children will suffer the consequences.

The signature achievement of the Ninety-Ninth Congress, however, was tax reform. Sentiment for major reform of the federal tax code had been building for some time. As Fowler put it in his May 1985 newsletter,

> It is a widely held view that over the past few decades our tax structure has become more complicated, less equitable, and more disruptive to our economy. In 1982, tax exclusions, itemized deductions and tax credits for individuals offset some 34 percent of income, compared with 18 percent in 1954. This growth in preferential income has meant that the remaining income, typically the wages earned by middle-income Americans, has had to be taxed at far higher rates than would otherwise have been necessary.

Fowler's Ways and Means Committee began holding public hearings on tax reform on February 27, 1985, and conducted twenty-nine more days of such hearings through the end of July. In May 1985, President Reagan submitted his proposal to reduce tax rates while eliminating a number of tax breaks in order to achieve near neutrality in revenues raised, thus not exacerbating the deficit. Though Fowler supported the broad outlines of the Reagan plan, he objected to its skewing of benefits toward the wealthy, who had been the biggest beneficiaries of the 1981 tax cut, and its net loss of $25 billion in federal revenues, which would add to the already large federal deficit.

Citing a Treasury Department report that disclosed that 55,000 taxpayers with incomes of more than $250,000 a year had paid an effective federal income tax rate of less than 10 percent because of tax breaks compared to an average rate of 13 percent for those with incomes between $30,000 and $75,000, Fowler reiterated his support for limiting tax deductions to no more than 40 percent of a taxpayer's income. "People who get up every morning and work hard for their paycheck should not have to pay more in taxes than those whose money does the working for them through investments," he said.[58]

After the completion of the hearing phase, the committee began drafting its tax reform bill on September 18, 1985, with a total of twenty-six days spent marking up the legislation, which concluded on December 3 when the Tax Reform Act of 1985 was introduced and favorably reported to the House by a vote of 28 to 8, with Wyche Fowler as one of twenty original cosponsors, which included his Georgia colleague Ed Jenkins. On December 17, the House took up the measure under a rule limiting the time for debate and the amendments that could be considered. After rejecting a Republican substitute, in a vote of 133 to 294, with all members of the Georgia delegation, including Fowler and Republican Newt Gingrich, voting no, except for Republican Pat Swindall, who supported the substitute, the House adopted the Ways and Means Committee bill by voice vote.

The House-passed bill was similar to the Reagan proposal but provided more tax relief to lower- and middle-income individuals than had the president's plan. Among its major features, the measure

- removed more than six million low-income households from the federal income tax rolls;
- lowered individual tax rates and reduced the number of brackets from fourteen to four (15 percent, 25 percent, 35 percent, and 38 percent) and retained the 1981 law's indexing of brackets to account for inflation;
- increased the personal exemption (from $1,080 to $2,000 for non-itemizers) and the standard deduction (for example, for a joint return from $3,670 to $4,800);
- increased the maximum Earned Income Tax Credit from $550 to $700;
- limited itemized deductions to those in excess of $500 times the number of personal exemptions claimed; and
- reduced the maximum corporate tax rate from 46 percent to 36 percent, created a graduated rate structure for small businesses that ranged from 15 percent to 36 percent, and broadened the corporate tax base while expanding the corporate minimum tax.

Fowler was pleased with the House-passed measure, which accomplished much of what he sought in his Bracket-Flattening/Mega Cap plan, and improved the fairness of the tax code. "People around [Georgia] know that when somebody pays nothing, the rest of us pay more. We were determined to put in stiff minimum taxes so that everybody—even the largest corporations—pays something. This bill takes a gigantic step to assure that everybody pays their fair share, but no more. The special interests are put in their places with this proposal and we'll all be the better for it."[59]

The Senate passed its own tax reform bill by a 97 to 3 margin on June 24, 1986, and a conference committee was held to reconcile the competing measures, with the final version approved by the conferees on September 18, 1986. The House adopted the conference report on September 25, 1986, by a vote of 292 to 136 (with Fowler joining fellow Georgia Democrats Barnard, Hatcher, and Jenkins, along with Republican Gingrich, in voting for the bill), and the Senate followed suit two days later by a margin of 74 to 23. President Reagan then signed the Tax Reform Act of 1986 into law on October 22, 1986.

The new law was similar in most respects to the House bill, though differing in the individual rate structure (with just two brackets—15 percent and 28 percent, but a 5 percent surcharge imposed on certain higher incomes, creating a 33 percent rate), how the tax base was broadened (with specific deductions, including the consumer credit deduction, being eliminated instead of an overall limit), and the corporate tax rates (with a top rate of 34 percent and no graduated scale for small businesses). In the end, though, Fowler felt it accomplished his key objectives for tax reform. Writing after the conference agreement had been reached but before final floor action had occurred, Fowler reported to his constituents in his August 1986 newsletter.

> The conference committee was able to take the best that each bill had to offer and meld them together into a tax code that, above all, guarantees fairness, particularly for the average taxpayer.... Congress must pass a tax reform bill which is more fair for lower and middle income taxpayers and closes the floodgates to the special interests who are seeking to restore their preferences. This type of tax bill will help strengthen our economy by eliminating inefficient subsidies and tax loopholes so that business and investment decisions will not be made on the basis of sheltering profits but in terms of what will help our nation maintain and further develop a healthy and growing economy.

The 1986 Act, passed with bipartisan input and support, remains the last major tax reform and simplification measure to be enacted into law.

Iran-Contra Affair

With his departure from the Intelligence Committee at the end of the Ninety-Eighth Congress, Wyche Fowler was no longer in a position to play a lead role in the battle over US policy toward Central America. Yet he remained active in the debates that followed in the ensuing years. The policy itself became increasingly divisive not only in producing bitter fights in Congress over the wisdom (and legality) of administration policies, but also by harming US relations in the international community. It resulted in the worst scandal of the Reagan presidency.

In June 1985, the House took up a supplemental appropriations bill that authorized the funding of $14 million for "humanitarian" assistance to the Nicaraguan contras, provided that such aid was not delivered by the Defense Department or the CIA. The bill also offered $2 million in support for the Contadora nations in implementing a negotiated end to the Central American armed conflicts based on the Contadora Document of Objectives of September 9, 1983. In nonbinding language, the legislation "urged" the president to: 1) pursue diplomatic and economic steps to resolve the conflict in Nicaragua; 2) suspend military maneuvers in Honduras and off the Nicaraguan coast and lift the trade embargo against Nicaragua if Nicaragua agreed to a ceasefire, to holding a dialogue with the contras, and to end its state of emergency; and 3) resume bilateral discussions with the Nicaraguan government.

Fowler took an active role in the debate that accompanied the proposed easing of the Boland Amendment restrictions. In a series of votes on June 12, 1985, the House refused to reinstate the Boland language (defeated 196 to 232); delay the provision of aid to the contras for six months to allow more time for the Contadora peace negotiations to continue (defeated 172 to 259); or ensure the "humanitarian" aid was actually provided for that purpose by having it distributed by the Red Cross or the UN High Commissioner for Refugees (defeated 174 to 254). In each case, Fowler was the lone member of the Georgia delegation to vote in favor of the amendment. He addressed the House during the action.

> I believe that our current attempt to win the battle in Nicaragua runs the risk of our losing the wider war for power and influence in the Americas. Our mining of harbors, our abandonment of the international legal system we helped to create, our economic embargo, and our preoccupation with a tiny country of three million people and a Gross Domestic Product of under $3 billion have served to isolate us from our key friends in Latin America and Western Europe.... Between calling for the Sandinistas to cry uncle and actually forcing them to do so lies a wide gulf that can only be bridged by an ever-expanding U.S. commitment to the contras, and, as a last resort, direct U.S. military intervention. These facts would be clearer if the Administration would de-classify the material it has transmitted to the Intelligence Committees about this no

> longer secret covert operation.... The alternative is to achieve a negotiated end to the fighting in Nicaragua and to the threat posed by Nicaragua toward its neighbors. That possibility was tantalizingly close last year with the draft treaty proffered by the Contadora Group, a treaty which the Nicaraguans pledged to sign. We and our Central American allies raised objections to the draft, some legitimate and necessary having to do with verification, others peripheral and questionable such as preserving our military maneuvers in Honduras. If we were to put the same effort into finalizing a Contadora Peace Treaty as we have into prosecuting the contra war, I believe that we can achieve...reducing hostilities in the Americas, building respect for peaceful and lawful settlement of disputes, increasing U.S. prestige and influence among the nations of Latin America, and allowing us to turn our attention to far more important questions such as the economic and political health of the new democracies in the Western Hemisphere like Argentina, Brazil, Uruguay, Peru and El Salvador.

It soon became clear that the Reagan administration had a very different approach in mind. Less than two weeks after the House action in loosening the restrictions on aid to the contras, a *Miami Herald* story first identified Lt. Col. Oliver North of the National Security Council staff in connection with the contras. It was later learned that in early 1985, representatives of the Islamic Republic of Iran, then at war with Saddam Hussein's Iraq, approached the Reagan administration about buying arms and that, in opposition to the official US arms embargo against Iran, the administration agreed to do so, according to subsequent testimony, with the understanding that the Iranians would assist in persuading the Hezbollah terrorist group in Lebanon to release seven American hostages it was holding. The first arms delivery (made via Israel) was in August of 1985, and by the end of the year more than 1,500 American weapons had been delivered to the Iranians.

In December 1985, Oliver North devised a modification to the Iranian arms sales under which the US would directly supply the arms and use a portion of the proceeds from the sales to support the contras. The plan was approved, though President Reagan's precise role in the process is still disputed. In any event, by November of 1986, 1,500 missiles had been sold to Iran, three of the American hostages had been released (only to be replaced by three more), and the contras had received $2 million in assistance. On November 3, 1986, the day before the US general election, including the Georgia Senate race, a Lebanese newspaper exposed the operation. Though the president initially denied these allegations, in a nationally televised address on November 13, 1986, he acknowledged that the arms sales had occurred with the hope that Iran would "use its influence in Lebanon to secure the release of the hostages."

As American news media continued to pursue what became known as the Iran-Contra Affair, the president and the Congress both appointed investigatory commissions, with the presidentially appointed panel criticizing the president for not adequately supervising his staff and the congressional commission finding that Reagan bore "ultimate responsibility" and his administration had displayed "secrecy, deception and disdain for the law." Fourteen administration officials were indicted as a result of their role in the Iran-contra operation, and eleven were convicted.

Further damage to American prestige had occurred in June 1986 when the International Court of Justice—an entity that the United States had helped found—ruled that the US had violated international law by supporting the contras in their attempt to overthrow the government of Nicaragua and by mining Nicaraguan harbors. The US was subsequently forced to block enforcement of the court's decision by using its veto in the UN Security Council. In November of 1987, the United States was one of only two countries (Israel being the other) to oppose a UN General Assembly resolution calling for "full and immediate compliance" with the decision.

One can debate whether the original Reagan policy made a positive contribution toward the eventual peaceful settlement in Nicaragua in 1989. A year later, elections turned the Sandinistas out of power. Fowler believed that the willingness of President George H. W. Bush and his secretary of state, James Baker, to seriously pursue a negotiated agreement is what produced the positive result. However, few informed observers would question that the consequences of the contra policy, including arms-for-hostages deals, obstruction of justice trials, and the US being found in violation of international law, were very damaging to the Reagan administration and to America's national interests. And the Sandinistas returned to power again in 2006 when Daniel Ortega was elected president of Nicaragua, a post he retains at present, though through increasingly corrupt and authoritarian methods.

Fowler commented on the impact of the contra operation on the CIA in a March 1985 interview in which he also reflected on what he had learned during his seven and a half years on the Intelligence Committee.

> **Q.** Why does it bother you that the CIA is doing what Reagan wants by supporting the Nicaraguan rebels?
> **A.** For one thing, it spreads them too thin and jeopardizes our relationship with other countries who might be reluctant to pass information on to us if we're running around starting wars.... I think the director of intelligence should be apolitical. He should not be the spokesman advocating a foreign policy, especially a military foreign policy. What happens is all of a sudden you see the analysis from the area in which you are running those kind of covert activities automatically support the policy....
> **Q.** What shape is the CIA in now?
> **A.** Technologically it is without peer in the world. There is no question we are technologically superior to the Soviets.... But much remains to be done on the human intelligence-gathering side. It takes years for proper language training and moving people around the world to establish proper covers, and all sorts of training in technical areas to make a good spy. We had let that go for a good while....
> **Q.** Did your views of the CIA change while you were on the committee?
> **A.** I have a greater respect now for the professionals in the CIA at all levels and the difficulty of their tasks than I did before. And I'm extremely impressed by their dedication and their competence. What disturbs me is what I've already said. I'm afraid that the bipartisan attempt to build up the CIA's capability as an information collection and analysis agency...is being seriously compromised by using the CIA to run paramilitary operations.... I've been trying to convince the administration that they are still undercutting the competence of the CIA, and losing the confidence of the American people, by politicizing it and using it to run wars.[60]

The Iran-contra scandal did indeed take a political toll on President Reagan, at least in the short run. His job approval ratings dropped from 67 percent to 46 percent in November 1986, "the largest single drop for any US president in history," according to the *New York Times*/CBS poll. (Most of Reagan's popularity had returned by the end of his presidency, when he received a 64 percent approval rating.)

Aviation Security

The October 1983 bombing of a US Marine barracks in Beirut, the June 1985 hijacking of TWA Flight 847 that killed one American and led to beatings and threats against many more, and the October 1985 seizure in the Mediterranean of the Italian cruise ship *Achille Lauro* (resulting in the death of an American citizen and the holding hostage of four hundred passengers and crew) served as early warnings to the American government about the growing threat of international terrorism.

Fowler offered a specific proposal to bolster aviation security, as well as anti-drug trafficking efforts, with his April 17, 1986, introduction of the Airport Security Act. The legislation provided that any person who delivers property for air shipment or seeks to board any aircraft subject to US jurisdiction would, by that act, give consent to the search of their person, belongings, and baggage by duly authorized law enforcement officials. The law at that time provided for such searches only in the event that the law enforcement officer had probable cause to do so. In announcing his proposal, Fowler stated,

> While I am sensitive to the need to preserve our rights against intrusive searches, I believe this proposal, limited to air travel, is a prudent and reasonable step to deter the growing threats of terrorism and drug trafficking. Airport security systems were first implemented in the 1970s in response to the skyjacking crisis, and they have been successful in meeting this threat. But the professionally-trained, suicidal terrorists operating today are a far cry from the deranged hijacker of 15 years ago. Mass killing of innocents, not a free trip to Havana, is the goal of the modern terrorist. Most experts believe that our airport security, while quite effective so far, might not detect certain types of explosives which have great destructive potential. The fewer specifics [known] about our vulnerabilities the

better, but suffice it to say that we should strengthen our defenses now. To use an old truism, an ounce of prevention is worth a pound of cure.

No action was taken on the Fowler legislation at the time, but the notions about the need for improved security against onboard explosions and suicidal hijacking were prophetic of the tragedies to come in the 1988 bombing of Pan Am Flight 103 and the 9/11 hijackings. Fowler's proposal to make passenger and baggage screenings more intrusive was a sign of things to come.

Space

In October 1985, Representative Fowler resumed his efforts to promote American leadership in the field of space science. First, he introduced three resolutions expressing congressional endorsement of specific space science missions. Two were updated versions of the measures he had authored in the previous session, backing the recommendations of the National Academy of Sciences' Astronomy Survey Committee and of NASA's Solar System Exploration Committee for future programs in their fields of expertise. The third similarly endorsed the proposals made by the National Academy of Sciences' Committee on Solar and Space Physics.

Then, from October 8 to 10, 1985, Fowler hosted a conference in Washington, DC, on the future of the US space science program, featuring participants such as noted astronomer Dr. Carl Sagan, former astronaut and United States Senator Harrison Schmitt (R-CO), and Dr. James Van Allen, discoverer of the radiation belts circling the Earth that bear his name.

The Fowler resolutions boosted the profile of space science programs on Capitol Hill, and the advisory groups' recommendations helped shape US space science programs in the years ahead. At the time, however, the resolutions attracted limited support, with only a total of thirteen other members of the 435-seat House of Representatives signing on as cosponsors. One who did so, and the only other Georgian on the list, was Rep. Newt Gingrich. A newspaper article titled "Fowler, Gingrich agree: US Must Maintain Lead in Space" drew attention to their common ground on this issue.

> Democrat Wyche Fowler and Republican Newt Gingrich don't always see eye to eye on the issues, but the two Georgia congressmen do share the goal of keeping America at the forefront of space science and exploration. As members of the Space Caucus, both have been outspoken about the need to establish spending priorities for NASA and to keep research and development money flowing to universities such as Georgia Tech, where they believe many of the nation's future space scientists will be trained. In a joint interview last week, they talked about their desire to rekindle the spirit and drive for space exploration that put Americans on the moon, and the necessity of establishing specific, long-range goals for America's space program.[61]

In his spring 1986 newsletter, Fowler commemorated the January 28, 1986, *Challenger* space shuttle explosion and the loss of its seven crew members: "Let us go forward with the investigations of what caused the loss of our seven fellow countrymen and women who gave their lives on board the Shuttle, but let us honor their memories by rededicating ourselves to the great work which they sacrificed so much for."

Other Fowler Activities and Awards

In 1985, the Solar Energy Industries Association presented Fowler with its Solar Man of the Year Award for the second time. His bill to extend the solar residential energy tax credit won 145 cosponsors, and his legislation to extend both residential and business solar tax credits obtained forty-five cosponsors in the Ninety-Ninth Congress, but neither received further action, owing to executive branch opposition and the overriding focus on tax code simplification in the Tax Reform Act of 1986.

On the local front, Congressman Fowler testified in support of funding for MARTA before the House Appropriations Subcommittee on Transportation in both 1985 and 1986, and his efforts helped the transit agency obtain the funding that allowed it to complete the North-South Line from Chamblee to the airport by mid-1988. He also continued his work on behalf of the Martin Luther King Jr. National Historic Site by working to obtain federal funding and by sponsoring legislation to create a revolving loan fund to finance redevelopment within the entire MLK Jr. National Preservation District on and around Auburn Avenue in Atlanta.

In January 1985, Fowler traveled to southern Africa. In the Republic of South Africa, he met with government officials and the opposition to try to determine the current status of reforms of the apartheid system there. In Mozambique, he explored the ongoing civil conflict between the Soviet- and Cuban-backed government and the rebel Mozambique National Resistance.

It was during his stay in Mozambique that Fowler experienced a "funny in retrospect" incident, which was recounted in a column by Ron Hudspeth.

> We may have to outlaw jogging to save Wyche Fowler. We mentioned that Wyche was nabbed by a Palm Beach cop a couple of springs ago for jogging without a shirt in that stuffy little town of millionaires. Seems topless doesn't fly even if it is a U.S. congressman. Well, Wyche reports that was kid stuff compared to a recent jog in Maputo, the capital of the African country of Mozambique. Wyche arose one morning, "put on my Palm Beach jogging attire" (shorts and no shirt) and was off for a run down a deserted beach. Suddenly, from nowhere charged a half-dozen soldiers with Russian AK47s pointed directly at Wyche. They weren't smiling. "They were...about 15 years old," says Wyche. "I held up my hands and tried to say 'friend' or 'tourist.' It didn't help much. They only spoke Portuguese." The soldiers marched Wyche back to his hotel where he was released and discovered his sin—he had jogged within the security perimeter of the Presidential Palace.[62]

Pre-Legislative Forum (1985)

One of Fowler's biggest undertakings during the Ninety-Ninth Congress straddled the line between his role as a member of the US House and his campaign for the Senate. Between November 4 and November 14, 1985, he participated in the Georgia Chamber of Commerce's annual Pre-Legislative Forum. The forum, then in its thirty-second year, provided an opportunity for local business and community leaders to meet with representatives of the Georgia congressional delegation and the Georgia General Assembly to discuss pending public policy issues expected to be taken up during the following year's legislative sessions in Washington and Atlanta. The 1985 forum featured Speaker of the Georgia House of Representatives Thomas Murphy along with Fowler, and visited eighteen cities over the eleven days: Columbus, Americus, Bainbridge, Albany, Valdosta, Douglas, Waycross, Savannah, Macon, Atlanta, Elberton, Athens, Toccoa, Gainesville, Cartersville, Dalton, Rome, and Griffin.

With Fowler then in his ninth year in the US House, it was his turn to appear, but his all-but-announced candidacy for the Senate seat produced some uneasiness among event organizers, and they cautioned him to avoid overt politicking. Fowler was more than happy to oblige and prepared a series of detailed policy addresses covering a wide span of issues, including national defense, crime, terrorism, and tax reform, among other topics. Of course, the exposure to local leaders and, through media coverage, to voters all over the state was of great value to his campaign efforts, even without any direct political appeals.

One of Fowler's topics, addressed at several stops, was agriculture, a subject that he had seldom been called upon to address while representing the City of Atlanta and the Fifth District, but one that he felt was important for several reasons.

> My grandfather was a farmer in Warren County. I spent the weekends and summers of my childhood on his farm. He used to pay me a penny for every boll weevil I could pick off his cotton plants—and I never made more than ten cents at a time. I learned to preach and sing hymns without a hymnbook on visits to relatives around Wilkes County. And I learned then that farming is no easy life. My grandfather, like many Georgia farmers today, had to work two jobs to support his family. Those aren't the only reasons, though, that this city boy cares about farming in Georgia. The people I represent live in the city—but they depend heavily on our state's farm economy. The supply of food they eat, and the prices they pay, depend on a stable farm economy. Literally thousands of city jobs, in law firms and banks and other businesses, depend heavily upon Georgia agriculture and on the export of Georgia's farm products. If our state's farm economy suffers, Georgia cities feel the impact. People crowd into the cities—and the cities feel the pressure in unemployment, crowded housing and other problems.... And unfortunately,

> Georgia's rural economy, and Georgia's agriculture are not in the best of health right now.

He went on to endorse the recently passed Farm Credit Bill that "shores up the ailing Farm Credit System," call for stronger measures to protect fragile topsoil, support gradual reform of the federal subsidy programs for wheat and corn and continuation of the tobacco and peanut programs, and advocate the development of a national trade policy that "makes it costly for our overseas trade partners to unfairly subsidize their own products or to erect artificial trade barriers to keep out American farm exports."

In addition to all this, Fowler was committed to helping to heal the longtime divisions in Georgia between urban and rural areas and between Atlanta and the rest of the state. His service in the House may not have yielded a large record of accomplishment on behalf of agriculture and rural interests, but a great deal of his time and effort in the Senate would be devoted to those issues he articulated in the legislative forum speech.

In another of those speeches, Fowler returned to the theme of the role of government and political labels by invoking the memory of one of Georgia's most illustrious senators.

> Throughout his career, [Senator Richard Russell] helped advance the economy of Georgia—by supporting federal programs to help his relatively poor state: rural electrification; farm-to-market roads; Social Security; water and sewer projects; airport construction—dozens and dozens of programs which enabled a poor, rural state to share in the bounty of a rich nation. He realized that Georgia—and Georgia's people—couldn't go it alone....
>
> I am concerned that the attack on government in our country has become so intense and so strident that it endangers our capacity to act nationally in response to national problems. The attack upon government has virtually drowned out those noble words, "we, the people," and planted instead the notion that our government is somehow an alien, hostile force: "they, the government." As a result of this unrelenting—and often unthinking—attack, the very idea of government has been called into question. We are in danger of throwing out not only programs that don't work, but those that

> have proven their worth over the years. And our children, who have no first-hand memory of great moments of national cooperation like the New Deal and World War II, are in danger of concluding that the national government is at best incompetent and at worst illegitimate....
>
> Now, I admire President Reagan for many of his achievements. He has been an eloquent spokesman for our country. He has underscored the importance of a strong national defense.... But when it comes to the role of our national government in domestic affairs, the president's rhetoric bothers me because it seems to ignore and even discredit what the American people have achieved, and can achieve, together. Our national government opened up the West and built the railroads. It established the land-grant colleges and the farm extension program. Our national government has helped states like Georgia build roads and schools and hospitals and other vital facilities that would have been beyond the ability of a poor, rural state left to its own resources. Our national government has mounted successful national efforts to reduce poverty, support people in their old age and eradicate diseases like smallpox and measles.
>
> Time and again—especially here in the South—we, the people, have used our national government as an instrument of progress and enlightenment and economic growth. We have not always succeeded—but neither have we always failed.... We need to remember, before we discredit "they, the government," that in our system, the government in reality is "we, the people." And there are times when we, the people, need to act together in support of worthwhile national goals.

The issue of the role of government, and of what kind of representation Georgians and Americans needed in Congress, would be a key part in both of Fowler's Senate races, and, indeed, remains at the center of the national political debate in the twenty-first century.

Voting Record

The conflicting demands on Fowler's time and energies as representative and Senate candidate exacted a toll, and one that showed up most clearly in his voting record. The use of "voting participation"—percentage of total recorded votes in which an official voted—as a measure of legislative performance is problematic for a number of reasons. It counts all votes as equally important even though a significant proportion of those in both the House and Senate are on noncontroversial procedural or commemorative questions on which the vote is unanimous or nearly so. It ignores altogether the work in committee, where a majority of the legislative work is done (including hearings, drafting of legislation and committee reports, voting on amendments and reporting the bill out, etc.) However, its relative simplicity (a single percentage figure), apparent comprehensiveness (covering all votes, and not just a small selection), and objectivity (avoiding the biases inherent in vote ratings by interest groups) make it a sometimes useful tool for campaigns, especially in making the case that an incumbent was shirking his or her responsibilities by "not even showing up to vote."

For members of the House seeking to run statewide, the dilemma was clear: stay in Washington to vote and fail to adequately introduce oneself to all those voters who have little or no knowledge of the candidate, or campaign vigorously back home and get attacked for a poor attendance record. Fowler was far from the first to face such a choice, even within the Georgia delegation during the 1980s. In 1980, southwest Georgia congressman Dawson Mathis ran and lost in the Democratic primary for the Senate seat held by Herman Talmadge, and in the process participated in only 41 percent of the recorded votes in the US House. Two years later, coastal Georgia Congressman Bo Ginn ran in the Democratic primary for governor, eventually losing in a runoff to the ultimate victor, Joe Frank Harris. Representative Ginn voted 51 percent of the time that year. Note that in both of these cases, the House member was defeated in the primary, and thus did not have to campaign in the general election.

Coming in to 1986, Wyche Fowler had maintained a solid vote participation level that was never below 85 percent and was in keeping with average House voting rates throughout the period. Indeed, in the record-setting Ninety-Fifth Congress, in which a total of 706 recorded votes were held in the House in 1977, and an all-time high of 834 took place in 1978, Fowler exceeded the House average both years.

Faced with a multi-candidate field of opponents in the August Democratic primary and a well-funded incumbent in the November general election, Fowler—who had never run for office beyond the confines of Fulton and DeKalb Counties—made the choice to campaign back in Georgia as vigorously as possible while carrying out his Fifth District duties as best he could. And, as we have seen, even under these circumstances, he was able to leave his mark in fields as diverse as tax reform, foreign policy, and space policy. However, his voting participation rate in 1986 fell to just 36 percent, by far the lowest score in his entire congressional career (it was never below 96 percent while he was in the Senate). And this fact became one of the most effective attacks made upon him in the upcoming Senate race.

Chapter 9

1986 Senate Election: "Georgia's Man"

He was born and raised in Georgia
And her values made him strong.
He knows her small towns and family farms,
And he knows what's right and wrong.
Georgia taught him simple things, like family, work and faith,
And the spirit of her working folk that made this country great.
With a vision for the future and the wisdom of the past,
He works to keep us strong and free and build the dreams that last.
Wyche Fowler, raised on Georgia's land.
Wyche Fowler, he's Georgia's man.
—1986 Fowler campaign song

1980 Senate Race

By 1980, the growing clout of urban Georgia was increasingly a decisive factor in Georgia statewide elections even though memories of the rural-dominated past continued to exert a powerful influence on perceptions about the electability of urban, and especially Atlanta-based, candidates. In 1956, the five close-in metro Atlanta counties (Fulton, DeKalb, Cobb, Gwinnett, and Clayton) cast 23.4 percent of the total vote in the Democratic primary and 25.4 percent of the general election vote. By 1974, when Herman Talmadge was reelected to a fourth term, these proportions had grown to 26.8 percent of the primary and 36 percent of the general election totals.

Talmadge's Republican opponent in 1980 was Mack Mattingly, a forty-nine-year-old Indiana native who had first become familiar with Georgia while serving in the US Air Force in the early 1950s at Hunter Army Airfield near Savannah.

Though he trailed in most pre-election polls, was vastly outspent by the incumbent, and was running in one of the few states where he did not benefit from Ronald Reagan's huge national triumph over Jimmy Carter (with the Georgian president managing to carry his own state by a 56 percent to 41 percent margin), Mattingly managed to eke out a narrow 27,543 vote victory in the general election in one of the closest races in Georgia history up to that point.

Mack Mattingly (R)	803,686	50.87%
Herman Talmadge (D)	776,143	49.13%

Mattingly carried only twenty-nine of Georgia's 159 counties, but he took advantage of the increasing clout of the state's urban areas, especially metro Atlanta, which he won by just under 160,000 votes while losing in the rest of the state by more than 130,000 votes.

Another key factor in the 1980 Senate race was the disposition of African American voters toward Herman Talmadge. For most of the senator's career, this had been relatively straight-forward, with Talmadge's longtime opposition to civil rights measures and his association with staunch segregationists (including his father) producing mostly opposition from the Black community. By 1980, however, Talmadge had significantly increased his outreach efforts to Black voters, especially through use of his incumbency in providing constituent services to individuals and federal funding help to communities. In the 1980 primary, Zell Miller won the support of most Black leaders, and he beat Talmadge by approximately four-to-one among African American voters during the runoff. In the general election, with President Carter heading the ticket (and winning more than 90 percent of the African American vote), Talmadge won the overwhelming majority of Black voters, but in spite of his own limited campaign efforts directed toward them, these voters gave Mack Mattingly approximately 30 percent of their votes, providing a crucial part of his razor-thin majority.

Preparation for the 1986 Senate Race (1984–1985)

Though he had decided not to run for the Senate in 1980, Wyche Fowler continued to be interested in a future bid to represent Georgia in that body. He felt the Senate, with its smaller size and rules, which allowed its members to be involved in a wider range of issues than House members, was better suited to his own strengths and interests. In addition, he had never sought to be the "white hope" in the Fifth District and did not look forward to a revisitation of the race issue every two years for as long as he remained in the House. Finally, unlike many other officeholders, Fowler actually enjoyed the act of campaigning, and the notion of running as an underdog in the "largest state east of the Mississippi" was a challenge too tempting to pass up.

In mid-1984, Fowler directed his longtime aide Bill Johnstone to develop a detailed plan for a 1986 Senate race. That September, the first draft of that document was completed.

> A Wyche Fowler victory in the 1986 Democratic Primary and General Election for U.S. Senate, while not probable, is possible. A 1979 poll gave Fowler between 13 percent and 19 percent statewide support, an amount just short of the 20–25 percent vote likely to be needed to qualify for a position in the Run-off in a crowded Democratic Primary field. The major positive factors in a Fowler Senate candidacy include:
>
> - A strong, established base in the Atlanta media market, which reaches about 55 percent of the state's electorate (30 percent reside in the ten county Metro Atlanta area)
> - A significant potential for a hard-core, "first choice" constituency that would be most likely to vote in the August 1986 Primary (Fulton and DeKalb constituents, Blacks—who will make up about 25 percent of the electorate, liberals, community activists, etc.)
> - A candidate who is an effective campaigner both in the media and face-to-face (the latter being especially important in winning the support, or at least the neutrality, of political activists, campaign contributors, and media leaders)
> - The weaknesses of the likely Democratic primary opposition.
>
> The principal disadvantages for a Fowler candidacy are:
>
> - The historical bias against Atlanta candidates in statewide elections

- A probable shortage of funds, preventing the waging of a full-scale, statewide, paid media-intensive campaign
- A candidate with a liberal image (though outside of Metro Atlanta this perception is largely confined to elites, with the general public having little impression of the candidate)
- A strategy that is "self-sufficient" in reaching the Democratic Runoff, but that requires external factors to achieve victories in the Runoff and General Election (underdog status and an anti-opponent vote in the Runoff, and an anti-Republican mood in the General).

The plan went on to set out strategy. For the primary, "maximizing the Fowler vote in Metro Atlanta—largely through expanding the direct voter contact methods of the Fifth District campaigns to cover the whole Metro area, mobilizing the support of key groups outside of Metro Atlanta—Blacks, liberals, etc., and avoiding building up high negatives with non-supporters—to improve chances of winning their support in the Runoff and general elections" would be emphasized. In the General Election, the approach would be "adjusted to place greater emphasis on the traditionally Democratic non-urban areas...[and] a certain amount of negative campaigning by attacks on the incumbent's record...will be employed." Tactics were also outlined, with the headquarters' metro Atlanta phone bank termed the "centerpiece of the campaign organization" and fundraising objectives were set, with a goal of raising an additional $1 million between September 1984 and July 1, 1986.

With regard to campaign themes, it stated that

> the most important message to be conveyed is that the candidate is safe, responsible, and effective (that "he does not have horns"). The campaign cannot afford to go on the defensive about the Liberal record, because such an effort would convey a sense of weakness, would lack credibility with important opinion leaders around the state, and might weaken the commitment of key hard-core support groups. To combat the Liberal problem, the candidate must try to set the terms of debate, placing himself in the mainstream of Georgia's progressive tradition, pointing to Georgia's unmet needs (education, health, jobs, etc.), and emphasizing moderate, responsible

positions on the economy, the deficit, arms control, and similar issues.

A major factor underlying Fowler's interest in the 1986 Senate race was his strong belief that Mattingly was beatable based on the narrowness of his 1980 victory and the fact that it required him to win a third of Black voters and 70 percent of the votes cast by metro Atlanta's white constituents. Fowler believed he could run well ahead of Talmadge among both of these groups. In its May 25, 1985, edition, the respected *National Journal* ranked Mattingly as the most vulnerable of all senators up for reelection in the following year.

Throughout 1985, Fowler was an undeclared Senate candidate while he continued to represent the Fifth District in the US House, voting on 86 percent of all recorded votes. In January, the campaign conducted another statewide poll, this one of likely Democratic primary voters. In a hypothetical race with several other potential candidates, Fowler led with 27.3 percent, followed by state attorney general Michael Bowers (17 percent), Fourth District Congressman Elliott Levitas (9.9 percent), and former aide to President Carter Jack Watson (9.2 percent), with 31 percent undecided. (None tested in this survey, except for Fowler, ultimately ran.)

In addition to the November Pre-Legislative Forum tour of nineteen Georgia cities, other important campaign-related occurrences during the year included the hiring of pollster Cooper Secrest & Associates in March and media consultant Greer & Associates in August, and the development of a detailed budget for the primary. That budget, which was overseen by longtime campaign comptroller Harriett Muldawer, established the following objectives for campaign spending between January 1, 1985, and the primary in August 1986:

Mass media (including media buys and production)	$740,025
Direct voter contact (including phone banks and direct mail)	$281,145
Campaign organization (including HQ and staff)	$223,965
Fundraising	$136,725
Research (including polling and opposition research)	$77,695
Candidate travel	$39,205
Special events (mainly campaign kickoff)	$30,510
Other	$40,830
TOTAL	$1,570,100

In 1985, fundraising activities and the shaping of the Democratic primary field of candidates emerged as two of the most important developments for the Fowler campaign. With respect to the former, the campaign ended 1984 with $354,297 cash-on-hand and was able to raise an additional $591,582 in 1985, leaving approximately $625,000 to be raised in the first half of 1986 in order to meet the projected budget. While well behind Mattingly's resources, these amounts placed Fowler far ahead of his emerging primary opposition.

In late September 1985, Cooper Secrest & Associates (CSA, headed by Alan Secrest) conducted its first poll for the Fowler campaign, which focused on the general election. Mattingly held a 55 percent to 30 percent lead, which was not particularly alarming to the Fowler camp at this early stage. More importantly, Fowler was already in possession of decent name recognition (63 percent statewide) and was receiving a generally positive reception among those who did know him, with a personal appeal of 58 percent positive, 26 percent neutral, 16 percent negative. As expected, he fared best in metro Atlanta (68 percent positive, 16 percent negative) and among African Americans (77 percent positive, 11 percent negative). However, at this point, he trailed well behind the incumbent in the metro area (Mattingly 50 percent, Fowler 39 percent, undecided 11 percent) and Mattingly was still holding on to a third of the African American vote (Fowler 57 percent, Mattingly 33 percent, undecided 10 percent).

In 1985, it appeared that Fowler's most formidable likely primary opponent would be Atlanta attorney Dave Garrett. Given the fact that he had never previously run for office before, this perception was fueled almost entirely by Garrett's early fundraising success, in which he raised more than $300,000 while spending approximately $175,000 during 1985, ending the year with a cash balance of more than $140,000.

A profile of Fowler as he prepared to enter the Senate race appeared in the September 5, 1985, *Atlanta Constitution*:

> A moderate centrist—by conviction and voting record—Fowler has represented the state's most liberal congressional district for eight years, but he's thinking seriously of running for the Democratic nomination to challenge Republican U.S. Sen. Mack Mattingly next year. If he enters the race, he'll be an underdog....

Today, Fowler leads a "relatively modest" dual life, divided between Washington and Atlanta. In Washington, he rises at 5 or 6 A.M., reads the newspapers, breakfasts on coffee and fruit and then walks the five minutes from his Capitol Hill home to the Rayburn Office Building, usually to swim for a while before settling into work. Generally, he's returning phone calls by 7:30 A.M. and works straight through, with a break for a hot dog at lunch, until 9 or 10 P.M. He enjoys "an occasional medicinal drink" of King George IV Scotch, and he tries to go to bed early.... On vacations, he enjoys the great outdoors. "I'm not political like some people who have to live it and breathe it," he says. "I like to get away from it. Fishing and hiking are my second loves to baseball. My hiking and fishing are not just sports but that is a way of stepping back...." In his spare time at home, Fowler reads and occasionally sees a movie. "I just have to have a mental wash of fiction. I have to have somebody telling me a story and get away from all the realms of facts." He likes potboilers by Robert Parker, the poetry of William Butler Yeats, the novels of his favorite author, Sir Anthony Trollope. Most weekends, the congressman flies—tourist class—to Atlanta and visits with friends, constituents and his parents, at whose home he stays, though he owns a house in Virginia-Highland. In his travels around the Fifth District, he drives a 1970 Oldsmobile Cutlass, well broken in with 150,000 miles but a symbol of modernity compared to the '66 Buick Riviera he drives in Washington. In addition to attending Braves games, he catches three or four Falcons football games a year and likes to stop by Manuel's Tavern or the White Dot. He's occasionally seen jogging around the park near Peachtree Battle and Northside Drive. Sunday mornings, he goes to church: a few times a year to his own, Central Presbyterian, more often to the churches of his constituents. "I love to go to church with all its forms of worship," he says. He's comfortable meeting constituents there, too.[63]

An updated version of the Fowler campaign plan, dating from January 1986, summarized the previous year's major developments.

Thus far, the preliminary phase of the Wyche Fowler Senate Campaign has been successful. There is more reason to be optimistic about its chances for success now than there was at the beginning of 1985. All of the strongest potential opponents in the Democratic Primary have taken themselves out of the race. Several public opinion surveys have verified that Mattingly is vulnerable, and that Fowler starts out with a relatively strong base in Metro Atlanta. The campaign's low-profile strategy has been successful in avoiding attacks from the media and other candidates, and in keeping down Fowler's "negatives" with the general public. The fund-raising effort has gotten off to a promising start. The campaign plan is proceeding on schedule. On the other hand, the expected strength of the Mattingly fundraising effort has indeed materialized and Garrett has raised a considerable sum in 1985 (though Garrett's funds were mostly obtained from core supporters in Georgia, while the Fowler campaign has yet to tap its core group). Also, much remains to be done in meeting the overall fund-raising goal ($4.25 million by November) and in broadening the candidate's support base outside of Fulton County. The one major development during 1985 was that a larger and stronger field for the Democratic Primary failed to materialize. Thus, the Fowler campaign will have to continually assess the possibility for a first ballot victory in the Primary, though the entrance of Hamilton Jordan would appear to substantially reduce the chances for this.

1986 Democratic Senate Primary

CSA administered a detailed survey of Democratic primary voters in January 1986. It found Jordan had the highest name recognition, but Fowler held the most personal appeal among the potential field of Senate candidates, including, in addition to Fowler, Garrett, and Jordan, state Rep. John Russell of Winder, who was a nephew of the late Sen. Richard B. Russell.

	Name ID	Positive	Neutral	Negative
Wyche Fowler	61 percent	63 percent	24 percent	13 percent
David Garrett	18 percent	28 percent	57 percent	15 percent
Hamilton Jordan	77 percent	50 percent	32 percent	18 percent
John Russell	30 percent	42 percent	48 percent	10 percent

This translated into a small lead for Fowler in the trial heat, leaving him well short of the 50 percent required to avoid a runoff.

Fowler	32 percent
Jordan	27 percent
Russell	12 percent
Garrett	3 percent
Undecided	26 percent

On February 3, 1986, Wyche Fowler formally announced his candidacy for the US Senate at a 6 P.M. event attended by about two hundred supporters, in the studios of Atlanta TV station WPBA. The announcement was carried live by several television stations around the state.

> It is with a great sense of pride in our state and its potential, and with a deep sense of my duty and obligation to my fellow Georgians, that I declare my candidacy for the United States Senate. We have come to expect a lot from those we send to represent Georgia in the most important legislative body in the world. I believe Georgians want a Senator who will stand up for family farmers and small businessmen, who will be a voice for average working people, who will fight against unfair foreign trade that steals our jobs, and who will work to bring economic prosperity to small towns as well as big cities. I will be that kind of Senator for Georgia. For the past nine years, it has been my privilege to represent the people of Georgia in the United States Congress. I have listened, I have learned, and I know how to get things done for Georgia. Coupled with my years of experience in local government, I am prepared to offer the kind of progressive, effective leadership we need to build this great state.

Atlanta Journal and Constitution columnist Frederick Allen observed the announcement and the follow-up interviews Fowler gave shortly thereafter.

> Wyche Fowler spent Monday afternoon in the windowless confines of Studio B at WPBA, the Atlanta public television station, grinding out interviews one after the other by satellite with anchormen at various TV stations around the state. The Atlanta congressman was making his announcement of formal candidacy for the U.S. Senate. But instead of following the usual, time-wasting practice of flying around by private plane to Georgia's seven major media markets for seven airport press conferences in the same day, Fowler was letting the Westar 5 satellite do the work for him. It was in the midst of this high-tech display that Fowler complained, "I'm a flatbed truck man, myself." Fowler went on to explain that he would be happier conducting an old-fashioned campaign, driving from town to town, setting up on the back of a flatbed truck, working a crowd revival-style, using the unadorned power of oratory to hold the voters' attention. And he has a point. Fowler is handicapped in the era of the 30-second TV spot. It isn't just that the incumbent, Sen. Mack Mattingly, can outspend him, nor is it just that Fowler's message takes a good deal of time to impart. It is that Fowler is an old-fashioned politician. He is a storyteller. He is, in the best sense of the term, a character. He needs time to perform his magic, and he needs a bigger platform than a 19-inch diagonal screen. As he worked through his interviews Monday afternoon, Fowler showed that he knows the tricks of the TV trade: the right makeup, responses in 30-second "bites," voice soft and conversational, good side to the camera. But the restraint was practically killing him. Between interviews, Fowler's personality burst out. At one point, a TV reporter from Macon kept ruining her "cut-aways"—shots taken after the actual interview, in which the interviewer pretends to be listening soberly and nodding intelligently—because Fowler was breaking her up with a story: He had been booked on "Face the Nation" and was in the studio trying to compose himself for a serious foreign policy discussion when, 10 seconds before air time,

a woman came rushing at him with a makeup brush yelling, "Your hands are the wrong color!"[64]

After the announcement, the candidate embarked on a four-day tour of the state's other television media markets in Augusta, Savannah, Macon, Albany, and Columbus. Then, starting on February 17, his campaign ran two weeks of TV spots (the first Fowler had ever employed), produced by Greer & Associates, in those same markets, but excluding the very expensive Atlanta market. These spots were introductory in nature and designed to boost his name recognition in central and southern Georgia while stressing his Georgia roots and values. The first was a two-minute ad featuring the campaign theme song and visuals of Fowler in a variety of Georgia settings. (This spot later earned Greer an award from the American Association of Political Consultants for the best sixty-seconds or longer spot during the '86 campaign.) The second, at the more traditional thirty-second length, dealt with the correct pronunciation of his unusual first name—Wyche: "ch" like in church—while employing a number of value-laden visual symbols (a classroom of children saying the Pledge of Allegiance to an American flag). Fowler explained that the thirty-second ad "was totally my idea. Nobody is going to lean over their neighbor's fence and say 'I'm for Wyche' unless they know how to say Wyche. It's an unusual name, and I don't want people to be uncomfortable pronouncing it."

In late June, Dave Garrett withdrew from the Senate contest citing fundraising problems and lagging poll numbers. On the latter point, a WAGA-TV poll released just days before Garrett's withdrawal showed him with only 1 percent of the vote compared to 25 percent for Fowler and 24 percent for Hamilton Jordan.

As the primary campaign got underway in earnest, three other candidates filed to face Fowler in the August 12 Democratic primary: Jordan, Representative Russell, and Jerry Belsky, a fringe candidate associated with the controversial Lyndon LaRouche. Of the three, it was clear from polling and other indicators that Jordan would be the most formidable.

William Hamilton McWhorter Jordan had won national acclaim as the campaign manager—at age twenty-six—of Jimmy Carter's successful run for governor in 1970 and then again as a key advisor in Carter's winning 1976 presidential bid. But the most important factor for him leading up to the 1986 Senate bid was his successful battle in overcoming non-Hodgkin lymphoma. Jordan predicated his candidacy on the widespread belief that Fowler, thanks to his relatively liberal record and Atlanta base, would stand little chance in November against the incumbent Mattingly, and he sought to position himself as the conservative, "down-state" alternative. Among his tactics, Jordan's campaign produced "Sam and Ham" campaign buttons and bumper stickers seeking to link him to the extremely popular Senator Nunn (who remained scrupulously neutral, however, throughout the primary).

The phone bank operation was key to the Fowler Senate effort's direct voter identification, persuasion, and turnout operations, as it had been during his House campaigns. In addition to the sixteen lines at campaign headquarters in Atlanta, which began operation on April 21 and continued all the way through General Election Day in November under the direction of volunteer coordinator Fran Weiss, additional phone banks operated in Bibb, Chatham, Clarke, Cobb, Dougherty, Douglas, Gwinnett, Hall, Houston, Lowndes, Muscogee, Richmond, Rockdale, and Whitfield Counties for at least part of the primary campaign. Once again, it was the volunteers themselves who made this key campaign instrument so successful. What differentiated the Senate effort was that this time, these volunteers were drawn from all over the state rather than solely from his longtime support base in Atlanta.

Budgetary considerations, including provision for a possible runoff as well as the general election, led to a campaign decision to not resume paid mass media advertising until July, with a small cable TV buy starting on July 9, and buys in the non-Atlanta TV markets starting the following week and continuing up to Election Day. The Atlanta TV buy did not begin until the week of July 23 and ran only during the final three weeks prior to August 12. Radio advertising commenced during the week of July 16, continuing right up to the election. The radio buys were concentrated on stations reaching mostly African American listeners as well as residents of areas that were largely outside the reach of Georgia-based television markets, such as extreme northwest Georgia.

The July ads, all thirty seconds in length, included one focused on defense issues and Fowler's service in the military plus two testimonials in which Georgians from various walks of life praised Fowler's efforts in Congress and on their behalf. Fowler ran no negative spots during the primary. Jordan ran ads in this period accusing Fowler of being "out of step" with the state, and the rest of its congressional delegation, in voting against the MX, the anti-satellite missile program, and aid to the contras while voting for the nuclear weapons freeze.

Over the course of the primary, a number of candidate forums or debates were held, beginning in April 1986 and continuing until shortly before the August 12 election date. After one of the first such encounters, Frederick Allen wrote,

> In the first full-dress, on-your-toes, big-city debate of the Senate race, Wyche Fowler proved what everybody already should have known. He's a gifted politician. In Atlanta Monday morning before an audience of hundreds of county officials, the 5th District congressman easily outpaced two other Democratic hopefuls, Hamilton Jordan and John Russell, and served notice on the absent incumbent, Republican Sen. Mack Mattingly, that one does not lightly undertake to exchange public badinage with a man who has spent the past two decades campaigning.... Once the opening statements were through, and a panel of reporters began needling the candidates with questions, Fowler displayed his talents. At one level, he merely flashed his famous wit. When Jerry Belsky, a Lyndon LaRouche candidate, attacked one of Fowler's answers, the Congressman simply smiled and said, "I could not be more flattered," and while this may not seem worthy of Oscar Wilde when reduced to cold print, its delivery earned Fowler a big laughter and round of applause.... But it was on substance that Fowler carried the day. He was particularly effective in deflecting the inevitable suggestions that he is too liberal, and, unlike the others, who could do no better than to echo him, Fowler came up with specifics in describing federal budget cuts. He earned the biggest applause of the morning by arguing forcefully against foreign aid for "tinhorn dictators."[65]

The last major candidate forum was an August 3 debate in Atlanta sponsored by the League of Women voters and televised by WSB-TV and various public broadcasting stations around the state. The candidates were quizzed on a wide variety of subjects, including abortion (Fowler was the only one to voice a pro-choice view), farm foreclosures, economic sanctions, relations with Cuba, revenue sharing, Social Security, and daycare. (One of the most remarkable developments during the debate was Belsky's claim that the Queen of England was involved in the international drug trade.) In their closing statements, Jordan indicated that the United States was at a crossroads and needed to make some hard decisions in order to reduce the deficit. Fowler highlighted his sixteen years of experience in local and national government and called on voters to take a close look at his total record on behalf of average Georgians in such areas as Social Security, tax relief, and education. Russell emphasized that, unlike the others, his campaign was financed solely by Georgians, and he had the strongest Georgia record.

All told, the Fowler campaign spent $1.379 million for the primary, $521,665 of which went for media buys, and raised an additional $718,500 from January through July of 1986. A crucial decision for the Fowler team was determining how much to expend to maximize the chances of winning an outright majority—thereby avoiding an expensive and potentially damaging runoff with Jordan—while reserving as large an amount as possible to be able to respond to the Mattingly campaign attacks that were sure to follow as soon as the Democratic nominee was chosen. In addition, the campaign was bound by its candidate's absolute injunction against incurring any campaign debt, so the prospect of borrowing to meet urgent campaign requirements was never an option. In the end, the Fowler campaign ended the primary with a surplus of $343,656, which was very close to the $354,297 it began with back in January 1985. The voters themselves would determine whether these spending decisions were prudent.

In the closing stages of the primary, Fowler picked up an impressive array of newspaper endorsements from across the state, including papers in Americus, Atlanta, Augusta, Dalton, Gainesville, Macon, Madison, Moultrie, Rome, Sandersville, Thomaston, Valdosta, Waycross, and Wrightsville, most of which highlighted his accomplishments in the US House.

> Fowler, as representative of a majority-Black district in Atlanta, has voted the views of his constituents on many issues. But he is basically a centrist. He has taken thoughtful positions on all issues and

his voting record is far more congenial with that of Sen. Nunn than Jordan has sought to portray it. Fowler has sought to represent all of Georgia in Congress as well as his district. Not only in votes and committee work, but in constituent services, he has served citizens throughout the state. We believe he would be capable of forming a strong partnership in the Senate with Nunn. That would give Georgia the kind of representation the state had when Sen. Walter F. George and Russell in the Senate and Rep. Carl Vinson in the House were national leaders.

—*Macon Telegraph and News*[66]

There's a clear front runner out there [in the Democratic senatorial primary] when one considers all the relevant factors. His name is Wyche Fowler, a sharpened public servant who responds directly to questions and who is not afraid to admit it if he doesn't know the answer.... The folks of south Georgia should be careful not to put any marks against Fowler simply because he's from metro Atlanta. While there are indeed two Georgias, that does not mean that a non-south Georgian, or more specifically, an Atlantan, would be less representative to those of us below the gnat line. Fowler recognizes the two-Georgia problem and exudes a genuine interest in that regard.

—*The Moultrie Observer*[67]

By virtue of [his] experience, Fowler is the one equipped best to hit the ground running.... The fact Fowler has ably represented an urban, heavily Black district and served previously on the Atlanta City Council does not mean he cannot serve just as ably the entire Georgia constituency, with all its diversities. The truth is Fowler is a highly-skilled politician—and that quality is essential in a good senator. He has shown he knows how to discern the needs and wishes of his constituents and to express those effectively in a legislative forum—and get results. There is no doubt he could do that for all of Georgia.... Wyche Fowler is one of the shrewdest and accomplished political campaigners ever to come along in Georgia.

—*Rome News-Tribune*[68]

> Fowler has not attempted to conceal or blur his record to win broad support. Rather, he has properly emphasized the portions of his record that have not gained widespread notice outside his metropolitan district. As an exceptionally bright and thoughtful representative, he earned prestigious committee assignments that gave him a front-row perspective on pressing national issues. As a member of the powerful House Ways and Means Committee, Fowler helped to shape the crucial tax-reform legislation. He has also served on the prestigious Select Committee on Intelligence and the International Affairs Committee. His voting record on domestic and foreign policy speaks for his impressive command of the issues. Even with the duties of important committee work, Fowler didn't neglect the 5th Congressional District or the state of Georgia. He reminds rural voters of his votes in favor of aid to depressed farmers and the sagging agriculture industry. Further, he has an excellent record of delivering constituent services.
>
> —*The Atlanta Constitution*[69]

Polling done over the course of the primary for Atlanta TV station WAGA showed a close race between Fowler and Jordan, with Fowler opening up a significant lead only in the latter stages, though a large portion of the electorate remained undecided.

	Mid-June	Late July	August 9–10
Fowler	25 percent	34 percent	38 percent
Jordan	24 percent	30 percent	23 percent
Russell	5 percent	7 percent	7 percent
Belsky	1 percent	0 percent	1 percent
Undecided	44 percent	29 percent	31 percent

The pollster stated that the August numbers indicated a "slim" possibility of an outright Fowler victory, but it was more likely that a runoff would be necessary to determine the Democratic nominee.

On Tuesday, August 12, 1986, Georgia voters went to the polls to vote in the Democratic and Republican primaries. A total of 626,340 ballots were cast in the Democratic senatorial primary, representing a turnout of 24.7 percent of the state's 2,531,554 registered voters. Wyche Fowler ran well ahead of the field, leading second-place finisher Jordan by 118,430 votes, but managing to avoid a runoff by only 1,568 votes, the amount by which his total exceeded 50 percent of the vote.

Wyche Fowler	314,737	50.26 percent
Hamilton Jordan	196,307	31.34 percent
John D. Russell	100,881	16.11 percent
Jerry Belsky	14,365	2.29 percent

Fowler carried seventy-five of the 159 counties but built his majority by a dominant showing in metro Atlanta, where he obtained more than 50 percent in each of the region's eleven counties, including

- 81.4 percent in Fulton County (Atlanta), the state's most vote-rich county
- 72.9 percent in DeKalb County (Decatur), the second largest
- 58.9 percent in Cobb County (Marietta), third largest
- 51 percent in Gwinnett County (Lawrenceville), fourth largest
- 60 percent in Clayton County (Jonesboro), ninth largest

Fowler also fared well in the remainder of the Atlanta media market (the zone in which viewers predominantly watch Atlanta television stations) throughout north and central Georgia, finishing first in 35 of these 39 counties. (The entire Atlanta TV market, including metro Atlanta, accounted for about half of the overall primary vote.)

The Atlantan also led the way in five of the state's nine other largest counties, including

- Bibb County (Macon), where he beat Jordan 49.5 percent to 36.5 percent
- Chatham County (Savannah), where he beat Jordan 46.1 percent to 38.2 percent
- Clarke County (Athens), where he received 50.1 percent of the vote to 23.7 percent for both Russell and Jordan
- Glynn County (Brunswick), where he beat Jordan 40.3 percent to 35.7 percent

- Whitfield County (Dalton), where he narrowly edged Jordan 36.8 percent to 36.7 percent

On the other hand, Jordan carried Dougherty (Albany: 52.7 percent to Fowler's 35.3 percent), Houston (Perry: 43.3 percent to Fowler's 36.3 percent), Muscogee (Columbus: 49.2 percent to Fowler's 44.1 percent), and Richmond (Augusta: 50 percent to Fowler's 38.5 percent) counties.

Avoiding a runoff, which would have been held on September 2, proved crucial to the Fowler effort in saving time and money for the general election against Mattingly, but also in burnishing Fowler's reputation and positive recognition throughout the state. A Fowler campaign release entitled "1986 Georgia Senate Race: Why Wyche Will Win," produced just after the primary and distributed to certain opinion-makers and potential contributors, summarized the Fowler team's take on the impact of the primary.

> Wyche Fowler did what he needed to do in the Primary to position himself for a win in November. He made a strong showing in metro Atlanta and in the Atlanta media market, which are by far the largest voting bloc in Georgia, and were the key to the Mattingly win in 1980. He established a good electoral base upon which to build in the traditionally Democratic other areas of the state. He came through the Primary with low negatives [in his personal appeal measured in polling], and with some money in the bank.

1986 Senate General Election Campaign

At the start of the election cycle, Mack Mattingly had been regarded as an extremely vulnerable incumbent, and polling results from the beginning of 1986 indicated that a third of the electorate still knew little or nothing about him. However, developments in 1985 and the first half of 1986 had strengthened his position. First of all, the incumbent senator had easily outdistanced Fowler with respect to fundraising, obtaining $1.74 million in campaign contributions during 1985 compared with Fowler's total of just over $590,000, and he would continue that funding dominance throughout the election cycle. Second, whereas his Democratic opponents engaged in a hotly contested primary that drained resources and effort away from the general election, Mattingly faced only token opposition in the Republican primary, which he ultimately won with more than 95 percent of the 74,743 votes cast. And most pundits continued to believe that Mattingly's solidly conservative voting record in the Senate would stand him in good stead with the Georgia electorate.

Mattingly's fundraising success, combined with continuing indications of limited voter awareness, led his campaign to begin airing TV spots throughout the state beginning in late January 1986 that continued with few interruptions for the duration of the election. The early spots were exclusively positive, featuring biographical material on the senator as well as his endorsement by President Reagan, his work for individual Georgians and Georgia communities, and his legislative efforts, including sponsorship of the line-item veto proposal. However, just fourteen hours after the Democratic primary was decided, the Mattingly campaign began airing a series of attacks on Fowler's record.

Fowler lacked the money to effectively counter the Mattingly attacks via his own paid advertising, with modest TV buys and minimal radio purchases until the final two weeks of the campaign. In contrast, the Mattingly buy was about double the Fowler level throughout this period. In any case, the Fowler campaign plan had always called for heavy concentration of his TV and radio buys in the final weeks of the election.

The earliest of the Fowler general election ads unveiled his legislative proposal to place a cap on credit card rates: "I think you're paying too much interest on bank credit cards. Why should you have to pay 18 percent when we've gotten most interest rates down to about 10 percent?... We need a Senator who will stand up to the big international banks. That's exactly what you'll get when you elect me your next Senator. And you can bank on it."

In addition to fundraising activities, Fowler spent much of September and early October consolidating his support from Georgia Democrats outside of the metro Atlanta area. To start, he received a telegram of support from all of his fellow Democratic members of the congressional House delegation the day after the primary, and, crucially, he also won the backing of popular US Senator Sam Nunn, which culminated in the senator cutting a television ad in mid-September expressing his endorsement. In the spot, Nunn praised Fowler for his "unprecedented interest in the rural problems of our state," and concluded, "I've known Wyche for 10 years. I've worked with him. He's an outstanding Congressman. He will be an outstanding Senator." At the state level, both House Speaker Tom Murphy and Agriculture Commissioner Tommy Irvin pledged their support, and both helped add many members of their own organizational networks around the state, but especially in rural Georgia, to aid the Fowler cause.

An important element in this outreach was Fowler's "stirring, podium-pounding, Bible-quoting" address to the state Democratic Party Convention at the Atlanta Civic Center on September 27 in which he urged Georgians to hold Mattingly and other Republican officials accountable for "trumpets that blare with an uncertain sound."[70]

But despite these positive developments, Fowler suffered under the onslaught of the Mattingly paid-advertising attacks. The first criticized the Atlantan's vote against a balanced budget amendment and cited the fact that he "was voted one of the biggest spenders in Congress by the National Taxpayers Union." Another, aired later in the campaign, hit Fowler for traveling on taxpayer-funded congressional "junkets" to thirty-eight different countries during his time in the House. A fact-check on campaign advertising prepared by newspaper reporters noted that "viewers weren't told that Fowler made most of the trips in his capacity as chairman of a House Select Committee on Intelligence subcommittee that oversees Central Intelligence Agency operations. They also weren't told that a Fowler trip to the Caribbean was made at the request of the Reagan administration. And Mattingly himself has gone to eight foreign countries at taxpayer expense in his six-year term."[71] (The Caribbean trip referenced here was in Fowler's capacity as a member of the Ways and Means Committee supporting the Reagan Caribbean Basin Initiative on trade, and not in connection with intelligence operations in Central America, where the president and congressman held sharply different views.)

And, starting in mid-September, the Mattingly team began airing spots criticizing Fowler for missing votes under the general theme of "Fowler: Absent for Georgia." These ads claimed that in 1986, Fowler missed more votes than any member of Congress, with one suggesting that he should repay the government two years' worth of his salary for missing two years' worth of votes. A post-election article in the *Atlanta Journal* summarized the impact: "For at least 6 weeks, the ads kept the

Fowler campaign on the mat both by making voters wary of the Democrat, and by blunting his [Fowler's] attacks on Mattingly's alleged ineffectiveness."[72]

The Fowler campaign attempted to respond via a press release on his full attendance record. The fact that this response was confined to this rather limited method, rather than appearing in an ad, for instance, demonstrated the campaign's belief that, based on polling and other indications, it lacked an effective reply. Although the response did not prove overly successful in blunting the attendance attack, the same document went on to suggest the Fowler team's counterattack strategy helped turn the contest around.

> The issue is not attendance, but effectiveness. Wyche Fowler has been a far more effective representative for Georgia than Mack Mattingly, whether the issue is tax reform, education, Social Security, policies affecting children and families, agriculture, environmental protection, or fiscal responsibility.... The issue that <u>should</u> be raised is Senator Mattingly's attendance in Georgia. For six years, he has preferred Washington's swank Georgetown area to Georgia. This year, when Georgia voters get their only chance for six years to examine those seeking to serve in the U.S. Senate, Mattingly is hiding from Georgians. He has already refused over 15 debates and public forums with Representative Fowler.... <u>Mack Mattingly was absent from Georgia</u>.

However, the benefits from this strategy did not materialize until very late in the campaign, and the Cooper Secrest polls for the Fowler campaign tracked the damage inflicted by the Mattingly ads on Fowler's standing with voters along with the incumbent's continuing large lead in the race.

August 15, 1986, Campaign Poll:
Fowler Personal Appeal: 52 percent positive, 20 percent neutral, 28 percent negative; 78 percent recognition
Senate Race: Mattingly 54 percent; Fowler 29 percent; 17 percent Undecided

September 15, 1986, Campaign Poll:
Fowler Personal Appeal: 43 percent positive, 23 percent neutral, 34 percent negative; 82 percent recognition
Senate Race: Mattingly 49 percent; Fowler 34 percent; 17 percent Undecided

October 16, 1986, Campaign Poll:
Fowler Personal Appeal: 38 percent positive, 26 percent neutral, 36 percent negative; 88 percent recognition
Senate Race: Mattingly 55 percent; Fowler 31 percent; 14 percent Undecided

These findings were also reflected in various media assessments offered at the time. As recounted in the 1989 book *Candidates, Parties, and Campaigns*,

> Through mid-October the challenger languished in the polls, consistently about sixteen to eighteen points behind Mattingly. The local media agreed with the assessment in the *New York Times* on September 30 that Fowler had "little chance to win unless he can somehow get off the defensive." On October 13 the *Atlanta Constitution* observed, "The Republicans have controlled the dialogue...giving a classic example of their highly developed skills in re-electing shaky incumbents." The "smart money" in Washington also appeared to agree with the gleeful assessment of Reagan-Bush consultant Lee Atwater, "I don't think Senator Mattingly could have had a better opponent from political central casting." By early October the Democratic Senate Campaign Committee, which had "maxed out" for challenger John Breaux in Louisiana and had contributed 62 percent of the maximum to Alabama challenger Richard Shelby, had given only $175,000 (44 percent of the maximum) to Georgia's Fowler. Mattingly, by this time, had received virtually his full allotment from the Republican Senate Campaign Committee.[73]

Fowler's general election ads were mostly either personality-centered spots featuring the candidate talking directly to the camera (and voters)—

and providing a clear contrast to Mattingly, who was rarely seen speaking on the campaign trail in the state or in his own ads—or response ads that aimed at refuting the incumbent's attacks while launching counterattacks on Mattingly's own voting record. Examples of the former included a television ad featuring Fowler appearing with a mule—Fowler: "Some folks might call this a horse. But the folks in Georgia know a mule when they see one. That's why you got to be careful when folks that don't know what they're talking about make political charges"—and another in which he held a puppy while sitting next to his mother—Fowler: "If even a tenth of the things Mack Mattingly's been saying about me were true, my mother wouldn't let me come home for Sunday dinner. I might not be perfect, but in this race, I'm definitely the pick of the litter." At this point, the puppy licked Fowler's face.

Two of the most important response ads were titled "Social Security" and "Effectiveness."

Social Security

Announcer: You may have seen this ad:
Mattingly ad: "...to protect their Social Security benefits. That's why I voted <u>every</u> time to strengthen our Social Security system."
Announcer: That's simply not true. According to the official *Congressional Record*, Mattingly has voted thirteen times against Social Security, against senior citizens. And now he's not telling the truth. Instead of debating the issues, Mack Mattingly is hiding behind false advertising. But we aren't going to be fooled. We can elect a senator we can trust to fight for us: Wyche Fowler.

Effectiveness

Announcer: Contrary to Mattingly's distorted ads, Wyche Fowler has an attendance record of almost 90 percent. But the real issue is effectiveness. The *Atlanta Constitution* said, "Wyche Fowler has proven himself to be an extraordinarily effective legislator." And he votes with Sam Nunn, for us. Mack Mattingly's voting—voting against Social Security 13 times, voting to cut farm programs, voting against education, voting to allow big profitable corporations to pay no taxes. Let's elect a Senator we can trust to fight for us: Wyche Fowler.

Polling and focus groups conducted by Cooper Secrest for the Fowler campaign found these spots to be quite effective in boosting support for the candidate, but at the modest levels the campaign was able to buy in September and early October, they had little impact in cutting into the sizeable Mattingly advantage. However, during the week of October 15, the Fowler TV buy almost doubled over previous levels, and the next week more than doubled again. The Fowler radio buy, which had been minimal in the general election up until that point, also rose dramatically from October 22 on.

Part of the late radio buy was the "Listening to Georgians" call-in show patterned after a similar effort undertaken by Joe Frank Harris in his successful 1982 gubernatorial campaign. Starting on Monday, October 27, and running each weekday until Election Day, the program featured Fowler, as host, joined by campaign press secretary Chuck Searcy, responding to phoned-in questions from listeners and interviewing guests that included Senator Nunn, Speaker Murphy, Lt. Gov. Zell Miller, Congressmen Claude Pepper (D-FL) and Charles Hatcher (D-GA), and Thomson Mayor Bob Knox. The show provided a discussion of issues that included Social Security, veterans affairs, tax reform, farm policy, the budget, and national defense but also included "a lively Fowleresque mix of jokes, songs, and tales from the campaign trail." The show originated from a different campaign stop each day, including Atlanta, Bremen, Augusta, Thomson, and Tifton, and was ultimately carried on nearly one hundred radio stations throughout the state.

On every program, the congressman invited Mattingly to join him on his show to debate. There was never a response. But in Tifton on the Friday before the Tuesday election, Fowler reported, "As we went on the air, I saw out the station window what looked like Birnam Wood approaching us. It was a forest of microphones and cameras surrounding—I couldn't believe my eyes—Rep. Newt Gingrich! He squeezed into the station with the press, and puffing himself up exclaimed, 'I am here to accept your challenge to Senator Mattingly, who must remain in Washington for an important set of votes.' 'Newt,' I blurted out, 'I am here to debate the organ grinder, not one of his monkeys.'"

The filmed confrontation was so politically dramatic that it was repeatedly shown throughout the weekend on television stations statewide.

Fowler, who was trailing in the polls, is convinced that this incident turned the tide and gave him his narrow victory.

With a substantial lead in all polls, Senator Mattingly remained in Washington throughout much of September and October. This was brought into sharp relief when the Republican senator missed his own large (12,000-person) campaign event in downtown Atlanta at the Omni on October 8 in order to attend a House-Senate appropriations conference committee meeting in Washington. Instead, President Regan filled in, accusing Fowler of voting "to make America weaker" and stating that Mattingly's reelection "will help me be the president you elected me to be." Fowler commented, "I find it absolutely incredible that Mack Mattingly...turned down a two-hour flight with his own president because he's scared to come and face the people he is supposed to represent. I would rearrange my schedule 10 times for a flight with the president to make the case for textile workers, to make the case for farmers, for my constituents."

Faced with increasing media criticism for his refusal to campaign in the state or to debate Fowler, and perhaps recalling Herman Talmadge's reflection that his own refusal to debate Mattingly had been a major factor in his 1980 defeat, the Mattingly campaign finally agreed to a single, one-hour debate with his Democratic opponent, to be held on Monday, October 20, at WSB-TV's White Columns studio in northeast Atlanta. (The Mattingly campaign consistently indicated that it was always the senator's intention to participate in a single debate, but that scheduling difficulties precluded finalizing plans until well into October.)

Two days before the debate, the Fowler campaign held the "Peter, Wyche and Mary" fundraiser in Atlanta.

> U.S. Rep. Wyche Fowler rewrote "Puff the Magic Dragon," the old Peter, Paul and Mary tune, to better suit his purposes Saturday night. With Peter Yarrow and Mary Travers—two-thirds of the famous folk-singing trio backing him up at a Buckhead fund-raiser, Fowler sang:
>
> "Mack's head was bent in sorrow, green scales fell like rain,
> Mack no longer went to play along the TV lane.
> Without his lifelong friend, Mack could not be brave,
> So Mack the mighty senator sadly slipped into his cave."

Despite his wishful lyrics, Fowler knows that winning the 1986 Senate race against incumbent Republican Mack Mattingly will require more than a prayer and a song. What he needs is money to combat Mattingly's superiority on the airwaves, and Saturday's fund-raiser should help by adding almost $50,000 to his treasury. An estimated 300 Democrats mingled with Yarrow and Ms. Travers, and then joined them in singing nostalgic favorites like "Blowin in the Wind" and "If I Had a Hammer." A committee of 47 Fowler supporters sponsored the $250-per-couple event in Newcastle, the stately West Paces Ferry mansion owned by Mrs. Reuben Garland....

Saturday's fund-raiser marked the second time that Yarrow and Ms. Travers have campaigned for Fowler, whom they consider an old friend. The twosome, who made music history in the 1960s along with Paul Stookey, also appeared at a Fowler fund-raiser two years ago. "He's just one of the most promising and energetic people on the political scene," said Yarrow. "He's a man of integrity, an independent person, and he's nobody's fool," said Ms. Travers.

The fund-raiser, dubbed "Peter, Wyche and Mary" by the Fowler campaign, caused a small political tempest because of Yarrow and Ms. Travers' well-known support of liberal causes and candidates, a reputation that Fowler is trying to shed. Both singers have been active in the civil rights and anti-nuclear movements, and they have protested U.S. involvement in Central America. Ms. Travers hosted a celebrity dinner for Nicaraguan president Daniel Ortega in New York earlier this year. Yarrow and Ms. Travers each emphasized that the Atlanta congressman does not necessarily share their political views. "It's not my position to have to defend myself, and I would hope that Wyche doesn't have to defend his association with us," Ms. Travers said. "These people are here because we love their music," said Fowler. "They're not here in support of any causes other than my campaign."[74]

The Fowler-Mattingly debate was broadcast live on WSB, one of Atlanta's "big three" television stations, which also provided the venue and the moderator, Monica Kaufman. The broadcast was also carried by WALB in Albany, the dominant TV station in southwest Georgia, by smaller stations in Columbus and Macon, and by public television outlets throughout the state. Some estimates placed viewership that night as high as 60 percent of the state's voting-age population.

Candidates, Parties, and Campaigns summarized the lead-up to the encounter. "The delay [in Mattingly's agreeing to a debate date], coupled with the crescendo of negative press coverage, made the debate of extraordinary public interest, doubtless much greater than earlier or more frequent encounters between the opponents might have been. In a tone reminiscent of the 'Rocky' films, the media dramatically described the debate as Fowler's last chance to get 'momentum for a campaign that is far behind in the polls.'"[75]

Though many analysts afterward indicated that they had always assumed "the more attractive and articulate challenger" would be the beneficiary, at the time many pundits indicated that, in part because of such presumptions and "expectations," the incumbent would fare well enough simply by avoiding major gaffes.

An article in the following day's *Atlanta Journal* summarized the course of the debate.

> Democratic Senate candidate Wyche Fowler vigorously attacked Republican Sen. Mack Mattingly on the issues of deficit spending, foreign policy and personal honesty in a televised debate Monday, while the GOP incumbent tried to paint his opponent as a tax-and-spend liberal. Coming into the debate with a big lead in the polls, Mattingly appeared to succeed in his strategy of avoiding any major blunders. But he also seemed generally passive during the encounter, compared to the constantly attacking Atlanta congressman. When Fowler accused Mattingly, for example, of voting to kill the federal peanut program and to "destroy" farm export markets, the incumbent didn't respond. When Fowler came close to calling Mattingly a liar, the senator again had no response. "Mack, I don't know whether you won't tell the truth, or whether your aides won't tell you right," Fowler said, after Mattingly had accused him of not voting for a recent anti-drug bill. "I left the campaign trail...to vote for the drug bill. I was an original cosponsor of the drug bill...."
>
> Fowler, who won a pre-debate coin toss—opened the encounter by saying that the issue in this election is "plain and simple truth."

> Then he sought to turn the Mattingly campaign's most potent issue thus far—congressional absenteeism—around on the senator. Mattingly repeatedly has attacked Fowler for having the worst roll-call attendance record in Congress during the 1985–86 session. "But Sen. Mattingly has missed over 80 percent of the votes of his own agriculture subcommittee...where we both know that all the work is done," Fowler said. Mattingly didn't respond directly to the charge, but repeated his own attack on Fowler's absenteeism. "The truth of the matter is that he's missed 812 votes," Mattingly said. "We get paid to come back and campaign, not only in our state, but mainly we get paid to work in Washington, D.C."
>
> Throughout the debate, Mattingly sought to draw a clear ideological line between himself and Fowler, and he referred constantly to interest groups' ratings of congressmen to make the point.... "The issue in this campaign is the contrasting record of the candidates, because we do have a different record. Mr. Fowler is a liberal. I'm a conservative," Mattingly said. Fowler's response was twofold. He pointed to Georgia Sen. Sam Nunn's endorsement of him as proof that his record was in the "mainstream." And he criticized the "borrow-and-spend" policies that he said Mattingly and the Reagan administration have supported.[76]

Most media analysts credited Fowler with winning the debate. For example, Frederick Allen wrote,

> Now we know why Mack Mattingly does not like debates. To get straight to the scoring, Democrat Wyche Fowler won Monday night's bout with Sen. Mattingly—and in persuasive fashion. The key to the debate's influence on the voters, however, may lie in the length of time viewers spent in front of their televisions, because the first half was fairly even. Anyone who switched channels at 8:30 missed the knockout. It was during the second half-hour that Mattingly, responding to a question about the fight against drugs, fell back on a familiar accusation of absenteeism, and charged that Fowler had missed last Friday's vote on final passage of an anti-drug bill in Congress. That proved to be a costly error, and Fowler struck

back swiftly. "Mack," Fowler responded, milking a tone of exasperation, "I don't know whether you won't tell the truth, or whether your aides won't tell you right." Fowler then went on to say that he had left the campaign trail and returned to Washington to cast the vote in question. Political debates frequently provoke comparisons with boxing matches, and this one was no exception. Mattingly seemed determined to maintain a passive, defensive posture—a rope-a-dope strategy—evidently in the hope that Fowler would exhaust himself and his credibility through an excessive attack. As it happened, though, the senator simply looked like a man incapable of defending himself, while his opponent was pummeling him into submission.[77]

Most importantly, the debate did indeed attract a wide audience. In the dominant Atlanta market alone, overnight ratings compiled by the A.C. Nielsen Co. indicated that the Fowler-Mattingly encounter was watched by approximately 225,000 households and beat out all other TV programs airing at the same time (including *Kate and Allie*, *ALF*, and *Amazing Stories*).[78]

Fowler's performance in the debate (and the media's reporting of it), coupled with the Fowler campaign ads finally airing with enough frequency to be competitive with the Mattingly spots, produced a dramatic tightening of the race. Fowler's own polling showed that the Mattingly lead had been cut from 55 percent to 31 percent in mid-October to 49 percent to 37 percent immediately after the debate, and a WAGA-TV poll taken at the same time had Fowler within eight points. And in one of the last surveys released prior to Election Day, the *Atlanta Constitution* reported on October 30 that the Senate contest was in a "dead heat."

The major Atlanta dailies split their endorsements, with the *Constitution* backing Fowler and the *Journal* opting for Mattingly.

Atlanta Constitution: Fowler the Best Bet for Georgia

The Atlanta Constitution endorses Democratic candidate Rep. Wyche Fowler for the U.S. Senate over Republican incumbent Mack Mattingly.... Fowler is the class of this election, and Georgia ought to be represented by its best.... Wyche Fowler is very much a known quantity and a proven performer. He has served with distinction on such prestigious committees as the House Select Committee on Intelligence, and he faced down a contrary Tip O'Neill to win a spot on the powerful Ways and Means Committee. Under both Democratic and Republican administrations, he has effectively looked after the legitimate interests of his district and state—for example, in funding for MARTA and Georgia highway projects, creation of the Chattahoochee River National Recreation Area, preservation of Cumberland Island, and agricultural disaster-relief aid. And if in a few instances he has taken up issues that had little to recommend them but their trendiness, Fowler overwhelmingly not only has represented Georgians well in Washington, he has represented us well to the nation. He speaks on public policy with knowledge, comprehension and insight.[79]

Atlanta Journal: On the Record and Issues, It's Mattingly for Senate

The records of both candidates on significant issues offer voters a clear choice. On those issues, we agree with the incumbent and enthusiastically endorse Mack Mattingly for the U.S. Senate, while hoping to see the able and witty Wyche Fowler offer for office again with a better program on a better day.... In making our judgment about the current race for the U.S. Senate seat from Georgia, we start with the belief that incumbent Mack Mattingly has done a good job. He has voted as a conservative, though not an extremist; as a supporter of most of President Reagan's legislative program; as an opponent of wasteful federal spending and higher taxes.... Those who want a U.S. Senator who will consistently oppose the president and pursue a more liberal agenda certainly have reason to favor a change, and this brings us to the challenger, Wyche Fowler. As president of City Council he was a constructive force in Atlanta; he has been an able and effective member of the U.S. House of Representatives from the 5th District, a post for which we were pleased to endorse him several times. On some issues he was more liberal than suited our philosophy as editorialists, but he represented a liberal district, and he did so responsibly. But since we believe Mack Mattingly has done a good job as U.S. Senator, we would expect Wyche

> Fowler to show us how he could do a better job in that post, and Fowler has not done so in this campaign.[80]

Although most attention to the 1986 Senate general election campaign focused on the "ad wars" and the lone candidate debate, direct voter contact operations, especially the volunteer phone banks, were a prime element in the Fowler campaign effort. For the November election, twenty-five phone banks operated on Fowler's behalf, including, in addition to the campaign headquarters in the Buckhead section of north Atlanta, locations in Cobb, Bibb, Chatham, Dougherty, Clarke, Muscogee, Lowndes, Richmond, Houston, Gwinnett, Whitfield, Rockdale, Hall, Floyd, Bulloch, Gilmer, Carroll, Cherokee, Clayton, Towns, Bartow, Spalding, Sumter, and Catoosa counties, with a total of approximately 180 phone lines.

In all, the Fowler campaign spent $1.57 million for the general election, for a total of $2.99 million for the entire election cycle, compared to $5.14 million expended by the Mattingly team. Just under a million dollars ($988,000) of the Fowler general election total went for media, with $593,000 going for TV ad buys, $288,000 of which went for Atlanta television spots, and another $230,000 spent on radio ads. In keeping with Fowler's "no campaign debt" requirement, his 1986 campaign ended with a surplus of $74,000, whereas Mattingly concluded with a $242,000 deficit.

Atlanta Constitution columnist Bill Shipp summarized the 1986 Senate campaign on the day before the general election vote.

> Mattingly seems to have advantage, and yet I have a certain feeling....
>
> On his final campaign swing around the state, a pensive Wyche Fowler looked across the airport tarmac and into his post-election future. "If I lose, I'm going to take a few months off to consider what I might do, whether I want to practice law again—but, of course, I'm not going to lose," he said. Then he laughed and began a half-serious rehearsal of the victory statement he would deliver Tuesday night, or, more likely, early Wednesday. Win or lose, Wyche Fowler has waged as vigorous a campaign for public office as any candidate in Georgia history. He has stumped the state and

the nation for 20 months, soliciting votes in Georgia and campaign money in his home state and elsewhere. If any Georgian did not have an opportunity to meet Fowler, it was not the Democratic congressman's fault. He made an average of 100 campaign appearances a month in the final half-year of his assault on the Senate seat held by Mack Mattingly. He debated his Democratic Primary opponents 13 times. His evasive GOP foe allowed only one debate, a disaster, as it turned out, for the Republican side, but not one from which it cannot recover.... The Republicans would have millions of dollars to spend on TV advertising. Any candidate who challenged Mattingly would be tortured as a liberal. Ronald Reagan would come into Georgia to aid Mattingly. The incumbent senator, barely visible in Georgia during his first term, would be even more elusive and impossible to confront. As it turned out, the race went exactly according to that dreary forecast—a textbook study of how to market and package an unknown product without revealing its ingredients or uses. If the pre-election surveys are correct, the campaign has worked.... Fowler had two strikes against him from the outset. He was an Atlantan (Atlanta-based politicians seldom win statewide elections) and a badly under-financed challenger going against not only an incumbent but also against the most popular president in modern times. Fowler, however, had some pluses, too. House Speaker Tom Murphy and Democratic chairman John Henry Anderson campaigned wholeheartedly for him. Sen. Sam Nunn, the Georgia giant, tried to turn the contest into a battle between himself and Reagan, who had painted Fowler as weak on defense. "Wyche has voted against some weapons systems; so have I. I voted against the B1 bomber, just like Wyche Fowler. I voted against the MX, like Wyche Fowler. National defense is not simple," said Nunn, scorning the GOP's "bumper sticker mentality...." As the curtain falls on the '86 campaign, Mattingly seems to have all the advantages. He has spent an estimated $6 million on his campaign. Going into election eve, polls show he remains ahead. Still, I have a feeling about this election...[81]

1986 Senate general election Results and Analysis

On Tuesday, November 4, 1986, 1,225,008 Georgia voters of the 2,575,819 then registered cast ballots in the US Senate race, for a turnout of 47.6 percent. As the returns were reported throughout the evening of the 4th, and into the early morning hours of the 5th, it was clear that—like the 1980 contest—this was going to be another exceedingly close outcome. With 1,145,000 votes counted, Fowler's lead was 28,000 votes (51.25 percent to 48.75 percent). With 1,204,000 counted, the margin had dropped to 21,000 (50.88 percent to 49.12 percent). As of 4 A.M. on November 5, Fowler was still not claiming victory (though by that time, his campaign was nearly certain he had won).

When the votes had all been tallied, Fowler beat Mattingly by 22,466 votes, a result even closer than Mattingly's record-setting 1980 victory.

Wyche Fowler	623,707	50.915 percent
Mack Mattingly	601,241	49.081 percent
Write-in	60	0.005 percent

Fowler carried one hundred counties to Mattingly's fifty-nine, but the keys to victory were in the turnarounds in the 1980 results in metro Atlanta and among African American voters. The five-county metro Atlanta core, which had provided Mattingly with a 160,000 margin over Talmadge six years earlier, this time went for Fowler, primarily because of his huge advantage in his home county of Fulton, and his narrowing of the GOP edge in Cobb, Gwinnett, and Clayton Counties. The incumbent senator actually ran better this time in the remainder of the state, though the Atlantan maintained a slim lead there as well.

Fulton:
Fowler 103,155 (66.37 %) Mattingly 52,262 (33.63 %)

DeKalb:
Fowler 70,012 (54.81 %) Mattingly 57,725 (45.19 %)

Cobb:
Fowler 31,163 (36.84 %) Mattingly 53,417 (63.16 %)

Gwinnett:
Fowler 19,796 (35.58 %) Mattingly 35,845 (64.42 %)

Clayton:
Fowler 14,956 (44.38 %) Mattingly 18,743 (55.62 %)

TOTAL: Metro Atlanta
Fowler 239,082 (52.31 %) Mattingly 217,992 (47.69 %)

Rest of State:
Fowler 384,625 (50.09 %) Mattingly 383,249 (49.91 %)

Among the other major population centers in the state, Fowler won in Bibb (57.78 percent to 42.22 percent), Clarke (54.12 percent to 45.88 percent), Hall (51.98 percent to 48.02 percent), Houston—home of Senator Nunn (51.34 percent to 48.66 percent), and Muscogee (55.12 percent to 44.88 percent), whereas Mattingly prevailed in Chatham (53.54 percent to 46.46 percent), Dougherty (51.86 percent to 48.14 percent), Glynn—Mattingly's home (61.42 percent to 38.58 percent), Richmond (51.65 percent to 48.35 percent), and Whitfield (59.67 percent to 40.33 percent).

Though Mattingly had trailed significantly behind Talmadge in 1980 among Black voters, the 30 percent he received from this group was crucial to his narrow victory. In 1986, Fowler was able to reduce the Republican's vote share among Black voters to 15 percent, according to Fowler campaign estimates.

So, why did Fowler win, and in the process become the first Atlantan elected to represent Georgia in the US Senate?

First of all, the key premise of the Fowler campaign plan—that is, that far from being a disqualifying hindrance, his Atlanta base, and its growing importance in Georgia elections, would help enable his victories in both the primary and general elections—proved to be true. The five-county metro Atlanta core, which Fowler won in both contests, cast 28.3 percent of all votes in the Democratic primary (up from 23.4 percent in 1980) and 37.3 percent of all general election ballots (compared to 34.8 percent in 1980). The entire Atlanta media market accounted for fully 59.7 percent of the 1986 general election vote.

Fowler's voter contact and turnout operations were of particular importance in the 1986 non-presidential election cycle that saw much lower turnouts in both the Democratic primary and general election compared to 1980 when Jimmy Carter was running for reelection: in 1980, 1.029 million voted in the Democratic primary and 1.580 million voted in the general election, while in 1986, 626,000 voted in the primary and 1.225 million voted in the general election. The executive director of the Georgia Democratic Party highlighted this point in his post-election analysis.

> Along with Fowler's personal close-to-the ground style, said Bobby Kahn, executive director of the state Democratic Party, was the ability of the Fowler campaign to establish a well-dispersed turnout machine throughout the state—identifying their supporters and getting them to the polls. "I think voter contact was clearly an important part, and Wyche used it better than anybody, in both the primary and general election," Kahn said. And he said Fowler was helped by the strengthening of the Democratic Party apparatus, which provided a computerized list of the state's 2.4 million registered voters, to fit "hand-in-glove" with Fowler's grass roots campaign.[82]

The role of the Fowler campaign was also recognized by the American Association of Political Consultants, which presented campaign manager Bill Johnstone with its Campaign Manager of the Year award for 1986. The Fowler paid-advertising effort, primarily under the direction of Frank Greer and pursuant to Alan Secrest's polling and focus-group research, also played an important part, and, along with the impact of the October 20 debate, likely made a decisive difference in the late Fowler surge that produced the victory.

But most observers at the time, and those who have analyzed the 1986 race since, gave the candidate himself the lion's share of the credit.

> "The Atlanta congressman's win...was a tribute to the political strength of state Democrats who backed Fowler, particularly U.S. Sen. Sam Nunn and House Speaker Tom Murphy. But most of all, it was a personal victory for Fowler, who overcame a barrage of negative television ads and his Atlanta political roots with intense, on-the-ground campaigning and an excellent performance in the election's single debate between the two candidates."
>
> —Hal Straus, *Atlanta Journal*, November 5, 1986[83]

> "A myriad of reasons for Fowler's upset poked through during the long night of vote counting, but one picture dominates: the tireless whistle-

stopping of a born campaigner, backed by a political party that was threatened into effectiveness by Republican encroachment."

—Jim Galloway, *Atlanta Journal*, November 5, 1986[84]

From its strategy to its execution, Fowler's campaign was a one-man show. And the result, shattering a host of comfortable presumptions about Georgia's politics, could only be attributed to the sheer magnetism of Fowler's personality. Making three and four appearances a day, shaking hands from Rabun Gap to Tybee Light, telling talking-parrot jokes and singing gospel songs, posing in TV spots with a mule one day and a puppy dog the next—and always with a warm smile and a twinkle in his eye—Fowler charmed the voters of Georgia. More important, he reassured them that there could not be much truth to the rumor that he was overly liberal.

—Frederick Allen, *Atlanta Journal*, November 5, 1986[85]

"In 1986 Fowler defeated incumbent Republican Mack Mattingly to win election to the U.S. Senate with 51 percent of the vote. No Atlantan had ever before won a Senate seat. He succeeded against long odds—he trailed by twenty-four points in the polls just three weeks before the election—by dint of his humor and folksy stories, personal magnetism, and indefatigable campaigning."

—Loch Johnson, current Fowler biographical entry
in *The New Georgia Encyclopedia*[86]

Years later, when asked why he won in 1986, Fowler cited campaign management for effectively husbanding resources and targeting campaign efforts as well as the volunteer phone banks that involved hundreds of Georgians reaching out to their fellow citizens on his behalf. He added, "I was a good personal campaigner because I like people, could relate to them, and they responded."

Chapter 10

One Hundredth Congress (1987–1988): Two Georgias

First Days in the Senate

When he was sworn in on January 6, 1987, using a family Bible, Wyche Fowler became the twenty-fifth person to hold the Georgia Senate seat originally occupied in the First Congress back in 1789 by James Gunn, a Virginia-born lawyer who moved to Georgia after the Revolutionary War. (Fowler was actually the twenty-fourth individual to occupy the seat because one person—John B. Gordon—held the post in nonconsecutive terms.)

The Georgia congressional delegation hosted a party for Fowler in the Senate Caucus Room the night before his swearing in. His proud parents were in attendance, but as the party continued on well into the night, Wyche Fowler Sr. told a reporter he would be leaving to go to bed. "I'm 77.... I like to say I've had seven bonus years. The Bible promises three score and ten. Everything over that is gravy. I'm living my gravy years."[87] After he was sworn in the following day, the new Georgia senator remarked, "I've walked down the aisles of the House hundreds of times. But it was a lot different walking down the Senate aisle. The weight of history is so much greater in the Senate. It is overwhelming. I was humbled."[88]

Fowler had been attracted to the Senate, in part, because of the enhanced public service role it afforded compared to his position in the House. Quite obviously, he could have a larger impact as one of one hundred senators, as opposed to one of 435 representatives. Furthermore, as someone who had long been interested in the foreign policy domain, and as a lawyer, he was particularly enthused about the Senate's unique responsibility in voting on treaties and judicial and other important nominations. And Senate rules were generally less restrictive with respect to amendments one could offer on the floor, thus allowing individual senators to be more actively involved in shaping policy in fields beyond their committee assignments.

Another key difference between the two chambers was, and is, the Senate's filibuster rules, which, on most matters, require a sixty-vote majority in order to take up legislation, thus affording the minority a much larger role than in the House. However, since Fowler was never in the minority during his ten years in the House, and the Democrats had regained the majority in the Senate for the first time since 1980 by picking up eight seats—including his own—in the 1986 elections, to produce a fifty-five-to-forty-five majority, this factor did not directly affect him.

Although committee assignments in the Senate may have been somewhat less determinative of a member's policy pursuits than in the House, they were still important in shaping a senator's focus and opportunities for accomplishment. In the One Hundredth Congress, Fowler sought and won assignment to the Senate committees on agriculture, energy and natural resources, and the budget, though he was not successful in his attempt to gain a spot on the Appropriations Committee.

> "I'm elated," said Fowler at a news conference in Atlanta. "It's particularly significant and a pleasure to me that I will be able to go to work on my commitment to rural development, rural health, and the rural economy." Fowler had lobbied hard for the Agriculture and Energy committees, both of which are considered in the top tier of Senate assignments. He said Friday that Sam Nunn, Georgia's senior senator, was a strong advocate on his behalf. Nunn, who sits on the committee that makes Senate appointments, "was extremely helpful as far as getting on the Agriculture Committee. I understand he made a very powerful speech for me," Fowler said. Fowler noted that the Energy Committee has jurisdiction over federal forestry programs, which are important to a timber producing state such as Georgia. He said the Budget Committee—which sets overall budget goals—would give him an opportunity to try to cut the federal budget deficit, "which I consider the most serious domestic problem facing our country." The Agriculture Committee, however, was clearly the biggest feather in the new Senator's cap.

> Georgia has not had representation on the committee since the defeat of Herman Talmadge in 1980.[89]

In addition to his committee assignments, Fowler once again won a vote of confidence from his colleagues when the Senate Democratic Caucus elected him and three others to the newly created position of assistant deputy whip, which was designed to improve communications between Democratic senators and the Senate Democratic leadership. As the representative for the Southern region, Fowler was made responsible for the seventeen Democratic senators in eleven Southern states. Fowler indicated it was his intention to use the role to "develop a legislative agenda that is productive, progressive, and in the best interest not only of the south but of the nation."[90]

During the first recess after he became senator, Fowler embarked on a series of "open meetings" throughout the state between February 7 and 14. He said he was "determined to use every opportunity I have to come home, to be available to the people I represent, and give them a chance to meet with me and discuss their concerns." This was the first of such outreach efforts, which culminated with the successful, but exhausting, fulfillment of a campaign pledge to appear in all 159 counties during his term.[91]

Rural Champion

Fowler's interest in rural America and his Agriculture Committee assignment was made clear on his very first set of visits back to the state, as reported in a February 15 newspaper article.

> Wyche Fowler stepped into the warm sunshine of South Georgia and out of Sam Nunn's shadow last week, taking a giant stride in establishing himself as a champion of rural America in the U.S. Senate.... As the week wore on, it became clear that the state's junior senator, in his wish to rescue rural Georgia from economic ruin, is destined to play a key role in legislation benefiting all of rural America.... At each stop through South Georgia last week, Fowler made it clear that his top priority in the Senate is bringing economic prosperity to rural communities. "The economic despair—and that's not too strong a word—isn't confined to Georgia," Fowler said....

"You can find it in every rural area of the country. And if anything is going to be done about it, it's going to take a city slicker like me to win over the other city slickers," he added. "There aren't even 30 senators representing agricultural states. So we've got to reach out...."

If voters in rural Georgia had any lingering doubts about Fowler's election, it was not evident among the hundreds of farmers who were drawn to the senator's town meetings last week.... But it was Fowler's knowledge of agricultural issues, after only a month in the Senate, that got the most approval....

And not one person stood to defend the president when Fowler blamed the administration for the economic problems experienced by rural areas. "Every rural-oriented program, if not targeted for abolition, is scheduled for cuts in the administration's budget," the senator said. "It's outrageous. It's penny-wise and pound-foolish...." Fowler said the administration's policies have forced rural communities to export "our most precious commodity—our children." He added, "They're leaving because they can't find jobs. But everybody can't, shouldn't and doesn't want to live in Atlanta.... We've got to develop a strategy for rural investment. And we've got to make sure farmers get a fair price for what they grow. That's where my brainpower and sweat is going to go."[92]

In a 1988 address to Georgians for Better Transportation, Fowler spoke further about what he had learned in his visits to rural areas in his home state.

Since 1980, investment in rural programs has been cut by 75 percent. At a time when rural poverty is increasing and rural populations are declining, we have seen the near dismantling of rural health, housing and small business programs. Under these circumstances, we are required to innovate, not to ignore the mounting problems because they are not in easy range of the cameras of the media markets.... I think any efforts to encourage rural development should bear these characteristics: 1) We have to provide support, not only for a stable agricultural base, but for the small towns and rural communities that are interdependent with the farm economy. Our young people have to have a choice in where they live and work and raise their families. Right now they are being forced to flee the countryside and flood the cities to seek a future for themselves and their loved ones. 2) We have to respect the diversity and integrity of existing rural communities. The federal government has to strengthen its partnership with local governments and encourage local initiative, because rural America truly does produce the raw materials with which we fashion our society. That includes the intangibles of character—of the values—that contribute to our national identity. They are an element of our national strength that we need to nurture, and that we cannot afford to neglect.

To focus attention on the need for action on rural development, Fowler conducted field hearings in 1987 in Moultrie and Tifton with Agriculture Committee chairman Patrick Leahy (D-VT) and in Fort Valley with Senator Nunn. Fowler's agricultural and rural development initiatives during 1987/1988 included:

• Sponsoring a successful committee amendment to the Agricultural Credit Act of 1987 to ensure that the farm credit relief provided in the legislation would result in a reduction in interest rates paid by farmers, and a successful floor amendment to secure farmer rights in loan repayment proceedings by clarifying the terms under which delinquent loans would be eligible for restructuring. Both Fowler provisions were retained in the enacted version of the bill.
• Sponsoring a bill (S. 2416) that helped persuade Secretary of Agriculture Lyng to improve the government's farmland Conservation Reserve Program (CRP) by including windbreaks and shelterbelts in the program.
• Sponsoring the Agricultural Diversification and Rural Development Bill, which authorized the use of business development loans and state incentive funds for agricultural diversification, and established a new Agricultural Diversification Loan Fund to be administered by the states. Though no action was taken on the bill, it embodied Fowler's call for increased investment in rural America by providing for "a modest investment in rural communities—in every

dimension, not just for farmers, but for the professionals, public servants, service providers, craftsmen and teachers that also make their home in the countryside."

Fowler also used his position on the Agriculture Committee to advance causes that reached far beyond rural America. One such issue was food safety, on which he was to emerge as one of the leaders in the Congress. In the One Hundredth Congress, he sponsored a successful amendment in the Agriculture Committee to the federal pesticide regulatory law to increase FDA monitoring of agricultural imports treated with chemicals banned in the US, and require US chemical exporters to disclose health risks associated with the exported product. Although the Fowler provision was dropped in the final bill, the importance of improving the safety of the American food supply was to receive much greater recognition in the future.

Another issue on which Senator Fowler proved to be well ahead of his time was water conservation. Whereas by the latter part of the 1980s many had realized the importance to future generations of moving to develop alternative sources of energy supply and to protect the environment, far fewer focused on the critical, finite resource of water. Wyche Fowler was one of the first in the Congress to promote more effective federal water conservation policy by sponsoring the following Acts:

• the Farm Conservation and Water Protection Act, which promoted low-input agricultural production systems and encouraged land, resource, and wildlife stewardship in federal farm programs;
• the National Plumbing Fixtures Efficiency Act, which established national standards for the manufacture and labeling of certain plumbing products in order to conserve and protect water resources; and
• the National Water Conservation Act, which required that a comprehensive review of federal water management practices be undertaken, and that water conservation alternatives be considered in all federal projects.

All three of these measures were introduced late in the session and were designed to prepare the way for positive action in the next Congress.

Although none of them, nor their successors in future years, were enacted into law, they did help to bring attention to a subject that has markedly grown in importance since then.

Energy and Natural Resources

The subject of water policy involved multiple congressional panels, including both of Fowler's primary committee assignments. In addition, he was engaged in a number of other matters that fell within the jurisdiction of the Energy and Natural Resources Committee. One of the key issues to come before the committee at this time was the proposal to open up the Arctic National Wildlife Refuge (ANWR) in northern Alaska for exploratory drilling for oil. Fowler had visited the area as a member of the committee, hiking for three days in the Brooks Range through the Refuge to the small village of Kaktovik on the Arctic Ocean. The remoteness of the village was made manifest to the senator when it cost $100 for a five-minute shower there. Fowler was struck by the area's great natural beauty in addition to its uniqueness.

Drilling in ANWR was a topic on which two important national objectives—energy development and environmental protection—came into direct conflict. In this case, the Georgia senator felt that the environmental considerations in preserving the unique ANWR habitat outweighed the short-term gain from potentially increased oil production. He made the case for that position in a June 25, 1988, letter-to-the-editor of the *Atlanta Journal-Constitution.*

> I must take issue with the June 8 letter from Secretary of the Interior Donald Hodel promoting exploratory drilling in the Arctic National Wildlife Refuge (ANWR). It comes as no surprise that Hodel would dispute the Constitution's May 13 editorial, which noted correctly that drilling in ANWR would despoil a national wildlife refuge while offering no prospect for energy security.... His letter...completely misleads the American public about the issues involved.
>
> 1. Hodel says our failure to explore ANWR sends a message to OPEC that we "lack the will" to take care of our own energy needs. That message has already been sent through this administration's

virtual annihilation of the conservation and alternative energy research and development programs that grew out of the oil shocks of the 1970s, under both Republican and Democratic administrations....

2. In his letter, Hodel extols the chances of finding oil reserves comparable to those at Prudhoe Bay, Alaska, which accounts for 20 percent of domestic production. What he does not say is that the chances of finding any economically recoverable oil at all in ANWR are slim. A Department of the Interior study boosted the statistical probability that enough oil would be found to meet the costs of extracting it by estimating the future price of oil at twice the level anticipated by the oil industry....

3. The most astonishing contradiction of the facts by Secretary Hodel is his assertion that our experience at Prudhoe Bay shows that Arctic oil drilling can be done without serious impact on wildlife and the environment. The secretary's letter follows hard on the release of a Fish and Wildlife Service report to Congress on environmental damage.... This report states that air and water pollution—and the deterioration of bird and wildlife habitat—from oil exploration next to ANWR, in Alaska's Prudhoe Bay, far exceeded the claims of the oil companies.

Finally, Hodel's letter proposes no real measure by which we can weigh the value of potential oil reserves against that of our last pristine Arctic wilderness. This is a question that must be carefully considered, keeping in mind both the energy preparedness and the natural heritage we will bequeath to future generations.

Energy and Natural Resources Committee chairman Bennett Johnston (D-LA), who supported drilling in ANWR, brought up a bill in the committee to authorize such drilling in February 1988. Fowler offered two amendments in an attempt to ameliorate the environmental consequences. The first, which was approved by an 11 to 8 margin, redistributed federal revenues from any ANWR oil production by allocating a portion of such funds to the Migratory Bird Conservation Fund and other fish and wildlife programs. The second, and more contentious, which was defeated on a 4 to 10 vote, would have required that any energy development within ANWR would have to meet the stricter "compatibility standard" used in all other national wildlife refuges. The Johnston bill, which Fowler opposed within committee, never reached the Senate floor in the One Hundredth Congress, but the subject was to reemerge in the following session, when it came before the full Senate as part of the original version of the National Energy Strategy Act of 1991. Fowler voted with the majority in rejecting ANWR drilling at that time.

The fight over drilling in ANWR has persisted all the way to the present. After dozens of unsuccessful attempts over many years by congressional Republicans to authorize oil exploration in the refuge, in 2017 the Trump tax-cut law did contain such a provision. However, although the Trump administration issued leases for ANWR drilling on its last full day in office, these leases were put on hold the very next day by the incoming Biden administration. On June 1, 2021, Interior Secretary Haaland extended the suspension indefinitely, pending a thorough review of the environmental impact of ANWR drilling, as sought by Fowler over three decades before.

The Georgia Senator sponsored several pieces of legislation that were referred to the Energy and Natural Resources Committee. One of these represented a continuation of his longtime efforts in the House to promote renewable energy and energy conservation. The Renewable Energy and Energy Conservation Technology Competitiveness Act of 1987 was introduced by Senator Fowler on July 28, 1987, and provided for federal assistance and leadership for the research, development, and demonstration of renewable energy and energy conservation technologies. The renewable energy technologies addressed in the measure included wind energy, photovoltaics, solar thermal energy systems, biofuels, solar buildings energy systems, ocean energy systems, and geothermal energy. In fact, Fowler's first formal address on the Senate floor was in promoting adoption of this legislation.

> Sen. Wyche Fowler warned Tuesday that the failure of the United States to reduce its dependence on imported oil has produced a "foreign policy quagmire" that threatens American lives in the Persian Gulf. In his first speech to the Senate, Fowler said U.S. reliance on foreign oil "is why...we have our finger on the trigger" and "are poised to risk military engagement—and American casualties" in

> the Middle East. And citing the Reagan Administration's recently exposed secret arms-for-hostages deals with Iran, Fowler added, "Does anyone think we would have tolerated this insolent blackmail if we weren't gluttons for the crude oil coming out of the Middle East?..." [Fowler] chose to use his first floor speech to call attention to his legislation that would require the federal government to renew its commitment to energy independence by helping American business market alternative and renewable sources of energy.[93]

The Fowler bill was approved, in amended form, by the committee on September 22, 1988, and attached to the unrelated H.R. 3048 by voice vote on the Senate floor on October 5. Although the Fowler language was dropped in the final, enacted version of H.R. 3048, Senate approval paved the way for a more successful ultimate outcome in the next session.

Late in the session, Fowler introduced the Parks, Preservation and Recreation Reorganization Act, which sought to elevate and improve federal management of national parks and recreation areas as well as historic sites. Specifically, the bill created the new position of assistant secretary of the Interior for Conservation, Preservation and Recreation, subject to Senate confirmation, and established a new preservation agency within the Department of the Interior headed by a director appointed by the new assistant secretary. The measure also provided for the appointment of directors of the National Park Service and the recreation division. As Fowler explained in his introductory statement, "This arrangement seeks to build upon the current National Park Service structure, but raises the profile of these programs by essentially elevating each part one 'notch' within the Interior Department." With its introduction near the end of the One Hundredth Congress, Fowler's intention was to provide a vehicle for further discussion and consideration of the issues it raised during the years ahead.

Historic Preservation

On the same day that he introduced the Parks, Preservation and Recreation Act, Fowler also submitted the Comprehensive Preservation Act (S. 2912), a proposal that was to occupy the senator and his staff for almost the entire remainder of his time in the Senate, culminating in one of his signature achievements as a member of the US Congress. The impetus for the legislation came from three major sources: (1) a September 1986 report by the congressional Office of Technology Assessment (OTA) entitled *Technologies for Prehistoric & Historic Preservation*; (2) draft legislation developed in 1986 to 1987 by the National Conference of State Historic Preservation Officers (NCSHPO) for revising the National Historic Preservation Act, creating an independent federal preservation agency, clarifying and strengthening the role of state historic preservation, and making provision for tribal historic preservation programs; and (3) the interest of Fowler and his staff in improving federal historic preservation and archaeological resource protection programs.

The Fowler effort began with staff contacts with organizations that had an interest and expertise in these matters, including, in addition to NCSHPO, the Society for American Archaeology, Preservation Action, the National Trust for Historic Preservation, the Congressional Research Service, the State of Georgia Historic Preservation Section, the National Alliance of Statewide Preservation Organizations, and others.

Over the course of the next year, the meetings helped identify specific problems and develop legislative language resulting in the Comprehensive Preservation Act that Fowler unveiled at an October 18, 1988, speech at historic Union Station in Washington, DC.

> How we conserve and protect our past says much about what our values are and what kind of society we are. Preservation of our country's prehistoric and historic heritage is essential if we and future generations are to truly know from whence we have come and where we are headed.... If we have made some progress in improving the protection of our nation's prehistoric and historic resources, there are still many gaps in that protection. If we have made some advance in saving particular parts of our national heritage from uncontrolled development, many more sites face current or future peril because of inadequate nation-wide standards. If we can take some encouragement from the smashing success of Union Station, it must be acknowledged that recent changes in the tax code have sharply reduced the financial attractiveness of preservation investments by the private sector. If we, the Congress, can take some justifiable pride in preventing Administration attempts to reduce or eliminate federal funding for historic preservation, the reality is that

actual appropriations for these programs have fallen far short of what was provided under the last Administration, and even further short of the actual need. Finally, if we have seen an explosion of interest and involvement in preservation by state and local governments and by the private sector, we have also witnessed in many ways an abdication of federal responsibilities, financial and otherwise. It is with this backdrop, of encouraging recent trends but long-term concerns, that I introduce the Comprehensive Preservation Act of 1988, legislation designed to strengthen the protections for our country's prehistoric and historic heritage, to provide adequate federal grant and tax incentives for preservation efforts, and to improve the clout and the accountability of the federal/state/tribal/local organization of preservation programs.

S. 2912 was a far-reaching proposal that contained a number of highly controversial provisions. Specifically, the bill was proposed to accomplish the following:

- create a new, independent historic preservation agency to oversee and coordinate the national historic preservation program by transferring existing functions and personnel from the Advisory Council on Historic Preservation (which would be abolished) and certain relevant "external" programs from the National Park Service. The proposed system aimed at increasing the visibility and accountability of preservation concerns within the federal government.
- strengthen the independence of the National Park Service within the Department of the Interior by making its director subject to Senate confirmation, transfer the secretary of Interior's responsibilities for the Park Service to the director, and create separate deputy director positions for the Park Service and for recreation, conservation, and open space. Per Fowler's introductory statement, "By reducing control of the Park Service by the large, and essentially development-oriented Interior Department, the Service's natural and cultural conservation responsibilities will receive clearer and more visible direction."
- create a new national center for preservation technology as a private, nonprofit subsidiary of the federal preservation program, and

charge it with the responsibility of developing and disseminating preservation technologies.

• provide recognition and facilitation for an expanded role for state, tribal, and local preservation programs along with additional resources to help finance these programs.

• make the Historic Preservation Fund into a true trust fund by guaranteeing that at least $100 million of the $150 million annually collected from Outer Continental Shelf oil receipts that was theoretically set aside for the Historic Preservation Fund actually be spent for that purpose. (At the time of the Fowler bill's introduction, only about $25 million a year from OCS receipts was being allocated for historic preservation, and the fund's accumulated unallocated balance was over $1 billion.)

• strengthen federal tax incentives for the protection of archaeological resources by making preservation expenditures for archaeological sites and historic landscapes eligible for the existing preservation tax credit, increasing the tax value for the donation of an archaeological site, and making donations of archaeological artifacts not registered under the bill's new voluntary artifact registration program ineligible for tax deductions.

• establish a comprehensive preservation education and training program, which aimed to increase public awareness of and participation in historic preservation, and to improve and expand training opportunities in preservation fields, including special assistance to historically Black colleges and universities to establish preservation degree programs.

• enhance federal protection standards by clarifying, coordinating, and strengthening federal agency preservation responsibilities, the National Register, and the National Historic Landmarks program, including expanded authorities for timely action to protect historic properties under imminent threat; and by extending federal protection to submerged historic properties lying up to two hundred nautical miles offshore.

• improve protection of archaeological resources by focusing federally sponsored archaeological work on important research questions and by requiring the professional certification of archaeologists wishing to engage in such research; curbing the looting and illegal trade of archaeological resources by establishing a voluntary antiquities registration program ("to both encourage the conduct of scientifically valid excavations and create a potential market incentive in favor of certified antiquities"); calling for an international conference on the antiquities trade; strengthening federal laws against unauthorized removal and trade of archaeological resources from federal and Native American lands; and providing information and incentives to encourage private owners of archaeological resources to protect those resources.

• set principles to govern federal policy with respect to the reburial of human remains and grave-associated artifacts in an attempt to reconcile the competing claims of scientific research and the desires of cultural descendants.

No further action was taken on the bill in the One Hundredth Congress.

Intelligence Oversight

As had been true in the House, Fowler's efforts in the Senate were not confined to his committee-related work, and the Senate offered even greater latitude for such undertakings. Though no longer a member of the Intelligence Committee, he continued to press for reform of congressional oversight of US intelligence operations.

On November 5, 1987, Senator Fowler introduced the Intelligence Activities Improvement Act. The new legislation retained the standards from Fowler's earlier House bill but substituted a requirement for prior presidential reporting of all major covert operations for the previous bill's provision for congressional authorization of military and paramilitary covert operations. The Intelligence Committee reported out an intelligence oversight bill (S. 1721) on January 27, 1988. The committee-passed bill placed a statutory obligation upon the president to keep the intelligence committees fully and currently informed of US intelligence activities, including covert operations, and established standards for the presidential approval and reporting of covert operations.

Although Fowler voiced support for the general thrust of the committee-passed measure, he sought to strengthen its standards by authoring three floor amendments to the legislation on March 1:1) require that covert operations be consistent with overt foreign policy; 2) require that covert operations be "essential" to national security; and 3) require that covert operations be annually reauthorized. In exchange for not forcing a vote on his proposals (which had little chance of passage), the floor managers of S. 1721, Senators Boren and Cohen, entered into a "colloquy" on the Senate floor with Fowler on March 4 with regard to the first two of his amendments. (A colloquy is a means by which members of Congress can clarify the intent of legislative language.)

Colloquy on Covert Operations and Publicly Avowed Foreign Policy

Sen. Fowler: I am most concerned about the effectiveness of covert operations which we undertake. I believe the record is clear, as documented from sources ranging from the Church Committee in 1976 to the Iran/Contra Committee in 1987 that these secret activities of our government can succeed only when they are consistent with, and in support of, the publicly avowed foreign policy of the United States. I note...that one of the Iran/Contra Committee principles adhered to by the Committee in developing S. 1721 was the following: "As the Church Committee wrote more than a dozen years ago, 'covert actions should be consistent with publicly defined United States foreign policy goals.' But the policies themselves cannot be secret." I would like to inquire about the intent of the distinguished authors of S. 1721 with respect to insuring that covert operations are in accord with our open foreign policy.

Sen. Boren/Sen. Cohen: First of all, I would like to say that I share the distinguished Senator from Georgia's concern about coordinating our overt and covert foreign policies. The Intelligence Committee has been deeply concerned about the harm to our national interests which has resulted from the inconsistencies between these two sets of policies in the Iran/Contra affair. I can assure the gentleman that it is the intent of the Committee that covert actions will be scrutinized in great detail in terms of consistency with our publicly defined foreign policy goals. That is what is contemplated under S. 1721 as the standard for both the president in initiating covert operations and the Intelligence Committees in overseeing these activities.

Colloquy on Standards for Covert Operations

Sen. Fowler: There have been in the past, and no doubt will continue to be in the future, extraordinary circumstances in which these risky covert operations are the only effective means to protect vital interests of the United States. The Committee bill recognizes the necessity for maintaining the covert option, and this Senator certainly agrees with that determination. However, I am concerned that in the recent past covert operations have become too routine, have sometimes been undertaken because they are more convenient than going through more regular and open channels. In short, I believe the standard used under current law has been too lenient, and certain covert operations have been proposed where the risks were clearly disproportionate to the anticipated benefits, or where alternative, less sensitive means were available, or where the goal of the operation did not really touch a vital national interest. This situation has occurred under current law's requirement that a covert action must be "important" to national security. I note that the Committee bill retains that same standard. I would like to inquire of the gentlemen about their intent with regard to the standards to be employed in reviewing the appropriateness of a given covert operation.

Sen. Boren/Sen. Cohen: We agree with the Senator that covert action should be seen by both the Executive Branch and the Congress as an exceptional act. The need for a high standard for the initiation and conduct of covert activities was made clear in both the Tower Commission and the Iran/Contra Committee reports. Furthermore, under the leadership of then-National Security Assistant Carlucci, the Executive Branch significantly improved its oversight of covert operations. Finally, the Select Committee on Intelligence has strengthened its oversight of these operations. We believe the combination of improved Executive and Legislative Branch oversight, and the mandatory reporting provisions included in S. 1721 will provide the mechanism to bring about the kind of stringent standard for covert operations sought by the Senator from

> Georgia. However, if that does not prove to be the case, we can assure the Senator of our intent to revisit the issue of tougher statutory standards in the Select Committee on Intelligence.

S. 1721 was approved by the Senate on March 4, 1988, in spite of opposition by the Reagan administration, which stated its view that the bill would unconstitutionally infringe on the president's foreign policy powers. The measure was subsequently killed in the House of Representatives. While he would retain a strong interest in intelligence reform throughout his Senate career, and returned to the subject during his 1995 to 1996 service on the Commission on the Roles and Capabilities of the United States Intelligence Community, the 1987 to 1988 effort marked Fowler's last attempt in the Congress to reform congressional oversight of intelligence operations. Fowler was frustrated by the lack of meaningful action on intelligence oversight reform, especially in view of the inadequacies revealed in the Iran-Contra affair.

Space

Fowler continued to play a leadership role in the field of space science. Chief among his efforts in the One Hundredth Congress was his championing of NASA's proposed Comet Rendezvous Asteroid Flyby (CRAF) and the Cassini missions.

In 1988, NASA decided to seek congressional approval for a combined new start for CRAF and what came to be called the Cassini mission to Saturn. Fowler took up the cause for the combined missions in a May 12, 1988, letter to Sen. Donald Riegle (D-MI), chairman of the Commerce Committee's Science, Technology and Space Subcommittee.

> Dear Mr. Chairman:
>
> .... I believe the Congress has a unique opportunity this year to assert Congressional leadership of the space program.... I believe it is both possible and desirable for the Congress to authorize a new start for the combined Comet Rendezvous Asteroid Flyby (CRAF) and Cassini mission. I am not suggesting any change in the funding profile for the combined mission currently planned by NASA (which assumes an FY1990 new start). Thus an FY1989 new start for CRAF/Cassini would utilize the $15 million included in the

budget for advanced technology development of the Mariner Mark II series of spacecraft. While this would represent a "slow new start," it would be sufficient to advance the missions toward their currently planned launch dates....

Some kind of affirmative action this year on the Cassini mission is especially important. As you know, Cassini is proposed as a joint mission between NASA and the European Space Agency (ESA), and represents a further step in the direction of effective international cooperation. This November, ESA will be selecting one new space science project for its next three-year cycle, and from the reports I have received Cassini is currently the leading candidate from among five proposals. A strong American commitment to Cassini by this Congress would certainly be useful to NASA in its negotiations with ESA.

The CRAF/Cassini missions are the next priority space science projects in NASA plans and offer substantial and unique scientific benefits in understanding the origin and evolution of the solar system by initiating intensive American study of the primitive, volatile-rich bodies in the outer solar system....

By combining CRAF and Cassini into a joint development program, significant economies are possible. I am told that each mission, if pursued separately, would have a total cost of approximately $1 billion while the joint program would have a total cost of $1.5 billion, thus representing a 25 percent savings.

Fowler's efforts were not successful in winning Commerce Committee support for a FY 1989 new start for CRAF/Cassini, and he prepared an amendment to be offered to the NASA Authorization bill on the Senate floor in June 1988. After sounding out colleagues, and in view of opposition from both the Democratic and Republican floor managers of the legislation, he opted not to force a vote on his proposal, but again obtained a colloquy on the Senate floor on August 9, 1988, in order to attain at least some expression of support for his position.

Sen. Fowler: I would like to address a question to the distinguished Chairman of the Subcommittee on Science, Technology, and Space, the gentleman from Michigan. I notice in the Committee report that "the Committee is hopeful that the fiscal year 1990 NASA budget request will contain a new start request for the Comet Rendezvous Asteroid Flyby/Cassini Mission and that the final approved budget will be able to accommodate these two missions critical to the leadership position of the U.S. planetary science program." Would the gentleman elaborate on this point?

Sen. Riegle: Yes. The gentleman from Georgia has correctly stated the Committee position. The CRAF/Cassini Mission is NASA's highest priority space science initiative which has not yet received a new start, and the Committee believes such a request should be included in the FY90 NASA budget request.

Sen. Fowler: I thank the gentleman, and would like to make one additional inquiry. The House of Representatives included in its FY89 NASA Authorization bill a mandate for NASA to proceed with a new start for CRAF/Cassini as the next major mission start after the Advanced X-Ray Astrophysics Facility (AXAF). Does the gentleman anticipate that the conference agreement will affirm the Commerce, Science, and Transportation Committee's support for an FY90 new start for CRAF/Cassini?

Sen. Riegle: Yes, that would be my expectation.

Authorization for the new start was not provided in 1988, and Fowler would resume his efforts on behalf of CRAF/Cassini in the next session.

Fowler's settling for colloquies in place of likely losing floor votes in the cases of intelligence oversight and CRAF/Cassini was indicative of his whole philosophy of legislating in which working for attainable objectives and compromising when necessary was valued over scoring political points by forcing polarizing floor votes. In the view of the Georgia senator, "Nobody can get everything. In our diverse, and often divided, country, to achieve needed changes, you've got to compromise."

Other Fowler Legislative Activities and the Bork Nomination

Senator Fowler remained interested in foreign policy. In 1987, he was named as a congressional representative on the Commission on Security and Cooperation in Europe, known as the Helsinki Commission, an independent agency of the US government that monitors and encourages compliance with the Helsinki Accords on human rights and other issues. For example, in 1987, the commissioners wrote to President Reagan urging him to forcefully raise the issue of human rights at his summit meeting with Soviet leader Mikhail Gorbachev.

And among numerous Senate floor votes on foreign policy-related matters, Fowler cast two in the One Hundredth Congress that would be relevant to a major event that occurred in 1990 and 1991: the war with Iraq. On July 15, 1987, he voted for an amendment to the Omnibus Trade Bill that called for a trade embargo against Iran, or any other Persian Gulf country, "that launched an attack against US interests," and on September 9, 1988, he supported the Pell Amendment (approved by voice vote) that would have immediately imposed sanctions against Iraq for the use of chemical weapons in violation of international law. Both amendments were opposed by the Reagan administration, which strongly opposed sanctions against Iraq and supported continued US financial assistance to that country.

Returning to domestic policy, Fowler remained a leading congressional champion of historically Black colleges and universities (HBCUs). In 1987, he helped obtain $1 million in supplemental appropriations for HBCU graduate school programs; Morehouse Medical School and Atlanta University were two of the five schools eligible for these funds. For this and other accomplishments, he was awarded the 1987 "Presidential Achievement Award" by the Georgia Association of Black Elected Officials (GABEO).

In June of 1987, Supreme Court Associate Justice Lewis Powell announced his intention to retire, and on July 1, President Reagan nominated the controversial judge Robert Bork to replace him. Opposition to Bork was led by civil rights and women's organizations concerned that his previous writings and judicial opinions indicated he would likely support a rollback of federal protections in such areas as voting and abortion rights. The Bork nomination immediately set off a flurry of activity among both supporters and opponents. Fowler addressed the subject in a July 14 interview following a related speech he delivered to the Atlanta Rotary Club.

> I am upset by those who have prejudged Judge Bork on both sides, putting their own, artificial sometimes, criteria ahead of reading his

> judicial opinions and, most importantly, ahead of very close questioning when he comes before the Judiciary Committee as to his judicial philosophy, how he makes his decisions, and whether or not he does have any predetermined ideas that he would try to force on the court.[94]

After holding its hearings, the Senate Judiciary Committee rejected the Bork nomination by a 9 to 5 vote on October 6. The following day, Fowler and six other Southern Democratic senators announced their opposition, with Fowler stating, "Judge Bork, for all the brilliant qualities he does possess, does not incorporate the attributes we need most at this time in our history. I do not believe he embraces the spirit that can unite our people today, the same spirit that certainly united the authors of the Constitution."[95] On October 8, three more senators came out against Bork, producing a majority of fifty-one senators who had publicly declared their opposition. With defeat certain, there were calls for Bork to withdraw his name and not force a floor vote, but the judge refused.

On October 23, forty-two senators, including three Democrats, voted to confirm Robert Bork, whereas fifty-eight, including both Georgia senators as well as six Republicans, voted against. Fowler's decision and vote was denounced by supporters of the nomination, but he also received criticism from opponents. For example, the Atlanta chapter of the NAACP took out a full-page ad in the *Atlanta Voice* and *Atlanta Inquirer* faulting Fowler for his delay in coming out against Bork.[96]

Local Projects

Not all of Fowler's efforts were aimed at national and international matters, and he retained a strong commitment to serving the local interests of his constituents, which now stretched across the entire state of Georgia.

- Talmadge Bridge (Savannah, GA): As he had promised during the 1986 campaign, Senator Fowler helped secure the approval of Senate conferees to the 1987 Highway Bill for reconstruction of the Talmadge Bridge. Out of the $54 million included in the House version of the legislation, $53.2 million was approved by the conferees in March 1987. Prior to that time, the Senate had blocked several House-passed attempts in previous years to fund the new bridge. The overall legislation became law when Congress overrode President Reagan's veto on April 12. In recognition of Fowler's work, the Savannah Port Authority adopted a resolution that read, in part, "Senator Wyche Fowler was the leading catalyst in securing funding for the new bridge and without the dedicated support of Senator Fowler and his staff, the project might have failed to be successful."

• Chickamauga-Chattanooga National Military Park: Fowler obtained approval by his Energy and Natural Resources Committee and the full Senate of Rep. Buddy Darden's (D-GA) bill (H.R. 2121) to authorize federal funding for the rerouting of US Highway 27 to bypass the park. The legislation was signed into law by the president in December 1987. The following year, Fowler worked with Senator Nunn in a successful effort to obtain $6 million for the park in the enacted FY 1989 Interior Appropriations Bill.

• Savannah Harbor: Working with Senator Nunn and Rep. Lindsay Thomas (D-GA), Fowler succeeded in obtaining $2.15 million in FY 1988 appropriations to complete widening the Savannah Harbor channel, $400,000 in FY 1989 appropriations for a comprehensive study by the Corps of Engineers on deepening of the harbor, and another $300,000 in FY 1989 appropriations for extending the Savannah Harbor channel up to Mulberry Grove. The Georgia Ports Authority supported such an expansion so that it could build a new port facility at Mulberry Grove and thereby expand the capacity of the Port of Savannah.

• Augusta Railroad Crossings: Fowler helped obtain $1.187 million in FY 1988 and $900,000 in FY 1989 in appropriations for the construction of highway overpasses over railroad lines in downtown Augusta.

• Bobby Jones Expressway (near Augusta, GA): Senator Fowler worked with Augusta officials, the Corps of Engineers, the Georgia Department of Transportation, and EPA to work out a compromise on routing of the highway that enabled the highway to be built while minimizing environmental damage to surrounding wetlands. The compromise was announced in Augusta in August 1988, with Senator Fowler in attendance.

• Chattahoochee River National Recreation Area (metro Atlanta): Along with Representative Darden, Fowler took the lead in seeking $5.8 million in the FY 1988 Interior Appropriations Bill for acquisition of the 130-acre Chattahoochee Polo Fields site in east Cobb County for inclusion in the Chattahoochee River National Recreation Area. The Senate approved $1 million (versus nothing in the House bill) and the conferees ultimately provided $3 million.

• MARTA (Fulton and DeKalb Counties): Fowler helped obtain $106 million in appropriations for MARTA in FY 1988, which enabled the extension of three lines of the system, and $70 million in FY 1989, which provided sufficient funding to allow for the completion of the originally planned system.

• Fort Frederica (St. Simons Island, GA): In concert with Representative Thomas, Fowler succeeded in obtaining $300,000 in the enacted FY 1989 Interior Appropriations Bill for acquisition of the last remaining archaeological site related to the Fort Frederica National Monument.

As always, not all was serious business for Mr. Fowler. In a March 1987 column in the *Atlanta Constitution*, Ron Hudspeth concluded his saga of Fowler outdoor exercise exploits.

> I pulled Wyche Fowler out of a Washington staff meeting to give him the news last week. He came quickly to the phone. Hey, our elected representatives are supposed to be accessible and accountable, right? And, anyway, I had a biggie. When I relayed the news to our state's newest senator, his response was: "Wonderful." He hadn't heard the news of the Florida jogger who had won his case against the city of Palm Beach. A federal court had overturned a lower court, ruling that a Palm Beach ordinance restricting topless appearances in public is unconstitutional. The jogger, who went shirtless, had been arrested two years ago after being stopped by a police officer on a Palm Beach jogging trail. He had nothing on

Fowler. Fowler was also arrested topless in Palm Beach. "Most expensive tan I've ever had," he laughed. He paid a $25 fine. Fowler had awakened on a bright Florida morning four years ago, exited his Palm Beach hotel and hopped on a bicycle. The sun was beating down so warm and inviting, he pulled off his shirt and went pedaling off down the beach in the little town of millionaires. "I was actually on my way to a Braves [spring training] game," he explained. "I rode a mile down the beach, then I made a right turn to head over the bridge to West Palm Beach and the ballpark and, suddenly, this squad car pulled up, put on his lights and ordered me over. He said, 'Sir, you're violating an anti-nudity law," explained Fowler. "At first, I thought he was kidding. I even looked to see if I was unzipped. But he was serious. Dead serious. He wasn't smiling a bit." Fowler, a congressman at the time, did not tell the officer who he was. "I explained to him I wasn't aware of the law, and I certainly didn't intend to break any kind of law. He looked at me and said, 'Sir, ignorance is no defense before the law.'" The court ruled the Palm Beach ordinance "cannot be distinguished satisfactorily from a regulation requiring all citizens when in public to wear a brown shirt, or from a regulation requiring all men appearing in public after sundown to wear a black tie and tails." "I'm delighted the court so ruled that the sun is a gift from the almighty to be enjoyed by all," added Fowler.[97]

1988 Presidential Campaign

The biggest political event of 1988 was, of course, the race for president, with the state of Georgia playing a significant role because of the Democratic Party's selection of Atlanta as host for its national convention. Massachusetts Governor Michael Dukakis had already wrapped up the Democratic nomination before the Democrats convened in Atlanta in July. There had been some talk that Dukakis might turn to Wyche Fowler as his running mate, but ultimately he selected Sen. Lloyd Bentsen of Texas. *Atlanta Constitution* editor Tom Teepen commented on the case for Fowler, as well as the lessons the Dukakis campaign could derive from Fowler's successful 1986 race.

For a while there, for a couple of heady weeks, it looked as though Wyche Fowler might—just might—be seriously considered by Michael Dukakis as the Democratic vice presidential nominee. It appears that a couple of folks in Dukakis' small group of veep-finders were intrigued that Fowler had overcome a Republican opponent to win a Senate seat from Georgia and that he always has run well with Blacks, even against Black opponents, an attractive ability should Jesse Jackson prove sulky. What is more, Fowler has a progressive record that, although not as liberal as some on the party's left would like, would withstand scrutiny from most of the party.... And Fowler had useful foreign policy experience as a member of the House Foreign Affairs Committee and the House Select Committee on Intelligence. One of the knocks on Dukakis is his lack of experience in international affairs. It was always a long shot, of course, and it does not appear Fowler has made the short list. It isn't even clear the long list exists any more, though the fact that Fowler was invited to campaign with Dukakis in Massachusetts today will revive the speculation. And after all, who knows?

But if Dukakis' folks have gone off Fowler in search of bigger names, they would do well to keep him in mind for the campaign even so. It is difficult to imagine anyone who could give them better advice about how to run in the South. His campaigns two years ago for the nomination and for the Senate were classics.... Fowler turned both tricks while carrying a 10-year House record that was far more moderate than his conservative detractors tried to make it out, but was unquestionably liberal on some key issues. The liberalism was especially glaring at the time in Fowler's long opposition to Reagan's policies toward Nicaragua. The Atlanta congressman had consistently opposed the contras, the Nicaraguan guerillas whom the president is pleased to see as "freedom fighters." Reagan was trying to make the issue one of patriotism. Fowler, however, managed to wrap his own position so tightly in the flag that it would have taken Indiana Jones two days to cut through it with his sharpest machete. So, too, with other issues where Fowler had potential liabilities and where opponents tried to tar him as liberal. There are two points in this that should interest Dukakis and his plotters. One: Despite contrary legend and slander, voters in the

> South are entirely capable of listening to, and agreeing with, more or less liberal propositions. Not all Southern knuckles drag the sidewalks and red-dirt roads. Not even most. But, two, it is important just how such positions are put. Fowler, on the stump, is a master of putting issues in ways that, no, don't mislead voters, but that make issues accessible to a broad range of attitudes. And he does it without clowning it up, without "'necking"; that is, "rednecking."[98]

Fowler was given national exposure when he was asked to deliver a five-minute address to the Democratic Convention on Wednesday, July 20. Shortly after he began, the teleprompter—which he rarely used—broke, forcing Fowler to "wing it."

> The fact that I am standing here testifies to what people can do when we all work together. City people and country people, rich and poor, office workers and farm workers, men and women, Americans first, affirming our citizenship by expelling sorriness and selfishness from the highest offices of our land. That is the ideal of America Democrats stand for, all the way from Andrew Jackson to Jesse Jackson, representing the makeup of our country in its entirety, in its every dimension, every view. The Democratic vision of America is the one that has expanded the partnership among citizens united by their patriotism and their quest for public service, by their hard work and their optimism. It is the model of the active, involved citizen required by our Constitution.... Well, I know Americans are tired of just being strong on paper. They know that our answers to the challenges we face abroad in trade, in national defense, rest right here at home with the American people, with motivated workers in productive jobs. This is our national strength, my friends. This is our national reputation. Michael Dukakis will lead us to the job that must be done, not with Democratic solutions or Republican solutions but the best solutions for our country. That's what the word Democrat means, that we put patriotism above partisanship, that we put principle above patronage.

Reporter Scott Shepard profiled Fowler toward the end of his first two years in the Senate.

The black 1966 Buick Riviera wheeled into the courtyard parking lot of the Richard B. Russell Senate office building, the low rumble of its engine heralding the morning arrival of Wyche Fowler, the would-be "good ol' boy" of the U.S. Senate. The Buick once belonged to Lester Maddox, the firebrand segregationist who wrapped his beliefs in populist rhetoric and became governor of Georgia in 1967, when Fowler was in his first year of law school. The irony is not lost on the car's current owner. Fowler, a white Atlantan, represented a predominantly Black congressional district in the city for a decade before he was narrowly elected to the Senate in 1986 with the overwhelming support of Black Georgians. But the Buick is more than a reminder of the political changes that have occurred in Georgia since 1967. Like the ax handle Maddox once brandished in defiance of federal desegregation laws, the car is an important prop in Fowler's effort to create a head-turning reputation in the nation's capital.... Equally important to Fowler is the message the Buick is supposed to send back home: that the guitar-strumming, gospel-singing congressman who gained the confidence of 51 percent of the state's voters two years ago is the same folksy character in Washington that he is on the back roads of Georgia. "Some people may think that I'm a kook," the senator said during a recent interview, "but with Wyche Fowler, what you see is what you get." Gazing at the Buick through the Senate office window, Fowler expressed frustration that "too many people assume everybody in Washington is wheeling around in limousines, going to cocktail parties in Georgetown...." A longtime friend, Georgia Supreme Court Justice Charles Weltner, agrees with Fowler's appraisal of himself but also finds amusement in the senator's ability to generate publicity. "Wyche Fowler doesn't need a public relations man," Weltner said. "He's his own public relations man. He's got a knack for it." But Weltner believes Fowler's knack for publicity is not so much a ploy, such as driving a 22-year-old automobile, as it is the result of his sincerity. "Wyche is a genuine person," Weltner said. "He moves comfortably in any circle because he is a genuine person. He's sincerely interested in what everybody thinks, what everybody has to say...." "There's an awful lot of good ol' boy in him," [campaign media consultant Frank] Greer said, "but he's also a real

Washington insider who can get things done for his state." Fowler readily admits he was "very much an insider" in the House, where he served on the Ways and Means Committee and the Democratic steering and policy committee.... The "good ol' boy" emerges during the town meetings Fowler hosts most weekends in Georgia, events he clearly relishes. "I like people, and I think it shows," he said. "People can tell whether you like them or not, or whether you're just there suffering because you have to. And they don't mind disagreement if you look them straight in the eye and tell them without mincing words. Most of them just want to see whether you have a good reason for your position, whether you can back it up or whether you weasel or not." In the first 18 months of his Senate term, he visited 141 Georgia counties. Before the end of summer, he expects to fulfill his campaign promise to visit all 159. As a House member, he represented a congressional district consisting of 1½ counties and about 600,000 people. As a senator, he represents 10 districts, 159 counties and about 6 million people. "So you have to work ten times harder," Fowler said with a laugh, only half joking.[99]

Chapter 11

101st Congress (1989–1990): Summit

The 101st Congress represented the pinnacle of Wyche Fowler's career in the Congress in terms of his achievements and impact on public policy across a wide range of issues. Certain developments late in the term, however, highlighted challenges he would face in his bid for reelection in 1992.

Assistant Floor Leader

The story of Fowler's policy ascendancy in 1989 actually began with the race to succeed Robert Byrd (D-WV) as Senate majority leader. Senator Byrd had served as the Democratic leader in the Senate for twelve years, but after the lopsided defeat of Michael Dukakis in the presidential race (426 electoral votes for George Bush to just 111 for Dukakis) and minimal gains for Democrats in the Senate (one seat) and House (two seats) in the 1988 general election, there was a general belief that new leadership was required.

When Byrd announced his decision to take over as chairman of the Appropriations Committee in preference to remaining as Democratic leader, three senators announced their candidacies to replace him in the November 30, 1988, caucus of Senate Democrats: Daniel Inouye of Hawaii, J. Bennett Johnston of Louisiana, and George Mitchell of Maine. Many presumed that Fowler, like most of his Southern Democratic colleagues, would support Johnston, who also happened to be chairman of the Energy and Natural Resources Committee of which Fowler was a member. However, the Georgia senator had been impressed with Mitchell's organizational and communications skills—as well as his pledge to Fowler that he recognized the diversity of Senate Democrats and would ensure that Southern Democrats would operate on an equal footing in policymaking should he prevail—and decided to back him.

The Mitchell team regarded Fowler's support as key in demonstrating Mitchell's appeal to a wide range of Senate Democrats, particularly those in the South, and the Georgia senator was chosen to deliver one of two nominating speeches for him before the Democratic Caucus. Afterward he said, "Mitchell has a better chance of earning respect inside and outside the Senate by the way he has faced up to the toughest challenges and by his ability to penetrate to the heart of some very confusing issues." At the caucus, Mitchell received twenty-seven of the fifty-five votes, with Inouye and Johnston each tallying fourteen. Though this fell one vote short of the requisite majority, the two trailing candidates withdrew, and Mitchell was then elected by unanimous acclamation.[100]

Mitchell's election as majority leader was followed by two important advancements for Fowler. First, in a move reminiscent of his elevation to the House Ways and Means Committee back in 1979, his Democratic colleagues selected him for a spot on the Appropriations Committee, which, along with the tax-writing panels (Ways and Means and Senate Finance) is regarded as among the most influential of all congressional committees. This assignment had been an objective of Fowler's since his election to the Senate. Due to its role in allocating federal funds, the senator deemed it particularly valuable for his state, with its considerable need for investments in infrastructure and education.

The fact that he had supported the winning side in the leadership race certainly boosted Fowler's prospects in obtaining the Appropriations seat, but there was also a conscious desire to provide him with a political boost in preparation for what was widely anticipated to be a highly competitive race for reelection. Similarly to his 1979 election to the Ways and Means Committee, Fowler placed first among eight contenders for three spots on the Appropriations panel, including winning the endorsement of incoming chairman Byrd. Fowler told a reporter that in his remarks to the Democratic Caucus prior to the vote, "I ran as a seasoned man, with 10 years...in the House before the Senate.... I assured all my colleagues that I wasn't expecting them to vote for me just as a Georgian but as somebody who will do what's best for the country."[101]

The other occurrence in early 1989 was Senator Mitchell's appointment of Fowler to the newly created post of assistant floor leader. According to Fowler, "He never told me he was appointing me: I saw it on television." Mitchell explained the reasons for the selection: "[Wyche] has a very nice, easy manner that causes other Senators to like him. He helps to referee disputes among Senators.... I rely heavily on his judgment.... [His skill is enhanced by his ability to] serve effectively as a southern Senator and still be a national Senator."

Columnist Durwood McAlister was impressed by Fowler's advancement.

> The United States Senate has been described as "the most exclusive club in the world." Inside this club is a smaller group, the even more exclusive "inner club"—the leadership. That is where much of Washington's power and influence are concentrated. And who is the newest member of that "inner club"? None other than Georgia's very junior senator, Wyche Fowler. Only two years ago, Mr. Fowler was the liberal representative of Georgia's Fifth District, given little chance of success in his statewide race for the Senate. He not only won the race; he has quickly established himself as a force to be reckoned with in the nation's capital. Despite his short tenure, he was chosen this week by Senate Majority Leader George Mitchell as assistant floor leader, a position that makes him an active participant in the agenda-setting deliberations of the Democratic leadership in the Senate.... Mr. Fowler obviously comes up short on seniority and some Republicans would argue that his seat is not all that secure; but it is apparent that Mr. Mitchell sees in him an abundance of the other qualities required for membership in the inner circle. He said as much in his announcement of Mr. Fowler's appointment. "One of the reasons I created this position, and one of the reasons I selected Senator Fowler for it," he said, "is that I want to encourage bipartisanship, and I know that Senator Fowler is widely respected among all his colleagues, including the Republican members of the Senate. It will be his job, among other things, to help build bridges to enable us to work cooperatively to deal with the serious challenges and problems facing our country." Citing Mr. Fowler's 12 years of experience in Congress, Mr. Mitchell went out of his way to stress the importance of the Georgia senator's new role. "I intend that he will become an active participant in the Democratic leadership in the Senate," he said. "And that involves not just activities on the floor, but right in this very room where we meet regularly to attempt to determine what our course of action

should be, what legislation to bring up, when to bring it up, how to present it." All in all, it is a remarkable development.[102]

As a new position, his role as assistant floor leader evolved throughout the remainder of Fowler's tenure in the Senate. It included participating in regular strategy sessions with Mitchell and the other senators in the Democratic leadership, performing outreach to other Democratic senators, and handling a significant part of the Senate's procedural business.

1990 Farm Bill

The major work product of the Senate and House Agriculture Committees is the omnibus Farm Bill that periodically reauthorizes and updates existing programs and sometimes creates new ones. In 1990, the Farm Bill was due for reauthorization, and Wyche Fowler played a major role in crafting that measure. As a member of the Agriculture Committee, Fowler, aided by his staff counsel and chief agricultural aide, Bob Redding, was instrumental in drafting much of the language that ultimately was enacted and signed into law (PL 101-624):

- *Environmentally sound agriculture:* Many provisions from the Fowler-authored Conservation Promotion Act were retained in the final version, including expansion of the Conservation Reserve Program, with eligibility extended to include marginal pastureland, shelterbelts, and windbreaks; establishment of a Wetlands Reserve Program; creation of a voluntary Integrated Crop Management program to facilitate the adoption of environmentally sound agricultural practices; and a requirement that the extension service annually train 20 percent of its current personnel, plus all new hires, in environmentally sound agricultural practices.
- *Forestry:* A large portion of Fowler's Timber Research, Education, and Enhancement (TREE) Act was included in the forestry title of the enacted bill, which represented the most significant revision in the national forestry program in fourteen years. The Fowler provisions strengthened forestry education and technical-assistance programs for owners of small, private forests; expanded forestry research; increased international trade opportunities for

forest products; created a Southern Forest Productivity and Regeneration Center to study Southern forests; and established a permanent disaster-assistance program to assist landowners in reforesting lands damaged by natural disasters.

• *Commodities check-off programs*: Sen. Fowler offered a successful floor amendment to the Farm Bill that added language creating farmer-funded national promotion, research, and consumer information programs for pecans, soybeans, limes, and mushrooms, while improving existing such programs for Vidalia onions, cotton, potatoes, and honey.

• *Peanut program*: The Fowler-Nunn bill (S. 2473) was one of the major sources of the section of the Farm Bill that reauthorized the federal peanut program.

• *Minority farmers:* A Fowler floor amendment added the provisions of the senator's Minority Farmers Rights Act to the Farm Bill. The Fowler language sought to reverse the decline in minority-owned farmland by establishing a national registry of minority farmers to monitor ownership, expanding USDA education and outreach programs for minority farmers, establishing demonstration programs for minority youth, requiring USDA to review the effectiveness of its appeals process for discrimination complaints and affirmative action policies, and requiring USDA to review the effect of its purchasing and contracting policies on minority businesses. Said Fowler at the time of the Farm Bill's approval by the Senate, "Our minority-owned farms are disappearing. Trends that have damaged farmers in general have hit minority farmers the hardest. If we don't act now, in a few short years we won't have any minority-owned farms left." Whereas the number of white-owned farms had decreased by approximately 7 percent between 1978 and 1987, the decline was 23 percent for African American farms during that period, and in the South, where 60 percent of Black-owned farms were located, five African American farmers had given up farming for each white farmer who had done so.

• *Food safety:* Fowler offered a successful floor amendment to require EPA to establish a National Agricultural Pest Control Information Program that would compile a record of chemical and nonchemical pest-control methods for use in health risk and benefit assessments, and another that required the Department of Agriculture to investigate the extent to which the standards governing the physical appearance of fruits and vegetables affect the use of pesticides in the production of these commodities. Both requirements were retained in the final, enacted version of the Farm Bill.

• *Rural education:* Language from Fowler's Rural Star Schools Act was incorporated into the bill. These provisions promoted the use of telecommunications, computers, and related advanced technologies to improve educational opportunities in rural schools.

Senator Fowler spoke of the significance of the Farm Bill to Georgia at the time of the Senate's adoption of the legislation in August 1990. "We've won a major battle for the continued success of Georgia's agricultural community. Over the last few months, we have hammered out a bill supported by members of the agricultural community, environmentalists, and consumers. I consider it is a great accomplishment to have participated in the development and adoption of the 1990 Farm Bill, which will dictate farm policy for the next five years."[103]

These Fowler efforts were well received by a variety of organizations. He received the National Association of State Foresters Award "for improving forest resources through leadership as Chairman of the Forestry and Conservation Subcommittee of the United States Senate and as a principal author of the Forestry and Conservation Title of the [Farm Bill] of 1990"; the Public Voice Award "for efforts in food safety, specifically cosmetic standards and low-input agriculture"; the Southeastern Pecan Growers Association Award "for dedicated support of the pecan industry"; a Vidalia Onion Committee resolution "for efforts to promote the Vidalia Onion"; the Georgia Organic Growers Association Award "for steadfast concern and commitment to the welfare of agriculture and the environment"; the Georgia Farm Bureau "First Annual Friend of the Farmer Award"; and the Southeastern Peanut Association Award. Relatedly, he also was named Conservationist of the Year in 1990 by the Georgia Wildlife Federation.

Forest Road-Building

Senator Fowler's initiatives in the Farm Bill were not the only instance in which he sought to exercise leadership in national forestry policy during the 101st Congress. In July 1989, he secured passage (by a vote of 55 to 44) of his floor amendment to the FY 1990 Interior Appropriations Bill to reduce what he felt was the fiscally unsound and environmentally harmful practice of federally subsidized road construction within national forests. Specifically, the Fowler amendment, which had the support of a diverse coalition, including most environmental groups but also the fiscally conscious National Taxpayers Union and the conservative Heritage Foundation, cut forest service funding for such construction by $65 million and shifted $40 million of the savings to the Fish and Wildlife Service's resource management and land-acquisition programs, national recreation and preservation programs, state and private forestry programs, and the National Park Service's anti-looting and technology-transfer programs. It used the remainder for deficit reduction.

The final version of the Interior appropriations measure retained $41.1 million of the road construction reduction and $10.85 million of the Fowler programmatic increases. Peter Kirby of the Wilderness Society stated, "What Senator Fowler has done is attack the most environmental destruction and biggest single item in the Forest Service budget. In doing so, he has built a coalition of environmentalists and fiscal conservatives." Tom Kuhnle of the Natural Resources Defense Council commented, "He attacked what had been a perennial sacred cow and attacked it with a lot of vigor. He's really been quite a leader."[104]

Fowler's efforts also drew editorial support by the *Atlanta Journal-Constitution.*

> Although the Forest Service has a long and impressive history of escaping attempts at reform, Mr. Fowler should not let up. For decades, the Forest Service has been selling off the nation's trees at a loss—actually using taxpayer money to harm the environment... Consider the example of the Tongass National Forest in southeastern Alaska. Throughout the 1980s, timber sales from the Tongass

have lost more than 90 cents on each dollar spent by taxpayers. Incredibly, the Tongass wood is sold to just two customers with exclusive 50-year agreements—and one of these is a Japanese company. In other words, U.S. citizens are paying to level big chunks of pristine forest—land that serves as home to bald eagles, salmon and grizzly bears—so that Japanese builders can get cheap wood.... Mr. Fowler plans to continue the fight to reform the Forest Service by reducing spending for new roads. Not only would that slow logging, but it would allow the government to spend more on programs for fish, wildlife, recreation and wetlands. In addition, Mr. Fowler wants to find ways to encourage more private landowners to get involved in environmentally sound timber production. In light of the worsening budget deficit and growing concerns for the environment, 1990 may be the year the Forest Service finally gets a long overdue reordering of its priorities.[105]

But it was not to be. Fowler made a similar attempt via a floor amendment to the FY 1991 Interior appropriations legislation that would have cut Forest Service road-building by $100 million, and transferred $40 million of the savings to forestry research, fish and wildlife habitat protection, wetlands restoration, and historic preservation. However, this time strong opposition from Western Republicans led to the amendment's defeat in October of 1990 by a vote of 44 to 52.

An Associated Press story highlighted Fowler's views of the Senate action.

> The Senate reversed its support for reducing logging road construction in national forests because Republicans put politics ahead of fiscal and environmental concerns, says Wyche Fowler, Jr. (D-GA). Fowler said GOP senators concerned about the re-election prospects of Sen. Mark Hatfield (R-OR) made the difference in Tuesday's 52–44 vote against his amendment.... Six of the 12 Republicans who supported the amendment last year reversed themselves Tuesday.... Fowler said timber companies pay for 85 percent of the roads in national forests, with the Forest Service using taxpayer funds to build only those roads that aren't profitable for timber

> companies to build. "The timber companies build and willingly finance the roads to get in where they get the timber because they can still make their profit," he said. "They don't have to go up to the top steep slopes, the older growth, places of scenic beauty. We ask the taxpayers to do that." Fowler said the Forest Service's timber sales program cost the taxpayers $365 million last year, primarily because of road-building expenses. He said existing roads in the national forests already stretch eight times as far as the interstate highway system.[106]

Renewable Energy, Water Conservation, and HBCUs

Fowler's efforts to boost renewable energy also experienced some notable successes during 1989 to 1990. First, he finally secured passage of his Renewable Energy and Energy Efficiency Technology Competitiveness Act, which was signed into law by the president on December 11, 1989. It represented the first serious boost for renewable energy programs since the Carter administration. Second, he won Senate passage of an amendment to the Clean Air Act amendments of 1990 to promote the use of renewable energy technologies to achieve an accelerated reduction of sulfur dioxide emissions. The Fowler language was retained in modified form in the final, enacted version of the legislation.

In recognition of his leadership in the Congress on solar energy and energy conservation, the Solar Energy Industries Association presented Fowler with its 1990 Solar Salute Award "for conception and support of initiatives to promote solar energy to become further cost-effective" and the Passive Solar Industries Council bestowed upon him its 1990 Advocate of Passive Solar Award "for efforts on behalf of passive solar energy and energy conservation techniques."

Yet another *Atlanta Constitution* editorial praised a Fowler initiative, this time his ongoing efforts to promote water conservation.

> Our planners can no longer count on the heavens as they try to assure that metro Atlantans will have enough drinking water in the future. Recent rainfall patterns have added up to a cosmic game of chance. Worse, plans to funnel more Lake Lanier gallons into home taps rest with Congress, and are only a little less iffy than the

> weather. Meanwhile, the region is adding new homes and new water consumers at breakneck speed. Do we have any other options, besides luck and reallocation of Lanier's water to use by metro consumers? There is one thing we can do. We can push Congress to enact water-efficiency standards proposed by Sen. Wyche Fowler (D-GA) and Rep. Chester Atkins (D-MA). The rules would force plumbers to install more water-efficient showerheads, faucets and toilets in new homes. The bill would also set standards for water-guzzlers like dishwashers and washing machines. The Atlanta Regional Commission has been recommending similar measures for years. They could deliver some surprisingly dramatic benefits. While the best estimates are now little more than guesses, backers believe the bill ultimately could prompt Americans to use up to one-third less water as they go about their daily lives.... By using less water, our supply—in Lake Lanier and elsewhere—would be greater. And as we cut back on our use of water, we would be reducing our volume of wastewater. This would be a godsend for beleaguered sewage treatment plants in counties like Gwinnett. Meanwhile, water and sewage treatment bills would drop.[107]

In light of future events—years of drought; the water compact fight between Georgia, Alabama, and Florida over allocation of water from the Chattahoochee River; water pollution concerns—the editorial was most prescient, but it, like the Fowler legislation, fell on mostly deaf ears, and very little was done at the time.

Fowler continued to champion the cause of historically Black colleges and universities. He chaired a Senate Budget Committee Hearing in Atlanta on the status of HBCUs, secured report language in the Senate's FY 1991 Energy and Water Development Appropriations Bill urging the Department of Energy to work with Clark Atlanta University to complete construction of its research center for science and technology, and inserted language in the FY 1991 Budget Resolution supporting increased funding for HBCUs. The National Association for Equal Opportunity in Higher Education gave Fowler a March 1990 award "for consistent and dedicated support of the Historically Black Colleges and Universities."

Historic Preservation

Fowler's effort to enhance historic and archaeological resource protections continued to progress in the 101st Congress, albeit at the slow pace typical of the legislative process. To build support for his proposals, Senator Fowler addressed the 1989 annual meetings of the National Conference of State Historic Preservation Officers (NCSHPO) and the Society for American Archaeology, two of the leading organizational backers of his legislation, as a prelude to his reintroduction of historic preservation legislation. On August 4, 1989, the Georgia senator submitted two bills to the Senate which were similar to the legislation he introduced in the previous session:

- *Historic Preservation Administration Act* (S. 1578), creating a) a new and independent historic preservation agency to oversee and coordinate the national historic preservation program; b) a preservation advisory committee to advise and assist the historic preservation agency; c) an archaeology advisory board to advise the historic preservation agency on archaeological policy and assist in the development of professional standards for archaeologists and of relevant archaeological research questions that may be addressed in federally conducted archaeological projects; and d) a national center for preservation technology to research, develop, and disseminate historic and prehistoric preservation technologies.
- *National Historic Preservation Policy Act* (S. 1579), which was aimed at strengthening and improving the accountability of US preservation policies. It would represent the first comprehensive update since 1980 of the National Historic Preservation Act and the Archaeological Resources Protection Act, the two cornerstones of the national preservation program. Among its major provisions were
  - clarifying, coordinating, and strengthening federal preservation responsibilities, including the protection of high-priority historic resources from imminent destruction or disruption;
  - improving the quality of federally sponsored archaeological research;

- combatting the looting and illegal trade of archaeological resources;
- clarifying and strengthening state preservation programs by allowing states to assume additional responsibilities for administering the national program within their territories, while ensuring that they would be reimbursed for the costs of carrying out these duties;
- establishing a role for Native American tribes within the national preservation program, allowing tribes to assume responsibility for issuing permits for archaeological work on tribal lands, and establishing a federal policy on the reburial of human remains and grave-associated artifacts that gave priority to the wishes of living descendants;
- defining the role of local preservation programs and allowing qualified local programs to take on additional responsibilities; and
- requiring the establishment of a comprehensive preservation education and training program in order to increase public awareness of preservation concerns, increase opportunities for avocational preservationists to participate in the federal program, and expand training opportunities, including the provision of special assistance to HBCUs and schools with large numbers of Native American students.

Shortly after the introductions, the Fowler office received letters of support for the two bills from the Society for American Archaeology, NCSHPO, the Navajo Nation, the National Indian Education Association, the American Institute of Architects, and the Society for Historical Archaeology.

The effort to obtain Senate cosponsors for the Fowler bills proved exceedingly difficult. Only two senators signed on to S. 1578—Tom Daschle (D-SD) and Patrick Leahy (D-VT)—and only four cosponsored S. 1579—Daschle, Leahy, Jeff Bingaman (D-NM), and Alan Simpson (R-WY)—underscoring the challenge in gaining adoption of the Fowler bills. However, two hearings were held on the legislation, the first in Washington on February 22, 1990, and the second in Savannah, Georgia, on May 19, 1990, which helped generate additional attention and interest in the proposals.

Most importantly, in the spring and summer of 1990, negotiations with key stakeholders began in earnest, when the Fowler staff met with representatives of NCSHPO, Preservation Action, the National Trust for Historic Preservation, the Society for American Archaeology, and Native American organizations. Staff from the National Park Service and the Advisory Council on Historic Preservation provided technical assistance as the groups worked to arrive at a consensus bill that all could support. The process highlighted points of controversy:

1. The creation of an independent Historic Preservation Agency (S. 1578). This was the single most controversial provision in the Fowler preservation legislation, which was favored by the States and NCSHPO but strongly opposed by the National Park Service and its congressional allies as well as by the National Trust for Historic Preservation, who felt that it would weaken the Park Service.
2. The provision in S. 1579 requiring federal agencies to follow the preservation recommendations of the Advisory Council on Historic Preservation except when there was no "prudent and feasible" way to do so. This would represent a significant strengthening of the role of the advisory council in the less than 1 percent of cases each year that were not successfully resolved via a consultation process. While this was generally backed by the preservation community, the National Trust expressed some concerns that it could disrupt the existing cooperative relationships between the advisory council and other federal agencies.
3. The provisions in S. 1579 that largely clarified and codified the existing system for the National Register of Historic Places and Historic Landmarks. These were generally supported by preservationists, but Preservation Action and the National Trust expressed some concerns about their potential impact on existing relevant case law.
4. S. 1579's artifact registration program, with archaeologists supporting its intent while questioning its practicality, and private collectors, including many museums, opposed.
5. S. 1579's section on disposition of human remains and associated grave goods. A Fowler staff memo detailed the evolution of concerns on these provisions.

> [This section] was the most contentious of all of S. 1579's provisions because it involved trying to resolve a (or the) major conflict between two of the bill's key support groups: Indian tribes and archaeologists. When this Section was in its first draft, the archaeologists were against any statutory provision in this area, preferring to rely on local mediation efforts, while the Indian groups were pleased to see any language which recognized the rights of descendants. By the time the current language was developed both sides had signed off on the language as a reasonable compromise of their conflicting interests on the reburial issue.... After the introduction of S. 1579, the Indian groups' position on [this section] changed. This was the result of the passage (by both Senate and House) of Sen. Inouye's Indian Museum bill and a change in policies of the Smithsonian, both of which gave priority to the return of human remains to descendants to the exclusion of any competing research interests. Therefore, while the archaeologists now strongly support [the S. 1579 provision] as much better than the Smithsonian/Inouye approach, the Indian tribes now specifically do not endorse [it] (though they call it a "well intentioned" effort which is better than current law).

6. S. 1579's amendment of the Abandoned Shipwreck Act, to extend that law's protections to shipwrecks beyond three nautical miles offshore. It was supported by archaeologists but strongly opposed by salvagers and sport divers.

The consultative process resulted in Fowler's introduction of the National Historic Preservation Act Amendments of 1990 (S. 3196) on October 12, 1990. The new bill retained the National Center for Preservation Technology from S. 1578 and many of the provisions in S. 1579, including the no "feasible and prudent" standard before an agency could undertake a project not in accord with advisory council recommendations. However, it dropped the following:

- the independent Historic Preservation Agency,
- the Archaeology Advisory Board and Preservation Advisory Committee,
- most of the changes in the National Register and National Landmarks programs,

- the artifact registration program, substituting a study on the feasibility of such a program and a requirement that archaeological materials produced by federally sponsored archaeological survey and recovery work be registered,
- the Human Remains and Associated Grave Goods section,
- the Abandoned Shipwreck Act Amendment, and
- the section on local preservation programs.

Though Fowler regretted the loss of many of these provisions, the development of this consensus bill was to prove crucial in the eventual enactment of much of the Fowler program.

Local Projects

Winning a spot on the Appropriations Committee facilitated Senator Fowler's ability to obtain federal assistance for Georgia projects. From this point on in his Senate career, these accomplishments were numerous. A partial list of Georgia-related appropriations in the 101st Congress in which Fowler played the lead role include the following:

- *University of Georgia (UGA) programs*: obtained $750,000 in FY 1990 and $744,000 in FY 1991 for a rural economic development program run by the UGA Office of Rural Economic Development and obtained $1 million in FY 1991 for construction of the Dean Rusk Center for International and Comparative Law.
- *Chattahoochee River National Recreation Area*: obtained $3 million in FY 1990 and $1 million in FY 1991 for acquisition of additional land for the national recreation area.
- *Andersonville National Historic Site:* obtained $435,000 in FY 1990 and $644,000 in FY 1991 for road and visitor-center work at the historic site.
- *Fort Benning Schools:* inserted language in the FY 1990 Military Construction Appropriations Bill directing the Defense Department to include $8.6 million in its FY 1991 budget for renovations at two Columbus-area schools that served children whose parents worked at Fort Benning, and led a successful effort to approve FY 1991 appropriations of $7.9 million for construction of Bouton Heights School and $1.5 million for additions to White School.

• *Tuskegee VA Medical Center:* obtained $624,000 in FY 1991 for design of the renovation of the Tuskegee VA Medical Center Nursing Home Unit, which served a large number of west Georgia veterans.

• *Bond Swamp:* obtained $11 million in FY 1990 for "High Priority Wetlands Acquisitions" and inserted report language singling out the Bond Swamp area near Macon for such acquisition. (The US Fish and Wildlife Service subsequently purchased the Bond Swamp land for inclusion in the Ocmulgee Wildlife Refuge.)

• *Glynn County Harbors and Beaches:* obtained $3.7 million for Brunswick Harbor Operations and Maintenance, helped obtain $400,000 for Glynn County beach restoration in FY 1990, and obtained $4 million in FY 1991 for an interim renourishment project for beaches on St. Simons Island.

Space

Fowler's efforts on the Appropriations Committee were not confined to Georgia-related projects. One key example was his service on the VA-HUD-Independent Agencies Subcommittee, which was the appropriations panel that funded NASA. This position enabled the Georgia senator to continue his work on behalf of space exploration in general, and the CRAF/Cassini missions in particular. He continued to take the lead role in the Senate with respect to the latter, writing to VA-HUD-Independent Agencies chair Barbara Mikulski (D-MD) in May of 1989:

> My highest priority within the FY90 NASA Budget is the combined CRAF/Cassini mission. I believe that providing a FY90 new start for this program, which has continually won the highest approval from all relevant NASA review groups, is essential to the survival of a strong and balanced American space science program. If we don't fund CRAF/Cassini this year: 1) the celestial mechanics (for helping to transport the missions to the outer solar system) are such that launch opportunities for similar missions would be many years in the future; 2) almost certainly the European Space Agency will remove its substantial commitment to the Cassini mission; 3)

with the projected FY91 request for the Earth Observing System (which I also support), a mission with a much higher price tag (at least $600 million a year for a number of years), the competition for scarce space science dollars will only grow more difficult; and 4) because of all of the above, the U.S. planetary exploration program would be placed in considerable jeopardy, with no new missions in sight for the outer planets, with the whole peer review system (as exemplified by the Solar System Exploration Committee's fine work) under question, and with diminished future research opportunities to attract today's high school students to pursue careers in space science.

Senator Fowler took the lead in the Senate in the successful effort to obtain the full $30 million requested by NASA in its FY 1990 budget to fund a new start for CRAF/Cassini, and he helped obtain $145 million in FY 1991 appropriations for the combined missions.

On a related note, Fowler was the author of a concurrent resolution expressing the sense of Congress that "1) the entire NASA/Jet Propulsion Laboratory team is to be commended for its achievement in the Voyager program of successfully reaching into the depths of the Universe and taking great strides in solving the mysteries of the solar system; and 2) the United States should remain preeminent in the field of planetary exploration, and will continue to support high priority science missions to maintain that leadership." The Fowler Voyager resolution was adopted by the Senate by unanimous voice vote.

Obscenity and Federally Funded Art

Ten days after the Senate's approval of the Voyager commemoration, Senator Fowler was involved in a far more controversial proceeding. Demonstrating both his strong parliamentary skills and keen interest in finding a workable compromise in a very polarized debate, on September 28, 1989, and without any advance notice to his own staff (who almost certainly would have recommended against the undertaking), Fowler entered into the political minefield of obscenity and federally funded artwork. Through his intervention, he broke an impasse that had developed in the Senate over an attempt by Senator Jesse Helms (R-NC) to attach an amendment to the FY 1990 appropriations bill for the Departments of

Commerce, Justice, and State that would prohibit the National Endowment for the Arts from funding "indecent or obscene materials." Supporters of the arts were determined not to let any bill—even one that provided funding for three key federal agencies—pass with the Helms language intact, and Senator Helms and his supporters were equally determined to hold up the bill until the amendment was acted on. Few senators wanted to go on record as either "supporting obscenity" or "opposing artistic freedom."

Stepping into this situation, in the words of a *New York Times* article, "[Fowler] strode onto the Senate floor waving a Bible and demanded to know if supporters of even more restrictive language were prepared to ban its contents, or to declare the paintings of the Old Masters obscene because they portrayed naked cherubs."[108] A discussion between Senators Helms and Fowler then ensued on the Senate floor.

> **Sen. Helms:** Mr. President, I have an amendment I send to the desk and ask for its immediate consideration.
>
> Helms Amendment No. 891:
>
> None of the funds authorized to be appropriated pursuant to this Act may be used to promote, disseminate, or produce—
>
> (1) Obscene or indecent materials, including but not limited to depictions of sadomasochism, homoeroticism, the exploitation of children, or individuals engaged in sex acts; or
>
> (2) Material which denigrates the objects or beliefs of the adherents of a particular religion or non-religion; or
>
> (3) Material which denigrates, debases, or reviles a person, group, or class of citizens on the basis of race, creed, sex, handicap, age, or national origin.
>
> **Sen. Helms:** I believe most Senators are familiar with the amendment that I offered to the Interior Appropriations bill and that it would prevent the NEA and other Federal so-called arts agencies from using Federal funds to pay for art that is obscene or indecent or which degrades religion. If artists want to go in a men's room and write dirty words on the wall, let them furnish their own crayons; let them furnish their own wall. But do not ask the taxpayers to support it with their hard-earned money. That is all the

amendment says. No tax funds shall be used for garbage just because some self-appointed "experts" have been foolish enough to call it "art...."

Sen. Fowler: I preface by agreeing with the Senator from North Carolina in his paragraph No. 1 that what he has attempted to do is to prohibit material, photographs, so-called art that is deeply offensive to the spirit and to the dehumanization of man [from receiving federal funding]. And for that effort, he has my support.

But if the Senator would reply, I am concerned...by the language of his amendment in article two and article three, which I submit is unnecessary to the attempt to get rid of smut, which we all share.... For instance, the language of the Senator's amendment says, and I specifically quote, "No funds may be used to promote, disseminate or produce material which denigrates the objects or beliefs of the adherents of a particular religion or non-religion." Would not the Senator admit that the Holy Scripture itself, that the words of Jesus in the Sermon on the Mount, in all of the Gospels, Matthew, Mark, Luke and John, depictions in this Bible, in any written work, much less 700 years of Christian art, can be conceived as being offensive to Jews, who are being asked to follow a man that we as Christians believe is the Son of God, but their faith, Judaism, denies that special status? Would not the Senator, who knows this Bible, know that when Jews deny that Jesus is the Son of God, the absolute rock on which all Christian faith is founded, that that denial by Jews, throughout all of the literature of our libraries, funded by public moneys, depicted in religious films, depicted in art, that that denial by Jews is deeply offensive in the words of the Senator's amendment to the particular religion of Christianity?

Others have spoken tonight far more eloquently than I...about the last clause, section 3; and I will not try [to repeat them] except to say that language can be written to cover pornography and obscenity, but when we get into these areas—exploitation of children, what about the great Titian of Herod slaughtering the first-born? Is that not a depiction of exploitation of children? Why did Sampson, blinded, pull down the temple on his head? Is that not self-masochism, a man who believes his faith so strongly that he would kill himself by pulling down the temple? We cannot let some bureaucrat decide these questions, because these questions, which are as deeply rooted and as old as all of our faiths, are not necessary to reach the intent of the Senator's amendment....

The question down the road if we adopt this amendment is whether or not we are going to fund libraries that have any literature that is covered under this act. The question down the road is whether or not we repeal the charitable deductions of taxpayers who give to their religion in order to disseminate, produce, and promote their religion, which happens to be offensive to the non-religious. That is where the public policy leads. All of you forgive me for sounding like I am preaching. I am not trying to do that. I am just trying to say...there is an easy way to deal with this and accomplish, I submit, the complete purposes of the Senator from North Carolina and that is to voluntarily delete sections two and three that cover areas totally extraneous to obscenity or pornography and art.

We can adopt the strong language [in section one] minus the word "indecent" [and including only "obscene"] because that has been the subject of all sorts of interpretations by the Supreme Court, and what the U.S. Senate would say is "No public money shall be authorized to promote, disseminate, or produce obscene materials, including but not limited to depictions of sadomasochism, homoeroticism, the exploitation of children or individuals engaged in sex acts." What could be stronger or more explicit to tell the country, no money for that, tell the bureaucrats you are gone if you do that, tell the NEA that you have to get back in touch with the American people, our values; we are not going to tolerate this.

The next day, Senator Helms modified his amendment as suggested by Senator Fowler, except for retaining the word "indecent." Fowler then offered a successful amendment, which passed the Senate 65 to 31 on September 29, that limited the Helms ban to "obscene" art. His reasoning was that, with taxpayers' money involved, there was a legitimate public interest in placing some conditions on federal grants, as indeed is done in virtually every federal grant program. However, he felt that artists should not be subjected to the arbitrary whims of federal bureaucrats left to interpret what is "indecent." The "obscene" standard retained in the Fowler measure at least had a long history of Supreme Court decisions to act as a guide. While the Fowler amendment did help end the gridlock in the Senate over this issue, it brought Fowler mostly attacks—from supporters of the arts who saw any conditions on federal funding as an improper restriction on artistic freedom, and from conservatives who believed the Fowler language significantly weakened the attack on what they viewed as obscenity.

In an October 12, 1989, commentary, *Constitution* editor Tom Teepen cited Fowler's efforts.

> Call it Fowler's Dodge. Georgia's U.S. Sen. Wyche Fowler has helped the arts avoid the rocket Sen. Jesse Helms had launched against federal support for them, but don't throw your caps in the air yet. The war isn't over.... [The National Endowment for the Arts] had been threatened by a Helms amendment that would have barred any federal aid to obscene or indecent art or, in effect, although the language was loftier, to art that anyone cared to take offense to because of its content or point of view. With his instinct for the vulnerable, Mr. Helms was taking advantage of the fact that 'round-about federal support had gone to two photographic projects of dubious taste. For every rare flap of that sort, the NEA supervises thousands of grants that cause no contrary stir, but Mr. Helms loves no advantage quite so much as an unfair one. He knew of course that the amendment would put his fellow senators in a painful political bind. Most recognized the amendment as wildly inappropriate but most feared—realistically—that Lee Atwater and other right-wing hard-ballers would incite election campaigns libeling Helms opponents as favoring using taxpayer money for child porn. Enter Mr. Fowler with a cute substitute. Inveighing on the floor against dirty art and citing Biblical sources like a preacher on a tear, the Georgian offered an amendment that emphatically forbids federal support for obscenity. It also, however, dropped the word "indecent," which has no legal meaning and was an open invitation to political manipulation, and eliminated the language that would have allowed art to be challenged because of its content. The Senate embraced the substitute like a drowning man grabbing at driftwood, and why not? The amendment does nothing more than

> repeat the operative Supreme Court definition of obscenity. Mr. Fowler's gambit protects the status quo while shielding his colleagues from political abuse: They have voted against obscenity. The senator has accomplished the most elegant of political maneuvers, the creation of legislation that beats the bad guys at their own game.[109]

Operation Desert Shield

On August 2, 1990, Iraqi forces invaded Kuwait and in a matter of days seized control of the country, with Saddam Hussein announcing its annexation as a province of Iraq. The international response to Iraq's actions was swift and largely unified. On August 3, the United Nations Security Council passed a resolution condemning the invasion and demanding the withdrawal of Iraqi troops. Three days later, the Security Council adopted another resolution imposing economic sanctions on Iraq, and shortly thereafter another resolution authorized a naval blockade to enforce the sanctions. At the national level, condemnation of the invasion and support for retaliatory sanctions was widespread, extending to countries such as China, France, India, and the Soviet Union, which had had close relations with the Hussein regime. For its part, the United States demanded the immediate and unconditional withdrawal of Iraqi forces from Kuwait, and on August 7 began "Operation Desert Shield," which involved the deployment of US military forces to Saudi Arabia to protect that country from a potential Iraqi invasion. Finally, on November 29, 1990, the Security Council adopted another resolution setting a withdrawal deadline of January 15, 1991, and authorizing member nations to use "all necessary means" to force Iraq out of Kuwait after that deadline.

Wyche Fowler strongly supported the coordinated international response to the Iraqi invasion, including the imposition of sanctions and the Desert Shield deployment of US military forces. Indeed, in the run-up to the invasion, he continued his consistent support for the imposition of sanctions against Saddam Hussein's government. In May 1990, he voted for a Senate bill requiring the president to impose trade and aid sanctions on countries—including Iraq—that used chemical or biological weapons, and in July 1990, he voted for an amendment to the Farm Bill requiring the president to invoke sanctions against countries that violated human rights and prohibit the extension of new financial credits to Iraq. Both of these measures were opposed by the Bush administration, which had actually doubled US financial credits to Iraq in 1989.

Both the Reagan and Bush administrations had hoped their policy of engagement with the Hussein government would produce significant benefits to the United States, including the possibility that Iraq could emerge as a strategic partner with the US, that it could serve as a regional counterweight to Iran, and that it could be a force for moderation on key regional issues such as the Arab-Israeli peace process. But, as Fowler later said, "We will never know whether we could have stopped Saddam in his tracks, without loss of American lives, if we had been more resolute in our dealings with him prior to August 1990."

At the time of the August 7 decision by President Bush to send US troops to Saudi Arabia, Fowler commented,

> I think it is the right decision, and I think [President Bush] has the overwhelming support of the Congress and certainly the American people. [Saddam] has got to be stopped now, and we hope we can stop him now without a fight...but we are prepared for a fight.... I'm so pleased we're going to have Arab participation on Arab borders. We hope this virtually unanimous show of force will make fighting unnecessary. [Saddam] would be and will be overwhelmed...if he forces a fight. But all of this is up to him now.

In an August 1990 interview, Fowler praised the Bush administration for its efforts in organizing international sanctions against Iraq after the invasion of Kuwait and presented his views about the way forward.

> A combination of worldwide economic sanctions against Iraq and U.S. military involvement in the latest Middle East crisis could take several months and Americans "will have to learn patience," U.S. Sen. Wyche Fowler said Thursday. The Georgia Senator said Iraq's President Saddam Hussein has no allies and Iraq can "be strangled...with a combination of economic sanctions and what I call the military wall.... We have to have some patience and shouldn't look at this thing as a one-week sort of deal.... It could take five, six, eight months and the American public will have to learn patience," said Fowler.[110]

As the year wore on, Fowler grew increasingly concerned about American policy in the Persian Gulf, which seemed to be shifting from defending Saudi Arabia to liberating Kuwait, with a vast increase in the size and scope of the American military commitment. On November 12, during his second stint as a participant in the Business Council's Pre-Legislative Forum in Columbus, Georgia, he called for a special session of Congress to debate the country's role and mission in that region. "We are now at a juncture where we must have a national debate. Questions must be answered responsibly." The following day, the president rejected calls for a special session and for congressional action on a formal declaration of war against Iraq. As Fowler continued his tour of the state, the Georgians he encountered expressed their own worries about the developing situation.

> Every question he got in Valdosta dealt with the war, and the spontaneous questions were the same from Cartersville to Savannah.... People are worried, he said. At Fort Stewart, for instance, a psychologist had seen 90 troubled children since their fathers went off to Saudi Arabia. People were "totally supportive" when President Bush's policy was defensive. But now it's offensive, and people are asking questions. If we invade Kuwait, how long might we stay? Will U.S. forces occupy Iraq? What about air war vs. ground war? "The approach I'm taking in doing my listening is to determine whether we are unified about a hot war, about going on the offensive." Some Georgians are telling him Saddam Hussein will have to be fought. But others ask, "Are we going to have forces stationed there until oil production is resumed—with all the oil wells blown up?" Like Sam Nunn, Fowler wants to know what the terms of victory are. How do we know if we've won? Egypt? It should send many more troops. Saudi Arabia? "There ought to be a five-fold increase in the money they're sending. I'm a burden-sharing man. Burden-sharing is very important to the Georgians I've been talking with." What if the allies don't come up with more? "I just don't have an answer." Fowler replied. He thinks a bombing war might not succeed, and he thinks a bloody ground war could radicalize the Arab world.... He wished Saddam would disappear. But what if someone just as bad replaces him? How can the American people

> distinguish between prudent congressional doubts and self-serving congressional carping? What's Congress's policy? His answer, then and later in the day, went like this: he doesn't have a full-blown policy, but the U.N. trade embargo should be given a chance to work. "I think you'll see some serious internal dissatisfaction in Iraq," he said, four or five months up the road. The American people, moreover, must be unified before going to war. Yet even Fowler (part of the Democratic leadership, a man interested in foreign affairs, a charter member of the House Intelligence Committee) does not know the answers to the questions people are asking, and he's appalled to hear the secretary of state saying we may go to war to protect U.S. jobs.[111]

As 1990 ended, the threat of war in the Persian Gulf continued to grow.

1990 Budget Summit

Back in January of 1990, President George H. W. Bush submitted a $1.2 trillion federal budget to the Congress for FY 1991, with a projected deficit of $64.7 billion, but in March the Congressional Budget Office estimated the actual deficit under the Bush plan would be $131 billion. Moreover, these figures did not include the costs for the federal bailout of the savings and loan industry. (A third of all S&Ls collapsed between 1986 and 1995, resulting in losses of $160 billion, of which $132 billion was ultimately paid for by taxpayers.) And though inflation remained a serious problem, the US economy was deteriorating, causing estimates of future deficits to escalate.

In the previous year, Bush had reached agreement with congressional Democrats, who had comfortable majorities in both houses, on measures to reduce the FY 1990 budget deficit to under $100 billion, as required by the Gramm-Rudman-Hollings Act of 1981. That agreement did not include any tax increases, consistent with the president's "read my lips, no new taxes" pledge at the 1988 Republican Convention, but many independent observers believed that that relatively modest deficit-reduction package only postponed difficult decisions about the spending cuts and tax increases that would likely be needed to reduce the federal deficit to more manageable proportions. In addition, the Bush administration faced pressure from Federal Reserve Board chairman Alan Greenspan, who indicated he would need to see a significant reduction in the deficit before the Fed would undertake the more stimulative monetary policy the administration (and many outside economists) felt to be essential if the economy was to get growing again.

With this as backdrop, on May 6, President Bush, along with key members of his economic team, including Office of Management and Budget (OMB) director Richard Darman, White House chief of staff John Sununu, and Treasury Secretary Nicholas Brady, hosted a White House meeting with key congressional leaders to press for negotiations on the FY 1991 budget. Darman told the group that failure to meet the Gramm-Rudman-Hollings deficit-reduction target, which would trigger that law's across-the-board "sequester" cuts, would be disastrous for the economy, and Senate Majority Leader Mitchell obtained a pledge from the president that he was willing to negotiate on taxes. At a follow-up meeting three days later, Mitchell got the group to agree that there would be no preconditions in the negotiations, and a bipartisan group of twenty-six congressional negotiators was named to negotiate a budget deal with Darman, Sununu, and Brady. The White House announced that the president "will not be a direct participant in the meetings but will be involved as necessary."

The congressional negotiators included the chairs and ranking Republican members of the appropriations, tax-writing, and budget panels in both chambers, along with representatives from the House and Senate leadership. This latter category included House Majority Leader Gephardt, D-MO, who was to chair the ensuing "summit" meetings, House Minority Whip Newt Gingrich, R-GA, and Senate assistant floor leader Wyche Fowler, who was to represent Majority Leader Mitchell in the meetings. Fowler's role was described in a June 29, 1990, *New York Times* article:

> George J. Mitchell, the Senate Majority Leader, has not given Mr. Fowler a precise job description, but it boils down to making sure that whatever the final deficit-reduction deal, it can be sold on the floor of the House and the Senate and that Democrats who vote for it do not get sold down the river in this fall's elections. It is a plum

> assignment for a first-term Senator.... The lanky Georgian, who describes himself as "a progressive by regional standards" lest someone label him a liberal, is in many ways a natural bridge connecting the competing concerns and personalities and ideologies of the Democratic negotiators. Mr. Fowler's assignment, said one Democratic strategist, is "being able to see the end game and how to get there, and Fowler has proven exceptional at that."[112]

The formal summit meetings began on May 15 in the Mansfield Room on the Senate side of the US Capitol building. Over the next month, the negotiators and their staffs met periodically, with limited results, as summed up in a June 8 Fowler staff memo.

> • The basic reason the President convened the summit was that, largely because of escalating costs associated with the S&L bailout, the Administration increased its estimate of the FY91 deficit from $93 billion in the President's January budget to $199 billion in the latest OMB estimate. This would mean that, absent deficit reduction agreements between the President and Congress, the across-the-board sequester under Gramm-Rudman would now be $135 billion...rather than $29 billion as contemplated in the President's January figures.
>
> • Within the summit, there has been some progress in determining the size of the deficit reduction package needed to bring the problem under control. The Administration, and many economists, have indicated that the largest deficit reduction package that they can safely approve (without triggering a recession) for FY91 would be in the $45–$55 billion range. Also, consensus seems to be developing that the full five-year deficit reduction package should total between $450–$550 billion, with the Democrats supporting the higher number.
>
> • One point of difference that has emerged thus far is that the Administration seems most anxious to remove all S&L bailout costs from the deficit calculations (in order to reduce the size of the needed package) while the Democrats are very interested in

taking the Social Security surplus off-budget (so it will not continue to be used as a backdoor method of reducing the deficit).

• The summit has heard presentations from the Administration and key Congressional committee chairmen and ranking members (including Sen. Nunn) on defense and entitlements. Next week, it is expected that discussion will focus on budget process reform and revenues. Both sides are anxious to accelerate the talks, but the Democrats still believe that without Presidential leadership in convincing the public that strong medicine is required and in laying out his proposed solution the summit cannot succeed.

It was during this period that one of Fowler's most talked about interventions during the summit meetings occurred. On June 14, OMB director Darman suggested that, in order to speed up the process and promote serious negotiations, a closed-door meeting should be held without the presence of staff. During that session, Sununu sought to clear staff from the room to carry out his colleague's suggestion. "According to one participant at the session, the Senator [Fowler] spoke up in mock amazement and said, 'But Governor, that means you and Mr. Darman will have to leave the room.' The staff members remained, a tactical victory for Democrats who contend that when their own technical experts are absent they are at the mercy of budget-number interpretations offered by Richard G. Darman, the White House budget director."[113]

Also around this same time, another Fowler witticism was injected into the proceedings. Sen. Robert Byrd, a noted defender of the constitutional role and prerogatives of the Congress, was dismayed by discussions of major "process" reforms concerning the budgetary and appropriations systems long in use. He was particularly disturbed about Bush administration support for a "line-item veto," by which the president could disapprove of a single item in an appropriations bill without having to veto the overall legislation. At a meeting of Democratic negotiators and staff, Senator Byrd expressed outrage at reports that Democratic and Republican staff members had been negotiating on such a proposal, and he demanded that he be included in any discussions on this topic. With tension in the room at a high point, Fowler asked Senator Byrd whether he was familiar with one of the shortest verses in the Bible. Byrd and others looked perplexed at this seeming non sequitur, but Fowler pressed on, paraphrasing the Good Book, "And Jacob leaned upon his staff and died." The remark lifted the tension in the room, gaining an affirmative nod from Byrd, bemusement from most of the other members present, and grimaces from many of the staff members.

The major impediment to progress in the negotiations was, however, taxes, as described in an article by Elizabeth Drew in the August 6, 1990, *New Yorker*.

> The President's aides had known for a long time that he would eventually have to break his pledge [on "no new taxes"]; they considered having him do it last year but decided to take more time while he built up a reservoir of popularity. The President's calling for a budget summit carried the implied assumption that he would have to agree to more taxes. His January budget had asked for about fourteen billion dollars in additional tax revenues, some of which the Administration knew that Congress wouldn't agree to, plus some new "user fees," bringing the new revenues to about twenty billion dollars.... The summit talks had become stuck, because neither side wanted to propose additional taxes. The Democrats had been saying that the President had to lay out his own new program, perhaps on national television. But the President wasn't interested in leading with his chin, or leading at all, so nothing happened. The Democratic negotiators, or most of them, had resolved that they wouldn't put forward tax proposals only to have Republicans beat them about the head as taxers; John Sununu...had already not so subtly telegraphed that this was the White House strategy.

Along with Sen. James Sasser (D-TN), chairman of the Senate Budget Committee, Wyche Fowler emerged as the leading voice among Democratic negotiators in calling for presidential leadership in putting taxes on the table. He came to that position for a variety of reasons. First was the obvious political one of avoiding the trap he had seen and personally experienced throughout the Reagan years of supporting bipartisan tax increases to offset a small portion of the enormous budget deficits caused in large part by Reagan tax cuts and defense spending increases, only to have the president disclaim responsibility and shift the blame entirely to Democrats for "forcing him" to accept the tax increases. Second, his role in the negotiations obliged him to look out for the political interests of fellow Democrats—especially those up for reelection in the 1990 midterms—who would be asked to support the certain-to-be politically painful deficit-reduction package but without having a part in its development. And, finally, he was also convinced from the outset that the success of any agreement was going to rest on President Bush, who had initiated the negotiations and who would necessarily have the lead role in selling any agreement to the American public.

Though not without dissent from some of the Democratic negotiators, the Fowler-Sasser position prevailed among the Democrats, and ultimately the president moved to break the impasse. At a June 26 White House meeting with Foley, Mitchell, Dole, House Minority Leader Robert Michel (R-IL), Gephardt, Sununu, Darman, and Brady, it was agreed that any budget deal would have to include entitlement reform, reduction of defense and other discretionary spending, budget process reforms, and tax increases, with this agreement expected to serve as the basis for serious negotiations in the immediate future. Bush issued a statement that same day:

> It is clear to me that both the size of the deficit problem and the need for a package that can be enacted require all of the following: entitlement and mandatory program reform; tax revenue increases; growth incentives; discretionary spending reductions; orderly reductions in defense expenditures; and budget process reform—to assure that any bipartisan agreement is enforceable and that the deficit problem is brought under responsible control.

In the short term, the Bush statement produced little movement toward an agreement, and most notably resulted in an outpouring of criticism from his fellow Republicans. For example, shortly after the statement was issued, a majority of House Republicans signed on to a letter to the president opposing any increase in tax rates (though remaining silent on other potential revenue raisers). Fowler indicated his belief that the endgame was still some distance off, stating, "Now we're like a couple of sumo wrestlers. We're circling each other, snorting and sniffing and throwing salt over our shoulders before we go to grappling." But the challenges facing the negotiators only intensified. In its midyear review issued on July

16, OMB raised its estimate of the looming FY 1991 deficit to $231 billion if S&L bailout costs were included, $168.8 billion if they were not.

In a July 20 newspaper story, it was reported that Newt Gingrich told summit negotiators the previous day that he was prepared to support tax increases as part of an "acceptable" plan to reduce the deficit.

> Gingrich, one of the staunchest foes in Congress of raising taxes, said he expected that he would have to ask House Republicans to support a deficit-reduction package that would seek to raise fiscal 1991 tax revenues by about $25 billion and that he expected to be able to deliver the votes, participants at the budget negotiations said. "It has always been my position that if we get an acceptable summit resolution, I would, of course, be an original cosponsor of that resolution," Gingrich said later. "If you're not willing to sponsor an agreement you think is good, you shouldn't be in the room." The assurances from Gingrich were made a day after House Republicans approved a resolution opposing higher taxes and the assurances were delivered to a budget bargaining session in which negotiators sought to calm the political apprehensions that have impeded the talks. Asked by House Majority Leader Richard A. Gephardt to explain the resolution, Gingrich told the group that House Republicans were responding to a statement by Senate Majority Leader George J. Mitchell that he would oppose any plan to cut the tax rate for capital gains without also raising the income taxes on the wealthiest Americans, participants said.... In a May fundraising letter, Gingrich declared, "I strongly believe that increasing taxes on working people will NOT solve our country's massive budget problems!... Keeping the Democrats from raising income taxes is one of my toughest jobs."[114]

With the congressional August recess nearing and no agreement in sight, in early August the White House and congressional leaders agreed that the budget negotiations would resume around Labor Day at Andrews Air Force Base outside of Washington for focused negotiations with a goal of producing completed action on a deficit reduction package by October 1. The task facing the negotiators was further complicated by Iraq's August 2 invasion of Kuwait.

The Georgia senator's thoughts on Democratic priorities for the upcoming Andrews summit were detailed in an August 29 staff memo.

A. *Protect the Purchasing Power of Middle Class Americans* in any spending cuts or revenue increases. This position is grounded in the following facts contained in a 1990 report by the bi-partisan Congressional Budget Office:
—From 1980 to 1990, the percentage of income paid by the poorest one-fifth of U.S. households in major federal taxes (income, payroll, excise) rose 16 percent, and their after-tax income fell by 5 percent.
—From 1980 to 1990, the percentage of income paid by the middle one-fifth of U.S. households in major federal taxes rose 1 percent, and their after-tax income rose by less than 3 percent ($660).
—From 1980 to 1990, the percentage of income paid by the wealthiest one-fifth of U.S. households in major federal taxes fell by 14 percent, and their after-tax income rose by 33 percent ($19,000).

B. *Protect the integrity of the Social Security Trust Fund.* This is perhaps the first accomplishment to come out of the summit: Agreement, already backed by bi-partisan majorities in both houses, to remove Social Security from the Gramm-Rudman deficit calculations, where its growing (but temporary) surpluses have been used by the last two administrations to hide the true size of the federal deficit.

C. Within the overall fiscal policy decisions made by the summit, *prioritize investments in America's future by adequately assisting education, infrastructure, scientific research, environmental protection, and energy security.* For example, to look at some specific considerations, there are a number of policy options consistent with reducing the deficit which would aid the environment and enhance our energy security....

D. Any deficit reduction summit agreement must produce 5-year savings of at least $500 billion. Otherwise, at the end of the period,

> the deficit will be only marginally reduced (if at all) from current levels, and members (and the public) could legitimately ask about the need for such an agreement....
>
> E. Any process reforms should be based on the following: 1) Our current constitutional arrangements concerning the separation of powers have served us well for over two hundred years, and no significant alterations should be made in those arrangements, or at least not without far more consideration and deliberation than is possible in an ad hoc summit whose supposed purpose is deficit reduction. 2) The problems in the present system have more to do with political will than with statutory/constitutional authorities. 3) Such problems reside equally with the president and the Congress, and any "fixes" must be aimed at the presidential, as well as the Congressional, budget process.

After a slow start, progress was made in the Andrews discussions to the point that they were extended beyond the original September 11 deadline. A September 12 *Washington Post* article highlighted the growing sense of optimism.

> White House and congressional budget negotiators buoyantly predicted yesterday that an agreement on a five-year, $500 billion deficit-reduction package can be reached in the next few days. In an exchange of proposals that began late Monday night and continued yesterday, the Democratic and Republican bargainers began moving toward each other and away from the positions they had maintained virtually unchanged since the beginning of the budget process in January, participants in the talks said. The negotiators are to return to the converted main bar in the Andrews Air Force Base Officers' Club this morning for a sixth day of bargaining. House Majority leader Richard A. Gephardt, who is presiding over the talks, vowed that, except for a brief gap this afternoon so lawmakers may go to the Capitol to cast votes, the negotiators will not leave the base without an agreement. "We'll work all day and, if necessary, through the night," said Sen. Wyche Fowler, a Democratic negotiator. "We're going to try hard to finish as soon as we can."

"I'm on the positive side of the mood swing," said White House Chief of Staff John H. Sununu. Participants predicted that a deal on a package of spending cuts and tax increases that would save $50 billion in the first year could be reached as early as Thursday. In the past days, administration officials have begun discussing a larger military spending cut than they had previously proposed and Democratic negotiators have nearly doubled the cuts they said they would be willing to accept in such benefit programs as Medicare. In addition, the most recent Democratic proposal, offered yesterday, dropped their plan to raise the marginal tax rate for the wealthiest Americans, an element they said was important to restore fairness to the tax system. The concession was made to accommodate the administration's demand that income tax rates not be raised, Democratic participants said. The Democratic offer still includes taxes on such luxury items as jewelry, boats and expensive automobiles and a temporary surtax on those with incomes higher than $500,000 a year, Democratic negotiators said. Revenue from the surtax would go to reducing the deficit. Bargainers are considering a military spending cut of between $10 billion and $12 billion in the first year, and between $170 billion and $200 billion over five years, participants said. The range of domestic spending saving is between $13 billion and $15 billion in the first year, and between $90 billion and $130 billion over the five years of the package, they said. Even with an agreement on the dimensions of various parts of a plan, large differences remain on the details. On taxes, for instance, the Bush administration has stood firm in its support for a cut in the capital gains tax rate, which Democrats oppose as a break for the rich.[115]

Those "large differences" on some items ultimately proved insurmountable in the Andrews talks, and on September 17, it was agreed that the negotiations should move to the White House, with Speaker Foley and Senate Majority Leader Mitchell now leading the Democratic negotiators. As Representative Gephardt explained, "The talks are not collapsed. We're just moving them to a different stage."

On September 30—the day before the new fiscal year was to begin, and with it the implementation of the Gramm-Rudman sequester cuts if no budget deal was reached—the Bush administration and congressional negotiators finally reached an agreement that was announced at a Rose Garden ceremony the next day at the White House. The accord outlined a plan to cut the deficit by $40 billion in FY 1991, and by $500 billion over five years. It provided for $134 billion in new taxes, the majority of which was to come from a phased increase in the gasoline tax; just under $120 billion in reductions in entitlement programs, including $60 billion from Medicare, $13 billion from farm programs, and $2 billion from student loans; and $182 billion in decreases in discretionary spending. (The balance of the $500 billion would come from lower interest payments.) Importantly, it also established a "pay as you go" requirement whereby any new federal program would have to be paid for at the time of its initiation by either offsetting spending cuts or higher revenues, or a combination of the two.

Accompanying the agreement, on October 1, Congress passed, and the president signed into law, a continuing resolution to fund the government until October 5 to allow for congressional action on its implementation.

Wyche Fowler joined all but one of the congressional negotiators in attending the Rose Garden announcement and backing the agreement with the president. The exception was his fellow Georgian Newt Gingrich.

> Sen. Wyche Fowler said Tuesday that he will reluctantly support the proposed $500 billion deficit reduction agreement reached over the weekend. Fowler, who helped negotiate the bipartisan accord, said the package of deep spending cuts and steep tax increases is "certainly not any good news document" for the public. "It's not something I find easy to support," the senator said during a meeting with reporters. "There are many things in it I do not like. There are many things not in it that I would have liked to see in." But Fowler said he considered the alternative "totally unacceptable"—$85 billion in across-the-board [FY 1981] spending cuts that could have taken effect this Monday if an agreement wasn't reached. "The alternatives to the deficit-reduction package are not only much, much worse, but they are totally unacceptable, hospitals literally

closing, airports ceasing to operate, layoffs...vast cuts in law enforcement, on and on and on," Fowler said.... "Despite this difficulty, this is the time to exhibit national unity and national resolve," Fowler said. "You're not strong as a nation if you have a weak, debt-ridden economy where interest rates and inflation continue to go up and up." Georgia's other participant in the budget talks, Republican Rep. Newt Gingrich, denounced the agreement Monday, saying Congress "can do better than this. It will kill jobs and weaken the economy with tax increases that are counter-productive," Gingrich, the second-ranking House Republican, said in announcing he would buck President Bush.[116]

Gingrich and conservative Republicans were not the only ones to oppose the budget summit agreement. Georgia Rep. John Lewis, for example, "said the agreement places too heavy a burden on low and middle income taxpayers, doesn't force the wealthy to pay their fair share, and cuts too little from defense spending."

The opposition of conservative Republicans and liberal Democrats, though motivated by diametrically opposed reasoning, combined to produce a "stunning defeat" for the president and congressional leadership on October 5, when majorities of both parties in the House rejected the budget resolution that would have implemented the agreement on a vote of 179 to 254 (Yes: 108 Democrats, 71 Republicans; No: 149 Democrats, 105 Republicans). The Georgia delegation was split right down the middle on the vote, with Democratic Representatives Darden, Hatcher, Ray, Rowland, and Thomas voting in the affirmative, and their Democratic colleagues Representatives Barnard, Lewis, Jenkins, and Jones joining Gingrich in voting against the resolution.

The defeat of the budget resolution set off a mad scramble to try to avert a government shutdown that was due to occur when the continuing funding resolution expired on October 6. On that day (Fowler's fiftieth birthday), Congress adopted another continuing resolution to fund the government through October 12, but President Bush vetoed it, stating, "It is time for the Congress to act responsibly on a budget resolution—not time for business as usual." The House then failed by six votes (on a 260 to 138 vote) to obtain the two-thirds majority needed to override the veto. Thus, portions of the federal government (mostly national parks) started to close down.

With the president unable to win over Gingrich and other GOP opponents, it was determined that the Democratic leadership would put together a slightly revised budget resolution that could win passage in the House and Senate by relying mostly on Democratic votes. The resulting resolution reduced the Medicare cuts and provided more flexibility to congressional committees in achieving the deficit-reduction targets agreed to at the summit. On October 8, the revised resolution was approved by the House on a largely party-line vote of 250 to 164 (Yes: 218 Democrats, 32 Republicans; No: 28 Democrats, 136 Republicans), with all nine Georgia Democrats voting yes and only Gingrich opposed. In the early morning hours of October 9, the Senate took up and passed the budget resolution by a more bipartisan vote of 66 to 33 (Yes: 42 Democrats, 24 Republicans; No: 13 Democrats, 20 Republicans), with Senator Nunn joining Fowler in voting to approve it.

Prior to the Senate action, Fowler spoke on the pending measure, including his assessment of the entire summit process.

> In response to last week's House defeat of the budget resolution, some changes have been made which make more explicit the role of House and Senate committees in shaping the final details of the deficit reduction package.... Yet, I do not want to mislead any member of this Senate into believing that this new conference report will ultimately lead to easier choices. It may be less difficult to vote for this less specific deficit reduction plan tonight, but you will still be faced with the specifics when the reconciliation bill comes out of our committees....
>
> Nonetheless, I believe that approval and implementation of the deficit reduction provided for in the budget conference report now before us is vital to our long-term national security. The budget package is about sacrifice: there are no easy ways to resolve the problems I have already alluded to. It is about commitment: now, with our servicemen and women on the front line in the Persian Gulf, is a time when we must demonstrate national unity and national resolve. It is about our nation's future: without finding a solution to

our budget, trade and investment deficits, we will continue mortgaging our children's futures. And, yes, it is about political courage: many of the things this agreement proposes to do are considered suicidal politically, and all of us who have signed on to the cause can look forward to "Monday Morning Quarterbacking," 30-second negative TV ads, and special interest attacks. This is a major effort, being the largest deficit reduction package in American history, by far, even if one takes the most pessimistic view of how our committees will implement its provisions. But, given the magnitude of the problem, no other course was possible....

There will be some difficult economic times ahead, whether or not this deficit reduction package is approved. But while, as I have said, no one could possibly endorse every item of this package with great enthusiasm, you must consider the alternatives if the agreement is not ratified. First, the Federal Reserve Board will conclude that there is insufficient political will to correct our fiscal policy problems, and will therefore, understandably, fail to reduce interest rates. Second, the Gramm-Rudman across-the-board sequester will be triggered, producing not only the undesirable policy outcomes I mentioned before, but also taking more than twice the amount of money out of the economy as envisioned in the summit agreement. Both of these factors will worsen, not improve, our economic situation....

If we fail to act now, how much longer will the country have to wait; how much more will our budget, trade and investment deficits have to grow; how much larger a share will have to go simply to pay the interest on the national debt; before action is taken? My answer is we cannot afford to wait. If we do nothing now, projections are that the federal deficit will grow to over $300 billion over the next five years, not even including the effects of an economic downturn. If left unattended, this deficit problem is going to grow and grow, and it will be much more difficult, not easier, to solve it in the future.

Clearly, the budget summit agreement is open to attack on many fronts. It represents neither what the Democrats nor the President and the Republicans would have produced if they were able to enact a plan on their own. A quick review of the initial offers which we presented to each other at Andrews Air Force Base should suffice as an indicator of what each side would like to have done. Compared to the final agreement, the Republican package had larger cuts in entitlements, including Medicare and agriculture, and in domestic discretionary spending, and lower cuts in defense. The Democratic offer was just the reverse. On taxes, they offered tax breaks for the wealthiest; we offered higher taxes on those who make over $125,000 a year. These are all legitimate and important differences which separate our two parties, and they are the very subjects which elections should be fought over, not the personal vilification or television attack ads which now dominate what passes for campaign debate. But the budget summit agreement, and this budget conference report which would start implementing it, is about governing, not campaigning, and all but one of the summit members understood that.

The progress in approval of the budget resolution and mounting public pressure led the president to sign a second continuing resolution on October 9 that provided funding through October 19. This time was to be used for further negotiations on the details of the reconciliation package that would implement the deficit-reduction package.

As these talks proceeded, two more continuing resolutions were signed into law (on October 20 and 25) to temporarily fund federal operations. Finally, on October 27, an agreement was reached between the White House and congressional negotiators on what became known as the Omnibus Budget Reconciliation Act (OBRA) of 1990. This package, which was indeed the largest deficit reduction measure in American history up to that point, contained the following major provisions:

- Reduced the deficit by $43 billion in FY 1991 and by $482 billion over five years, with $323 billion (67 percent of total) in spending reductions, including $189 billion in discretionary spending cuts, $75 billion in entitlement cuts, and $59 billion in debt service reductions, and $159 billion (33 percent) in increased revenues.

• Included the "PAYGO" requirement that any new tax cuts or spending increases must be offset through revenue increases or reductions in other spending.

• Took Social Security surpluses off-budget so they could not be claimed in deficit-reduction calculations.

• Made modest cuts in payments to Medicare providers and raised the cap on the portion of wages subject to the Medicare payroll tax from $53,400 to $125,000.

• Increased excise taxes on automobiles, boats, airplanes, furs, tobacco, alcoholic beverages, and cigarettes.

• Increased the top income tax rate from 28 percent to 31 percent and limited the value of tax deductions for high-income taxpayers.

• Increased the motor fuels tax by five cents per gallon. During debate on the Senate version of the reconciliation bill, which would have raised the tax by 9.5 cents per gallon, Fowler made an "impassioned" defense of the increases, reiterating his long-held belief that such a step would not only cut the deficit, but would also reduce American dependence on foreign oil and thereby lessen the need for sending American troops to the Persian Gulf. "Isn't there some patriotism tax? Isn't there something we can ask the American people to do that will make them participate...in backing up Americans abroad?"

On October 27, the House agreed to the reconciliation bill by a vote of 228 to 200 (Yes: 181 Democrats, 47 Republicans; No: 74 Democrats, 126 Republicans, the Georgia delegation splitting 8 to 2 in favor, with Barnard joining Gingrich in opposition), and the Senate followed suit later that same day, voting 54 to 45 (Yes: 35 Democrats, 19 Republicans; No: 20 Democrats, 25 Republicans, with Nunn joining Fowler in support) to approve the measure. President Bush signed the legislation into law on November 5, stating, "This Act is the result of long, hard work by the Administration and the Congress. No one got everything he or she wanted, but the end product is a compromise that merits enactment."

So ended the 1990 budget summit, but the event had significant and long-lasting implications. Politically, the breaking of his tax pledge and the economic downturn that accelerated after the summit agreement were cited by many as key factors in Bush's 1992 defeat by Bill Clinton. On the other hand, the prominence Newt Gingrich gained in leading the "Republican Revolt" further solidified his position as leader of the increasingly conservative House GOP rank-and-file, and positioned him to become Speaker of the House when the Republicans gained the majority after the 1994 elections. The agreement itself was panned by many (especially Republican) commentators at the time for exacerbating the recession, but in recent years has come to be regarded much more favorably. For example, in a 2010 article, former Reagan and Bush advisor Bruce Bartlett wrote,

> Budget experts now agree that the Budget [Reconciliation] Act of 1990, which was strengthened by another budget deal that was opposed by all Republicans in 1994, deserves much of the credit for the subsequent improvement in the deficit, which shrank from 4.7 percent of GDP to virtual balance in 1997 and gave us budget surpluses from 1998 to 2001. Economist Robert Reischauer, director of the Congressional Budget Office when the 1990 deal was enacted, told me it was "the foundation upon which the surpluses of the 1998 to 2001 period were built."[117]

In a 2012 report by the centrist Democratic group Third Way, the authors conclude,

> The 1990 Budget Summit Agreement set the stage for recovery and the Clinton budget surpluses. The improved fiscal outlook, combined with lower inflation, led Greenspan to lower interest rates in 1992. OBRA-90 and its successor, the 1993 Omnibus Budget Reconciliation Act (OBRA-93), ensured that as the economy recovered, deficits fell continuously from 1992 through 1998, when the government began a four-year run of surpluses. A CBO analysis credited OBRA-90 and OBRA-93 with ensuring that between 1991 and 1997, "most new revenue and mandatory spending laws" were deficit-neutral.[118]

For Wyche Fowler, the 1990 budget summit experience was, in many ways, emblematic of his congressional career. His participation was a result of the recognition by colleagues (in this case, Senator Mitchell) of his capabilities, and his conduct was marked by commitment to principle, but also the belief that politics was "the art of the possible" and that a better, if imperfect, outcome was to be preferred over the alternative. And his labors in this regard received little, if any, external praise, with ideologues on both sides of the spectrum finding fault with elements of the compromise package. Indeed, his association with the tax increases in the agreement was used against him in his 1992 reelection campaign.

George Mitchell wasn't the only one in this period to recognize Fowler's skills. In its January 27, 1990, edition, the respected *National Journal* named him as one of eleven "Rising Stars" in Congress.

> Wyche Fowler, Jr., has caught his colleagues' attention with his range of expertise and his ability to work with them on their own problems.... Unlike many of his colleagues, Fowler is comfortable on the Senate floor and in debate, and he likes to do his own legislative work. He said he was surprised when a Senate committee chairman told him that he should take his suggested changes in a bill to the chairman's staff. As a 10-year House veteran, former Atlanta City Council president and onetime youthful top aide to a House member, the 49-year-old lawyer appears to have taken to the freewheeling world of internal senate politics like a duck to water. William L. Armstrong, R-CO, acknowledged Fowler's parliamentary skills during the arts flap [on the Helms Amendment]. "I discovered a long time ago that the Senator from Georgia is so skilled in debate that if I were to yield for a question, he might embarrass me," Armstrong said when Fowler sought to respond to him.... Fowler plays down his own skills and emphasizes that he was appointed, not elected, to his leadership post.... With his quick mind—he may cite Marcus Aurelius to make a point—and political savvy, he often advises colleagues on their problems. "I'm more interested in other people's politics than my own," he said. As a House Ways and Means Committee member, he frequently helped other Members gain passage of their technical tax proposals—taxes being a subject, Fowler added, that he has intentionally avoided in the Senate.... Fowler has the ability to "synthesize" politics and policy, a close observer said. He has frequently displayed that skill in his home state, holding a House seat in a majority-Black district

and then, pulling off an unusual feat for a politician with a reputation as an Atlanta liberal, using his folksy campaign style to win statewide. His rhetorical superiority in debating Sen. Mack Mattingly, R-GA, played an important role in his 1986 victory. Georgia's narrowing Democratic majority in voter-identification makes Fowler cautious as he prepares for a 1992 reelection bid.[119]

Chapter 12

102nd Congress (1991–1992): War and Preservation

War against Iraq

When the 102nd Congress convened in early January 1991, the prospect of war in the Persian Gulf overshadowed all other issues. Iraq's occupation of Kuwait continued, in spite of international condemnation and the imposition of economic sanctions. Diplomatic initiatives to resolve the crisis proved unsuccessful, and the United States assembled a multinational coalition of 670,000 troops, including approximately 425,000 American servicemen and women, in the region. The UN's January 15 deadline for Iraqi withdrawal from Kuwait, with authorization of the use of "all necessary means" to force such withdrawal thereafter, drew nearer.

In early January, Senator Fowler responded to a questionnaire on US policy toward Iraq submitted by the Knight-Rider newspaper chain.

> President Bush has rights as Commander-in-Chief to act without advance Congressional approval to respond to attacks on Americans, or to defend Americans in imminent danger. But the Constitution is clear that Congress must be the one to declare war, and based on what the President, [Chairman of the Joint Chiefs of Staff] Colin Powell, and [Defense] Secretary Cheney have said, if force is used against Iraq, it will be all-out war. Therefore, I expect President Bush to fulfill his Constitutional responsibilities and seek a declaration of war, if he determines that a military offensive is our best policy. So far, the President has not requested this authority, but if and when there is such a vote, my final decision will be based on: A) whether there is clear evidence that economic and political sanctions cannot achieve our objectives; B) whether other nations, including Japan, the Western Europeans and Saudi Arabia itself, are doing their fair share (militarily and/or financially)—this isn't just our fight, and the American people have a right to know that

> others are sharing this burden; and C) what results are produced by diplomatic efforts over the next week or so. At the moment, there is not conclusive information on any of these points so I cannot make an informed decision. However, if the answers to these three questions convince me that military force is the best policy option, then of course I would vote for a declaration of war.... I don't think the administration has yet presented clear evidence that alternatives to military force are not working, and cannot work. My impression, admittedly based on incomplete information, is that Saddam is being weakened militarily (denial of spare parts) and economically (effective embargo against sales of Iraqi or captured Kuwaiti oil). If this is so, it seems to me that the longer the sanctions are in place, the worse off Saddam will be if and when a shooting war develops.

As the January 15 deadline approached, the Bush administration did decide to seek congressional authorization for use of military force against Iraq. During the January 11 Senate floor debate on the resolution, Fowler provided a detailed explanation of the reasons behind his decision to vote against the authorization of force.

> Is war with Iraq justified? Absolutely yes. The Iraqi invasion and occupation of Kuwait was a blatant act of aggression, and an affront to the international community of civilized nations, thus justifying an international response. But there is a difference between a war being just, and a war being necessary or prudent or immediate. What would determine whether this war was necessary and prudent? Given the high costs and uncertainties of war, I believe the answer is, we should choose the war option only when other less costly, less risky alternatives, such as the use of economic and political sanctions, are shown not to be able to achieve our objectives....
>
> What if we do go to war with Saddam Hussein on January 15 or 16, defeat and destroy him and Iraq in three weeks, with relatively few casualties? Will our long-range position in the Gulf, and regional stability be guaranteed, or undermined in the aftermath of our military victory? What if, after our victory over Iraq, the Arab masses throughout the Middle East perceive our successful war as an instance of Americans invading Arab land and killing Arabs, and

they hold their own non-democratic governments to blame for supporting us? What if, after our military victory, the Iranians, the Syrians and the Turks all press for immediate and favorable resolution of their border disputes with a badly weakened Iraq? What if, after our military victory over Iraq, the Kurds in Iraq attain, formally or informally, autonomy or outright independence, and exert a considerable, possibly destabilizing, influence on their fellow Kurds in the neighboring nations in the Middle East? What if the American and possibly other forces necessarily left behind to secure the new status quo in Iraq and the Arabian Peninsula are subject to frequent terrorist attacks, at a minimum? And, what if a devastated Iraq, facing potential starvation, is increasingly subject to the appeal of Islamic fundamentalism as a response to its total defeat?

Should not we, the United States of America, maintain our military threat, let the world know—as all of us are doing on all sides of this debate—that the military threat remains our option, that it will be used if all else fails? But should we not try all else and begin debate on what happens after we win and not look at this in terms of 3 days or 5 days or 7 days, when these overwhelming decisions have achieved no attention in the public debate or a discussion from the Executive Branch?

It is obviously my conclusion that now is not the time to lead with the military option.... I am not one who believes that it is never appropriate for the United States to use armed force to protect our interests. Quite the contrary. In the 14 years that I have served in the United States Congress, I have backed American military deployments in Grenada, in Panama, in Lebanon, and the ongoing defensive deployment in Saudi Arabia.... A military offensive to liberate Kuwait may well become necessary. It may well become our Nation's only option.... Let the world know that the American people are of one mind and one voice when it comes to resisting the naked aggression of the Saddam Husseins of the planet. We will continue to vigorously enforce sanctions in order to continue weakening his outlaw regime and to continue denying him any benefits from his occupation of Kuwait. At present, in my opinion, we should do everything, short of immediately initiating a war, to achieve our just aims. And if all else fails, then that option will be exercised.

On January 12, both the House (by a vote of 250 to 183) and Senate (by a 52 to 47 margin) approved the resolution authorizing the use of military force against Iraq. Senator Nunn joined with Senator Fowler in voting against the measure, whereas Representatives Lewis and Jenkins were the only Georgia House members to vote no. Fowler asked for, and was given, permission to address the Georgia House and Senate on January 15 to explain his vote.

> The dictator has not left [Kuwait] and the Congress has spoken. We have given the President authority to commence hostilities if the deadline is not met.... The men and women of Georgia are united.... Saddam Hussein will rue the day he took on the United States.... If [Saddam does not withdraw] please join me in praying that the war will be short and the casualties will be few. May God help us all.[120]

US and coalition forces began aerial attacks against Iraq on January 16 to 17, with the ground offensive into Kuwait and southern Iraq commencing on February 24. By February 27, Kuwait had been liberated and Iraq accepted ceasefire terms on April 6, effectively ending the war.

Once the authorization for war was given, Fowler was fully supportive of the ensuing Operation Desert Storm and the American military men and women who achieved a swift and decisive victory in evicting Iraq from Kuwait and in destroying much of Saddam's military. He later admitted that his misgivings about the likely destabilizing effects of the war proved to be ill-founded because of the president's and his senior military advisors' skill in carrying out the limited objective of freeing Kuwait, rather than the far more uncertain course of regime change in Iraq. However, many of these and related concerns resurfaced, and with a vengeance, in the aftermath of the overthrow of Saddam Hussein brought about by the 2003 invasion of Iraq initiated by the George W. Bush administration. Indeed, in looking back, it is clear that while what would prove to be the first Gulf War for the United States succeeded in evicting Saddam from Kuwait, it did not resolve any of the underlying sectarian, political, or economic problems afflicting the region and, in fact, only served to exacerbate them.

Energy Policy

In his fifth and sixth years in the Senate, Fowler continued to be active in many of the same fields that had drawn his attention in previous sessions, including energy, forestry, agriculture, water conservation, food safety, space science, and education. This continuing concentration was a reflection not only of his interests and committee assignments, but also of the realities of the legislative process in which most progress is incremental and slow-paced.

The major energy legislation to be acted upon in the 102nd Congress was the Energy Policy Act of 1992, which contained a wide range of initiatives to promote energy conservation and production. Wyche Fowler was involved in the development of this legislation both in committee and on the Senate floor, and four of his initiatives survived in the final enacted version of the legislation:

- Addition of certain solar and passive solar technologies to the energy efficiency mortgage pilot program established by the bill, which was included in a floor amendment by Senators Fowler, Graham (D-FL), and Wirth (D-CO) that was approved by the Senate by voice vote on February 5, 1992.
- Revision of the nuclear power licensing process to streamline the process for industry but preserve the citizen's right to public safety hearings, which was a modified version of the language in the Graham-Fowler amendment adopted by the Senate by a 52 to 43 vote on February 6.
- Authorization of energy efficiency and renewable energy grants to tribal governments, which was included in a Fowler amendment during the Senate Energy and Natural Resources Committee's markup of the bill.
- A study by the Department of Energy to determine the extent to which commodity futures and options could provide effective protection against unanticipated surges in fuel prices, which was another successful Fowler committee amendment.

Fowler also took the Senate lead in organizing support, in the form of authorship of a June 9, 1992, letter to the Senate Finance Committee cosigned by twelve other senators, for two other provisions retained in the bill: permanent extension of the existing 10 percent investment tax credit for solar and geothermal technologies and creation of a 1.5 cent production tax credit for wind energy.

In addition to the Energy Policy Act initiatives, Fowler won approval by voice vote of a floor amendment to the FY 1992 Energy and Water Appropriations Bill that shifted $14.7 million from lower priority Department of Energy programs to solar heating, photovoltaic, wind energy, and biofuels programs; the Fowler funding levels were retained in the enacted appropriations measure. During the Senate's consideration of that same legislation, Fowler obtained a colloquy with Energy and Water Subcommittee chairman Johnston clarifying that funding for renewable energy joint ventures (authorized by the 1989 Fowler Renewable Energy Bill) would be made available under the Energy and Water Appropriations Bill. In November 1991, the Department of Energy requested approval to transfer funds to the renewable joint venture program.

Forest Service Road-Building

From his position as chairman of the Agriculture Committee's Subcommittee on Conservation and Forestry, the Georgia senator continued to play a lead role in forestry policy, especially with respect to his efforts to curtail the practice of government-subsidized road construction in our national forests. In 1990, seventy-three of the 120 forests in the national forest system lost money on their logging operations, including the Chattahoochee and Oconee forests in Georgia. On June 6, 1991, he introduced the National Forest Timber Sales Cost Recovery Act of 1991 that required federal timber sales to recover the government's full costs (including for road construction) of selling timber from national forests and that authorized funding for community development, educational, and employment-training programs for communities adversely affected by the phasing out of below-cost timber sales:

> Timber production in our national forests is losing money for the taxpayers, and contributes to our budget deficit. At the same time, it does compromise the ecological integrity of our forests. These

> operations benefit a swelling Forest Service bureaucracy—and practically no one else. I guarantee we'll never miss the mountainside clear-cuts or $200 million logging-road budgets that support the activity. We can save money, woods and wildlife at the same time.

Though no further action was taken on this bill, Fowler introduced a revised version (S. 3115) on July 31, 1992, which prohibited the Forest Service from selling or offering to sell national forest system timber in cases in which revenues would be less than the minimum needed to meet or exceed sale expenses. The revised bill served as the basis for a floor amendment that Fowler offered to the FY 1993 Department of the Interior Appropriations Bill on August 5, 1992. Fowler described the amendment and his objectives during the floor debate on his proposal.

> The Forest Service admits that more than half of our national forests lose money on the Forest Service-administered timber sales, meaning that woodland resources and wildlife habitats disappear along with taxpayer funds from the Treasury. When the total costs of road building and bureaucratic overhead are figured in, many more of these timber sales come up losers for the American people, economically and ecologically. One study challenging Forest Service figures claims that timber sales in 101 of our national forests generate over $250 million a year in losses for the American taxpayer. In other words, the American people pay more and end up with less. Most timber sales do not cover the government's cost of producing the timber. It seems to me it is time for an honest accounting and responsible management of the public trust our national forests represent. That means no more ecological destruction at taxpayer expense. That means timber sales conducted according to sound business practices that do not depend on public subsidies. That means weaning the government off of this wasteful practice in the majority of our forests.... This amendment provides for a 25-percent reduction in national forest timber sold where cash returns to the Treasury do not cover the cost of growing and selling the timber. The amendment [also] reduces the Forest Service's budget by $35 million to reflect the reduction in appropriated funds to administer these sales. I believe this will force the Forest Service to

> consider the real costs of selling off our public forest lands. It will steer the Forest Service toward sounder management practices. It will get us on the road to eliminating timber sales that cannot be supported by the bottom line in these days of budget deficits, and it will force the Forest Service to begin making the most of our taxpayers' investment in these forest resources. Ideally, I would like to see the Forest Service at the forefront in the fight to protect our forests from excessive timbering and road building to assure wildlife diversity and survival of species and, most importantly, to preserve some semblance of this public trust for the future.

In spite of support once again from a broad-based coalition, including both environmentalists and fiscal conservatives, the Fowler amendment was tabled (killed) by a vote of 50 to 44, where a "no" vote was in support of the amendment (Yes: 12 Democrats; 38 Republicans; No: 41 Democrats; 3 Republicans). As in the last session, defeat of the effort to curb below-cost timber sales was achieved largely through near total opposition from President Bush and Senate Republicans.

The road-building controversy did not go away with the defeat of the Fowler amendment. In one of his last acts as president, in January 2001, Bill Clinton issued the so-called "roadless rule" that protected 58.5 million of the 191 million acres in the national forest system from road construction. The Clinton regulation has been contested ever since, but an October 2012 ruling by the US Supreme Court rejected a challenge to the rule, thereby leaving it intact. The issue has continued to be contentious, with President Trump removing the Clinton protections from 9.3 million acres in Alaska's Tongass National Forest three months before he left office. However, in June 2021 the Biden administration restored those protections.

A more successful fate awaited Fowler's second major timber policy initiative during the 102nd Congress. On May 21, 1992, Fowler and his Agriculture Subcommittee on Conservation and Forestry conducted hearings on the Bush administration proposal to sharply curtail the right of citizens to appeal timber sales in national forests. In response to the hearings' findings, on July 1, 1992, Fowler introduced the Forest Service Decisionmaking and Appeals Reform Act (S. 2921), which mandated that the Forest Service must maintain a public appeals process for project-level decisions and established a new notice and comment period prior to decision announcements for commercial sales of national forest timber. The measure was offered as a floor amendment to the FY 1993 Department of the Interior Appropriations Bill and approved by the Senate by voice vote on August 6, 1992. A modified version was retained in the enacted appropriations bill, resulting in the first statutory appeals process for the Forest Service, including provisions for notice, comment, agency decision-making, and appeals. Though revised somewhat over the years, it continues to serve as the basis for the Forest Service's appeals system.

These and related efforts earned Senator Fowler additional plaudits, including the 1991 Trust for Public Land Award, the 1991 Friends of the Mountains Award, and the 1991 Garden Club Award "for his honest rhetoric on environmental issues and continuing effort to enact strong environmental legislation."

Another Fowler undertaking arising out of his chairmanship of the Conservation and Forestry Subcommittee met with a more complicated outcome. In his oversight role for national forests, the Georgia senator was made aware of certain situations in which individuals engaging in lawful hunting in national forests were being subjected to harassment by anti-hunting groups. Though Fowler supported a number of gun control measures during his public career (thereby earning opposition by the National Rifle Association), he was also determined to protect legitimate and lawful hunting. There was, of course, a political dimension to this, especially in the period leading up to his reelection bid. It was a means of offering reassurance to hunters, and, more broadly, rural residents of Georgia, that he shared their values. In any case, on June 13, 1991, he introduced the Recreational Hunting Safety and Preservation Act, which was modeled on similar laws on the books in forty-four states (including Georgia) and sought to combat the harassment of lawful hunting in national forests by imposing a penalty of up to $5,000 for persons who intentionally obstructed, impeded, or otherwise interfered with such hunting. On June 28, Fowler introduced this proposal as a floor amendment to the Violent Crime Control Act, but certain Republican senators were able to block consideration of the amendment by the Senate. He tried again by offering a slightly modified version of his bill as an amendment to the Food, Agriculture, Conservation and Trade Act Amendments of

1991. The Fowler amendment passed the Senate by voice vote, but it was not included in the final enacted version of the bill.

Agriculture, Food Safety, Water Conservation, and Space

Although the omnibus Farm Bill had been enacted in 1990, a number of agricultural and rural policy issues were acted upon in 1991 to 1992, with Wyche Fowler's roles on both the Agriculture and Appropriations Committees affording him an opportunity for considerable input. First, he offered a number of successful amendments in the Agriculture Committee to the Food, Agriculture, Conservation and Trade Amendments of 1991 that were retained in the final enacted version of the bill, including authorizing the creation of a pilot program to increase farmer participation in the commodity futures market. Second, he helped obtain $995 million in agricultural disaster relief funds in the FY 1992 Dire Supplemental Appropriations Bill for farmers in Georgia and across the nation who had suffered extensive crop losses because of severe weather conditions in 1990 and 1991. Third, he obtained $5 million in FY 1992 appropriations for implementation of the Fowler Star Schools Initiative and for the Medical Link program, which uses satellite technology to improve access of rural hospitals to advanced medical procedures. Finally, he was instrumental in securing reforms in the USDA Market Promotion Program by winning agreement from the National Peanut Council to eight reforms in the program, including hiring an independent management consultant, increasing the public reporting of council marketing activities, and tightening the regulations for payment of travel expenses for council members and staff.

With regard to food safety, one of Fowler's successful committee amendments to the Food, Agriculture, Conservation and Trade Amendments of 1991 was taken directly from the Egg Products Inspection Act Amendments, which he introduced in July 1991 and which prescribed the temperature at which eggs must be maintained in order to protect consumers by reducing the potential for harmful microbial growth.

Although still ahead of its time, and producing limited results, Fowler advanced water conservation efforts by

- sponsoring the National Plumbing Products Efficiency Act of 1991, which established national standards for the manufacture and labeling of certain plumbing products in order to conserve and protect water resources;

• sponsoring the Municipal and Industrial Water Conservation Act of 1991, which provided for improved management of the nation's water resources by creating an Office of Water Conservation at EPA to oversee a technical assistance program, and by requiring the consideration of water conservation alternatives in environmental impact studies;

• sponsoring a successful amendment in the Energy and Natural Resources Committee to the National Energy Strategy Act of 1991 to set energy and water efficiency standards for showerheads. This language was retained in the enacted version of the energy bill and represented the one part of Fowler's ambitious water conservation agenda to become law.

Supporting the combined Comet Rendezvous Asteroid Flyby (CRAF)/Cassini mission remained a top priority for Fowler as a member of the VA-HUD-Independent Agencies Appropriations Subcommittee that funded NASA. In FY 1992, budgetary pressures seriously threatened both projects, with the House adopting a NASA funding bill that froze overall spending at FY 1991 levels. The House bill nominally retained CRAF and Cassini, though at unrealistically low funding levels that could have threatened both missions. In the Senate, VA-HUD-Independent Agencies Subcommittee chair Barbara Mikulski (D-MD) developed a proposal to add funding for NASA above the House-passed level, but incorporated a termination of the CRAF program and a one year delay in Cassini.

Senator Fowler proposed adding $113 million above the House level for CRAF/Cassini, while delaying them for one year. However, his effort was not successful, and the Senate-passed bill retained the Mikulski approach. He continued to support the combined mission because of the program balance they represented in providing for the only new missions then under consideration for the outer planets and the small bodies in the solar system (comets and asteroids), and termination of CRAF would be seen as a direct consequence of full funding for the Space Station as included in the Mikulski mark, thus exacerbating a split between the space science and manned spaceflight programs.

Prior to Senate passage of the FY 1992 NASA appropriations measure, Fowler entered into a colloquy with Senator Mikulski in an attempt to raise prospects for CRAF in the upcoming conference committee with the House.

> **Senator Fowler:** I am very pleased that the Senator from Maryland managed to produce a bill which repairs most of the damage to NASA's space science programs that would have resulted from the imposition of an across-the-board freeze. The major exception to this is in proposed termination of the CRAF portion of what Congress authorized in FY90 as the combined CRAF/Cassini missions. Madame Chair, it is my understanding that the Appropriations Committee came to this decision reluctantly, and based solely upon the severe financial constraints placed upon the VA, HUD, and Independent Agencies bill.
>
> **Senator Mikulski:** The Senator from Georgia is correct. I know of his long-standing, strong support for both the CRAF and Cassini missions, and I share his evaluation of the scientific value offered by both of these projects. The decision to terminate CRAF was, as he stated, a reluctant one based on the level of funding available for NASA within the Committee's 602(b) budget allocation this year and what is likely to be available next year.
>
> **Senator Fowler:** I would like to further inquire of the Senator from Maryland whether, given that the other body has adopted an appropriations bill which assumes a continuation of the combined CRAF/Cassini mission albeit at an unrealistically low FY91 spending level, she anticipates that the future of the CRAF mission will be an item for conference, and further that if sufficient resources can be found, she could support a continuation of CRAF?
>
> **Senator Mikulski:** I do believe that the status of CRAF will be an issue for conference. If the conferees can produce sufficient resources to fund a combined CRAF/Cassini mission without compromising the viability of the NASA core program funded in the

Committee bill, then the Senator from Maryland would be pleased to support a continuation of CRAF.

Fowler's efforts in the appropriations conference committee were successful, and the conferees restored CRAF and provided an adequate FY 1992 funding level for the combined CRAF/Cassini mission. However, that success proved short-lived, and in early 1992, the CRAF mission was canceled. It would be a number of years before its objectives were partially achieved by other, less ambitious NASA probes.

Once CRAF was eliminated, Fowler concentrated on ensuring that Cassini survived. His FY 1993 letter to Senator Mikulski outlining his priorities and requests for NASA stated, in part, that

> continuing support for Cassini is critical in order to maintain a viable American planetary exploration program. The recent restructuring of Cassini undertaken within NASA and at JPL has produced significant budgetary savings, and has substantially reduced the "ramp-up" problem. Therefore, I request that our Committee indicate in the strongest possible report language our support for the restructuring of the Cassini mission, and our commitment to having the mission carried out.

The effort to save Cassini was successful: the spacecraft was launched from Cape Canaveral on October 15, 1997, and reached the Saturn system on July 1, 2004. On December 25, 2004, the European Space Agency's Huygens probe was released by Cassini and successfully landed on the moon Titan on January 14, 2005. With more than ten years of ongoing discoveries, Cassini produced important scientific returns, including a 2014 finding of evidence for a large underground ocean of liquid water on Saturn's moon Enceladus, making that body one of the most likely locations in the solar system to find life beyond Earth. With its fuel running out, and in order to protect Enceladus and other Saturn moons that might have conditions suitable for life from contamination by the spacecraft, Cassini was plunged into Saturn's crushing atmosphere on September 15, 2017.

Other Fowler Initiatives

Fowler undertook additional efforts on behalf of historically Black colleges and universities in the 102nd Congress. He persuaded the Senate Energy and Natural Resources Committee to include language in the Department of Energy Laboratory Technology Partnership Act of 1992, which passed the Senate in July 1992, requiring the secretary of Energy to provide support for education and training to develop personnel resources needed for future research and development efforts by minority colleges or HBCUs in math, science, environmental restoration, and waste management. He also hosted a meeting at Morris Brown College in April 1992 concerning efforts to assist HBCUs and minority business enterprises in participating in the National Science Foundation's Small Business Innovative Research program. And Fowler authored a June 1992 letter (signed by six other senators) to Senator Byrd expressing support for the HBCU program within the Department of Energy's Fossil Energy Office, and requesting $2.5 million in FY 1993 funding for the program.

As part of his work for historic preservation, Fowler sponsored the Senate version of Rep. John Lewis's African American History Study Act, which directed the Department of the Interior to prepare a National Historic Landmark theme study on African American history, and to identify key sites eligible for National Historic Landmark and national park designation. Fowler won approval of the bill in the Energy and Natural Resources Committee and by the full Senate in June 1991, and it was signed into law in August of that year.

The Georgia Legislative Black Caucus presented Fowler with its 1991 Trendsetter Award "in recognition of dedication to the protection of the general welfare of minorities and disadvantaged citizens."

Local Projects

As usual, Wyche Fowler devoted considerable time and effort to Georgia-centered projects, including:

- *Moody Air Force Base:* Senator Fowler worked with local leaders in Valdosta and with Senator Nunn and Representative Hatcher to oppose Defense Secretary Cheney's proposal to close Moody AFB and testified on Moody's behalf in May 1991 hearings before the Base Closure and Realignment Commission in Washington and Jacksonville, Florida. The commission ultimately rejected the proposal to close the base.

• *Ocmulgee National Monument Donation:* Fowler introduced S. 638, the Senate version of the House-passed H.R. 749, and secured Energy and Natural Resources Committee and Senate approval of the House bill, which was signed into law on July 9, 1991. The measure authorized the Department of the Interior to accept a donation of the Drake Field parcel of land for addition to the Ocmulgee National Monument near Macon.

• *Chattahoochee National Forest Protection Act:* Fowler introduced S. 1949, the Senate version of the House-passed H.R. 3245, and secured Agriculture Committee and Senate approval of the House bill, which was signed into law in December 1991. The bill designated certain national forest lands in northern Georgia as wilderness areas.

• *State Medicaid Match:* At the request of Georgia and a few other states, Senator Fowler introduced legislation (S. 833) to allow states to continue using voluntary contributions as part of their state match for Medicaid. The Bush administration was attempting to sharply curtail this practice as potentially open to abuse, but at a time when Medicaid costs (along with other health care costs) continued to skyrocket, states like Georgia had few readily available alternatives. Ultimately, Fowler was able to get a one-year extension of the voluntary match program approved as part of the enacted Medicaid Moratorium Amendments of 1991. This proved long enough for a successful compromise to be worked out by the Bush administration and the affected states.

Fowler's position on the Appropriations Committee again meant that most of his initiatives that were targeted to benefit his Georgia constituents were accomplished through the funding process, including the following:

1) *Albany Courthouse*: obtained $921,000 in FY 92 appropriations for General Services Administration design work on a new US District Courthouse for the Middle District of Georgia in Albany.

2) *Tifton Agricultural Research*: obtained for Tifton $1.775 million in FY 92 appropriations for construction of the National Laboratory for Environmentally Sound Production Agriculture and $100,000 in FY 92 appropriations for research at the USDA Agricultural Research Station on biological control of pests on crops.

3) *Valdosta Geographic Information System*: obtained $1 million in FY 92 appropriations for the Geographic Information System Technology Transfer Center in Valdosta.

4) *Centers for Disease Control and Prevention (CDC)*: obtained $56 million in FY 92 appropriations for the Agency for Toxic Substances and Disease Registry (part of the CDC), including $4 million for the Association of Minority Health Professions Schools and $2 million for a study on the health impacts of consuming contaminated fish; helped obtain $5 million in FY 92 appropriations for design work on new lab facilities; and obtained $1.504 billion in FY 92 appropriations for CDC programs and infrastructure.

5) *Chattahoochee River National Recreation Area*: helped obtain $885,000 in FY 92 appropriations and $900,000 in FY 93 appropriations for Chattahoochee River National Recreation Area land acquisition.

6) *MARTA*: helped obtain $20 million in FY 92 appropriations for MARTA for design and construction of the North Line from Medical Center Station to Dunwoody Station.

7) *MLK National Historic Site*: obtained $400,000 for emergency structural stabilization and $645,000 for planning of headquarters and related facilities at the Martin Luther King Jr. National Historic Site in FY 92 appropriations; obtained $540,000 in FY 93 appropriations for the King Center.

8) *Olympics*: obtained $2 million in FY 92 appropriations for the Department of Defense to provide logistical support and personnel services for the 1996 Olympic Games in Atlanta, and $500,000 in FY 92 appropriations "for the Atlanta community and urban forestry project in preparation for the 1996 Summer Olympics." Relatedly, he helped obtain an authorization (in the enacted

Surface Transportation Reauthorization Act) for $58.1 million for a traffic signalization project and other transportation improvements needed for the 1996 Olympics.

9) *Augusta Courthouse Renovation*: obtained $3.5 million in FY 92 appropriations for renovation of the federal courthouse in Augusta.

10) *Augusta Railroad Crossings*: helped obtain $2.475 million in FY 92 appropriations for acquisition and engineering costs related to Augusta's 12th Street railroad relocation project.

11) *Sidney Lanier Bridge*: obtained $900,000 in FY 92 appropriations for design of the new Sidney Lanier Bridge in Brunswick. Fowler had previously helped obtain an authorization to make the replacement of the Sidney Lanier Bridge in Glynn County eligible for federal financial support (contained in H.R. 4009, the Federal Maritime Commission Act, which passed the House and Senate, and was signed into law by the president as PL 101-595).

12) *Federal Law Enforcement Training Center (FLETC)*: obtained $39.645 million in FY 92 appropriations for salaries and expenses at the training center in Glynco, and $8.309 million in FY 92 appropriations for facilities improvements at the center.

13) *Fort Frederica*: obtained $2.5 million in FY 92 appropriations to begin purchase of twenty-eight acres adjacent to the Fort Frederica National Monument and helped obtain $2.3 million in FY 93 appropriations for this purpose.

14) *Fort Benning*: helped obtain $4.55 million in FY 92 appropriations for construction of thirty-six family housing units at Camp Merrill near Dahlonega, which trains Fort Benning-based rangers in mountaineering skills.

15) *Bond Swamp*: obtained $700,000 in FY 92 appropriations for the Bond Swamp portion of the Ocmulgee National Wildlife Refuge.

16) *Appalachian Trail*: helped obtain $3 million in FY 92 appropriations for the Appalachian National Scenic Trail, which completed the Georgia portion of the trail.

17) *Chattooga River*: obtained $2.2 million in FY 92 appropriations and $1.8 million in FY 93 for protection of the headwaters of the Chattooga National Wild and Scenic River.

18) *Chickamauga-Chattanooga National Military Park*: obtained $3 million in the Senate FY 92 Transportation Appropriations Bill to complete construction of the Chickamauga-Chattanooga National Military bypass in northwest Georgia; the conference report provided $1 million.

19) *Bear Island*: helped obtain $812,000 in FY 92 appropriations for acquisition of the Bear Island addition to the Savannah National Wildlife Refuge.

20) *Fort Stewart*: obtained $6.951 million in FY 92 appropriations for renovation and expansion of Diamond Elementary School at Fort Stewart.

21) *McIntosh County Bombing Range*: helped obtain $2.881 million in FY 92 appropriations for completion of the acquisition of 5,192 acres for a multipurpose tactical bombing range. This project had been blocked by Senator Fowler, Representative Thomas, and others in 1989 because of strong local opposition, but in 1991, the local communities and Department of Defense reached a compromise agreement, which resulted in a lifting of the congressional block and allowed the project to continue.

Clarence Thomas Nomination

One of Fowler's most controversial actions during the 102nd Congress was his vote to confirm Clarence Thomas as a Supreme Court justice. After joining with the majority in rejecting the 1987 nomination of Robert Bork, Fowler subsequently voted for Reagan Supreme Court nominee Anthony Kennedy (in 1987) and George H. W. Bush's nominee David Souter (in 1990), both of whom were confirmed by the Senate.

In the summer of 1991, Thurgood Marshall, who was the first—and at that time, the only—African American to serve on the Supreme Court, announced his retirement, and on July 1, 1991, President Bush nominated forty-three-year-old Clarence Thomas, a Black man who was born in the small town of Pin Point, Georgia. On July 17, Fowler issued his initial take on the Thomas nomination.

> The outpouring of pros and cons about the Thomas nomination is part and parcel of the American system and is healthy in informing the debate which is to come. And, with all due respect to those

whose minds are made up, I look forward to learning something from that debate: from the confirmation hearings before the Senate Judiciary Committee, from the floor debate in the Senate, as well as from the public debate in print and on the airwaves. Speaking for myself, as one United States Senator, I believe that both Judge Thomas and President Bush deserve a fair hearing on the merits of the nomination, not on narrow partisan or ideological grounds. At the same time, the American public is entitled to more than a rubber stamp—it deserves a full examination of the qualifications of Clarence Thomas to sit on the highest court in the land.

One might well ask what is the proper way to evaluate a Supreme Court nominee: how to prevent advice and consent from becoming either obstruction or dereliction of duty. I have no perfect answer to that question because determining who is right for the Supreme Court is more art than science. And certainly when looking at those who have served on that high court, one can find examples of individuals whose elevation to the Supreme Court transformed an undistinguished career into one of greatness, as well as those whose lofty credentials were never really validated by their work on the court. To me, in examining a candidate for the Supreme Court, we should look for wisdom, not merely intelligence. We should require an understanding of the law, but also the values that underlie that law. We should seek men and women with sound judicial ideals, not political ideologues. We should, above all, search for those in whom respect for the law will be the guiding principle of their stewardship on the Supreme Court. Are these difficult standards? I certainly hope so, for the selection of the highest-ranking non-elected position in our Nation. Does Judge Thomas meet these criteria? The honest answer is that I don't know yet; that is what the confirmation process is all about. But I will say that these are the standards I have used and will use in evaluating all Supreme Court nominees to come before me, whether Democrat or Republican, liberal or conservative. In short, I intend to impose neither a higher nor a lower standard for the Thomas nomination. We need, we deserve our very best on the Supreme Court, and I will act on that belief when considering Judge Thomas or any other nominees to the Supreme Court.

During the ensuing judiciary committee hearings, Thomas repeatedly stated that he had not developed a position on the *Roe v. Wade* decision on abortion rights or on other controversial specific issues likely to come before the Supreme Court. Given his limited experience as a judge (he had served less than two years in that capacity at the time of his nomination) and the sparse record of his public writings and statements, aside from his critiques on affirmative action, there was considerably less material available to assess Clarence Thomas's views than there had been for Bork (or Kennedy or Souter, for that matter).

In a statement on the Senate floor on October 3, 1991, Wyche Fowler announced his intention to support the Thomas nomination.

> I rise in support of the nomination of Judge Clarence Thomas for the U.S. Supreme Court. I do so after reviewing this nomination for the last two months, including hundreds of pages of documentation submitted both for and against the nomination; and most importantly having watched Judge Thomas's testimony on his own behalf and the testimony of others before the Senate Judiciary Committee over the past two weeks. I have decided to cast my vote based on that review.
>
> My support is based primarily on three factors: First, based on all the evidence I have received, Clarence Thomas's record as a judge, although brief, has been a very good one. Indeed, I was very impressed by the American Bar Association's testimony on this point. And in determining fitness for the highest court in the land, it is the nominee's actual record as a judge which is most important. Second, in my personal meeting with Judge Thomas and in the testimony before the committee, I became convinced that he has both the proper judicial temperament for the Supreme Court and the necessary fundamental respect for the law and recognition of its real-life consequences. Finally, there is the personal trait that is very hard to describe, but which might best be simply called character or integrity. And as a native Georgian, as well as a U.S. Senator from Georgia, I can say with pride that I believe the Nation has seen something distinctly Georgian in Clarence Thomas, in the strong sense of self and purpose he traces back to a very close community.

I do want to stress that this decision has not been an easy one.... I must also confess that, unlike others, my vote is not cast without some doubt. But from the day that I met with Judge Thomas last July, I told him...that I would give both the president and the nominee the benefit of the doubt. I do not know—and I emphasize "know"—I do not know how Clarence Thomas will vote on any of the upcoming controversies facing the Supreme Court of the United States. And there are many, many examples in American history of Supreme Court Justices defying the expectations of those who appointed them. But even if we did know with certainty about the handful of cases that currently loom largest on the judicial horizon, it is more likely that future cases and controversies not yet articulated will prove at least equally important in setting the bounds for personal freedom and individual liberty in civil law as those currently pending.

So, in the final analysis, my vote is essentially one of hope and one based on what I consider to be Judge Clarence Thomas's promise, a hope that Clarence Thomas will demonstrate the same independence, the same self-reliance, and the same promise that have been the hallmarks of his struggle and his career; a hope that Clarence Thomas will not forget those who are seeking still to better this Nation and better themselves, yet who remain cloaked in the shadows of the injustice, intolerance, and inequality that still exist in our society; finally, a hope that Clarence Thomas will remain true to his promise to uphold the Constitution of the United States, to refrain from judicial activism, to approach each and every case before the court with an open mind, and to judge each case on its merits and its merits alone....

As I called Judge Thomas this morning and informed him of my decision, I asked him again simply, when he puts on the robe of judicial independence, to remember that there are still many, many people in our Nation who are left in the shadows, who seek to and deserve simple justice, and all they ask of an individual Supreme Court Justice or those who serve on the highest court of the land is to have the same manner toward all people when judging these cases and controversies. That is my hope for Judge Clarence Thomas. I have every belief that he will rise to that standard.

Left unsaid in the statement was the matter of symbolism. As a product of Atlanta, the Fifth District, and Georgia politics, Wyche Fowler was keenly aware of the importance of symbols and role models, especially with respect to race. Clarence Thomas was a Black Georgian from a poor, rural background nominated to replace the only African American on the Supreme Court. Had the Thomas nomination failed, it was highly unlikely any subsequent candidate George Bush nominated would have such a background. Related to this was the political dimension. Barely a year away from the November 1992 election, the Thomas nomination placed Fowler (and other Southern Democrats representing large African American constituencies) in a difficult position, with Black leaders and voters (especially in Georgia) deeply divided. For example, the Southern Christian Leadership Conference supported Thomas, as did a majority of the state's African American population, according to polling, whereas Rep. John Lewis, among others, opposed the nomination. And Fowler's very popular colleague Sam Nunn had already announced in favor of Thomas.

Late in the confirmation process, reports surfaced that Thomas was being accused by Anita Hill of making unwelcome sexually related comments to her when the two of them worked together at the Department of Education and at the Equal Employment Opportunity Commission. Ms. Hill testified before the Judiciary Committee on October 11, 1991, describing the incidents underlying the allegations, but indicating she wasn't sure whether they rose to the level of actual sexual harassment. In subsequent testimony, Thomas denied all of the accusations. Fowler was critical of the Senate Judiciary Committee's failure to inform him and other senators of the allegations, which the committee had been aware of for some time. Fowler observed, "I have heard from too many women that Professor Hill's behavior in this case is entirely consistent with that of a victim of sexual harassment.... However, there was nothing to prove the charges, either," and thus maintained his support for Thomas's confirmation. He did call for the Senate to review its own policies with respect to sexual harassment and expressed support for legislation to permit women to collect monetary damages in cases of sex discrimination.[121]

Women's organizations and pro-choice groups, which had provided significant support to Fowler over the years, were not divided with respect to the Thomas nomination. They strongly opposed it, viewing the nomination as a threat to abortion rights and believing the nominee was guilty of sexual harassment. They were unequivocal and persistent in their criticism of Fowler's decision.

On October 15, 1991, Clarence Thomas was confirmed by the Senate by a vote of 52 to 48, with 41 Republicans and 11 Democrats (including Georgians Nunn and Fowler) in favor, and 46 Democrats and 2 Republicans opposed. It is fair to say that Thomas's subsequent performance on the court did not fulfill Fowler's hopes.

National Historic Preservation Act Amendments of 1992

In the waning days of the 102nd Congress, President Bush signed into law the Reclamation Projects Authorization and Adjustment Act of 1992 (PL 102-575). Included as Title XL of this massive legislation were the unrelated National Historic Preservation Act Amendments, the final result of Wyche Fowler's multiyear effort to improve our national historic preservation and archaeological protection programs.

Building on the consensus reached with the preservation community in the previous session, on March 19, 1991, Fowler reintroduced his National Historic Preservation Act Amendments as S. 684, which eventually had seventeen cosponsors, all Democrats. An important difference from previous Fowler historic preservation bills was that this time, both the National Trust for Historic Preservation and Preservation Action joined with the National Conference of State Historic Preservation Officers, the American Institute of Architects, the Navajo Nation, and the Society for American Archaeology in endorsing the proposal.

The Senate Energy and Natural Resources Public Lands Subcommittee, on which Fowler served, held hearings on S. 684 in Macon and Augusta as well as Washington, DC. After these hearings, the Interior Department submitted a series of concerns about the measure, in spite of the largely positive review provided by the Advisory Council on Historic Preservation. In addition, full committee Chairman Bennett Johnston indicated that, in order to advance the Fowler bill out of the Energy and Natural Resources Committee, he wanted the bill to specify Northwestern State University of Louisiana in Natchitoches as the location for the new National Center for Preservation Technology and Training. Fowler's original intent was to have the center's location chosen through a national competition; he and his staff had been informed that Georgia Tech and the University of California at Davis would likely be leading contenders. Many in the preservation community were dismayed by the designation of the site in rural Louisiana, but as Fowler and his staff explained, that was the only way to get the chairman's active support to move the bill out of committee and through the Senate. After making some modifications in response to Interior's concerns, and adding the Natchitoches designation, S. 684 was favorably reported out by the Energy and Natural Resources Committee on June 24, 1992.

With time running down on the 102nd Congress, Senator Johnston determined that, in view of the administration's lack of support for the measure, the only way to ensure action on S. 684 would be to attach it to a popular, must-pass House bill. To achieve this, he chose H.R. 429, which authorized a whole range of water projects mostly located in Western states. Thus, after further negotiations with the administration and Senate Republicans, and a few additional modifications, S. 684 was attached to H.R. 429, and the combined bill was adopted by the Senate by voice vote on July 31, 1992. The House decided not to act separately on the preservation provisions and went right to conference with the Senate.

Negotiations between the relevant House and Senate committee staffs ensued in September. Among the key issues involved in these "end game" negotiations was the Fowler bill's provision to require federal agencies involved in projects that adversely affect properties listed in or eligible for listing in the National Register of Historic Places to implement the recommendations of the Advisory Council on Historic Preservation unless there was no "feasible and prudent" means of doing so. Although this language had strong support from House Democratic conferees, opposition by Senate Republicans killed it in conference. An agreement was reached by conferees on October 5, which was then approved by voice vote in the House on October 6 (Fowler's fifty-second birthday), and by an 83 to 8 margin in the Senate on October 8, before being signed into law by the president on October 30.

In its final, enacted form, the National Historic Preservation Act Amendments of 1992 included, among its many provisions, the following:

> **Section 4003** directs the Interior Department, in consultation with the Advisory Council on Historic Preservation and State Historic Preservation Officers, to review threats to historic properties

and report to Congress on such threats at least once every four years.

Section 4004 provides a more explicit description of the federal review process for state preservation programs, expands the list of state historic preservation responsibilities to include consultation with federal agencies on federal undertakings that may affect historic properties in the state and assistance in the review of rehabilitation tax credit applications, and authorizes the Interior Department to make agreements with state historic preservation offices to expand their responsibilities (including reaching agreement on the terms of any additional federal financial assistance, if any, for the costs of carrying out such responsibilities).

Section 4006 establishes tribal historic preservation programs.

Section 4007 makes religious properties eligible for matching historic preservation grants "provided that the purpose of the grant is secular, does not promote religion, and seeks to protect those qualities that are historically significant" and authorizes direct federal historic preservation grants to Indian tribes, Native Hawaiian organizations, and certain US territories and possessions.

Section 4008 establishes a comprehensive federal preservation education and training program, including "technical or financial assistance, or both, to historically Black colleges and universities, to tribal colleges, and to colleges with a high enrollment of Native Americans or Native Hawaiians, to establish preservation training and degree programs."

Section 4012 further defines and strengthens federal agency historic preservation responsibilities by requiring the agencies to identify, evaluate, and nominate eligible properties to the national register and to do so in consultation with state historic preservation offices, local governments, Indian tribes, Native Hawaiian organizations, and the interested public; authorizing agencies to deny federal assistance in cases of anticipatory demolition (where "an applicant, with intent to avoid the requirements of Section 106, has intentionally significantly adversely affected historic property to which the grant would relate"); and requiring the agency to document any instances in which the agency did not reach agreement with the Advisory Council on Historic Preservation in undertakings that adversely affect properties listed in or eligible for listing in the National Register of Historic Places.

Section 4014 requires that historic preservation and archaeological protection activities undertaken by federal employees or contractors meet professional and qualification standards to be developed by the Department of the Interior and the Office of Personnel Management; provides that "records and other data produced by historical research and archaeological surveys and excavations are permanently maintained in appropriate databases and made available to potential users"; and directs the Department of the Interior to: (1) provide information to private owners of historic or archaeological resources "about the need for protection of such resources and the available means of protection"; (2) encourage such owners to preserve such resources "intact and in place and offer the owners...information on the tax and grant assistance available for the donation of the resources or of a preservation easement of the resources"; (3) encourage the protection of Native American cultural resources; and (4) encourage owners undertaking archaeological excavations to do so in accordance with standards for federally sponsored excavations, donate or lend recovered artifacts of research significance to an appropriate research institution, allow access to artifacts for research purposes, and consult with the appropriate Indian tribe or Native Hawaiian organization prior to excavating or disposing of a Native American cultural item.

Section 4015 directs the Department of the Interior to "study and report on the suitability and feasibility of alternatives for controlling illegal interstate and international traffic in antiquities" and report to Congress on the findings within eighteen months of the bill's enactment.

Section 4016 adds the requirement that a member of an Indian tribe or Native Hawaiian organization be appointed to the Advisory Council on Historic Preservation.

Section 4017 authorizes funding of $5 million per year for FY 1993 through FY 1996 for the Advisory Council on Historic Preservation.

Section 4019 amends National Historic Preservation Act definitions, including a revision in the definition of "undertaking" that clarifies and extends it to include federal actions delegated to states and localities, and an explicit designation of the National Park Service as the agent for the Department of the Interior in carrying out the provisions of the act.

Section 4022 creates a National Center for Preservation and Technology located at Northwestern State University of Louisiana in Natchitoches to "(1) develop and distribute preservation and conservation skills and technologies for the identification, evaluation, conservation, and interpretation of prehistoric and historic resources; (2) develop and facilitate training for Federal, State, and local resource preservation officials, cultural resource managers, maintenance personnel, and others working in the preservation field; (3) take steps to apply preservation technology benefits from ongoing research by other agencies and institutions; (4) facilitate the transfer of preservation technology among Federal agencies, State and local governments, universities, international organizations, and the private sector; and (5) cooperate with related international organizations including, but not limited to the International Council on Monuments and Sites, the International Center for the Study of Preservation and Restoration of Cultural Property, and the International Council on Museums."

Though falling short of its author's original intent, the 1992 Fowler amendments to the National Historic Preservation Act were well received in the preservation community, as reflected in a December 1992 article in *Historic Preservation News*.

> In the waning days of the 1992 presidential campaign George Bush signed into law a legislative package containing amendments to the 1966 National Historic Preservation Act. The preservation legislation, officially the National Historic Preservation Act Amendments

of 1992, is widely known as the Fowler bill for Sen. Wyche Fowler, Jr. (D-GA), who initiated it, orchestrated provisions and mediated compromises among preservationists and others, and introduced it in the Senate.... Enactment of the 1992 amendments is the culmination of more than four years of research and study. The goal was to "fine tune," as Fowler puts it, the landmark 1966 legislation. "We are quite simply facing the permanent loss of historical resources, on an unprecedented scale throughout the country," Fowler says. "We need to strengthen the partnership between the federal government and the vigorous forces of preservation that have developed in the private sector and in state and local government. Above all, we need a commitment at the highest level to our preservation responsibilities. The legislation of 1966 got us started. The preservation legislation passed...this year takes another strong step in that direction...."

Despite the inevitable compromises, the preservation legislation [signed into law] retains measures that please those who worked for its passage. Nellie L. Longsworth, the president of Preservation Action, praises the provision that is designed to discourage demolition of historic properties in order to avoid review under Section 106 of the 1966 act by the federal advisory council. "We've lost many buildings because of anticipatory demolition," says Longsworth. "Now that we have this prohibition in the law the people at the grassroots level have more of a chance to say to those who seek federal aid for a project, 'Don't be in such a hurry to tear down that building.'" She also commends the recognition in the amendments of such indigenous populations as Native Americans and Native Hawaiians.

Elizabeth Merritt, the National Trust's associate general counsel, believes the amendments' new definition of what constitutes a federal "undertaking" will "actually save a lot of litigation. Over the last ten years we have had to fight this issue one agency at a time. Each agency has its own regulatory framework, and each one has its own excuses as to why certain types of decisions should be exempted from historic preservation review. This amendment should settle that issue once and for all. Congress has confirmed our [preservationists'] position by making it crystal clear that the full range of agency programs and decisions will be subject to the historic preservation laws. The message to federal agencies is, 'No more excuses; just do it.'"

For Eric Hertfelder, the director of the National Conference of State Historic Preservation Officers, the big achievements of the amendments are their strengthened protection provisions and simplified administrative relationship between the National Park Service and the states. "This will allow the states to do more preservation and less paperwork," he says.... As the amendments' author, Fowler credits the work and time of "all of the people involved, not only in historic preservation but also people concerned with economic development." It is, he says, "a law we can all be proud of."[122]

Fowler's work on the preservation legislation also received a number of formal endorsements. In January 1992, the American Institute of Architects gave Senator Fowler its Presidential Citation Award "in acknowledgement of consistent leadership in historic preservation," and after the bill's enactment, the National Conference of State Historic Preservation Officers unanimously approved a resolution of appreciation "for his efforts to strengthen the nation's preservation program, for his ongoing consultation of the preservation community throughout the legislative process, and for his leadership in securing passage of the 1992 Amendments to the National Historic Preservation Act." NCSHPO executive director Eric Hertfelder commented, "Without Senator Fowler, there would be no Preservation Act Amendments. In 1987, Senator Fowler was the only member of Congress interested in a preservation bill. During the following six years, he kept at it, working with preservation and tribal organizations and the Congress until the bill was passed."

Constituent Services and Voting Record

Wyche Fowler was easily one of the most accessible politicians in modern Georgia history. In the Senate, with the second highest number of counties in the nation (after Texas) and the largest geographic territory east of the Mississippi to represent, his person-to-person communication efforts were extensive and physically demanding:

- Fowler visited every one of Georgia's 159 counties at least once during his Senate term, with most being traveled to multiple times;

• He conducted more than two hundred town meetings all over the state that were open to all citizens—Republican, Democrat, or Independent, supporter or not; and

• He made more than four hundred additional appearances throughout the state, from speaking to Rotarians and touring nursing homes to shaking hands at farmers markets and bringing congressional hearings to grassroots Georgia.

Another form of access to constituents was in his office's attention to the problems individuals experienced when dealing with federal bureaucracy. His entire Georgia Senate staff—headed by state director Charles Jackson and located in Atlanta as well as eight other Georgia cities (Albany, Athens, Augusta, Columbus, Dalton, Macon, Savannah, and Waycross)—was devoted entirely to this casework. During Fowler's six years in the Senate, his office handled more than twenty thousand requests for help from Georgians.

While making sure his office could handle the legislative and casework load outlined above, Fowler made a conscious effort to ensure that taxpayers got their money's worth. During his Senate term, he saved, on average, more than $200,000 each year from his office budget allocation, and these savings totaled more than $1.2 million over the six years, representing 18 percent of his allocation.

Despite his heavy Georgia travel schedule, Senator Fowler missed very few votes while he served in the Senate, and his attendance record exceeded the Senate average in all six years.

1987: Senate average 94 percent, Fowler 97 percent
1988: Senate average 92 percent, Fowler 96 percent
1989: Senate average 98 percent, Fowler 99 percent
1990: Senate average 97 percent, Fowler 98 percent
1991: Senate average 97 percent, Fowler 99 percent
1992: Senate average 95 percent, Fowler 96 percent

This time, voting attendance would not be an issue in the upcoming campaign.

Chapter 13

1992 Senate Election: Runoff

In 1992, Georgia was unique as the only state in the nation that required a runoff if no candidate won a majority in a general election. (Louisiana also required, and continues to require, a runoff in general elections, but its electoral system is quite different in that a runoff is triggered when no candidate wins a majority in a single primary in which candidates from all parties compete. Mississippi adopted a system like Georgia's effective for the 2024 general election.) Though this had been the state law since 1964 (when its author had proclaimed that its intent was to "thwart election control by Negroes and other minorities"), it had never been put into effect until 1992; in response to the events of that year, Georgia's Democrat-controlled general assembly changed the election law in 1994 so that general election runoffs would be triggered only when no candidate received less than 45 percent of the total vote. This change was to prove crucial in the 1996 Georgia Senate race in which the Democratic nominee, Secretary of State Max Cleland, defeated his Republican opponent, Guy Millner, by a 30,024-vote plurality (48.87 percent to 47.54 percent). Partisan calculations then produced another revision in the state's election code, with the absolute majority requirement being reinstated in 2005 by the Republican-controlled legislature, resulting in another runoff in 2008 in which Republican incumbent Saxby Chambliss easily defeated (57 percent to 43 percent) his Democratic challenger Jim Martin in a December runoff, after holding a narrow (49.8 percent to 46.8 percent) lead in the general election. Georgia's unique "general election runoff" requirement was placed in the national spotlight in 2020 when partisan control of the US Senate was decided by the January 2021 runoff victories of Democrats Raphael Warnock and Jon Ossoff, with Warnock again prevailing in a 2022 runoff.

Early Stages

A survey conducted for the *Atlanta Journal-Constitution* and WSB-TV in November 1991 underscored the competitiveness of the 1992 Georgia Senate race from its outset.

> Sen. Wyche Fowler, Jr., could be vulnerable to a strong Republican challenge in next year's election, but the two announced GOP opponents are virtual unknowns, even in metro Atlanta.... The poll of 970 voters found that Mr. Fowler has not expanded his base of support beyond the majority that supported him in 1986. His job approval and popularity ratings hover around 50 percent, and only 38 percent of voters said they would vote for the Democrat if the election were held today. Another third said they would consider voting for another candidate, but the poll...suggests Republicans have their work cut out for them if they hope to recapture the seat Mack Mattingly lost five years ago. The two announced Republicans, former Peace Corps Director and longtime state Sen. Paul Coverdell and former U.S. Attorney Bob Barr, are unknown by at least 80 percent of the voters.

Interestingly, especially in view of later analyses of the 1992 election results, the AJC/WSB poll found that whereas Fowler's vote against the Persian Gulf War was costing him some support (more likely to vote for Fowler: 14 percent; less likely: 35 percent; not much difference: 47 percent; no opinion: 4 percent), his vote to confirm Clarence Thomas was actually a net positive overall (more likely: 31 percent; less likely: 18 percent; not much difference: 47 percent; no opinion: 4 percent).[123]

The Georgia electorate that would decide the outcome had continued to evolve over time and was considerably different compared to the one that had chosen Fowler just six years before. The number of registered voters had grown by more than six hundred thousand (23 percent), with most of this increase occurring in the partisan-divided five-county metro Atlanta area (Clayton, Cobb, DeKalb, Fulton, Gwinnett; +286,000) and the heavily Republican Atlanta "exurbs" (Cherokee, Douglas, Fayette, Forsyth, Henry, Newton, Paulding, Rockdale, Walton; +93,000). African

Americans accounted for 22 percent of Georgia's registered voters in the 1992 election.

One of the crucial challenges facing the Fowler campaign was in defining him and his record for Georgia voters. In the words of a January 1991 Secrest report, "Let's be frank here. Most of the problem is that Georgia voters don't have any idea what the hell Wyche Fowler is doing for them in Washington." The source of this "information deficit" remains unclear to this day and is one that afflicts many (if not most) incumbents. In the absence of paid advertising—most of which generally does not occur until the months and weeks just before an election—the source of voter information is limited to "free media": TV, radio, newspapers, and now (though not in 1992) the Internet and social media, with the media operations in incumbents' offices largely devoted to attempting to get their message across to citizens via these means.

Initially, the Fowler team decided that their thematic focus would highlight the senator's specific accomplishments for localities across the state and emphasize his accessibility and accountability to his constituents, as exemplified by his two hundred-plus town hall meetings and visits to all of Georgia's 159 counties. However, the campaign's own polling revealed that this approach was not very appealing in the 1992 election cycle, during which a strong anti-incumbent sentiment was prevalent. This was particularly true for conservative white Democrats and political Independents, who represented key, and potentially decisive, segments of the electorate.

An independent perspective on the 1992 Georgia Senate race was provided by political scientist Richard Fenno, who approached Fowler in the summer of 1991 with a request that he be allowed to follow the senator's reelection efforts from the "inside" in order to provide research for a book he planned to do. In the end, the book project was shelved, but Professor Fenno did use his research (gleaned from twenty-one days of visits with Fowler and his campaign team in both Washington and Georgia between August 1991 and November 1992) as the basis for two chapters in his 1996 book, *Senators on the Campaign Trail.*[124]

> I asked him why a campaign theme like "fighting for Georgia" or "Georgia first" had not been the obvious choice [for the principal theme]—given his success with that theme in 1986, his available

record of accomplishment in the Senate, and his fear of the anti-incumbency mood. "That was our original idea of what the campaign should be," he answered. "We even picked out the things I had done for each area.... About a year and a half out, that was our plan. Then our later polls seemed to tell us that it would sound like too much pork, and that was not what people wanted to hear, that they wanted to hear about the major policies. So we switched. We were moved by the 'superior intelligence of new information.'"[125]

More specifically, the polls suggested that an emphasis on key domestic policy issues—including jobs, health care, and education—offered a more effective pro-Fowler message, and this was certainly in keeping with the "It's the economy, stupid" approach of the ultimately successful Bill Clinton campaign for the presidency.

Fenno offered his take on the challenges the Fowler campaign faced in translating his policy record into a political asset.

> [Fowler] described himself always as a "public policy person" who examined problems "from a public policy standpoint." He saw himself as someone who was in public service to make good public policy in the Senate. That is what he most enjoyed; that was where he could best exercise his independence, and that was the reputation he most wanted. The dozen or so campaign speeches I heard focused, Clinton-style, on the need for domestic policy change—in health care, education, and jobs.... He showed a sophisticated understanding of these issues, as a Senate policy broker might. Even so, he was unable to identify himself closely with any of those policy areas. They were not part of his observable legislative record. And he never put forward any specific, recognizable plan for coping with any of them. Neither could he derive any electoral leverage from his two major legislative accomplishments in the Senate. Historic preservation and alternative energy research had tiny constituencies. Nor did his personal policy passions—for the environment and foreign affairs—have any visible saliency in Georgia in 1992. Nor could he capitalize on his facilitative work in the Democratic leadership, since it was done on the inside and out of public view.[126]

1992 Senate General Election Campaign

Fowler's Atlanta campaign office in Buckhead opened in January 1992, and he used the same campaign team as in 1986, including media consultant Frank Greer, pollster Alan Secrest, and campaign manager Bill Johnstone. Unlike in 1986, he was unopposed in the Democratic primary. He officially announced his candidacy for reelection in April. His announcement speech represented an attempt to mesh local accomplishments with national policy priorities as well as to respond to the growing anti-incumbent sentiment.

> Public office should not be about special privileges, but about service to our neighbors and our country. That's why I have a 97 percent voting record in the Senate. That's why I voted against the pay raise, why I have always driven myself to work in my own car, why I've insisted that Congress and the Executive Branch live under all the same laws applied to everyone else.... A lot of people in Washington, DC, have forgotten the one simple rule that should guide public service: people are the first priority. That's how I make decisions. Will it help the people of Georgia? Will it help you? That's why I've been fighting to protect American jobs. To get you affordable health care. To protect the right to choose. To protect everyone's right to equal treatment and opportunity. To help educate our children and to care for our parents....
>
> It is time to invest in America, to make sure our country and our people are in position to take advantage of the dramatically changed world of the 21st century. That's why I helped Columbia County teacher Marcia Bailey get the tools she needs to teach math to 10th graders like Billy Neal and Eric Strang, who will need those skills to successfully compete for future jobs with kids now growing up in Tokyo, Paris, and Berlin.... And why I have worked so hard to bring jobs to Georgia, to help small businesses and farmers expand their markets, and to stop the exporting of American jobs to Mexico and overseas.... That's why I'm fighting for reform of our health care system—for cost control, improved access, and more emphasis on prevention. The money we invest now in education, in the infrastructure—the roads, bridges, airports, in all of our

> transportation and communications systems—will pay off quickly in an enhanced ability to attract and provide good paying jobs for well-educated, highly skilled workers. That's why I am proud to be the author of the Rural Star Schools Act, which the President signed into law, and which will use space age technology to give the children of rural Georgia the educational opportunities they deserve. That's why I've voted for full funding for Head Start and the TRIO programs for disadvantaged youth, and why I've sponsored legislation to make college tuition aid available to children of middle-class families. That's why, with the goal of improving the productivity of Georgia's economy in mind, I have worked hard to improve airport facilities in Athens, Dublin, Gwinnett County, Savannah and Valdosta.

As Fowler was kicking off his reelection bid, Georgia Republicans were engaged in a hotly contested primary to choose his November opponent. In a multi-candidate field, former Peace Corps director and state Senator Paul Coverdell led the way in the July primary with 100,016 votes (37 percent). Former US Attorney Bob Barr finished second with 65,471 (24 percent), edging out Waycross Mayor John Knox (64,514; 24 percent). Businessman Charles Tanksley finished fourth (32,950; 12 percent). Though these results were still well below the number of votes cast in Democratic primaries (Fowler won more than 314,000 votes in the uncontested 1986 Democratic primary by comparison), they marked a continuing advance in Republican identification in the state (Mattingly, for example, won the GOP nomination in 1980 with slightly more than 28,000 votes). Since Georgia law required an absolute majority in the primaries as well as the general election, Coverdell and Barr were pitted in a runoff three weeks later, which Coverdell won by a scant 1,548 votes (80,435 to 78,887).

In the first Fowler campaign poll taken after the Republican runoff, Fowler held a substantial lead, but his vote share was barely above 50 percent, and his positive job performance rating, usually one of the better predictors of an incumbent's ultimate vote, had declined to just 43 percent.

August 18, 1992 Campaign Poll:
Fowler Personal Appeal: 50 percent positive, 20 percent neutral, 30 percent negative; 91 percent recognition
Fowler Job Performance: 43 percent positive, 46 percent negative, 11 percent not sure
1992 Vote: 51 percent Fowler, 30 percent Paul Coverdell, 19 percent undecided

Originally, the Fowler campaign plan had called for three weeks of introductory, pro-Fowler TV ads, costing approximately $750,000, sandwiched around the Republican primary in July and August. However, in June, the campaign team decided to forego this early round in order to ensure there would be sufficient funds to finance a massive, uninterrupted eight-week effort at the end of the campaign.

On August 11, Fowler proposed to Coverdell that both campaigns forego paid advertising and instead have the candidates participate in an ongoing series of "Lincoln-Douglas" debates on TV and radio in which the candidates would directly question each other rather than respond to queries from media representatives. The proposal also called on television and radio stations to make a half hour of free air time available to both campaigns each week during the last eight weeks of the election. "There is no way that a 30- or 60-second broadcast ad can give voters adequate information about candidates and their platforms," Fowler said. In addition, it called for limitations on overall spending by each campaign and on expenditures made on their behalf by third parties. Other than the debates, the proposal was rejected by the Coverdell campaign.

The Fowler paid-media effort began the week of September 8 with a shorter (sixty-second), slightly revised version of the 1986 biographical "Born and Raised in Georgia" TV ad running in all Georgia markets: Albany, Atlanta, Augusta, Columbus, Macon, and Savannah. This was followed with two weeks of positive, policy-oriented spots on education and health care reform. The buy level for these three spots was moderate. Five weeks out from Election Day, the campaign began ramping up the buy level, resulting in a doubling of the original level for the final two weeks of the general election campaign. The content for these spots was again predominantly positive, and included "Nunn," which featured Georgia's senior senator offering his endorsement of Senator Fowler and citing his colleague's specific accomplishments for the state.

The issue that would become the focal point for the Coverdell campaign for the remainder of the race surfaced in late August when a Republican Party operative directed a reporter to a deposition given by Fowler in 1986 concerning his child support payments, as recounted in a September 1 article.

> Republican Senate candidate Paul Coverdell challenged U.S. Sen. Wyche Fowler Monday to release records from his account at the now-defunct House bank, saying statements by Mr. Fowler in a 1986 child-support deposition raised questions about possible overdrafts. Mr. Fowler, who served in the House from 1977 to 1986, has denied bouncing any checks. Mr. Coverdell, seeking to tie Mr. Fowler to the House banking scandal as a campaign issue, said his statement in the deposition suggests otherwise. The deposition became public after a Republican Party member pointed a reporter to it during the recent Republican National Convention in Houston. In it, Mr. Fowler was asked about his monthly cash flow. He replied, in part, "Thankfully, we have a bank that doesn't zap me when I bounce a check because we have our own bank." In March, Fowler stated flatly that he never bounced a check written on the House bank. "Who did Wyche lie to?" Mr. Coverdell said during a news conference Monday. "The voters are not going to tolerate that kind of arrogance and attempts to deceive by status quo politicians in Congress." Last week, Mr. Fowler angrily refused to answer a reporter's questions about the deposition, saying it had nothing to do with his Senate record. "We decry this continual mudslinging from the Coverdell campaign," Bill Johnstone, Mr. Fowler's campaign manager, said Monday. "They now may have reached a new low in bringing divorce proceedings into the political arena."[127]

A few days later, Fowler made public all his bank statements from the House bank and released monthly summaries of account activity for the entire 1977 to 1986 period. Citing the fact that the Mattingly campaign was aware of the same document but chose not to use it in the 1986 race, Fowler criticized Coverdell, stating, "No person of integrity...would fish in this dirt." However, because the House bank provided what amounted to overdraft protection, meaning the bank statements never reflected a negative balance, the released documents could not substantiate Fowler's denial. The whole situation was made more confusing by the outdated operating procedures of the bank, which included use of a "pencil and ledger" accounting system instead of a computerized system, lack of regular account statements or overdrawn notices to House members, and failure to post deposits in a timely manner. However, regardless of the actual facts, the scandal was doubly damaging to the Fowler reelection effort: it provided the Coverdell campaign with perhaps its single most effective line of attack and soured Fowler's relationship with the news media, particularly the Atlanta papers. He repeatedly attacked the media for focusing on the House bank issue and not reporting on more substantive policy matters, commenting, "I didn't bounce a check and everybody knows it. I was angry about the fact that certain people in the press allowed themselves to be used by anonymous Republican sources."[128]

Coverdell's general election TV ads began airing the week of October 6 and continued through Election Day. As described in the Fenno book,

> [Coverdell's] television campaign began with the "too liberal" theme, packaged in a singing jingle by a small-town grandmother, tying Fowler to Ted Kennedy and telling voters to "vote Paul Coverdell in and vote Wyche Fowler out...." The challenger's commercials charged that Fowler lied about not bouncing checks at the House bank when he served in that body; that he voted for pay raises and perks for himself and higher taxes for his constituents; that he deceived the voters by leading a "double life," voting one way in Washington and talking another way at home.... The Coverdell television campaign was the most completely negative and the most completely personal attack of any, save one, of the thirty-six campaigns I observed.... And it was a faceless campaign. The challenger never spoke and never appeared in any of his television ads. And not one of them ever mentioned what he would do if elected. As commentator Bill Shipp said, "It was totally negative. It failed to articulate a single time why Paul Coverdell should be a Senator." The challenger was campaigning on television as Mr. X.[129]

The two most frequently aired Coverdell attack ads were one that criticized Fowler over congressional pay and pensions, along with his support of the 1990 budget agreement that raised taxes, and another that invoked the House bank issue and closed, "What's the truth, Wyche? Did you lie under oath about bouncing checks or are you lying now to try to keep your job? The truth is, after 16 years in Washington, you can't trust Wyche Fowler."

As was the case in 1986, a key decision for the Fowler team was over whether, when, and how to respond to the opposition attacks. Based on research into Coverdell's record and polling and focus group results, the campaign prepared a small number of "counterattack" ads, criticizing the opponent's record in the state senate, as Peace Corps director, and as an insurance executive. One of those spots, titled "Crime," was considered to be particularly hard-hitting and, perhaps not coincidentally, consistently tested as the most effective of these "negative" ads. It centered on a Coverdell vote in the Georgia Senate in favor of a furlough program that "made it easier for convicted murderers to be temporarily released into the community." From the time it was first presented to him, Fowler was uneasy about this spot, which he felt was an oversimplification of the vote itself and excessively inflammatory in the manner of the 1988 George Bush attack on Michael Dukakis in the infamous "Willie Horton" ad.

Turning to Fenno once more:

> When Coverdell's attacks came, the Fowler campaign retaliated in very measured fashion. For a while, nothing, then with one, then two of the three [negative] ads—but always holding back the third, most hard-hitting "crime spot...." [Toward the end of the general election campaign] the Fowler campaign decided to prepare a response ad, replying to each one of the various personal attacks in turn, with "supporting editorial comment," and with attribution for each comment flashed across the screen.[130]

In addition to the advertising battles, another important feature of the latter stages of the 1992 Georgia Senate race were the three Lincoln-Douglas style candidate debates, the first of which was held on October 9 in Thomasville and broadcast on radio stations around the state.

> Under questioning from his Republican challenger, Sen. Wyche Fowler Jr. on Friday defended the bipartisan 1990 budget accord that raised some taxes, saying it would keep the budget deficit $500 billion smaller than it would have been.... GOP nominee Paul Coverdell suggested that Mr. Fowler was the lead Democratic figure who "forced' President Bush to sign the agreement, thus breaking his pledge not to raise taxes. Mr. Fowler replied, "I'm very flattered you accorded me the power to force the president of the United States to do anything.... Were it not for the 1990 budget summit, the deficit would be—three years from now—at least $500 billion more than it will be." At times more aggressive than his opponent, Mr. Fowler also made his case in this rural South Georgia town that he is a friend of Agriculture, noting his seat on the Senate Agriculture Committee. When Mr. Coverdell addressed the same topic, there was little he could say to counter Mr. Fowler.... Trailing Mr. Fowler in fund-raising, Mr. Coverdell was hoping to use this forum and two televised debates, planned for next weekend, to raise his own profile while trying to undermine Mr. Fowler's record and image. But the freshman Democrat dictated the pace of this first meeting.... Near the end of the hour-long debate, Mr. Coverdell raised the issue of whether Mr. Fowler had overdrafts at the House bank during his 10 years representing the 5th Congressional district. "I don't believe you have been candid with us," Mr. Coverdell said. Mr. Fowler replied that he, unlike Mr. Coverdell, has released his income tax returns. After the debate, Mr. Coverdell said he hasn't decided whether to release his tax returns.[131]

The next debate was in Savannah on October 17, telecast live that day on Savannah station WTOC-TV and tape-delayed for rebroadcast statewide on the Georgia Public Television Network the following day.

> The second debate between Democratic U.S. Sen. Wyche Fowler Jr. and GOP challenger Paul Coverdell deteriorated Saturday into an acrimonious exchange about personal ethics. Mr. Fowler accused Mr. Coverdell of voting as a state senator for insurance legislation that would benefit his business. "Give us your tax returns, and we'll let the public see who has profited from public service,"

> Mr. Fowler said near the end of the hour-long debate in an elementary school here. Mr. Coverdell last week released tax returns for the last three years, but has yet to produce his returns for earlier years. He served in the Georgia Senate from 1971 to 1989. Asked after the debate whether he has reason to believe Mr. Coverdell acted improperly in the Senate, Mr. Fowler replied, "Yes." He would not elaborate. The Republican, meanwhile, tried to link Mr. Fowler to the scandal over loans to Iraq made by the Atlanta branch of the Italian bank Banca Nationale del Lavoro (BNL), noting that Mr. Fowler made a government-paid trip to Iraq in 1990. "Who did you meet with in Iraq?" Mr. Coverdell asked in the debate.... There has been no indication that Mr. Fowler had anything to do with the BNL affair or acted improperly in meeting with government officials in Iraq.... The personal attacks overshadowed an issues-based discussion in the first part of the debate. While Mr. Coverdell criticized Mr. Fowler for his support of the 1990 budget summit agreement that raised $137 billion in new taxes over five years, Mr. Fowler rattled off budget items he has opposed as a way of reducing the deficit. He criticized Mr. Coverdell for his support of a balanced-budget amendment and the line-item veto for the president.... Mr. Fowler appeared to have his opponent on the defensive when he challenged Mr. Coverdell on his opposition to fully funding Social Security benefits for "notch babies"—retirees born between 1917 and 1926 who receive smaller payments because of a quirk in the benefit formula. Mr. Fowler supports legislation to increase benefits to those retirees. Mr. Coverdell opposes it.[132]

The final general election debate occurred in Atlanta on October 18 and was broadcast on WSB-TV.

> Three debates down and two weeks to go, GOP Senate nominee Paul Coverdell is hoping a steady stream of attacks in debates and television ads is narrowing the gap with Democratic Sen. Wyche Fowler Jr. Pursuing a line of attack that questions Mr. Fowler's character and integrity, Mr. Coverdell on Sunday accused the senator of lying about his involvement with the House bank, overstating his support for budget reductions, and misleading voters about

congressional pay raises.... Mr. Fowler returned the favor and complained of the Republican's desire to attack him. Mr. Coverdell has provided few specifics of what he would do if elected. "In all three debates now, you have not proposed a single cut [to reduce the deficit]," Mr. Fowler said. The two Atlantans also claimed the title of reformer, pledged to cut the deficit, advocated an overhaul of the health-care system without specifying how that would be done, and derisively labeled each other as millionaires.... The bitter tone of the campaign, which peaked in a debate in Savannah Saturday, continued Sunday in the candidates' only planned joint appearance in Atlanta. Mr. Coverdell set the tone even before the afternoon debate when he debuted a television ad about the House bank that ended: "The truth is, after 16 years in Washington, you can't trust Wyche Fowler." He pressed the theme during the hour-long debate, saying, "The senator has lied a few times." Mr. Fowler replied that he has released whatever records he has and repeated that he never had any overdrafts at the now-closed bank. The only definitive answer could come from the checks themselves, and Mr. Fowler says he no longer has a complete set. Mr. Fowler, in turn, challenged Mr. Coverdell to release his income tax returns from his 19 years in the state Senate. Mr. Coverdell previously has resisted, but said Sunday he would make those records available.... As he has in earlier debates, Mr. Coverdell tried to focus his fire on Fowler's support for the 1990 budget agreement, which raised $137 billion in new taxes over five years. "He was the promoter, the organizer, the driver of the one of the nation's largest tax increases," Mr. Coverdell said. President Bush proposed the increases, "mainly on the wealthy, that we went along with," Mr. Fowler countered. The Democrat waited until the last exchange between the candidates to question Mr. Coverdell's support for abortion rights, bringing up a 1973 vote. "He voted against the implementation of Roe v. Wade when he was a state senator," said Mr. Fowler, who supports abortion rights. Mr. Coverdell, without acknowledging that vote, replied he supports current Georgia law, providing for abortions in the first trimester and increasing restrictions afterward. But he did vote against a bill, on the last day of the 1973 legislative session, that established the framework for legal abortions in Georgia.[133]

Based on his personal observations, Fenno wrote,

> Whenever straightforward policy confrontations occurred during the debates, Fowler came across as an active, thoughtful, constructive member of the Senate. And he did carry the debate. The problem was that such clear confrontations occurred only in the interstices of the challenger's all-purpose anti-incumbent attack. On these more numerous occasions, Fowler's performance consisted of personal counterattacks and scattershot sallies that sometimes scored and sometimes didn't.[134]

Fowler's record of accomplishment in the Congress once again won him editorial endorsements from leading newspapers across the state.

> Senator Fowler's decision to give up his seat representing a metro Atlanta district to move into the Senate and have a state-wide constituency was a politically brave one. But Mr. Fowler was able to succeed in his personal challenge to be accepted by the South Georgia farm community and other citizens below the "gnat line" as he had been for five terms representing "city folk." It was a major obstacle to overcome, but Wyche Fowler made a promise if elected to never forget the Southern part of our state, to visit it often and work for the needs of this section. We have watched this factor closely over the last half dozen years and are happy to declare that the Senator kept his promise. He has returned to the area time and time again and he has received enormous support and praise from citizens in all walks. Not only in the field of agriculture, but in many others as well, Fowler has proven his abilities in obtaining sorely needed legislation, along with economic and business pluses that have been of tremendous benefit to all Georgians.
>
> —*Americus Times-Recorder*[135]

Wyche Fowler has served Georgia well as an effective member of the Senate. He has earned the support of voters and deserves re-election. Far from being the "Ted Kennedy liberal" the GOP has portrayed, Mr. Fowler has fashioned a mostly moderate record, with forays into conservative ground on some issues.... Some supporters from days past feel he has shifted too far, but Mr. Fowler has shown that he remains at the core progressive and compassionate. He has managed to climb the Senate hierarchy to a degree that is unusual for a freshman.

—*Atlanta Constitution*[136]

It is true that Fowler...is more liberal than many Georgians he represents, but it is also true that he has his head screwed on right. The senator from Atlanta understands the basic issues that confront us all, namely the need for more and better jobs for Georgians, better health care and especially the imperative that we educate and prepare our people for the highly competitive work world of tomorrow. Moreover, Sen. Fowler has a good record on the environment, historic preservation, women's issues (though he had a falling out with NOW over his endorsement of Clarence Thomas for the U.S. Supreme Court), and, for a city boy, he has shown a surprising sensitivity to the concerns of farmers and rural residents. In fact, Fowler is one of the few men in the Senate who appears to possess an understanding of both urban and rural problems.

—*Columbus Ledger-Enquirer*[137]

Sen. Wyche Fowler's worthy opponent has attempted to tar him with, among other things, the "Ted Kennedy liberal" brush. Under scrutiny, the tar won't stick. Actually, Fowler's overall voting record as a freshman senator indicates a distinct movement toward the moderate center. The vast majority of his Senate votes have coincided with those of his senior colleague, Sam Nunn, who is rarely counted in the liberal column. Discerning voters will find the junior senator in good company. But Fowler can stand on his own merits. Ideology aside, he has steadily climbed the ladder of influence, a tough ascent for any first-termer. He is assistant floor leader and already a voice in agribusiness policy and other issues critical to

Georgia. He will doubtless accumulate more clout during a second term, all the better to serve his constituents and help shape this country's challenging future.

—*Macon Telegraph*[138]

At a time when it has become fashionable to talk of term limits and throwing the rascals out, Fowler is an exception. He is not, and never has been, a part of the problem. Rather, he has always been viewed as part of the potential solution. It has been for some time apparent to the people, if not their representatives, that Congress must drop all its posturing for political purposes and get down to the serious business of finding solutions, both logical and innovative, for national troubles. Many of the old ways have ceased to work and Fowler, like the state's senior senator, Democrat Sam Nunn, has been among those relative few who have steadily offered new ideas and approaches for exploration—if, alas, not always for implementation.... While this newspaper does not always agree with the senator's positions, it totally agrees with his attitude toward his responsibilities to the people. It is that attitude, coupled with a proven willingness to act independently of party and be his own man, by which Fowler commends himself to the favorable attention of the electorate. He deserves another six years in the Senate and has earned it.

—*Rome News-Tribune*[139]

This newspaper believes that [Fowler's] re-election would be of benefit to Savannah and the Coastal Empire. Two recent letters to the editor explain why we take this position. One was from the head of a Georgia farmers' organization. It lauded the Senator for the help he had given soybean farmers. The other letter was from an official with the Lucas Theatre project in Savannah, an undertaking vital to the future of the downtown area. The official thanked Sen. Fowler for seeking funds for restoration of the Lucas.... Mr. Fowler is an ardent Democrat, but he can work with a Republican administration when it's important to his constituents. He showed that when he supported President Bush's request for planning, engineering and design work on the Savannah harbor. He also voted for

> Savannahian Clarence Thomas for the Supreme Court. At times we have disagreed with the senator. We may well do so again. But this fact does not temper our conviction that he has done an excellent job of serving his constituents. He has also learned to listen to those who don't necessarily identify with his views.
>
> —*Savannah Morning News/Savannah Evening Press*[140]

Organizationally, direct voter contact via telephone continued to be the mainstay of the Fowler operation, though this time that effort was supplemented by a significantly expanded coordinated campaign effort undertaken in conjunction with the state Democratic Party and the Clinton presidential campaign.

As General Election Day approached, concerns were raised about a drop-off in support for Fowler among groups that had backed him in 1986. The National Organization for Women (NOW) withheld its support because of the senator's vote to confirm Clarence Thomas. In acknowledging Fowler's otherwise strong record on women's issues, the group's leaders indicated they were not advocating a vote for Coverdell, but rather that they, and like-minded people, should consider not voting in the Senate race. On the other hand, the Gay and Lesbian Alliance Against Discrimination (GLAAD) actively opposed Fowler's reelection, expressing extreme disappointment with his record, especially his failure to support legislation to expand civil rights protections for gay men and lesbians.

The 1992 general election campaign bore a striking resemblance to the 1986 race from a polling standpoint, only this time with Wyche Fowler in the incumbent position. Fowler maintained a lead in all of his pre-election surveys, though never much exceeding the crucial 50 percent support mark, with relatively low job performance and personal appeal positives (which experienced significant declines after Coverdell's attack ads began to run on October 6). And challenger Coverdell did not make up much ground until the late-stage debates and his end-game equality in level of media-buy finally solidified his partisan base and produced the narrow result that actually occurred on Election Day.

October 5, 1992, Campaign Poll:

Fowler Personal Appeal: 58 percent positive, 17 percent neutral, 25 percent negative

Fowler Job Performance: 52 percent positive, 41 percent negative, 7 percent not sure

Vote: 56 percent Fowler, 31 percent Coverdell, 13 percent undecided

October 11, 1992, Campaign Poll:

Fowler Personal Appeal: 53 percent positive, 18 percent neutral, 29 percent negative

Fowler Job Performance: 43 percent positive, 48 percent negative, 9 percent not sure

Vote: 52 percent Fowler, 31 percent Coverdell, 17 percent undecided

October 18, 1992, Campaign Poll:

Fowler Personal Appeal: 52 percent positive, 15 percent neutral, 33 percent negative

Fowler Job Performance: 47 percent positive, 46 percent negative, 7 percent not sure

Vote: 51 percent Fowler, 33 percent Coverdell, 16 percent undecided

October 25, 1992, Campaign Poll:

Fowler Personal Appeal: 48 percent positive, 16 percent neutral, 36 percent negative

Fowler Job Performance: 44 percent positive, 49 percent negative, 7 percent not sure

Vote: 50 percent Fowler, 33 percent Coverdell, 17 percent undecided

October 29, 1992, Campaign Poll:

Fowler Personal Appeal: 44 percent positive, 15 percent neutral, 41 percent negative

Vote: 45 percent Fowler, 39 percent Coverdell, 16 percent undecided

And much as was the case in 1986, the news media, which, after the fact, excoriated the incumbent candidate and his campaign for a "desultory" performance, pointed to Fowler's likely success and Coverdell's failure throughout most of October, as Fenno describes.

> On October 11, an Associated Press story reported that "polls and pundits say Wyche Fowler is a safe bet for re-election." Four days later, the *Atlanta Journal-Constitution*'s campaign story began,

> "Holding a big lead in the polls [Fowler] also has seven times more money available than [his] GOP challenger...." At the time, Fowler was holding a twenty-two-point lead in the latest Mason-Dixon poll and a twenty-four-point lead in the *Atlanta Journal-Constitution* poll. Georgia's pundits talked in mid-October as if there were no race, no issues, and no reason to replace the incumbent. Coverdell, they said, had been his party's "weakest candidate."[141]

In its editorial endorsement of October 23, the *Atlanta Constitution* wrote,

> Long, long ago, in the early days of this political season, Georgia's Wyche Fowler was consistently among the top names on the Republican Party's "hit list" of vulnerable Democratic U.S. senators targeted for defeat at the polls Nov. 3. From the GOP perspective, it was easy to see why. Mr. Fowler's election six years ago was considered a fluke that came about through a poor campaign run by Republican Senator Mack Mattingly, and an off-year for the GOP in congressional races in general. Mr. Fowler's first term was supposed to reveal him as too liberal for a conservative state. The country's anti-incumbent fervor also was supposed to work against him. Moreover, Republican chances for the seat seemed to improve when questions surrounding the U.S. House of Representatives bank arose. There was an opportunity to taint Mr. Fowler at least indirectly with that "scandal." He was supposed to be on the defensive throughout the campaign. So far, it hasn't worked out that way. Polls indicate Mr. Fowler has maintained a comfortable lead over his Republican opponent, Paul Coverdell. While it was easy to see why the GOP thought Mr. Fowler would fare poorly, it is just as easy to see why he has not. Wyche Fowler has served Georgia well as an effective member of the Senate. He has earned the support of voters and deserves re-election.[142]

And an October 25 article in the *Atlanta Journal-Constitution*, headlined "Incumbent Fowler Finds Himself in Good Shape Heading into Stretch," observed, "Unlike six years ago, when he needed the help of Speaker Tom Murphy and U.S. Sen. Sam Nunn to edge out a Republican incumbent, Mr. Fowler appears to be on the winning side of a potential rout. He has a double-digit lead in the polls, and he has a huge edge in money."[143] Four days later, reporter Tom Baxter wrote of Fowler's having inherited Herman Talmadge's base in rural Georgia.

> Just as Talmadge did, Fowler polls best by far among native Georgians, worst among people from outside the South. He is very strong among self-described core Democrats. And the biggest eye-opener: the former 5th District congressman polls several percentage points better outside metro Atlanta than he does inside it. His best region, in fact, appears to be southwest Georgia, which was also where Talmadge was strongest. That is not accidental. Fowler has carefully tended the Agriculture Committee appointment, and he has invested considerable time in small-town and rural Georgia during his six years in office. At the same time, he has done some things that have caused portions of his old central Atlanta constituency to look askance. Some gay and lesbian organizations are actively opposing him this year, and he got a cool reception this week at a gathering of Atlanta businesswomen, who seemed particularly unimpressed with his rationale for voting for Thomas. Fowler does not seem to have lost support among Black metro Atlanta voters, however—something Talmadge didn't have—and that plus the downstate vote gives him a formidable edge. This is not to say this race is over. Fowler trailed Mack Mattingly by double digits in 1986, and Mattingly wasn't given much chance against Talmadge in 1980. But Fowler had a Democratic surge working for him, and Mattingly the Reagan landslide. Coverdell hasn't been as lucky, in his timing or his opponent. Bush might still win Georgia, but he has no coattails. And Fowler, for all his vulnerability a year ago, is a politician who takes few chances, and isn't likely to be surprised by anybody.[144]

1992 Senate General Election Results and Analysis

Georgia voters went to the polls on Tuesday, November 3, 1992. Unlike in 1986, when only a one-sided gubernatorial race was present, in the

1992 general election two other contests were on the ballot that produced equal, or higher, levels of media and public attention than the Senate race: the presidential election involving Republican President George Bush, Democratic challenger Bill Clinton, and Independent Ross Perot, and a referendum on the establishment of a statewide lottery whose proceeds would be earmarked for higher education. This combination of tightly contested, high-profile races resulted in a major upsurge in voter interest and turnout.

More than 2.32 million Georgians voted in the presidential race, representing a turnout rate of 73.1 percent of the state's registered voters. In the closest result of all of that year's contests for president, Bill Clinton won Georgia's electoral votes by a razor-thin plurality of 13,714 votes.

Bill Clinton	1,008,966	43.47 percent
George Bush	995,252	42.88 percent
Ross Perot	309,657	13.34 percent
Andre Marrou (Libertarian)	7,110	0.31 percent

Just under 2.2 million voters (69.16 percent turnout) made it all the way through the lists of candidates for office to cast ballots for the lottery referendum, with the "Yeses" prevailing by fewer than 100,000 votes.

Yes (for lottery)	1,146,349	52.17 percent
No (against lottery)	1,050,674	47.82 percent

Falling between these two on the ballot, as well as with respect to turnout, 2,251,606 Georgians (70.87 percent) voted for US senator. In a reprise of the 1980 and 1986 contests for the same seat, the margin was exceedingly small, with Wyche Fowler winning by a plurality of 35,104 votes (12,638 more than in his victory over Mattingly), but, crucially, falling 17,388 votes short of the requisite "50 percent plus one" majority because of the presence on the ballot of a Libertarian candidate who drew almost 70,000 votes.

Wyche Fowler	1,108,416	49.23 percent
Paul Coverdell	1,073,312	47.67 percent
Jim Hudson	69,878	3.10 percent

Fowler won a majority in ninety-one counties and a plurality in eleven more, with Coverdell leading in the remaining fifty-seven. Fowler's margin in metro Atlanta fell slightly (from +4.6 in 1986 to +3.7 in 1992), but more importantly, the presence of the Libertarian candidate helped reduce his vote share in this area from 52.3 percent to 50.3 percent. (Likewise, Coverdell's percentage was below what Mattingly received.) Fowler again eked out a narrow lead in the remainder of the state, but this time his percentage fell slightly below the 50 percent mark.

Fulton:
Fowler 155,975 (60.50%) Coverdell 95,001 (36.85 %)

DeKalb:
Fowler 130,372 (60.76 %) Coverdell 77,573 (36.15 %)

Cobb:
Fowler 73,213 (37.47 %) Coverdell 115,558 (59.15 %)

Gwinnett:
Fowler 51,543 (34.50 %) Coverdell 92,467 (61.89 %)

Clayton:
Fowler 28,682 (49.76 %) Coverdell 26,766 (46.44 %)

TOTAL Metro Atlanta:
Fowler 439,785 (50.27 %) Coverdell 407,365 (46.57 %)

Rest of State:
Fowler 668,631 (48.56 %) Coverdell 665,947 (48.37 %)

A key factor in boosting the Republican candidate beyond the five-county metro Atlanta area was his showing in the increasingly important Atlanta exurbs, which he won by more than forty thousand votes (Coverdell: 112,358, 58.70 percent; Fowler: 72,289, 37.77 percent). Fowler led in most of the other population centers, obtaining majorities in Bibb (61.05 percent to 36.84 percent), Clarke (55.96 percent to 39.43 percent), Dougherty—which he had lost to Mattingly (55.54 percent to 42.42 percent), Houston (50.54 percent to 46.26 percent) and Muscogee (55.21 percent to 42.28 percent), and pluralities in Chatham—won convincingly by Mattingly (49.31 percent to 48.49 percent), Floyd (48.82 percent to 48.42 percent), and Richmond—also carried by Mattingly (49.58 percent to 47.62 percent). On the other hand, Coverdell won only in Glynn (53.70 percent to 44.10 percent), Hall (52.82 percent to 44.21 percent), and Whitfield (62.43 percent to 35.17 percent).

Regionally, Fowler improved upon his 1986 showing throughout south and central Georgia while losing ground in north Georgia (especially in the extreme northwest corner).

Although turnout increased substantially across-the-board, it was higher for white voters (over 70 percent) than for African Americans (63 percent), producing an electorate in which the latter constituted 18 percent to 19 percent of the total, down slightly from 20 percent in the 1986 general election. Wyche Fowler won an even larger share of the Black vote this time, garnering 93 percent (compared to 85 percent in 1986) but saw his vote among white voters decline slightly from 41 percent to 39 percent.

Fowler ran 5.6 points, or just under 100,000 votes (99,450), ahead of Democratic presidential nominee Bill Clinton. The referendum on the Georgia lottery appears to have had no significant direct impact on the Senate race, as Fowler ran almost identically in both the 105 counties that voted against the lottery (Fowler: 49.1 percent) as he did in the fifty-four that supported it (Fowler: 49.3 percent).

1992 Senate Runoff Campaign

The failure of any candidate to win a majority in the general election resulted in Georgia's first-ever general election runoff, which would take place three weeks later, on Tuesday, November 24, two days before Thanksgiving. Actually, there would be two races on the ballot that day because the contest for public service commissioner (the entity that regulates utilities) between Democrat John F. Collins and Republican Bobby Baker also failed to produce a winner, with Republican Baker holding a 48 percent to Collins's 47 percent lead.

With Bill Clinton having just won the presidency and Democrats having already secured a fifty-six to forty-three majority in the Senate while retaining a large majority in the House, both parties focused attention on the Georgia Senate runoff, the only race of national significance left in 1992. For President-Elect Clinton and the Democrats, it was an opportunity to further build on the general election successes and lessen the prospects for Republican filibusters in the Senate. For the GOP, it represented a chance to reduce Democratic momentum going into 1993 and to provide an early political setback to the new president.

All told, the national Democratic and Republican Parties poured more than $1 million into the three-week Georgia runoff campaign, and large numbers of field operatives on both sides were dispatched to aid their party's candidate's get-out-the-vote operation. Coverdell garnered support from the defeated Libertarian candidate as well as from the Ross Perot organization whereas Fowler had the backing of the Clinton-Gore team.

A major question for the Fowler campaign was whether, and how, to directly use the president-elect and vice president-elect. The issue was summarized by campaign pollster Secrest in his analysis of the first post-general election survey conducted for the Fowler campaign on November 5–6.

> Bill Clinton...edged George Bush 44 percent to 43 percent among general election voters. Among likely runoff voters (a different electorate), however, Bush won 48 percent to 41 percent, commanding fully 55 percent of white voters and 61 percent of younger voters. Clinton won only 32 percent of white runoff voters and Perot is reduced to 11 percent.... Despite his win, Clinton's profile remains mixed (49 percent positive, 38 percent negative overall...41 percent positive, 45 percent negative in the white community).... However, he is extremely well regarded among Fowler voters, who, of course, we will need to motivate to come back to the polls (81 percent positive, among strong Fowler voters; 68 percent positive among weak Fowler voters). Senator Gore's numbers are somewhat stronger in the aggregate (56 percent positive, 28 percent negative overall; 77 percent positive, 8 percent negative among weak Fowler voters; 51 percent positive, 32 percent negative among white voters). We feel there is <u>some</u> room for Bill Clinton (or at least part of his message) in the next few weeks, essentially to fire up our troops. Those [campaign] arguments which involve the president-elect AND are grounded in issues (economy or health care) or concern Georgia, prove effective. However, considering the fact that most likely runoff voters did not support Clinton, it would be a mistake to craft the runoff as merely a referendum on the presidential results. Also, Al Gore might be a less risky advocate for Wyche than Clinton,

> especially among metro Atlanta voters and younger women where Gore sparks more enthusiasm. If money is involved (fundraising) it probably makes sense to bring in the president-elect. But short of that, the downside risk—both to Clinton and Senator Fowler (in this latter case, among white Independents)—may well be too much.

In the end, the Fowler team employed Clinton-related themes in its messaging and advertising and brought in both Clinton and Gore, though only near the end of the runoff, in an attempt to maximize the impact on pro-Fowler turnout while avoiding provoking an extended debate on the upcoming Clinton presidency.

One Clinton-related issue rose to prominence in Georgia and nationally during the runoff: whether or not to lift the ban on gay men and women serving in the US military. Shortly after his election, Clinton announced his intention to promptly seek an end to the US military's prohibition on homosexuals serving in the armed forces once he was sworn in as president. Fowler announced his support for the proposal while Coverdell opposed it. Senator Nunn immediately indicated his opposition to the plan, believing it would be harmful to military cohesion and discipline. Eventually, Clinton and Nunn reached a compromise resulting in the "don't ask, don't tell" policy, which continued the ban on gay men and women serving in the military only in cases where the individual disclosed their sexual orientation, and which was official US policy from February 1994 until September 2011, when it was repealed and the ban was finally lifted.

In the context of the 1992 Georgia Senate runoff, however, the main effects of the debate were to focus attention on a controversial matter that divided many of the Fowler campaign's key target groups, including lower-income white voters and white Independents, as well as the top two political figures supporting Fowler (Clinton and Nunn).

The November 5–6 poll report highlighted the challenges now facing the Fowler reelection bid.

> The die is pretty much cast in this runoff. Almost without exception (just 4 percent undecided) voters have already decided who they will support two days before Thanksgiving.... Wyche's success

> now will depend more on motivation than persuasion. As we anticipated, we face a challenging runoff. Although likely runoff voters are currently divided in their support, Wyche is burdened with substantial negatives, partially driven by Coverdell's media, partially the result of the larger climate, but mostly the result of the Senator's still-tentative profile.... Also, this is not the same electorate which went to the polls November 3rd. For example, likely runoff voters provided George Bush with an electoral plurality and voted to defeat the state lottery. The younger/suburban white voters who showed up to defeat George Bush and the Independents who pulled the lever for Ross Perot are a bit less likely to show come runoff day. As a result, Wyche's support is substantially balkanized and contained among Blacks, lower income whites, white Democrats, and to a lesser degree, older whites. That is to say, that the path to a win is extremely narrow.... Wyche will be competing in an electorate that is slightly less Independent, and slightly more Republican than general election voters are. Overall, 38 percent of likely runoff voters regard themselves as Democrats, 27 percent are Independents, and 34 percent Republican. This is the strongest Republican showing we have found for a Georgia statewide electorate.... The runoff is a dead heat (48 percent Fowler, 48 percent Coverdell) with very few persuadable voters for either campaign.... Fully 42 percent of voters now indicate a negative personal opinion of Wyche, similar to the 41 percent negative in our last poll. Another 49 percent suggest a positive opinion (44 percent previously) and only 9 percent are neutral. Wyche's negatives in the white community now stand at 49 percent (just 42 percent positive).

Voters were also asked to rate the persuasiveness of a number of arguments being made by the two campaigns (typically in commercials). In this format, a score of 45 percent or higher rating a proposition as "very persuasive" was considered a benchmark of effectiveness. Most relevant to Fowler campaign decisions, among the pro-Fowler messages tested, supporting Clinton's health care reform plan (45 percent very persuasive), followed by supporting the president-elect's job creation plan (42 percent) led the way, whereas Wyche Fowler's efforts to save Georgia jobs trailed somewhat behind (38 percent). The leading anti-Coverdell propositions included his vote "to make it easier for convicted murders to be temporarily released into the community" (53 percent very persuasive), his vote against "a bill that would have required minimum penalties for those convicted of certain violent crimes against senior citizens" (47 percent), his opposition to "federal efforts to control health care costs" while proposing "a voucher system that would give money to insurance companies and leave cost reform up to them" (45 percent), and his missing many votes as a state senator (45 percent).

In response to these findings and other input, GMMG Associates (formerly Greer & Associates) produced a number of TV and radio spots for the Fowler campaign in the runoff (some recycled from the general election).

A substantial direct mail effort was also mounted, allowing for appeals to more targeted audiences. One such communication was sent out on November 16 from "Concerned Women for Wyche," a group of fifty-five women mostly from the metro Atlanta area.

> We are writing this letter as a plea and a wake-up call. Senator Wyche Fowler is in the fight of his career on November 24 and must have your vote to win. While Wyche disappointed many of us with his support of Clarence Thomas, it is time to face reality. Wyche has been a stalwart friend over the years and has staunchly supported every cause that we consider of the utmost importance, including a woman's individual right to choice, family medical leave, health care and education programs.
>
> Wyche cosponsored the Freedom of Choice Act which would codify into law the Roe v. Wade Supreme Court decision and allow a woman the right to decide without government intervention matters personal to her own conscience and body. He also voted to overturn the Reagan-Bush gag rule which prohibits the provision of abortion information and counseling.
>
> In 1991, Wyche cosponsored a bill to combat violence against women. He cosponsored the Equal Rights Amendment to declare that equal rights under law shall not be denied due to gender. He has twice cosponsored the Parental and Family Medical Leave Act as well as voting for many other critical pieces of legislation on early childhood education, maternal health and domestic violence issues.

In sharp contrast, Paul Coverdell, who now claims to be pro-choice, voted against the Roe v. Wade decision during his tenure in the Georgia legislature. Mr. Coverdell has not and will not support the Freedom of Choice Act or the Family Leave Act. He would also be under tremendous pressure to support the Republican Party's right wing platform, and is there any question at all as to how President Bush's friend would have voted on Clarence Thomas?

If you do not vote for Wyche Fowler on Tuesday, November 24, 1992, you have effectively voted for Paul Coverdell. The runoff will be decided simply by which candidate gets his supporters to the polls, and you better believe that the Moral Majority and the Right to Lifers will do everything possible to get their man elected.

Wyche has always been and will continue to be an effective legislator. With Bill Clinton in the White House, the possibility of passing long-delayed legislation of great importance to women is within our grasp. Seize the opportunity and do not allow one vote in a long and effective career to turn against someone who has been our friend for over 20 years.

Candidate debates were also a feature of the runoff. The first was held in Augusta on November 16 and broadcast by Augusta television station WJBF on November 22.

Waving a copy of his opponent's letter as evidence, GOP challenger Paul Coverdell on Monday claimed that U.S. Senator Wyche Fowler Jr. supports lowering the tax exemption on inheritances—bringing a vehement denial from Mr. Fowler.... Mr. Fowler bitterly denounced Mr. Coverdell's claim during the debate and in campaign appearances elsewhere Monday. Retiring U.S. Rep. Ed Jenkins held a news conference of his own in Albany to call it "a flat-out, bald-faced lie," noting that he and Mr. Fowler helped raise the exemption from $240,000 to $600,000 a decade ago. "Mr. Coverdell has the most unbelievable, unbelievable gall to say to me, face to face that I want to take my own law down from $600,000," Mr. Fowler said during the debate. The issue is of particular importance to farmers and Mr. Fowler has been campaigning hard for rural voters. Short on cash but holding land and farm machinery, family

> farmers have used the exemption when passing ownership of farms to children or other survivors.... Monday's debate also produced spirited exchanges over television advertisements. Mr. Coverdell called Mr. Fowler's ads "as scurrilous and vicious as any I've ever seen." Mr. Fowler said, "Mr. Coverdell has never run an advertisement on what he would do for our state...has never spoken for himself in the ads, only hired agents who are totally dishonest about my record."

At another point in the debate, Coverdell charged that Fowler was an "architect" of the 1990 budget summit agreement with President Bush that raised taxes, producing the following exchange:

> **Coverdell:** You were a principal author of the tax increase and you voted for it.
> **Fowler:** Absolutely. I stood up for the president of the United States and you denied him.... We have (seen) a lot of changes in Mr. Coverdell now that his president has been defeated.[145]

The second debate was another thirty-minute encounter, taped at Atlanta TV station WAGA on November 19 for broadcast on November 22. As reported by Frank LoMonte of Morris News Service,

> Each candidate tried to claim the support of Sen. Sam Nunn for his position on allowing homosexuals in the military. Mr. Fowler supports the policy, which President-elect Bill Clinton promises to enact, while Mr. Coverdell opposes it. Mr. Fowler, who supports legalized abortion, accused Mr. Coverdell of "trying to have it both ways" by telling liberals he is pro-abortion rights and conservatives that he supports restrictions. The contenders had their most detailed debate on health-care reform. Mr. Coverdell proposed making benefits "portable," so people who lose their jobs don't automatically lose health coverage; Mr. Fowler called for controlling the charges of insurance and drug companies, and for offering basic health insurance to everyone. The hottest dispute came when Mr. Fowler, a first-term Democrat, attacked Mr. Coverdell's ads that

claimed Mr. Fowler may have bounced checks at the now-closed House bank.

The third and final debate was broadcast live on Atlanta television station WXIA, also on November 22. As reported in the *Atlanta Constitution*, during the hour-long session, the candidates "offered starkly different visions Sunday of how they would vote on key issues in the next Congress. Mr. Coverdell...said he would oppose gun-control measures—including a waiting period—raising taxes on the wealthy and the Freedom of Choice Act [which would have codified the *Roe v. Wade* decision into statutory law]. Mr. Fowler...voiced support for these proposals.... The debate lacked much of the open hostility that dominated their (previous) meeting."[146]

In the final stages of the runoff, both Bill Clinton and Al Gore made appearances on behalf of Wyche Fowler. At an appearance in Athens, Gore said, "Bill Clinton and I need Wyche Fowler in the United States Senate to break the gridlock,"[147] and at an African American church in Savannah, he observed, "The margin of one vote can make a difference in the changes Bill Clinton and I have been elected to make in this country. Those who care, those who want to be part of that change will go ahead and vote."[148] In Macon, President-Elect Clinton stated, "I know Georgia is tired of politics, and people get tired of voting. I came here because I believe Wyche Fowler represents the type of change we need. I believe he'll help me reform the political system."[149]

The major Atlanta dailies once again split their endorsements.

> The Atlanta Constitution endorses incumbent Democrat Wyche Fowler in the upcoming U.S. Senate runoff over Republican Paul Coverdell.... Having just emerged from elections in which voters across the country made clear their dislike for ads meant to attack rather than articulate a vision for the future, it is disappointing to witness the way Mr. Coverdell and Mr. Fowler have chosen to conduct themselves.... Notwithstanding criticism of campaign tactics, this election must be decided on the basis of which candidate is best able to serve the interests of Georgia and the nation in the U.S. Senate. Clearly, Wyche Fowler is that candidate. The nation has made clear that it is ready for change, ready to move forward on

issues that have been neglected for too long. President-elect Clinton is poised to place before Congress an agenda for change. Mr. Fowler is the candidate best suited to help his fellow Democrat implement that agenda and to be an effective advocate for Georgians during the process. Mr. Coverdell and his party, on the other hand, have focused not on how to get things moving, but on how to keep them from—in their view—going too far.... Anyone can stand in the way. Wyche Fowler has shown he can lead. In his first term he sponsored legislation to help rural schools take advantage of technological innovations in education; to offer incentives for renewable energy and conservation technologies that will steer the nation toward energy self-sufficiency; and to encourage preservation of historic landmarks. He has been a strong advocate of keeping government out of citizens' most private decisions, including a woman's choices about abortion. Mr. Fowler has helped Georgia by his membership on the Senate Appropriations and Agriculture committees. Mr. Coverdell could not hope to match such influence as a freshman member of the minority party. Some who have enthusiastically supported Mr. Fowler in the past have been upset by some of his Senate votes, most notably his support of Clarence Thomas for the Supreme Court. The question they should ask themselves, however, is whether Mr. Coverdell would have voted their way on those few issues and would match Mr. Fowler's progressive stand on others. The answer, surely, is no. A new picture is being painted in Washington, one that shows a government can be bent to the will of the people and act in their interests. Georgians can add a powerful stroke by re-electing Wyche Fowler.[150]

—*Atlanta Constitution*

The Atlanta Journal endorses Republican candidate Paul Coverdell in the general election runoff Tuesday, Nov. 24, over Democratic incumbent Wyche Fowler, for the U.S. Senate.... The conduct of the runoff leads The Journal to endorse with more vigor the candidacy of PAUL COVERDELL. Both campaigns have become too nasty and too personal of late, but for the most part Mr. Coverdell campaigned on the issues and on the voting record of Sen. Wyche Fowler, Jr., while Mr. Fowler resorted to spurious attacks on Mr.

> Coverdell's business activities.... Mr. Fowler, it must be said, has been no foe of higher taxes. As an assistant majority leader, he was a key negotiator in the disastrous budget deal and tax increase of 1990. He voted against shutting off debate to allow the Senate to vote on a constitutional amendment to balance the federal budget. On many issues, he has waffled. He says that for now he opposes making the District of Columbia a state, but reserves the right to change his mind. On whether to admit homosexuals to the military, his position is unclear. With the exception of his vote for Justice Clarence Thomas, he has been hostile to the nominations of conservative judges with well-defined views in favor of capital punishment. It also should not go unnoticed that Mr. Fowler voted against the use of force in the Persian Gulf. It is a vote that long will be questioned. Voters are fortunate that in Paul Coverdell they have a worthy replacement for Mr. Fowler. It gives them a chance to even the balance of power and to vote for change that is both positive and more in line with the conservatism of the Georgia electorate.[151]
>
> —*Atlanta Journal*

The 1992 Fowler Senate campaign had more resources at its disposal than had the 1986 effort. Over $4 million ($4.012 million) was raised for the general and another $1 million ($1.007 million) for the runoff, for a grand total of $5.02 million.

The campaign spent $4.1 million in the general and another $1.274 million in the runoff, with the lion's share of expenditures going for media buys ($1.77 million, or 43 percent in the general; $735,000, or 58 percent in the runoff), and TV ads consuming most of those expenditures ($1.62 million in the general; $500,000 in the runoff). With the leftover surplus from the 1986 campaign plus interest earned on the contribution deposits, true to his commitment, Fowler once again finished the campaign with a small surplus ($56,000).

The Fowler direct campaign efforts were supplemented by approximately $500,000 in media buys paid for by the Democratic Senatorial Campaign Committee and by an extensive Democratic Party coordinated campaign effort that was integral to Bill Clinton's success in the general election and played a key role in direct voter contact activities for the

Fowler campaign in both the general and runoff. In the latter, the coordinated campaign had a total budget of more than $800,000 and funded phone banks, direct mail, get-out-the-vote field operations, and materials distribution, among other things.

Repeating the pattern of the 1980 and 1986 Georgia Senate races, the challenger (in this case, Coverdell) was at a considerable financial disadvantage overall, with $3.2 million in total expenditures, but he was at near parity in the runoff, and in fact outspent Fowler in terms of television and radio ads. A key factor in Coverdell's funding during the runoff was the purchase by the National Republican Senatorial Committee (NRSC) of a half million dollars' worth of TV ads on his behalf. On November 18, the Fowler campaign filed a formal complaint with the Federal Election Commission alleging that the Coverdell campaign and the NRSC violated federal election law by exceeding the maximum contribution limit for national parties in US Senate races. Specifically, the allegation stated that the NRSC had already expended the maximum level—$17,500 in direct contributions, $535,000 in media buys—in the general election but then continued to make such contributions in the runoff. Prior to the runoff election, the Coverdell campaign flatly denied the charges, indicating the problem was simply a clerical error in listing the NRSC rather than the Coverdell campaign as the sponsor of the ads in question. However, immediately after the runoff, the Coverdell campaign admitted that the NRSC had, in fact, contributed another $500,000 in ad purchases for Coverdell. More than three years later, in February 1996, the FEC found the NRSC guilty of an election law infraction and imposed a penalty of 1 percent of the violation ($5,000).[152]

Though subject to some fluctuations (all within the surveys' margin of error, but with the movement toward Coverdell again coinciding with his achieving parity in TV advertising), the runoff remained tight throughout, as reflected in Fowler campaign polls:

November 6, 1992: 48 percent Fowler, 48 percent Coverdell, 4 percent undecided
November 16, 1992: 52 percent Fowler, 43 percent Coverdell, 5 percent undecided
November 19, 1992: 45 percent Fowler, 51 percent Coverdell, 4 percent undecided

That final November 19 survey found that the likely runoff electorate was even more GOP-inclined than before, with Republican identification equaling Democratic affiliation for the first time in a Secrest Georgia statewide poll (37 percent Democratic, 37 percent Republican, 25 percent Independent). The same poll also presented respondents with a battery of questions on which candidate would do a better job with respect to specific issues.

Issue	Fowler better	Coverdell better	Fowler +/-
Better able to work with Senator Nunn to help Georgia	61 percent	24 percent	+37
Working to make health care more affordable and available	49 percent	31 percent	+18
Cares about and fights for the special needs and concerns of women	40 percent	25 percent	+15
Having Georgia values	42 percent	38 percent	+ 4
Representing your views on the issue of gun control	32 percent	30 percent	+ 2
Willing and able to fight for the kind of changes we need in this country	42 percent	44 percent	- 2
Being trustworthy, a man of his word	37 percent	39 percent	- 2
Being independent from the special interests	34 percent	37 percent	- 3

Being honest, having integrity	37 percent	42 percent	-5
Will work to keep taxes in line	34 percent	46 percent	-12

1992 Senate Runoff Results and Analysis

Two days before Thanksgiving, on Tuesday, November 24, 1992—a day with rainstorms and tornadoes in north Georgia—1,251,370 Georgia voters returned to the polls to vote in the state's first-ever general election runoff, one million fewer than had cast ballots three weeks before and representing a turnout rate of 39.4 percent of registered voters compared to almost 71 percent in the general election.

Consistent with the razor-thin margins of 1980 (Mattingly won by 27,543 votes), 1986 (Fowler won by 22,466 votes), and the 1992 general election (Fowler led by 35,104 votes), the outcome of the runoff was again extremely close—indeed, the closest of them all—with Paul Coverdell securing a narrow 14,990-vote victory.

Paul Coverdell	633,18050.60 percent
Wyche Fowler	618,19049.40 percent

Turnout declined in all 159 counties, ranging from decreases of 11 percent in rural Pickens and Dawson Counties to more than 40 percent in the Atlanta-area counties of Gwinnett, Forsyth, Dawson, Douglas, and Paulding. Fowler carried eighty-four counties to Coverdell's seventy-five. Fowler's vote share actually increased in metro Atlanta, but Coverdell secured his majority by winning in the rest of the state by just under 35,000 votes.

Fulton:
Fowler: 89,936 (62.52 %) Coverdell: 53,923 (37.48 %)

DeKalb:
Fowler: 76,313 (61.54 %) Coverdell: 47,702 (38.46 %)

Cobb:

Fowler: 37,469 (37.64 %) Coverdell: 62,071 (62.36 %)

Gwinnett:
Fowler: 26,205 (35.54 %) Coverdell: 47,523 (64.46 %)

Clayton:
Fowler: 15,124 (51.73 %) Coverdell: 14,110 (48.27 %)

TOTAL Metro Atlanta
Fowler: 245,047 (52.10 %) Coverdell: 225,329 (47.90 %)

Rest of State:
Fowler: 373,143 (47.78 %) Coverdell: 407,851 (52.22 %)

As was true in the general election, the heavily (94 percent) white Atlanta "exurbs" were crucial to the Republican's success, accounting for more than 21,000 of his 35,000-vote margin outside of metro Atlanta (Coverdell: 61,397, 60.69 percent; Fowler: 39,761, 39.31 percent). Fowler's vote share fell off, slightly in most cases, in many of Georgia's other urban areas, though he once again managed to carry most of them, including Bibb (58.27 percent Fowler, -2.8 vs. general election), Chatham (50.69 percent, +1.4), Clarke (58.11 percent, +2.1), Dougherty (55.24 percent, -0.3), Floyd (51.51 percent, +2.7) and Muscogee (53.23 percent, -2.0). However, this time he lost in Richmond (45.22 percent, -4.4) and Houston (44.25 percent, -6.3), where he had led three weeks earlier, and Coverdell again won in Glynn (Fowler 39.55 percent, -4.5), Hall (43.51 percent, -0.7), and Whitfield (32.39 percent, -2.8) and by increased margins.

Regionally, metro and exurban Atlanta were somewhat less predominant among the runoff electorate (more on this point below), though both, and especially the latter, still constituted a larger share of the total vote than had been the case in 1986. Wyche Fowler once again ran ahead in metro Atlanta and Southwest and central Georgia, but he trailed in eastern and north Georgia. In a race decided by fewer than 15,000 votes, even small changes can be decisive; even so, what is once again most striking about the regional vote patterns is their similarity to the 1986 and 1992 general elections.

A 1997 analysis by Charles Bullock and Robert Furr found that turnout dropped to 40 percent among white voters and 33 percent among Black voters, with Fowler winning 96 percent of the African American vote and 38 percent of the white vote.

> Turnout rates were lower for both Blacks and whites but the rate of drop-off for the latter group exceeded that of Blacks so that Blacks contributed a larger share of the electorate in the runoff than in the general election. Thus, expectations that it might be more difficult to mobilize African American voters for a second election were not supported.... The polls show that white Fowler followers were less motivated to vote in the runoff than were Coverdell's legions. Especially helpful to Coverdell were Republicans, conservatives, and voters in the 18–29 and 40–49 age categories who shifted in his direction during the runoff. Each candidate got his strongest supporters back to the polls for the runoff.[153]

Though scant consolation, the Fowler runoff campaign exceeded its own and others' predictions in terms of getting out its vote. A look at subsequent Georgia general election runoff history offers some perspective. Between the 1992 Fowler-Coverdell contest and 2019, there were six other such runoffs: for the Public Service Commission (PSC) on the same day as the Fowler-Coverdell runoff in 1992, for the PSC in 2006, for the US Senate and PSC in 2008, and for secretary of state and the PSC in 2018. The GOP candidate won in each case with an average improvement between the general election and runoff of eight percentage points. Fowler was the only Democrat whose vote share actually increased after the general election, albeit by a very small amount. By comparison, in the only other Senate runoff in that period, Republican Saxby Chambliss saw his margin over Democratic challenger Jim Martin grow from three points in the general election (49.8 percent to 46.8 percent) to almost fifteen points in the runoff (57.4 percent to 42.6 percent). In the PSC runoff held on the same day as the Fowler-Coverdell contest, Republican Baker's lead grew from one point on November 3 (48 percent to 47 percent) to fourteen points on November 24 (57 percent to 43 percent).

As mentioned above, this pattern was broken in both January 2021, when Democratic challengers Raphael Warnock and Jon Ossoff prevailed over Republican Senate incumbents in runoffs, and 2022, when Warnock won reelection in another runoff. These results illustrate Georgia's increasing competitiveness, in partisan terms, as a result of demographic and other changes in the state's electorate since 1992.

In keeping with Georgia's population growth, the number of registered voters rose from 3.2 million at the time of the 1992 runoff to more than seven million by January 2021. In 1992, non-Hispanic white voters accounted for almost 80 percent of those who voted, and African Americans represented 20 percent, but the far more diverse electorate of 2021 was 60 percent non-Hispanic white, 31 percent African American, and 9 percent other (mainly Hispanic or Asian American).

Geographically, whereas the five-county metro Atlanta core—Fulton, DeKalb, Cobb, Gwinnett, and Clayton—still represented 37 percent of the total vote, the Atlanta exurbs of Cherokee, Douglas, Fayette, Forsyth, Henry, Newton, Paulding, Rockdale, and Walton almost doubled their share—from 8 percent in 1992 to more than 15 percent in 2021—with the rest of the state seeing its share drop accordingly (from 54 percent in 1992 to 47 percent in 2021). These shifts helped Rev. Warnock improve on Fowler's vote (51 percent versus 49 percent overall), even though Warnock ran well behind Fowler among white voters (27 percent Warnock, 38 percent Fowler) and in the rest of the state beyond the Atlanta area (Warnock 38 percent, Fowler 49 percent). The two each won about 95 percent of African American voters. The key to the Warnock win was his far better showing in metro Atlanta (Warnock 70 percent, Fowler 52 percent) and, to a lesser extent, exurban Atlanta (Warnock 45 percent, Fowler 39 percent).

Returning to the 1992 contest, a story in the November 26 *Atlanta Journal-Constitution* attributed Fowler's narrow loss to "several factors—a change in any one of which might have swung the election in Mr. Fowler's favor. Mr. Fowler's problems with gay and women's organizations, a healthy dose of anti-incumbent sentiment, Mr. Coverdell's success in getting the party's religious right wing behind him and perhaps even Tuesday's bad weather all contributed to the Senator's ouster."[154]

However, most of the analyses of the 1992 Georgia Senate election focused on Senator Fowler's failure to win an outright majority on November 3. Atlanta journalist Bill Shipp provided an assessment that was fairly typical.

[Fowler] landed on the run in the Senate in 1987. He became a freshman power immediately. Senate Majority Leader George Mitchell created the new post of assistant majority leader and named Fowler to it in 1988. Fowler was a leading negotiator in the budget summit meetings with the White House. Fowler's ideological votes mostly fit the national Democratic agenda. He opposed Robert Bork for the Supreme Court, said no to the Persian Gulf War, fought restrictions on funding for the National Endowment for the Arts, and voted against the confirmation of a Circuit Federal Judge Edward Carnes, an advocate of capital punishment. Fowler tried to mollify conservatives back home by supporting the nomination of Clarence Thomas to the Supreme Court. Instead of picking up praise, he set off an explosion of anger among women activists, many of whom refused to vote for him Nov. 3. On the pragmatic side, Fowler brought home the bacon. He saw to it that the new Talmadge Bridge in Savannah was finally funded. He kept millions rolling into MARTA's coffers, even as federal money for mass transit was drying up. He made certain peanut subsidies were protected. He held town meetings in every Georgia county, and his aides fielded reams of complaints about Social Security, VA benefits and IRS matters. As a Senator, he deserved at least a B-plus. His detractors say he might have become a Grade A lawmaker, except he developed a mean streak and, like many other public figures, he believed his own press clippings.... He ignored advice to support a balanced budget amendment. He failed to make peace with the women's and gay organizations he had alienated. He refused to take seriously the barrage of negative TV ads launched by the Coverdell campaign. At one point, his campaign virtually stopped. He was stunned by the death of state Supreme Court Justice Charles Weltner, his friend and mentor. On election day, Fowler ran far ahead of Democratic presidential contender Bill Clinton. Still, it wasn't enough.... So how was Fowler to hang onto his seat against the onrushing Coverdell? Get most of his Nov. 3 supporters back to the polls for the Nov. 24 runoff. He was betting that the anti-lottery and the Perot crowd wouldn't return in large numbers, and neither would many mainstream Republicans not enthralled by Coverdell's candidacy. That was a long-shot wager.[155]

In *Senators on the Campaign Trail*, Richard Fenno offered a lengthy critique of the 1992 Fowler campaign. "Fowler's miscalculations were probably sufficient to have cost him his seat in the Senate. My view is that Fowler's self-confidence caused him to underestimate certain things he needed to do in the campaign to win: to settle on a campaign theme, to take his opponent seriously, to win back disaffected supporters, to use television effectively, to cultivate the media."

As mentioned above, Fenno pointed the finger at the Fowler campaign team (including not just the candidate, but the campaign manager, media consultant, and others as well) and their failure to develop a positive theme as one of the biggest shortcomings of the 1992 reelection effort.[156] In addition, he highlighted the Weltner factor.

> There was his constant preoccupation with the health and comfort of his most valued "friend and mentor" Charles Weltner, who was battling cancer and who died in late August. During the 1992 April recess, when senators facing an election invariably go home to make reelection hay, Fowler took his sick friend, a lifelong student of ancient religions and owner of a world-class library on the subject, on a trip to Turkey and Iraq to pursue their mutual interest in ancient religion and archaeology.... Throughout the campaign period, Fowler devoted himself to two urgent projects designed to brighten his friend's last days. He worked to arrange and helped fund a special room in the library at Oglethorpe College (Weltner's alma mater) to memorialize Weltner and to house his personal library. He proposed and pushed through the construction of an eternal flame and plaque outside the Georgia Department of Justice building memorializing Chief Justice Weltner. And he rushed it to completion so Weltner could see it on his final trip from the hospital to his home. During my August visit, Fowler began each day with a visit to the hospital to talk with Weltner and keep him abreast of his various activities.... I have described Fowler, basically, as a person who wanted to be his own man and to operate free of all encumbrances. In this case, the campaign itself had become the

unwanted encumbrance. If, at times, Fowler seemed to treat the campaign that way, it may have been because a big piece of his heart was never in it.[157]

Additional factors not generally cited by those seeking to explain the outcome of the 1992 Georgia Senate race include the following:

- *The presence of a third-party candidate, unlike in the 1986 election.* With another very close race in 1986, a third-party candidate would have needed just over 35,000 votes to have forced a runoff in which Mattingly would have been the clear favorite.
- *Physical exhaustion.* Fowler's demanding six-year travel schedule across Georgia, particularly his commitment to visit all 159 counties, undoubtedly took a toll on the candidate. It is true that Fowler increased slightly his vote percentage in the one hundred least-populous Georgia counties (from 54.5 percent in 1986 to 54.7 percent in 1992)—presumably locations most affected by his honoring his promise—but these counties accounted for only 16.2 percent of the total vote in 1992, down from 17.5 percent in 1986. From a campaign standpoint, whether it was worth the effort is highly debatable, and Fowler and his staff concluded long before the 1992 general election that it was not.
- *Use of the entire 1986 campaign team.* Fenno noted that the success of the 1986 campaign increased demand for Fowler's media and polling consultants, who by 1992 were stretched across many more campaigns, resulting in reduced attention to Fowler's reelection effort.[158] His campaign manager and organizational leadership remained unchanged as well and may have fallen victim to past success by being resistant to changes in strategy and operations.
- *The impact of the presidential race and lottery referendum on turnout.* The 1992 electorate differed in size and composition from its 1986 counterpart, being much larger and with a higher proportion of Republican suburban and white voters. The three-way race for president and the referendum on the lottery were almost certainly major contributors.
- *The emergence during the runoff of the issue of gay men and women serving in the military*, a matter that divided Fowler (and Clinton)

from Senator Nunn. For example, it could be speculated that this was a major reason for the large drop-off in Fowler's vote share in Nunn's home county of Houston in the runoff.

• *The illegal $500,000 contribution by the National Republican Senatorial Committee* which enabled the Coverdell campaign to remain competitive in TV advertising during the runoff.

Given the extreme closeness of both the November 3 and November 24, 1992, races, even small factors could have made a decisive difference, so a case could be made for most of the oft-cited reasons as key determinants. For example, one of the most commonly invoked explanations for the Fowler campaign failure was the purported "lack of a positive message or theme." Fenno hypothesized that the campaign would have been better served if there had been a focus on the senator's Georgia achievements. Perhaps this was crucial, though it is worth remembering that the Fowler team was aware of this approach and indeed had planned on utilizing it before its own polling indicated voters in 1992 were not particularly persuaded by it. It is, of course, not possible to "re-run" the campaign to see if this change would have made a major, or any, difference in voter choices.

What can be measured is the turnout patterns of 1986 and 1992, and, as noted previously, the Atlanta exurbs were far more important in the latter campaign. A closer look at both metro Atlanta and those exurbs is even more revelatory.

The predominantly Republican nine-county Atlanta exurbs plus the two GOP strongholds within metro Atlanta (Cobb and Gwinnett) increased their share of the total statewide vote from 18.22 percent in 1986 to 23.81 percent in the 1992 general election, a gain of 5.59 points. Combined with a slight reduction in Fowler's vote in these counties, which dropped from 39 percent to 37 percent, and almost certainly a result of the increased Republican identification in the exurbs, this produced a net increase of 73,722 in Fowler's vote deficit in these counties. At the same time, the vote share of the core Democratic counties of Fulton and DeKalb dropped by 2.14 points, from 23.12 percent in 1986 to 20.98 percent in 1992. The significant expansion of African American registration in DeKalb offset Coverdell gains in his home county of Fulton, leaving Fowler's vote at 61 percent in both races and allowing the incumbent to actually increase his margin in the two counties by 50,593. The net result of this shift of the electorate was thus 23,129 against Fowler, not a large amount in an election with more than 2.25 million votes cast; but with Fowler falling just 17,388 votes short of an outright win on November 3, this was clearly an important factor in his failure to obtain a majority.

In the runoff, the vote shares of the various Atlanta area components partially reverted to previous patterns, with the vote share of the exurbs, Cobb, and Gwinnett declining by 1.88 points (with the latter two experiencing the largest drop-off by far among all 159 counties) while that of Fulton and DeKalb rose by 0.43. This helps explain why the Fowler camp was able to perform better than expected in the runoff, and furthermore suggests that the Senate race itself was not the major cause of the extraordinary November 3 turnout in the key eleven Republican-dominated counties in the Atlanta area, with the presidential contest and the lottery referendum the likeliest contributors.

With all of the many postmortems and explanations of Wyche Fowler's 1992 defeat offered by pundits and analysts considered, the one presented in the 1994 *Almanac of American Politics* appears to come closest to the truth.

> [The 1992 Georgia Senate] results indicate not fickleness but steadiness; they are uncannily similar to the 51 percent–49 percent margin by which Fowler beat Republican Senator Mack Mattingly in 1986 or the 51 percent–49 percent margin by which Mattingly beat Democratic Senator Herman Talmadge in 1980 or, for that matter, the narrow margin by which Bill Clinton edged George Bush here.... When Coverdell won after Vice President-elect Gore and President-elect Clinton campaigned for Fowler, there was talk in Washington that Fowler had run a "desultory" campaign. Actually, he was in trouble because he was seen for what he was, a national liberal on most issues, with strong convictions and great political skills, blessed with a folksy rural manner, but also one of Majority Leader George Mitchell's chief lieutenants.[159]

As the returns late on the evening of November 24 indicated a likely defeat, Fowler told his gathered supporters, "Shed no tears for me. Whether I am Senator Wyche Fowler or citizen Wyche Fowler, I will find other ways of public service."

Chapter 14

Mr. Ambassador (1993 to Present)

FEC

Shortly after the runoff, Senate Majority Leader Mitchell appointed Fowler as the Senate's nonvoting representative to the Federal Election Commission (FEC). The commission was composed of six voting members appointed by the president and confirmed by the Senate (with no more than three of these members coming from the same political party) and two nonvoting members, one representing the House and the other the Senate, who were to play a liaison role in providing information and advice to the commission. Mitchell appointed Fowler because of his trust in the latter's communications skills, ability to get things done in highly charged partisan environments, and commitment to campaign finance reform, which included his service on an informal, bipartisan working group on the subject in the Senate.

The FEC is responsible for enforcing limitations on contributions to and expenditures by and on behalf of candidates for federal office, administering campaign finance disclosure requirements, investigating and prosecuting violations of these provisions, conducting a limited number of compliance audits, administering the public funding of certified presidential candidates, and defending federal campaign finance laws and regulations against legal challenges. The even partisan division of the voting members (three Democrats and three Republicans), the four-vote requirement for official action, the lengthy process of investigating and resolving complaints (often long after the alleged violation), and the agency's limited budget and staffing ($21 million and 276 full-time positions in FY 1993) combine to seriously limit the FEC's effectiveness.

During Wyche Fowler's time there, the FEC received a small increase in funding and staffing, expanded public access to its records, worked to implement new government-wide ethics standards, and assumed responsibility for assisting states in implementing the National Voter Registration Act of 1993. Designed to enhance voter registration opportunities and signed into law by President Clinton on May 20, 1993, the National Voter Registration Act included provisions for voter registration when individuals applied for a driver's license, earning it the nickname of the "Motor Voter" law. Regarding enforcement, it was estimated that the commission oversaw more than nine thousand political committees that spent more than $2 billion in the just-completed 1992 election cycle and was facing a three-fold increase in enforcement cases since 1988. In response, during 1993 it implemented a new prioritization system designed to produce more timely resolution of significant cases.

Fowler's tenure with the commission was brief, however. Since 1991, a case in which the FEC had sought to enforce its finding that the National Rifle Association (NRA) had made illegal corporate campaign contributions in 1988 was making its way through the courts. As part of its response, the NRA challenged the constitutionality of the FEC's composition, especially the inclusion of the two nonvoting congressional representatives. Against this backdrop, Fowler resigned from the commission in June 1993.

When Fowler was appointed to the FEC, there was some criticism about his assuming this role when one of the cases before the commission was the complaint filed by the Democratic Senatorial Campaign Committee (DSCC) alleging that its Republican counterpart, the National Republican Senatorial Committee (NRSC), had made illegal campaign contributions to the Coverdell campaign in the 1992 Georgia Senate runoff. Fowler made clear at the time that he would take no part whatsoever in any cases involving his campaign. Furthermore, he had no vote, and the FEC's lengthy enforcement process meant that any formal action would likely take several years. In fact, that is what happened, and Fowler was long gone from the commission before there was any resolution.

On November 19, 1992—five days before the runoff—the DSCC filed its complaint with the FEC, which then deadlocked along partisan lines on whether to begin an investigation. The three-to-three tie vote (with the Democratic commissioners voting in favor and the three Republicans opposed) resulted in dismissal of the complaint on April 27, 1993. The DSCC then brought the case to the US District Court for the District of Columbia. On November 14, 1994, the court issued its decision declaring the FEC's dismissal of the DSCC complaint contrary to law and ordering the commission to vacate the dismissal and initiate appropriate enforcement proceedings against the NRSC within thirty days. The commission unanimously voted on December 31, 1994, to implement the court decision and proceeded to enter into the "conciliation" stage with the NRSC, which is the final stage in the commission's enforcement process. On December 5, 1995, it found there was "probable cause" to believe the NRSC violated federal campaign finance law.[160]

On February 13, 1996, the commission accepted a signed conciliation agreement submitted by the NRSC indicating that the NRSC violated federal election law by making expenditures in excess of the legal limit and imposing a $5,000 civil fine on the committee. The agreement included the following key points.

> National and state political party committees may each make a limited amount of expenditures in connection with the general election campaign of a candidate for U.S. Senate affiliated with such party. The 1992 limit for each party in the general election campaign in Georgia was $267,803.52. Both the Republican National Committee and the State Republican Party of Georgia authorized the NRSC to expend their share of [this] limit. Thus, the total combined 1992 Section 441a(d)(3) limit for the general election campaign in Georgia was $535,607.... The NRSC's disclosure reports show that it made coordinated expenditures totaling $535,607 on behalf of Coverdell for media services in connection with the November 3, 1992, election. The NRSC's disclosure reports reflect additional coordinated expenditures totaling $509,570 on behalf of Coverdell in connection with the November 24 runoff election. The district court concluded that under the plain meaning of the [FEC] regulations at 11 C.F.R. Section 100.2, the November 24, 1992, election was a runoff election and thus, no additional Section 441a(d)(3) limit was available.... In light of the court's decision, the NRSC exceeded the Section 441a(d)(3) expenditure limit by $509,570 in connection with the 1992 U.S. Senate campaign in Georgia.[161]

Transition (1993 to 1995)

While still at the FEC, speculation in the spring of 1993 centered on the possibility of Fowler being named as the new commissioner of Major League Baseball (MLB), to replace Fay Vincent, who had resigned in 1992 following ongoing disputes with the team owners. Fowler's longtime friendship with Bill Bartholomay, Atlanta Braves chairman of the board and chair of the MLB commissioner search committee, and the fact that more than half of MLB team owners had contributed to Fowler's campaigns plus his indisputable love for the game helped fuel the rumors. He was interviewed twice by the owners, both times in Chicago.[162]

The second session was attended by most of the owners and led by Jerry Reinsdorf, owner of the Chicago White Sox, and New York Yankees owner George Steinbrenner. As Fowler remembers it, he made the case for fans' widespread discontent with the major leagues, and especially their ownership, largely caused by the ongoing labor discord between owners and players. Reinsdorf indicated he did not accept this assessment and saw no evidence that the public was dissatisfied with the product or the owners. Fowler reiterated that in his view the owners had a "black eye" with the fans, media, and players: "Everybody hates you." Steinbrenner retorted that if that was the case, why should the owners choose for commissioner a "has-been politician" like Fowler when they could select a distinguished statesman like Colin Powell? Fowler said, "That's brilliant, if you want someone of such stature that you owners can never fire him, no matter how much he might side against you."

It is not clear whether Fowler was ever under serious consideration, but this meeting effectively ended his candidacy. After it was over, Fowler worried that he might have inadvertently damaged the chances for selection of General Powell, whom he had gotten to know when the general headed up the United States Army Forces Command (FORSCOM) at Fort McPherson in Atlanta. Fowler tried to reach the general that night but was told by Powell's wife that he was traveling in Japan. When the former senator finally reached him and told him about the Chicago meeting, Powell simply laughed and told Fowler he had no interest in the position.

After leaving the FEC, Fowler resumed the practice of law in July 1993 by accepting a position in the Washington office of the Atlanta-based law firm of Powell, Goldstein, Frazer & Murphy. Fowler informed the partners that he did not want to engage in lobbying, and particularly did not want to lobby his former colleagues on Capitol Hill, citing legal restrictions that had been put in place to prevent such actions by former members of Congress for a period of years after they left office. The partners told him they could accept those conditions and hired him. However, not long after he began, it became clear to him that the firm viewed his chief value to be in gaining access for their clients to senators and representatives. At that point, Fowler reiterated he would not perform this function. Though the firm's members did not press the issue and largely left him alone, he accomplished little, bringing in only a few clients, and was let go after just over a year.

Fowler remained close to his parents throughout all of his years of public service. His father, Wyche Fowler Sr., died of cancer on January 27, 1994, at the age of eighty-three. The memorial service was held at Second-Ponce de Leon Baptist Church in Atlanta, where the Fowlers had been members for more than forty years. The younger Fowler described his father as "a strong man and a strong influence on my life. He was a tough mentor, demanded excellence from his children and had enough of the old-time schoolteacher in him to enforce that through discipline." Wyche Jr.'s mother, Emelyn Barbre Fowler, passed away, also from cancer, a year and a half later, on July 15, 1995. She was eighty-one. Her son spoke of her lifelong interest in helping others. "She retrieved hundreds of Medicare checks for the elderly, found day care openings for the young and even coached a distraught widow on how to coax a raccoon off her porch. When folks didn't want to pay for a long-distance call to [my] Washington [office], they called my mother. She spent thousands of hours during my 26 years of public life helping citizens in her calming, pragmatic and caring way."

In June of 1990, Wyche Fowler married Donna Hulsizer of Poughkeepsie, New York, at Central Presbyterian Church in Atlanta. It was the second marriage for both. They divorced in 1998 while he was serving in Saudi Arabia but remain close friends.

Intelligence Commission

In October 1994, Congress created a commission on the roles and capabilities of the United States intelligence community, which was to conduct a comprehensive review of American intelligence, examining the effectiveness and appropriateness of intelligence operations in the post-Cold War world and making recommendations for improvements. The commission consisted of seventeen members: nine appointed by President Clinton and two each by the Speaker of the House, the House minority leader, the majority leader of the Senate, and the minority leader of the Senate. Senate Majority Leader Mitchell once again turned to Wyche Fowler by naming him to the commission on November 30, 1994. It was chaired by former congressman and defense secretary Les Aspin (D-WI) until his death in May of 1995, when former defense secretary Harold Brown assumed the chairmanship. The vice chairman was former Sen. Warren Rudman (R-NH). Fowler's longtime friend and intelligence expert, University of Georgia professor Loch Johnson, served on the commission staff.[163]

The commission began its work on March 1, 1995, and held regular monthly meetings through December 1995. It received testimony from eighty-four witnesses, with the staff interviewing two hundred others. The commission also reviewed a large number of documents on intelligence issues, and the commissioners visited several nations with which the US maintains cooperative intelligence relationships. For Fowler, this service presented him with another opportunity to contribute to US intelligence policy, an ongoing interest of his from his days in army intelligence. On the commission, he critiqued the failures of several CIA covert operations and sought to reduce waste in the US intelligence budget.

Fowler was one of the more active participants in the commission's deliberations and displayed particular interest in covert action, congressional oversight, counterintelligence, potential spending cuts, and environmental intelligence.[164]

The commission's report and recommendations were hammered out in a series of meetings in January 1996. They were approved by unanimous vote on February 2 and transmitted to Congress on March 1. The following were among its key findings and recommendations:

> The Commission concludes that a capability to conduct covert actions should be maintained to provide the President with an option short of military action when diplomacy alone cannot do the job. The capability must be utilized only where essential to accomplishing important and identifiable foreign policy objectives and only where a compelling reason exists why U.S. involvement cannot be disclosed. [This was one of the few references to covert action in the report, and represented a far cry from Fowler's earlier proposals in the Congress.]
>
> The Commission believes...that [congressional] oversight would be strengthened if appointments to the [congressional oversight] committees were treated like appointments to other committees, with new members added as result of normal attrition [rather than the existing arrangements that limit service on these committees to eight years]. The choice of new members, however, should continue to be made by the respective congressional leaders. If this is not feasible, the maximum period of service should be extended to at least ten years.

In the final report, "covert action was essentially ignored, and counterintelligence was discussed in less than a page." Despite his disappointment over these and other omissions, Fowler joined all other commissioners in endorsing it.[165]

The immediate response to the commission's recommendations was limited, with "modest results" and "the intelligence community...unaffected in any large degree by the...inquiry." However, in the years to come, this work helped set the stage for debates and policy changes strengthening the role of the overall director of central intelligence (DCI), consolidating certain intelligence functions, and helping prepare the public, the news media, and congressional and executive branch policymakers for the intense scrutiny afforded to intelligence operations in the wake of the terrorist attacks of September 11, 2001. It was of specific assistance to Fowler in bringing him up to date on the current state of US intelligence just prior to his becoming ambassador to Saudi Arabia.[166] However, these responses were mostly confined to the executive branch, and questions about the effectiveness of congressional oversight of intelligence programs, including covert operations, remain.

Ambassador to Saudi Arabia (1996 to 2001)

Fowler's work for the commission was part-time and unpaid, but in 1996 Fowler was presented with the opportunity for a full return to public service in a capacity that represented a capstone for the Georgian's governmental career. On April 4, the Clinton administration announced its intent to nominate Wyche Fowler as United States ambassador to the Kingdom of Saudi Arabia. The post was considered one of the most important of US diplomatic assignments, given Saudi Arabia's roles as the largest supplier of oil to Western nations, a key participant in the Middle East peace process, and a significant source of commercial investments. It was also an important US ally, though major differences in history and culture presented an ongoing challenge in that relationship.

Fowler's knowledge on a range of relevant policy issues—including energy, intelligence and foreign policy, his familiarity with the region (based on the number of official trips he made to the region over the years), and his political skills—all likely played a role in his selection. This last was perhaps particularly important in that the Saudis had long preferred (and received) political appointees as the American ambassador because of their belief that the ambassador's personal relationship with the president, his administration, and the Congress was the most important factor in sustaining the alliance. Fowler's desire for the job was heightened by his interest in Middle Eastern and biblical history and archaeology. "It's very exciting, not only to have the chance to help the country, but to get back into public policy. Saudi Arabia is our center in the Middle East," he commented.[167]

Ambassadorial appointments are subject to confirmation by the US Senate, and as a former senator who was generally well regarded by his colleagues (another reason for his selection), he was almost certain to be confirmed. Two factors, however, complicated the situation: 1996 was a presidential election year, and with Republicans in control of the Senate, delays in action on Clinton nominations were a strong possibility. Second, the chairman of the Senate Foreign Relations Committee, through which the nomination must pass, was Jesse Helms, an often-fierce Fowler adversary.

The need for a US ambassador in Saudi Arabia was greatly heightened by the June 25, 1996, terrorist bombing of the Khobar Towers housing complex in Saudi Arabia. Nineteen US servicemen were killed and almost five hundred individuals of various nationalities, primarily US and other foreign military personnel and their dependents, were wounded. On that day, the US government cited Hezbollah as the responsible party. The attack came just over two weeks after the formal submission of the Fowler nomination to the Senate. It was hoped that in light of the Khobar bombing, Senate action might be expedited, but that was not the case.

Just before the Senate's customary August recess, a State Department spokesman commented, "Given the number of issues on our plate with the Saudis—the continuing concerns about terrorist threats to Americans in Saudi Arabia, the protection for our military officers and soldiers and our diplomats, some of the discussions that the Defense Department has had over the last couple of weeks, this really requires the presence of a senior person, an ambassador. We very much want Ambassador-designate Fowler to be out there." Fowler, who was studying Arabic for up to six hours a day in anticipation of confirmation, said, "I'm ready to go."[168]

The Senate took no action on the Fowler nomination at that time, with no committee hearing even scheduled by Chairman Helms, so President Clinton used his prerogative to fill an ambassadorial vacancy by presidential appointment without Senate confirmation during periods when the Congress was not in session. Such appointments were effective for the current congressional session (which would end in January 1997) and had to be affirmed by the Senate in the following session. Thus, on August 16, 1996, at a White House ceremony, Fowler was sworn in by Vice President Al Gore, who praised his former Senate colleague for "the incisive nature of his mind, [and] the deep thoughts he brings to the questions of great importance to our nation." Gore called on him to enhance the US-Saudi relationship and to advance US "deterrence of rogue states, such as Iran and Iraq, and the determination to fight those who murder innocents in order to spread fear.... We're sending Wyche Fowler off to an extremely important mission.... We will never bow to terrorism and Wyche Fowler will be our strong and resolute point man on this issue," said the vice president.[169]

Before departing Washington, Fowler received intensive briefings from the State Department as well as the Federal Bureau of Investigation with respect to its investigation into the Khobar bombing. He then participated in diplomatic consultations in London before arriving in the Saudi capital of Riyadh at the end of August.

At the very beginning of Fowler's ambassadorial assignment, relations with Saudi Arabia's neighbor Iraq were a major focus of American foreign policy in the aftermath of the 1991 Gulf War. In August 1996, Iraq moved a large number of troops into the US-protected Kurdish zone in northern Iraq, prompting the Clinton administration to order air- and sea-based missile strikes against military targets in southern Iraq, which led to an Iraqi withdrawal from the Kurdish area.

In an October 29, 1996, letter to a family friend, Fowler recounted his first days on the job and his initial impression of the country and its people.

> I arrived here literally 36 hours before our strikes against Saddam, and it was my duty to inform the King and the senior Cabinet members, his brothers, what we were about to do under the guise of "consultations." For 36 hours, I ricocheted from palace to palace and from city to city—Riyadh and Jeddah on the Red Sea—making my initial acquaintances by asking the Government to allow us to use our Air Force stationed here to strike Iraq. No poker face could contain the amazement at what we were asking ([Chairman of the Joint Chiefs of Staff] Shalikashvili was with me on one such round of visits; Secretary [of Defense] Perry with me on the other), as well as their inability to conceal concern that we were about to strike within hours. So within hours of arriving, I got my first glimpse of the mind of the Kingdom, and my first glimpse of the disconnect between Western and Islamic perceptions of place and duty. The King explained patiently that he was the Custodian of the Two Holy Places (Mecca and Medina) and that his duty to his people was both temporal and spiritual. According to the Qur'an, Saudis could not allow this holy ground to be used to launch attacks against other Muslim nations. The exception being defense of the Kingdom, he said the Saudis would willingly fight alongside their fine American allies if and when attacked. This was not the case today, however, as the Kingdom saw the Kurdish fighting as an internal Iraqi affair and not one that required defensive measures on

behalf of the Saudi Government. Request denied. And so it went. We went through the same drill ten days later after Saddam rebuilt his missile sites that we had partially destroyed. This time Secretary Perry came back with me for several more 2:00 A.M. meetings with the King, but to no avail. The issue of holiness and spiritual sanctity claimed for the Arabian Peninsula is not one easily debated by Western representatives. We shake our heads in frustration over the inability to use our military, but secretly I believe appreciate the convictions and rationale behind the Government's decision, especially if one factors in the domestic reaction and discontent already evident. Any American politician would lead with his domestic concerns, and whine that his people simply would not permit such-and-such an action. The Saudis should be given credit for a deep-seated belief that they have been chosen for a special place in spiritual history, and their ability to continue to rule depends on their living up to their duty of this (God-given) custodianship. I like these people a lot. They are open, candid and have a wonderful ability to laugh. Of course, their reputation for hospitality and generosity cannot be exaggerated. At any given time on any given evening, enough food is prepared for the foreign guest to feed twenty. I have learned to take two bites, launch into a story, and continue that story until plate one is removed. Then comes plate two laden with every kind of morsel imaginable and three, four, five, six, seven, ad infinitum. At a recent meal, food was brought continuously from 9:30 until long after midnight even though it lay untouched by all of us in the later "innings."

After Bill Clinton's reelection victory in the 1996 presidential election, the Fowler nomination was resubmitted to the Senate on February 25, 1997, and the Foreign Relations Committee finally held a hearing on it on September 18, 1997. A newspaper article reported on those proceedings.

> The U.S. ambassador to Saudi Arabia, Wyche Fowler, Jr., said Thursday that searching for those responsible for the truck bombing of a U.S. military building in Saudi Arabia 15 months ago is

"my highest personal priority...." Fowler, an Atlanta native and former Democratic Senator from Georgia, said containing Iraq also remains essential to protecting U.S. interests in the Persian Gulf region.... He praised the Saudi government for its assistance in helping U.S. bases in Saudi Arabia try to improve security by moving the bases to isolated areas since the bombing at the Al-Khobar tower near Dhahran in June 1996. "Cooperation by our hosts has been forthcoming and extensive" in the effort to improve security for American forces in Saudi Arabia, Fowler noted in written testimony submitted to the committee. He was more circumspect in characterizing Saudi cooperation in the Al-Khobar bombing investigation. The State Department has offered a reward of up to $2 million for information leading to the arrest of the bombers. Asked by Sen. Sam Brownback (R-KS) about Saudi cooperation in the investigations, Fowler said only that "both us and the Saudis have a common objective." He then shifted the focus away from the Saudis to add, "and it's certainly my personal highest priority to bring those murderers to justice...." Fowler has been at the post for 13 months but still awaits confirmation. Thursday's hearing was a step in that direction. The committee has not scheduled a vote on whether to forward Fowler's nomination to the Senate. He is expected to be easily confirmed. "Senator Fowler's proven himself in the course of his recess appointment," said Sen. Paul Sarbanes (D-MD) in a comment that seemed to sum up the general sentiment in the 20-minute hearing.[170]

The article's last assessment proved accurate because when the Fowler nomination was finally called up for action in the Senate on October 27, 1997, it was approved unanimously on a 90 to 0 vote in which Senator Helms joined with Georgia Senators Coverdell and Max Cleland (D-GA) in voting in the affirmative, with ten senators not present for the vote.

Sen. Ernest (Fritz) Hollings (D-SC) praised Fowler in a statement submitted to the Senate the following day.

I rise today to congratulate my good friend and former colleague Wyche Fowler on his confirmation as United States Ambassador to Saudi Arabia. This is a great and well-deserved honor for the former

> Senator from Georgia. Even more important, it is a blessing for America. Because his was a recess appointment, Wyche Fowler already has served with great distinction and success for over 1 year in Saudi Arabia. President Clinton appointed him to this post just days before the June 25, 1996, terrorist bombing of the United States military residence in Dhahran. Although he took the ambassadorship at one of the most tenuous moments in United States-Saudi diplomatic relations, Wyche embraced the challenge and helped cement the United States relationship with Saudi Arabia, one of our most important allies.... His appointment came at an important moment in the relationship between the United States and Saudi Arabia. Despite the difficulties that have surrounded the bombing investigation, he has served his country well and protected American interests in the region with tenacity and skill.... And, Wyche is genuinely fascinated by Saudi Arabia's people and culture. He has begun to learn Arabic, and already has indulged his enthusiasm for Arabian history and archaeology by trekking on camel through the deserts of Saudi Arabia's Empty Quarter. America is fortunate to have Wyche Fowler as its Ambassador to Saudi Arabia. His diplomatic skills will see us successfully through a delicate and vital period in our relations with that nation. In this instance, Georgia's loss was the Nation's gain.

An August 1998 interview with the *Atlanta Journal-Constitution* addressed some of the major issues of Ambassador Fowler's first two years on the job. Notably, Fowler brought up the threat posed by Osama bin Laden, fully three years prior to the 9/11 attacks upon the United States.

> **Q:** Has security been heightened at your embassy since the bombings [of the US embassies] in Nairobi [Kenya] and Dar es Salaam [Tanzania]?
>
> **A:** We have been on great alert for quite a time because of Osama bin Laden's public threats against civilians and the military in Saudi Arabia, which he issued about two months ago on television, calling for the first time that it was legitimate to attack American civilians as well as military. The Saudis have been extraordinarily cooperative in providing us external security as well as the

shared intelligence to protect ourselves to the greatest possible extent. Bin Laden went further than anyone could have believed when he publicly urged his followers to declare a holy war against Americans and specifically included civilians as targets as well as military. He's thought to be hiding out in Afghanistan, but the investigation is ongoing. Obviously because of his proclamation against Americans he is certainly under suspicion [in connection with the East Africa embassy bombings]. It's unquestioned to all the people in the intelligence business that if you've got two bombs going off within a minute of each other in two different countries that that requires a degree of sophistication that only a handful of terrorist organizations could probably accomplish. That doesn't mean there is not a new one that has emerged. But it was a very sophisticated operation.

Q: Can you update us on the relationship between the United States and Saudi Arabia and your mission there?

A: We have a unique bilateral relationship with the kingdom of Saudi Arabia that goes back over 50 years now. We've had a unique path of development in our relations. It began with the American companies discovering oil in Saudi Arabia, and it has broadened to include now most of the American multinational giants doing an extraordinary amount of trade and business with the kingdom. As a result, there are over 50,000 Americans working in Saudi Arabia across the whole gamut of business activity. We also have between 5,000 and 6,000 American military forces stationed in Saudi Arabia at a given time, as well as a huge training mission whereby we train the Saudi military and air force with sophisticated weaponry that they have bought from us....

Q: What's been the most difficult part about your job?

A: My responsibility for security of all my people [at the embassy] as well as the security, to the greatest extent I can provide it, of the Americans working in the kingdom. It has been a large challenge.

Q: How would you characterize the level of tension in the Middle East today?

A: It is undoubtedly in America's interest to have a politically secure and economically vibrant Middle East. We believe that the key to that success is a peace process that leads to a final end to Israeli-Palestinian hostilities. There's no question that the greatest springboard to economic success anywhere in the [Persian] Gulf [region] is a cessation of all hostilities. But there will remain political instability of some sort throughout the region until those governments in the Gulf have confidence that peace in the region will be long-term. The Arab states do believe that we have a disproportionate influence with the Israeli government. But what is very hard for any Arab government to understand is the nature of democracy—that another country cannot dictate to a democracy what their policies should be or what security needs they believe are required for their own interests. Our goal should be to not allow ourselves to be isolated with just one friend but to maintain our historic ties with the nation of Israel and at the same time, by our policies and actions, convince the Saudis and our other allies in the Gulf that they are an equal partner with us on regional interests and global interests.

Q: What are the main things you want to accomplish in Saudi Arabia?

A: I hope first of all, God willing, there will be no terrorist attack under my stewardship, and we reinvigorate ourselves every day with fresh eyes to see what can be done to protect the people and families who are there, both in the embassy and the private American community. I hope that we will succeed in training, through our military, Saudi armed forces to such an extent that they can defend themselves without question from any regional threat, including Saddam Hussein. And, of course, I hope to bring to the kingdom a better understanding of the economic and political fruits of moving toward democratization and the unquestioned insurance of human rights.[171]

The most remarked upon aspect of Fowler's ambassadorship was undoubtedly his role in the investigation of the Khobar Towers bombing. Throughout his service in that position, "there was never a day that went by that I didn't have a conversation about the Khobar investigation," he later said. According to Clinton national security adviser Sandy Berger, Fowler was "very much the instrument" in helping to forge cooperative ties between American and Saudi officials investigating the bombing.

Particularly key was the strong working relationship he developed with the FBI, which established a permanent liaison office in Riyadh and took charge of the investigation. There were reports at the time of friction between the Bureau and some Clinton administration and Saudi officials who were said to be concerned that discovery of links between the attacks and the government of Iran could precipitate further conflict with that nation. However, Fowler retained the confidence of FBI director Louis Freeh, and when the Bureau announced the indictment on charges of terrorism of thirteen Saudis and one Lebanese member of the pro-Iran Saudi Hezbollah on June 21, 2001, shortly after Fowler left his post after the change of presidential administrations, Freeh singled out the ambassador whose "unswerving commitment to seeing progress made played a critical role in today's development." Earlier, on April 17, 2001, Fowler was awarded the Jefferson Cup, the FBI's highest civilian honor, "in grateful recognition of your leadership, dedication to duty, service to the nation and extraordinary contributions to the rule of law in the fight against terrorism and crime."[172]

As is customary in the case of political appointees, Ambassador Fowler resigned from his post in March 2001, shortly after the George W. Bush administration assumed office. In reflecting on his tenure as ambassador a few weeks after his departure, Fowler again spoke to the *Atlanta Journal-Constitution*.

> "Much of my time the first year and a half was spent trying to improve security to ensure that we weren't bombed again," he said. At least a third of each day was devoted to coordinating with the military, which was taking steps to move American personnel to locations where they could really protect themselves. "I could not have been more impressed with the quality of our military leadership," Fowler said. The presence of the U.S. military is a delicate issue, and "there was always tension in the air and real danger...." The Saudis, Fowler said, were very supportive of Clinton's Camp David peace effort. Most countries in the region appreciated the

administration's active efforts to secure peace, he said. "The Arabs for the most part understood America's special relationship with Israel," he said. "They frankly wish it weren't so special. But they understand, and have adapted, with some extremist exceptions, to the permanent existence of the state of Israel."

The same article contained an assessment of Fowler's ambassadorial record.

> As ambassador, Fowler handled the usual ceremonial duties that come with such posts, including cutting numerous ribbons. Like many ambassadors, he devoted time to helping promote American goods and services.... But more than many ambassadors, the former Democratic senator and congressman—who knew Clinton, National Security Adviser Sandy Berger and Secretary of State Madeleine Albright—also worked closely with the administration on policy issues affecting the region, from Iraq and Iran, to the Middle East peace process, to the price of oil. "Wyche is, of course, not a wallflower in expressing his views," Berger said. But he also brought "enormous value added" to his role because he quickly developed rapport with the inner circle that rules Saudi Arabia and because he understood Saudi views as well as those in the wider Arab world. The fact that the Saudis recognized Fowler "had good access to the president" increased his effectiveness, Berger said.[173]

Looking back in 2023 on his time in Saudi Arabia, the Georgian focused on the people and culture of that country.

> From the moment of my arrival, I found Saudi Arabia fascinating and totally unique. It was unique in its history (it had never been invaded or colonized), unique in its geography and topography (95 percent desert), unique in its resources (oil production at 90 percent of gross domestic product), unique in its religion (Islam—no Christian churches allowed), and unique in its interpretation of Islam (Wahabism, a conservative strain emphasizing the secondary status of women). As a tribal desert society, I found no primary allegiance

to the concept of nation. Focus was loyalty first to the family, second to one's tribe, and lastly to the nation. A desert warrior, Saud, and his tribe, had defeated all other desert tribes in the late 1930s and united the conquests by marrying the daughters of his defeated chiefs. The new country took his name: Saudi Arabia. It was poor and illiterate. Oil was discovered in 1938 by the American Standard Oil Company of California. Oil wealth soon made it one of the richest countries in the world.

The Saudis, as I have mentioned, value their family ties and history, not unlike those of us from the American south. When I expressed interest in memories of their childhood and family influences, they readily engaged, creating narratives of a primitive society surviving by cooperation and tribal loyalty. I was able to respond in kind, telling of my childhood adventures, my parents' struggles as schoolteachers during the American depression, and my paternal grandfather being the first to go to college. Thus a personal relationship with royals and business leaders that was often unusual between foreign service trained diplomats and leaders was born. I also violated ambassadorial protocol by calling on the Saudi royals—including the Custodian—when I had no message from the president or the State Department to impart. I simply went to see them to chat and build our relationship, a technique (or was it a strategy?) they seemed to relish. I was seldom denied an audience with the king, the crown prince, or the foreign minister whereas many of my colleagues in the ambassadorial corps went months, or even years, without securing a private audience with top officials. I realize this was principally because I was the AMERICAN ambassador, but the intimate relationship that I had developed ensured top-level contact when needed.

I traveled extensively throughout the Kingdom, indulging my interest in archeology, skin diving in the Red Sea near Jeddah, but also meeting local chiefs, mayors, and tribal functionaries who had never had a high-ranking foreigner show interest in their villages or community problems. They were hospitable to a fault, always insistent on a meal of roasted lamb or goat eaten with our fingers and washed down with Arabic tea. Through translation we shared family stories and desert lore. These Saudis, rich in tradition but with

> little material wealth, had never been far from their village or cluster of tents. Their eyes widened as I struggled to describe life in America, impossible for them to imagine.
>
> Once, at a tiny village near the Yemeni border, I was feasting with four octogenarians when I was startled by a question: "Have you tried Viagra (the erectile dysfunction pill)? Does it work?" Replying honestly that I had not tried the pill, I said, teasingly, "but I'll order some of those little green pills." "They're BLUE," shouted all four men in unison. I had them. It was the first time I had ever seen Arabs blush.

Crossing the Great Nafud Desert

He recalled in particular the genesis and details of one of his travels that left a deep impression on him.

> Vern Cassin, an American lawyer who was fluent in Arabic, had established a law practice in Riyadh and became a friend and fellow adventurer. He introduced me to his many Saudi friends and was a guide to the social and cultural complexities of the country. We often discussed the age of exploration in the Middle East, and the many—mostly British—pioneers of the 19th century: Lawrence of Arabia, Gertrude Bell, Wilfred Thesinger and particularly Lady Anne Blunt, who had crossed the Great Nafud desert in Saudi Arabia in 1878–79 on horseback. I became fascinated with her courage and daring and determined to replicate her trip across the desert but on camels, not horses. The idea stewed in my brain until one night, having a desert dinner with Dr. Ziad Sudeiri, a descendent of a prominent family (and ancient rival to the throne), I mentioned my hope. "You must do it," he exclaimed, and instantly volunteered his camels for the journey.

When asked on another occasion for his advice to those who would journey by camel, Fowler, who over the years has been known to do an evocative impression of the beast, replied, "I suggest one's legs be very strong so that when the softer part of the anatomy goes you can walk most of the way. But camels are easy to ride, and, in many aspects once you lose your fear of them, are a lot more comfortable than a horse."[174]

Three months later, in mid-December 1997, after several weekends of camel training, Vern Cassin, his friend James Phipps, my Sudanese embassy driver, and I arrived in al-Jouf for our journey across the Great Nafud desert! As guides we had been provided two unschooled desert Bedouin, who had been asked to provide our food and water. The weather was cold, and the wind was fierce and gusting. Our patron, seeing we were ill-prepared, gave us knee-long heavy wool cloaks, which served as wind buffers while riding in the cold and an indispensable cover of warmth at night while attempting to sleep. Sleep was the first challenge. I feared that the heat of my body would attract scorpions, whose sting, without immediate treatment, can be deadly, or the infamous camel spider, a six-inch Solifuge ("those who flee from the sun" in Latin). Although not technically a spider, this opportunistic carnivore got its name from eating the underbellies of camels. I learned years later that it seldom attacked anything larger than itself, but sleeping in the desert sands, my great fear was the legend that the "spider" anaesthetized the cheeks of sleeping humans, then gorged on their hapless, unaware victims. I had also learned that the camel spider, like scorpions, primarily hunts at night. Bedouins say that a scorpion surrounded by a circle of fire will sting itself to death. Needless to say, I had no ring of fire to protect myself, but physical exhaustion proved to be my antidote to fitful nights of fear.

We had no tents, only thin, frayed sleeping bags. My "bed" was a shallow trench (think grave) dug each night behind my seated camel, its four legs delicately folded and tucked under his belly for the night. The trench kept me under the gusting wind, but the camel provided a massive windbreak, making a restless sleep possible. There was only one problem: Sleeping camels persistently fart all night, the noise alarmingly loud, followed by a perfuming of the gusting wind. We arose at daybreak, had tea and milky rice, saddled our reluctant beasts, and with the rising sun at our backs, headed into the dunes.

A word about camels. Understandably perhaps, they don't like to be ridden, but once saddled and mounted they accept their fate and do not buck or try to throw the rider. All camels have triple eye lashes, enabling them to see—and survive—the inevitable sand storms by constantly "washing" and cleansing the camel's eyes. The storms appear without warning, can last for hours, and make sight impossible for the rider. Desert sand is made of ancient rock, eroded by the wind, and consisting of mostly quartz particles. Depending on the topography of the landscape, the sand changes its shades and hues when the light strikes. Muslims pray five times a day while facing Mecca. Our guides dismounted for all prayers (although technically the Muslim is excused from prayer while traveling) and washed ritually with sand before kneeling in prayer.

Probably history's premier expert on desert sands and the mysteries of their formation was an English aristocrat, Ralph A. Bagnold, who explored the sands of Libya in the early 1930s. In 1941, his findings and conclusions were published in *The Physics of Blown Sand and Desert Dunes*, now considered a classic. Hear the awe echoing in this passage from his book: "Here, instead of finding chaos and disorder, the observer never fails to be amazed at a simplicity of form, an exactitude of repetition and a geometric order unknown in nature on a scale larger than that of crystalline structure. In places vast accumulations of sand weighing millions of tons move inexorably, in regular formation, over the surface of the country, growing, retaining their shape, even breeding, in a manner which, by its grotesque imitation of life, is vaguely disturbing to the imaginative mind."

Here is a revelation of wonder and scientific precision that I do not possess, although I experienced, like Bagnold, similar emotions as I rode and walked in the tracks of Lady Blunt.

I could only ride for a few hours at a time, as the wind and bitter cold made me struggle on foot to warm up from exertion. With every step my foot would sink several inches, and when walking uphill the effort was increasingly tiring, until breathless I mounted again. Thus rotating my riding and walking, I struggled on for approximately ten hours a day, until the approach of sundown brought relief and a hot meal of tea and rice—the only provisions that the Bedouin had thought to bring. This was my fault, as I had told Ziad that I wanted to imitate Lady Blunt's crossing as faithfully as possible, including rationed food. (I was greatly chastised by my companions for not including a bottle of brandy in our saddlebags. Every night in camp we mourned its omission.)

We judged our trip would take four days, but it soon became obvious that we would be lucky to arrive in Hail by the seventh day. On we trudged, admiring the beauty and contours of every approaching dune, while silently steeling ourselves to the effort—of man and beast—to climb them. By the third day I could feel my weight loss, and my stomach groaned at night from the lack of substance and protein. No one complained, and the daily exercise, although exhausting, actually made me feel stronger.

On the fifth day we detected nervousness in our guides, and it was somehow communicated that we must pick up the pace by riding at night. I had fought sleep for the first few nights to revel in the kaleidoscope of stars, but sleep came too quickly from exhaustion. Riding at night unveiled the magnificence of the cosmos. Many stars appeared as large as our full moon; others mere sprinkles of salt billions of light-years away. The familiar constellations conveyed the myths of creation and the mythology of the early Greeks: I saw the red beating heart of Orion, the scorpion highlighted in Scorpios, and the magnificence of the seven sisters in Taurus. But most of all, my mind dwelled on the Christmas legend of Joseph and the pregnant Mary traveling by donkey—and possibly camel—to give birth in a manger in Bethlehem. It was two weeks before Christmas, and I was transported back 2000 years in time marveling at this seminal point in Christianity and how the belief in a supernatural birth had transformed mankind. During these eons, many wars have been fought in the name of various religions, but the Christian belief that the birth in Bethlehem, foretold by angels, is when God became human to redeem his creation and promise eternal life, remains. I have never experienced such a moment of transcendent illumination and satisfaction before or after. It was a gift of profound peace in my soul.

In our six days of travel, we had met no one, but, thanks to our native guides had found an ancient waterhole to replenish our camels. Nearby, through binoculars, we spied a solitary tent wavering against a massive dune. Suddenly, the skies opened (as occasionally happens) in this part of the desert and we were deluged with rain.

As we passed by the tent we had seen, a man darted out to invite us inside. Readily complying, we dismounted. He made tea as we shivered, and continued to rush about unrolling rugs and refilling our glasses at every opportunity. Suddenly, I realized he was insistent on our staying for the night, the Bedouin code of hospitality for anyone in need wandering—as we had done—into his home. I immediately protested, to no avail. Without a wave goodbye, he dragged a rug and ragged blanket outside into the storm and was gone for the evening. At first light the next morning, we thanked him and departed, embarrassed that we had no gifts as a token of our appreciation. His last words to us, conveyed in sign language and drawings in the sand: "My great grandfather told me once that a foreign lady had once come this way. I have never seen anyone until you." His great grandfather had seen Lady Anne Blunt.

On the eighth day we arrived in Hail wind-burned and spent. A message awaited me on arrival from Crown Prince Abdullah: come immediately to the palace.

Abdullah had been crown prince since 1982, but became regent and de facto ruler of the kingdom when King Fahd suffered a serious stroke in 1995. He assumed the throne upon Fahd's death in 2005, and served as king until his own death in 2015.

I rushed to my residence to bathe and shave. Peering in my shaving mirror I could scarcely believe my eyes. Who was this creature staring back at me, a face gaunt with sunken cheeks and eyes widened by weight loss? My skin was a wind-burned reddish-brown, the color of sand. Whiskers and hair jutted out at weird angles, my teeth in contrast so white they shone like stars. I appeared the modern version of John the Baptist returning from the wilderness, lacking only a loin-cloth to complete a vision of wildness.

Approaching the Crown Prince, he exclaimed, "You told the truth. You have been in the desert. Sit and tell me all about it." We talked for two hours. He asked me to recall, day by day, impressions of everything from small lizards and scorpions to the wonders of the night constellations. He asked about the personality of my camel, and whether the camel had responded to my commands. He inquired as to whether I had come across any "green," meaning small plants (I had, but very few). Suddenly: "You are now one of us. You see from whence we came." Embarrassed, I lowered my eyes, then he asked, "Will you go again next year?" Suddenly alert, I replied, "Your Royal Highness, my experience was an exciting journey of mind and body, but it was truly a ONCE in a lifetime experience!" He smiled a smile of recognition.

As I rose to leave, he bade me remain. "I go to the desert often to clear my mind and reflect on man and his temptations. Where does this lust for things come from? Why does man need fancy cars and bracelets and trinkets that rust in the sun and do nothing for his spirit? My sons (I knew at least three) would never ride a camel into the desert. They only want expensive cars and jet skis. They are soft. They care nothing of their family history or traditions. I fear they will not become strong men. They would not have given a stranger their tent for shelter in a sudden storm."

"When I die, I will be buried as a Bedouin in an unmarked grave in the desert. (Sadly, his wishes were not fulfilled. Abdullah is buried in a cemetery in Riyadh, but his grave is unmarked.) I came from dust and I will return to dust. I deserve no recognition after death. My deeds—good and bad—will live after me. It is as Allah wishes it."

I said goodbye to Abdullah for the last time at his horse farm north of Riyadh. It was one of the saddest days of my life, as he had come to treat me as a friend, or even confidant. He trusted me to tell him when I disagreed with the U.S. policy I was told to advocate before him. And I did, knowing that I was violating the duties and responsibilities of ambassadors. The foremost example of my dereliction of duty involved the constant pressure by the U.S. to sell major weapons systems to the Saudis, including jet fighters, tanks, and missiles. I did what I was told by the State Department, but when asked by the Crown Prince what I thought, I told him honestly I believed that his country would be better served by investing in vocational education, education of women, and training that would produce livable wages for his citizens—jobs needed to maintain the infrastructure of the Kingdom—plumbers, masons, electricians, and carpenters to name a few. He never revealed details of future plans to me, but years after his death at age 90, his legacy is chiefly the universities, trade schools, and advancement of women's opportunities he initiated and fulfilled. But the Kingdom still buys the most sophisticated American weapons at every opportunity.

Post-Ambassadorship (2001 to Present)

It was ultimately concluded that Osama bin Laden and al Qaeda had not been involved in the Khobar bombing, but only a few years later they perpetrated the worst terrorist attack on American soil in history with the September 11, 2001, hijackings that resulted in nearly three thousand deaths and produced more than $100 billion in damage to the American economy. On that day, Wyche Fowler was flying into New York's LaGuardia Airport at the same time the first hijacked plane was crashing into the World Trade Center not far away. "As we circled.... I saw the smoke from the first attack. I knew instinctively that was not smoke coming from a wastebasket fire," he said. After his plane landed and he saw the television coverage, Fowler was certain it had been a terrorist operation, but his thoughts turned to the safety of his daughter Katherine, who was working for American Express's restaurant marketing division in an office in the World Trade Center. He tried to call her but the phone lines were down, and then sought the best way to reach her in the chaos that gripped New York's surface transportation systems. Four hours later, at 12:30 P.M., he finally met up with Katherine at her apartment. She told her father that she had been in a concourse on her way to her office when the first plane struck the tower and that she had run outside as soon as someone started yelling, "Bomb! Bomb!" "She was totally shell-shocked. The next day was pretty bad," Fowler said. He spent the next two and half days with Katherine, watching the news coverage of the attacks and talking with her about what had occurred.

Fowler has continued to remain actively involved in Middle East policy. For example, from 2005 to 2011, he served as chairman of the board of governors of the Middle East Institute, the oldest (founded in 1946) Washington-based organization devoted entirely to Middle Eastern studies. The institute carries out its mission by publishing *The Middle East Journal*; hosting scholars and sponsoring research; organizing events, including its annual conference featuring international experts; offering language classes for Arabic, Hebrew, Persian, Urdu, Pashto, and Turkish; and responding to media inquiries.

Fowler is frequently asked by the news media to comment on current developments, especially with respect to Saudi Arabia, as illustrated by the following excerpts from two articles he wrote for the *Atlanta Journal-Constitution* that are reflective of official American policy as well as the state of US-Saudi relations at the time. (Those relations have deteriorated in recent years, especially after the October 2018 murder of journalist and Saudi dissident Jamal Khashoggi at the Saudi consulate in Istanbul, Turkey.)

> U.S. Well-Served by Saudis: Rulers Are Key to
> Mideast Peace, Keep Oil Spigots Open
> By Wyche Fowler Jr. and Mark Weston
> January 7, 2008
> Of the six Arab nations President Bush is visiting this week, four are monarchies: Saudi Arabia, Kuwait, Bahrain and the United Arab Emirates. Three of the royal families control over 40 percent of the Earth's oil reserves: the al-Saud of Saudi Arabia, the al-Sabah of Kuwait and the al-Nahayan of Abu Dhabi in the UAE. We are fortunate that all three families are American allies.... By far the most powerful royal family is the al-Saud, the rulers of Saudi Arabia, the world's only country named after a family. Saudi Arabia is easy to criticize. Women cannot drive, work with men or travel without a man's permission, and the religious police, though less assertive than they used to be, still harass women if they see the slightest bit of hair, arm or ankle. Worse, until 2001 the Saudi people carelessly sent millions of dollars abroad to schools that taught Muslim extremism and to charities that turned out to be fronts for al Qaeda. In November 2007 a Saudi court sentenced a female victim of gang rape to 200 lashes and six months in jail because prior to the rapes she had been in a car with a young man who was not her relative, a verdict overturned only when King Abdullah issued a pardon. Yet Saudi Arabia has also been a steadfast ally of the West since 1915, first of Britain then of the United States. Even during the Arab oil embargo of 1973–74, when relations were at their

worst, the Saudis still sent oil to the U.S. military forces in Vietnam.... To cite cultural differences, however great, as a reason to end America's longstanding alliance with the Saudi kingdom makes no sense, for the prospect of another government friendlier to the United States assuming power in Saudi Arabia is nil. The royal family mediates between conservative clerics and Western-educated businessmen and reformers. Neither group is satisfied. Clerics warn of the danger of changing too fast, liberals warn of the peril of moving too slowly—which suggests the royal family performs its mediation with care and skill. Americans on both the right and the left who want the Saudi monarchy to fall are shortsighted and naïve. They ignore the hard fact that the Saudi people are more conservative, anti-Israel and anti-American than the royal family. The alternative to Saudi Arabia's royal family today is not some Arabic-speaking version of the Swedish parliament, but a Sunni version of Iran's Shi'ite theocracy. America's 60-year friendship with the Saudi government needs to be nurtured, not censured. Without Saudi Arabia as an ally, the world's oil supplies would be less secure, and peace between Israel and Palestine would be improbable.

Thoughts on the Terrorist's Death: Fowler Lauds U.S. Actions; Recalls bin Laden's Rise on World Stage; Calls Successful Secret Mission "A Matter of Intense Satisfaction"
By Wyche Fowler (as told to Tom Sabulis)
May 3, 2011
My first reaction [to the death of Osama bin Laden] is one of immense relief that a murderer on this scale has been silenced now forever. The Americans ordered killed by him on 9/11 and before that in the bombings of the embassies in Kenya and Tanzania, and before that the attack on the U.S.S. Cole in Yemen, have also been brought some justice. I think that bin Laden has been what the poet Dylan Thomas called the "worm beneath the nail" of American foreign and military policy, preventing us from examining the larger strategic interest of the United States in the Middle East and South Asia because of our almost single-minded focus on terror and terrorism, and specifically bin Laden. Praise is due to President [George W.] Bush and President Obama for the single-mindedness

of their constant efforts that finally enabled him to be discovered and killed. Now that irritant has been removed, and I hope it will enable us to turn a new page in our relationship with Muslim countries in particular. I think [Saudi Arabia's] celebrations over this are like ours. You'll recall that it was Osama bin Laden who first called for the overthrow of the Saudi monarchy, which [took] his citizenship away and expelled him from the country. He declared war on Saudi Arabia many years before declaring war on us and our people. And I would not be surprised if there was a very large element of Saudi intelligence involved, in conjunction with American intelligence, that led to this discovery and this attack. This is a matter of immense satisfaction.... This is a tremendous blow to al Qaeda and all the would-be al Qaeda followers, that their leader has been tracked down and killed. They're not going to recover from that. It may still be a slow death. There very well may be attacks in retaliation for his death. It might not be next month, it may be six months from now. But we've proven to the world that we don't give up, that no matter what these terrorists throw at us, we are determined to bring the rule of law and justice to those who would murder our people and attempt to do us harm anywhere in the world. I think this strength of resolve in America will be a lesson to our would-be enemies.

In recent years, Fowler has remained active on a number of fronts. He taught politics and constitutional law at a number of universities (including Harvard, the University of Georgia and Rice) and served on the boards of a number of private and public institutions, including the Morehouse School of Medicine, the Carter Center, and the Shubert Theaters and Shubert Foundation in New York. He also started a consulting business, with a focus on American companies doing business in the Middle East, and he retains his passion for public policy, baseball, opera, and fishing.

Wyche and Becky Hendrix, his partner of many years, split their time between homes in Atlanta and St. Simons Island, Georgia. Becky's career mirrors Wyche's, with more than thirty-five years of public service including at the White House, the US Senate, and the US Environmental Protection Agency, from which she retired in 2014. Wyche and Becky continue to travel extensively, maintaining contact with their many friends.

Fowler takes great pride in his two children, Katherine Fowler Ernest and William Connel Fowler, and two grandchildren, Wyche McPherson Ernest and Clayton Fowler Ernest.

Conclusion

In his aforementioned statement to the Senate upon Wyche Fowler's confirmation as ambassador to Saudi Arabia, Sen. Fritz Hollings of South Carolina offered a summation of his former colleague's public service.

> Of course, [Fowler's nomination] is no surprise to those of us who have followed Wyche Fowler's career of public service or worked closely with him during his 16 years in Congress. Elected to the Senate in 1986, Wyche served on the Appropriations, Budget, Energy, and Agriculture Committees. As assistant floor leader, he helped fashion a bipartisan consensus on major public policy issues. Many of us remember Wyche Fowler as an unusually reflective Member of this body, who talked often of conserving our natural resources and energy sources. I can remember listening with humor and fascination as he used electric toothbrushes to point out the danger of decadent applications of technology. Before becoming the first Atlantan elected to the Senate, Wyche Fowler represented Atlanta's Fifth District in the House of Representatives. First elected in 1977, he served on the Ways and Means and Foreign Relations Committees, as well as the Select Committee on Intelligence and the Congressional Arts Caucus. Wyche's legislative record is long and distinguished: he tried to stop oil drilling in the Arctic National Wildlife Refuge and protect national wetlands; recodified and strengthened the national historic preservation law; established joint public/private ventures in alternative energy; and ensured interest-free relief for farmers in the Farm Credit System overhaul. The consensus-building skills Wyche learned in Congress have stood him in good stead in Riyadh. Just as valuable is his affable personality. All his colleagues in the House and Senate remember Wyche Fowler as a genial and charismatic fellow, not to mention a great singer of hymns and a superb storyteller. In fact, Wyche used to entertain us with the same country songs he performed as a teenager on an Atlanta talent show. Though the Saudis may not appreciate country ballads, I am sure that they will find Wyche

Fowler every bit as hard-working, engaging, and honest as the people of Georgia and his colleagues have.

Wyche Fowler has been an aspiring preacher, a would-be singer, a consummate storyteller, and above all, a performer. After exposure to the civil rights movement and under the influence of Charles Weltner, he found his true calling in public service. Fowler was what is usually referred to disparagingly as a "career politician," but he pursued this career with determination and dedication, and he was very good at it.

The performer in him came out most clearly as a campaigner, where his affinity for people and enjoyment in being center stage served him well, whether at rallies, debates, or town hall meetings.

As an office holder, Fowler consistently received recognition and responsibilities from those he worked with, whether on the Atlanta Board of Aldermen (where he was elected vice president by his colleagues), the US House (elected to the Ways and Means Committee) or US Senate (elected to the Appropriations Committee). He was given responsibilities in institutional leadership as well, including by House Speaker O'Neill (appointed to House Intelligence Committee and ABSCAM investigation), Senate Majority Leader Mitchell (appointed as assistant floor leader and to 1990 budget summit) and President Clinton (nominated and then served as ambassador to Saudi Arabia).

Wyche Fowler can point to a wide range of legislative accomplishments including, but not limited to, updating and improving the nation's historic preservation policy; reforming agricultural, forestry, and rural programs; obtaining federal funding for a large number of infrastructure and other projects throughout Georgia; jump-starting federal support for renewable energy technologies; and promoting American leadership in space science. And though his multiyear effort to strengthen congressional oversight of covert operations and other intelligence programs did not meet with legislative success, it has nonetheless drawn attention to the subject and helped expose the excesses ultimately revealed in the Iran-Contra affair.

In pursuing his objectives, Fowler had little time for ideological labeling or philosophical debates about "big government" versus "small government." His goal was always to try to find a way to promote "good government," and to that end, he was very often to be found in the role of coalition-builder and negotiator. He played important roles in obtaining passage of such landmark bills as the Social Security Amendments of 1983 that preserved its solvency; the Tax Reform Act of 1986, which remains the last major tax reform proposal enacted into law; and the Omnibus Budget Reconciliation Act of 1990, the largest deficit-reduction measure in American history up to that point, which helped pave the way for the budget surpluses of 1998 to 2001.

Wyche Fowler Jr. concluded his public service career with a five-year term as the American ambassador to Saudi Arabia, making him one of the longest serving individuals in that key posting. His experiences and expertise in foreign policy, intelligence, and energy issues served him, and the United States, well. Throughout his career, Fowler sought to serve his constituents—local, state and national—with integrity and ethics. Although his specific legislative accomplishments, including those in agriculture, historic preservation, energy policy, and space science, may not have always generated "front page" material, they have served as a base for further progress in the twenty-first century. But perhaps Wyche Fowler's greatest legacy is in having demonstrated that our democratic system *can* work when it's built on compromise and good will, for, as the great British parliamentarian Edmund Burke noted on the eve of the American Revolution, "all government—indeed every human benefit and enjoyment, every virtue and every prudent act—is founded on compromise."

Notes

[1] Keith Graham, "Wyche Fowler Is a Man on the Run," *Atlanta Constitution*, September 5, 1985.

[2] John F. Kennedy Library and Museum 1991 Profile in Courage Award, May 29, 1991, https://www.jfklibrary.org/events-and-awards/profile-in-courage-award/award-recipients/charles-weltner-1991

[3] Graham, "Fowler."

[4] 1991 Profile in Courage Award.

[5] John Fuller, "Republican, Democrat Clash in Opening Political Forum," *The Battalion*, October 20, 1967.

[6] Margaret Shannon, "Year of the Young Politicians," *Atlanta Constitution*, May 4, 1969.

[7] "Aldermanic Races," editorial, *Atlanta Constitution*, October 1, 1969; "Tuesday Is the Day Atlanta Votes," editorial, *Atlanta Journal*, October 6, 1969.

[8] Charles Longstreet Weltner, "New Faces on Aldermanic Board," *Atlanta Constitution*, January 1970.

[9] Tom Roeser, "Flashback: Andrew Young Wins the Primary and the General Election Despite All," May 2005. http://blog.tomroeser.com/2007/05/flashback-andrew-young-wins-primary-and.html.

[10] "President Candidates," *Northside Neighbor*, September 26, 1973.

[11] "The New Team," editorial, *Atlanta Constitution*, October 17, 1973.

[12] Reg Murphy, "The Smart Voter's Candidate Wins," *Atlanta Constitution*, October 19, 1973.

[13] "Fowler Sees Harmonious Council," *Atlanta Constitution*, October 22, 1973.

[14] Jim Merriner, "Hearing Set on Superchief," *Atlanta Constitution*, July 31, 1974.

[15] Frederick Allen and Jim Stewart, "Fowler Hits Jackson's Choice," *Atlanta Constitution*, August 6, 1974.

[16] "Who's in Charge Now?" *Harper's Weekly*, May 16, 1975.

[17] Frederick Allen, "Concentrate on Violent Crimes, Fowler Urges," *Atlanta Constitution*, January 8, 1975.

[18] Jim Merriner, "Eaves, Fowler Settle Feud over Crime," *Atlanta Constitution*, January 22, 1975.

[19] Jim Merriner, "Mayor and Fowler Bury the Hatchet," *Atlanta Constitution*, November 21, 1975.

[20] Warren Brown, "A Free-for-All Race for Young's seat," *Washington Post*, February 15, 1977.

[21] Margaret Ballard, "Tensions Mount for Fifth Race," *Northside Neighbor*, March 9, 1977.

[22] John Lewis, *Walking with the Wind* (New York: Simon & Schuster, 1998) 444.

[23] "Front Yard Congressman—Wyche Fowler," *Buckhead Atlanta*, June 1977.

[24] Jim Merriner, "Fowler Finding Things Different," *Atlanta Constitution*, June 20, 1977.

[25] Jim Merriner, "Fowler Opposes Plan to Sell Warplanes to Arab States," *Atlanta Constitution*, February 20, 1978.

[26] "Fowler to Lead Delegation," *Atlanta Journal*, August 17, 1977.

[27] Jeff Nesmith, "Fowler Gets Intelligence Panel Spot," *Atlanta Constitution*, July 28, 1977.

[28] Jeff Nesmith, "Fowler Urges Charter for Spy Agencies," *Atlanta Constitution*, October 5, 1977.

[29] Ibid.

[30] Sarah Dunbar, "Wyche Fowler Jr. Now Aging 'Boy Politician'" *Buckhead Atlanta*, June 1977.

[31] Craig R. Hume and Frederick Allen, "River Park Plan Floats through House," *Atlanta Constitution*, February 15, 1978; Charles Hayslett, "Fowler: River Park Vote a 'Valentine for Future,'" *Atlanta Journal*, February 15, 1978.

[32] Suzanne Dolezal, "Buck Stops at Congressman's Door," *Atlanta Journal*, December 13, 1977.

[33] Julia Wallace, "Atlanta's 10 Most Eligible Bachelors," *Atlanta Journal* and *Atlanta Constitution*, September 11, 1977.

[34] Bill Montgomery, "Fowler Hiding, Foe in 5th Charges," *Atlanta Journal*, July 14, 1978.

[35] Numbers do not add due to rounding.

[36] Charles Hayslett, "Talmadge Challengers under the Gun," *Atlanta Journal*, December 19, 1978.

[37] Henry Eason, "Wyche Fowler Proclaims the Politics of Change," *Atlanta Constitution*, September 10, 1979.

[38] Ann Woolner, "Nunn, Ginn Rise in Power; Fowler Loses Bid for Key Post," *Atlanta Journal*, January 17, 1979.

[39] Ann Woolner, "Fowler Wins Seat on Potent Committee," *Atlanta Journal*, January 24, 1979.

[40] "Fowler Wins," editorial, *Atlanta Journal*, January 25, 1979.

[41] "Fowler's Energy Plan," editorial, *Atlanta Journal*, January 2, 1980.

[42] Gordon Freedman, "Fowler 'Hardnosed' on Ethics in Congress," *Atlanta Journal*, March 31, 1980.

[43] Charles R. Babcock, "Jurors See and Hear Myers Meet FBI Agent," *Washington Post*, August 14, 1980.

[44] Gordon Freedman, "Fowler: Nigerians, Saudis Wary of Soviets," *Atlanta Journal*, January 16, 1980.

[45] Gordon Freedman, "Trip to Africa, Mideast Gives Fowler a Big Jolt," *Atlanta Journal*, January 20, 1980.

[46] Henry Eason, "Ambitious Senate Hopefuls Testing Talmadge's Muscle," *Atlanta Journal* and *Atlanta Constitution*, August 25, 1979.

[47] Gordon Freedman, "Fowler Won't Rush to Senate Race," *Atlanta Journal*, December 2, 1979.

[48] *Busbee v. Smith,* 549 F. Supp. 494 (DC Dist. 1982).

[49] Charles S. Bullock III, "Racial Crossover Voting and the Election of Black Officials," *Journal of Politics* 46 (February 1984): 238–51.

[50] *Busbee v. Smith.*

[51] Charles S. Bullock III, "Changing Standards for Legislative Redistricting and Their Consequences." Prepared for the US in the 1980s: The Reagan Years Conference, sponsored by the Rothermere American Institute, Oxford University, Oxford, England, November 10–12, 2005.

[52] "The Supreme Court, Racial Politics, and the Right to Vote: *Shaw v. Reno* and the Future of the Voting Rights Act," September 9, 1994, *American University Law Review* 44:1 (1994): 113–14, https://digitalcommons.wcl.american.edu/aulr/vol44/iss1/1/.

[53] Loch K. Johnson, *The Threat on the Horizon* (New York: Oxford University Press, 2011) 305.

[54] Alfonso Chardy, "U.S. Ignoring Covert-Activity Curbs, Lawmaker Says," *Miami Herald*, April 8, 1983.

[55] "Fowler's CIA Bill Thoughtful," editorial, *Atlanta Constitution*, May 3, 1983.

[56] Joanne Omang, "Hill Learns That Being Tightfisted Is Its Only Way to Collar CIA," *Washington Post*, September 26, 1983.

[57] Michael Barone and Grant Ujifusa, *The Almanac of American Politics 1986* (Washington, DC: National Journal Group, 1985) 343–44.

[58] Paul Bernstein, "Fowler Proposes Limiting Tax Deductions," *Atlanta Constitution,* August 13, 1985.

[59] Renee D. Turner, "Fowler Touts Tax Plan from House Panel," *Atlanta Journal,* November 25, 1985.

[60] Greg McDonald, "Wyche Fowler on Spies, Gadgetry and Politics in the CIA," *Atlanta Journal-Constitution,* March 24, 1985.

[61] Greg McDonald, "Fowler, Gingrich Agree: U.S. Must Maintain Lead in Space," *Atlanta Journal-Constitution,* October 27, 1985.

[62] Ron Hudspeth, "Jogger Fowler Keeps Running into Trouble," *Atlanta Journal-Constitution,* March 16, 1985.

[63] Keith Graham, "Wyche Fowler Is a Man on the Run," *Atlanta Constitution,* September 5, 1985.

[64] Frederick Allen, "On a Flatbed Truck, Fowler Could Work His Magic Best," *Atlanta Constitution,* February 4, 1986.

[65] Frederick Allen, "Fowler Easily Outpaces Senate Hopefuls at Forum," *Atlanta Journal,* April 22, 1986.

[66] "Senate Battle Close on Democratic Side," editorial, *Macon Telegraph and News,* August 10, 1986.

[67] "Fowler Is Man for Demo Ticket," editorial, *The Observer* (Moultrie, GA) July 12, 1986.

[68] "Fowler for Senate," editorial, *Rome News-Tribune,* August 10, 1986.

[69] "Fowler at Top of Primary Field," editorial, *Atlanta Constitution,* August 12, 1986.

[70] Kevin Sack and Hal Straus, "Fowler Fires Up Democrats at State Convention," *Atlanta Journal-Constitution,* September 28, 1986.

[71] Hal Straus and Kevin Sack, "What the TV Spots Didn't Say: Senate Candidates Fudge on the Facts," *Atlanta Journal* and *Atlanta Constitution,* November 2, 1986.

[72] Hal Straus, "Fowler WINS!" *Atlanta Journal,* November 5, 1986.

[73] Barbara G. Salmore and Stephen A. Salmore, *Candidates, Parties, and Campaigns: Electoral Politics in America,* 2nd ed. (Washington, DC: CQ Press, 1989) 198.

[74] Kevin Sack and Hal Straus, "Peter, Wyche and Mary a Hit Fund-raiser," *Atlanta Journal and Constitution,* October 19, 1986.

[75] Salmore and Salmore, *Candidates, Parties, and Campaigns,* 200.

[76] Hal Straus, "Mattingly, Fowler Both Say Debate Went Their Way," *Atlanta Journal*, October 21, 1986.

[77] Frederick Allen, "Fowler Beats Mattingly, but Only in Late Rounds," *Atlanta Constitution*, October 21, 1986.

[78] Hal Straus, "Mack and Wyche Top 'Kate & Allie,'" *Atlanta Journal*, October 22, 1986.

[79] "Fowler Is the Best Bet for Georgia," editorial, *Atlanta Constitution*, October 23, 1986.

[80] "On the Record and Issues, It's Mattingly for Senate," editorial, *Atlanta Journal*, October 24, 1986.

[81] Bill Shipp, "Mattingly Seems to Have Advantages, and Yet I Have a Certain Feeling," *Atlanta Constitution*, November 3, 1986

[82] Jim Galloway, "Fowler Style Proves to Be the 'X-Factor,'" *Atlanta Journal*, November 5, 1986.

[83] Hal Straus, "Fowler WINS!" *Atlanta Journal*, November 5, 1986.

[84] Galloway, "Fowler Style."

[85] Frederick Allen, "Fowler Triumph a One-Man Show Using Sheer Personal Magnetism," *Atlanta Journal*, November 5, 1986.

[86] Loch Johnson, "Wyche Fowler," *New Georgia Encyclopedia*, https://www.georgiaencyclopedia.org/articles/government-politics/wyche-fowler-b-1940/.

[87] Lewis Grizzard, "Sen. Fowler Is Treated to Capital Party," *Atlanta Journal*, January 7, 1987.

[88] Scott Shepard, "Fowler, Lewis Take Oath in D.C.," *Atlanta Journal*, January 7, 1987.

[89] Hal Straus, "Fowler 'Elated' after Gaining Seats on Agriculture, Energy Committees," *Atlanta Journal and Constitution*, November 22, 1986.

[90] Scott Shepard, "Fowler Elected as an Assistant Deputy Whip," *Atlanta Constitution*, February 4, 1987.

[91] Scott Shepard, "Fowler Plans Tour of State during Break," *Atlanta Journal*, February 5, 1987.

[92] Scott Shepard, "Fowler Making Strides as a Rural Champion," *Atlanta Journal and Constitution*, February 15, 1987.

[93] Scott Shepard, "Fowler blames U.S. Reliance on Foreign Oil For 'Finger on the Trigger' in Gulf," *Atlanta Constitution*, July 29, 1987.

[94] Brian O'Shea, "Fowler Urges Senators Not to Prejudge Bork," *Atlanta Constitution*, July 14, 1987.

[95] Staff and Wire Reports, "Bork Opponents in Senate Reach Majority at 51," *Atlanta Journal*, October 8, 1987.

[96] Lorri Denise Booker, "NAACP Ad Faults Nunn, Fowler for No 'Stand' against Bork," *Atlanta Journal*, October 15, 1987.

[97] Ron Hudspeth, "Wyche Fowler Takes His Hat Off to Court Ruling," *Atlanta Constitution*, March 25, 1987.

[98] Tom Teepen, "Fowler's Campaign Strategies Could Help Dukakis Win in South," *Atlanta Constitution*, June 23, 1988.

[99] Scott Shepard, "Fowler Fosters 'Good Ol' Boy' Image in DC: He's Savvy Insider in Spite of Props, Such as 1966 Buick," *Atlanta Journal and Constitution*, July 10, 1988.

[100] Jackie Calmes, "Democrats Tap Mitchell to Be Senate Leader," *Atlanta Constitution*, November 30, 1988.

[101] Jackie Calmes, "Fowler Plucks Plum Assignment," *Atlanta Journal* and *Atlanta Constitution*, December 2, 1988.

[102] Durwood McAlister, "Fowler Emerges as Senate Leader in Only Two Years," *Atlanta Journal* and *Atlanta Constitution*, February 5, 1989.

[103] *Thomaston Times*, "Fowler Reports on Farm Bill Impact on State," August 8, 1990.

[104] John Harmon, "Trying to Cut Federal Funds for Logging Roads," *Atlanta Journal-Constitution*, September 3, 1989.

[105] "U.S. Forest Policy Waste Must Stop," editorial, *Atlanta Journal-Constitution*, November 12, 1989.

[106] "Fowler Blames GOP Politics for Defeat of Logging Roads," *Waycross Journal-Herald*, October 25, 1990.

[107] "A Bill That Is Righter Than Rain," editorial, *Atlanta Constitution*, March 27, 1989.

[108] Susan Rasky, "For Freshman Senator, A Unifying Budget Role," *New York Times*, June 29, 1990.

[109] Tom Teepen, "Fowler Helps the Arts Win Early Battle in Long War," *Atlanta Constitution*, October 12, 1989.

[110] Lee Parkam, "Senator Says Sanctions Take Time," *Gwinnett Daily News*, August 10, 1990.

[111] Colin Campbell, "Colin Campbell's Diary," *Atlanta Journal* and *Atlanta Constitution*, November 25, 1990.

[112] Rasky, "A Unifying Budget Role."

[113] Ibid.
[114] John E. Yang, "Rep. Gingrich 'Prepared' to Back Increase in Taxes," *Washington Post*, July 20, 1990.
[115] John E. Yang and Steven Mufson, "Budget Negotiators See Agreement within Days," *Washington Post*, September 12, 1990.
[116] Mario Christaldi, "Fowler: I Will Support Painful Budget," *The Tifton Gazette*, October 3, 1990.
[117] Bruce Bartlett, "A Budget Deal That Did Reduce the Deficit," *The Financial Times*, June 25, 2010.
[118] David Brown and Jim Kessler, "It Can Be Done: Five Lessons from the 1990 Budget Summit Agreement," *Third Way*, November 2012.
[119] Richard E. Cohen, "Congress's Rising Stars," *National Journal* (January 27, 1990): 172.
[120] Jeanne Cummings and Rhonda Cook, "The 1991 Legislative Session," *Atlanta Constitution*, January 16, 1991.
[121] Mike Christensen, "The Supreme Court Showdown: The Politics," *Atlanta Journal* and *Atlanta Constitution*, October 16, 1991.
[122] Allen Freeman, "Amendments to 1966 Act Become Law: Fowler Bill Strengthens Nation's Preservation Program," *Historic Preservation News*, December 1992.
[123] Mark Sherman, "Poll Shows Fowler May Be Vulnerable to GOP Challenger," *Atlanta Journal-Constitution*, November 26, 1991.
[124] Richard F. Fenno Jr., *Senators on the Campaign Trail* (Norman and London: University of Oklahoma Press, 1996).
[125] Ibid., 186–87.
[126] Ibid., 178–79.
[127] Steve Harvey, "Fowler Foe Hints at False House Bank Statements," *Atlanta Journal-Constitution*, September 1, 1992.
[128] Peter Mantius, "Fowler Discloses Documents Showing No Bounced Checks," *Atlanta Journal-Constitution*, September 5, 1992; Mark Sherman, "Fowler Bank Records Sought," *Atlanta Journal-Constitution*, September 16, 1992.
[129] Fenno, *Campaign Trail*, 205–207.
[130] Ibid., 208–10.
[131] Mark Sherman, "Fowler, Coverdell Have First Debate," *Atlanta Journal-Constitution*, October 10, 1992.
[132] Mark Sherman, "Fowler, Coverdell Trade Accusations in Bitter Debate," *Atlanta Journal-Constitution*, October 18, 1992.

[133] Mark Sherman, "In Debate, Coverdell Says Fowler Lied," *Atlanta Journal-Constitution*, October 19, 1992.

[134] Fenno, *Campaign Trail*, 213.

[135] "Wyche Fowler, A Senator Georgia Can Be Proud Of," editorial, *Americus Times-Recorder*, October 30, 1982.

[136] "Re-elect Wyche Fowler," editorial, *Atlanta Constitution*, October 23, 1992.

[137] "Fowler for U.S. Senate," editorial, *Columbus Ledger-Enquirer*, October 30, 1992.

[138] "State Fares Better with Fowler in Senate Race," editorial, *Macon Telegraph*, October 26, 1992.

[139] "For Senate: Wyche Fowler," editorial, *Rome News-Tribune*, October 26, 1992.

[140] "Return Fowler to Senate," editorial, *Savannah Morning News* and *Savannah Evening Press*, October 17, 1992.

[141] Fenno, *Campaign Trail*, 201–202.

[142] "Re-elect," *Atlanta Constitution*.

[143] Mark Sherman, "Incumbent Fowler Finds Himself in Good Shape Heading into Stretch," *Atlanta Journal-Constitution*, October 25, 1992.

[144] Tom Baxter, "Fowler Inherits Talmadge Base in Rural Georgia," *Atlanta Journal-Constitution*, October 29, 1992.

[145] Ben Smith III and Mark Sherman, "Senate Debate Turns Testy," *Atlanta Journal-Constitution*, November 17, 1992.

[146] Mark Sherman and Jingle Davis, "Fowler, Coverdell Define Differences in Last Debate," *Atlanta Journal-Constitution*, November 23, 1992.

[147] Frank LoMonte, "Coverdell, Fowler Call on Stars," *Augusta Herald*, November 19, 1992.

[148] Lauren Neergaard, "Gore, Clinton Throw Weight behind Fowler," Associated Press, November 24, 1992.

[149] Frank LoMonte, "Runoff Blitz Goes to Wire," *Augusta Chronicle*, November 24, 1992.

[150] "Wyche Fowler for Senate," editorial, *Atlanta Constitution*, November 18, 1992.

[151] "Coverdell for U.S. Senate for Change and Candor," editorial, *Atlanta Journal*, November 23, 1992.

[152] Dawn M. Odrowski to Jan Witold Baran, February 13, 1996, Washington, DC.

[153] Charles S. Bullock III and Robert P. Furr, "Race, Turnout, Runoff and Election Outcomes: The Defeat of Wyche Fowler," *Congress & the Presidency* 24 (Spring 1997): 1–16.

[154] Mark Sherman, "Coverdell Savors 15,000-vote Victory over Fowler," *Atlanta Journal-Constitution*, November 26, 1992.

[155] Bill Shipp, "How Fowler Tripped on Second Term Attempt," *Bill Shipp's Georgia*, December 1992.

[156] Fenno, *Campaign Trail*, 172.

[157] Ibid., 221–22.

[158] Ibid., 187–88.

[159] Michael Barone and Grant Ujifusa, *The Almanac of American Politics 1994* (Washington, DC: National Journal Group, August 1, 1993) 330.

[160] Federal Election Commission, FEC Litigation-Court Case Abstracts, *FEC v. NRA Victory Fund* (1994), https://www.fec.gov/legal-resources/court-cases/fec-v-nra-political-victory-fund/.

[161] Odrowski to Witold Baran, February 13, 1996.

[162] I. J. Rosenberg, "Fowler Is Unclear on Future," *Atlanta Journal*, March 16, 1993: WF candidacy for MLB commissioner.

[163] For a comprehensive account of the work of the commission, including Wyche Fowler's participation therein, see Loch K. Johnson, *The Threat on the Horizon* (New York: Oxford University Press, 2011).

[164] Ibid., 370, 337–38, 343.

[165] Ibid., 350, 345.

[166] Ibid., 360, 366, 367–68.

[167] Kathey Alexander and Maria Saporta, "Fowler Picked for Saudi Arabia Post," *Atlanta Journal-Constitution*, April 5, 1996.

[168] Bob Deans, "Fowler Waits for Chance as Envoy," *Atlanta Journal-Constitution*, August 2, 1996.

[169] Bob Deans, "Fowler Sworn in as Saudi Ambassador," *Atlanta Journal-Constitution*, August 17, 1996.

[170] Bob Deans, "Bomb Case Tops Agenda, Fowler Says," *Atlanta Journal-Constitution*, September 19, 1997.

[171] Keith Graham, "Q & A on the News: Saudi Mission Puts Fowler Near Pulse of Region," *Atlanta Journal-Constitution*, August 20, 1998.

[172] Keith Graham, "A Bridge between Two Worlds," *Atlanta Journal-Constitution*, June 28, 2001.

[173] Ibid.

[174] Staff, "Envoy Treks Saudi Desert," *Atlanta Journal-Constitution*, August 20, 1998.

Index